LA PRINSE ET MORT DU ROY RICHART D'ANGLETERRE

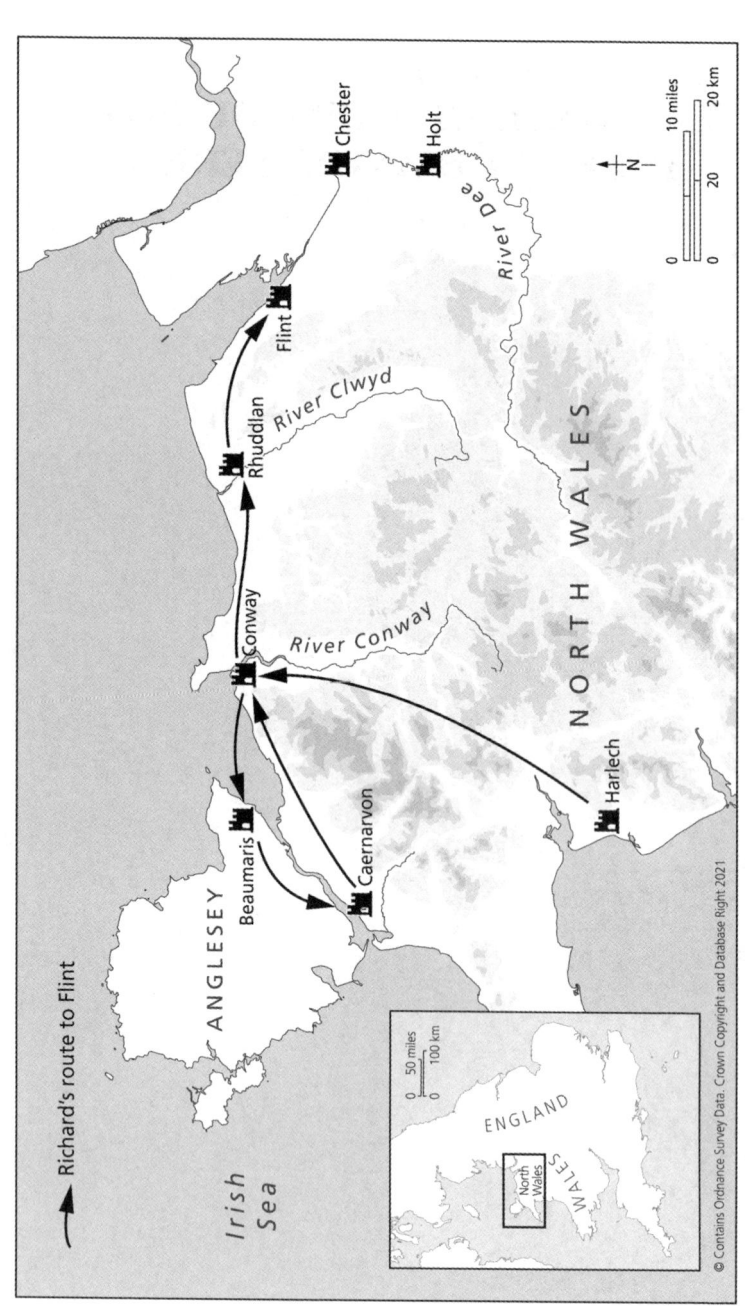

Richard II in North Wales in August 1399, prior to his capture by Henry Lancaster.

LA PRINSE ET MORT DU ROY RICHART D'ANGLETERRE, based on British Library MS Harley 1319, and Other Works by JEHAN CRETON

edited and translated by
LORNA A. FINLAY

CAMDEN FIFTH SERIES
Volume 65

CAMBRIDGE
UNIVERSITY PRESS

FOR THE ROYAL HISTORICAL SOCIETY
University College London, Gower Street, London WC1 6BT
2023

Published by Cambridge University Press on behalf of The Royal Historical Society
Shaftesbury Road, Cambridge CB2 8EA, United Kingdom
One Liberty Plaza, 20th Floor, New York, NY 10006, USA
477 Williamstown Road, Port Melbourne, VIC 3207, Australia
314–321, 3rd Floor, Plot 3, Splendor Forum, Jasola District Centre,
New Delhi – 110025, India
103 Penang Road, #05-06/07, Visioncrest Commercial, Singapore 238467

© The Royal Historical Society 2023

First published 2023

A catalogue record for this book is available from the British Library

ISBN 9781009387248 hardback

SUBSCRIPTIONS. The serial publications of the Royal Historical Society, *Royal Historical Society Transactions* (ISSN 0080-4401) and Camden Fifth Series (ISSN 0960-1163) volumes, may be purchased together on annual subscription. The 2023 subscription price, which includes print and electronic access (but not VAT), is £245 (US $409 in the USA, Canada, and Mexico) and includes Camden Fifth Series, Volumes 65, 66 and Transactions Seventh Series, Volume 1 (published in December). The electronic only price available to institutional subscribers is £189 (US $314 in the USA, Canada, and Mexico). Japanese prices are available from Kinokuniya Company Ltd, P.O. Box 55, Chitose, Tokyo 156, Japan. EU subscribers may be required to pay import VAT at their country's rate on receipt of physical deliveries. EU subscribers for electronic deliveries who are not VAT registered should add VAT at their country's rate. VAT registered subscribers should provide their VAT number.

Subscription orders, which must be accompanied by payment, may be sent to a bookseller, subscription agent, or direct to the publisher: Cambridge University Press, Shaftesbury Road, Cambridge CB2 8EA, UK; or in the USA, Canada, and Mexico: Cambridge University Press, Journals Fulfillment Department, One Liberty Plaza, Floor 20, New York, NY 10006, USA.

SINGLE VOLUMES AND BACK VOLUMES. A list of Royal Historical Society volumes available from Cambridge University Press may be obtained from the Humanities Marketing Department at the address above.

Printed in Great Britain by Henry Ling Limited, The Dorset Press, Dorchester, DT1 1HD

CONTENTS

PREFACE	ix
ABBREVIATIONS	xi
LIST OF FIGURES	xiii

INTRODUCTION	1
Description of the Manuscripts	2
Manuscript Tradition and Choice of Base Manuscript	13
Previous Editions	16
The *Prinse et mort du roy Richart d'Angleterre* and the *Chronicque de la traïson et mort de Richart Deux roy dengleterre*	17
Jehan Creton: His Life	19
Jehan Creton: His Writings	26
Historical Value of the *Prinse et mort*. By J.J.N. Palmer	36
EDITORIAL PRINCIPLES	43

LA PRINSE ET MORT DU ROY RICHART D'ANGLETERRE

by Jehan Creton (composed 1399–1402), Complete verse text plus prose section, with a facing-page translation	45

EPISTLES AND *BALLADES*

by Jehan Creton, with a facing-page translation   300

Epistle [I to King Richard] written by the said Creton   300

Ballade [I] by the said Creton   308

[Epistle II to Philip the Bold, duke of Burgundy]   310

Ballade [II] by Creton   320

Another *ballade* [III] by the said Creton   322

Another *ballade* [IV] by the said Creton   326

ILLUSTRATIONS

Reproductions of the pages containing all sixteen miniatures (Figures I–XVI)   330

NOTES ON TRANSLATION   347

BIBLIOGRAPHY   367

INDEX OF NAMES   375

To the memory of my dear parents:

Jamesina Gault Smith
Charles Kennedy Smith

PREFACE

It was my great good fortune to begin this edition as a pupil of †A.H. Diverres, Carnegie Professor of French in the University of Aberdeen; an eminent medievalist, Armel Diverres was yet a most kindly and painstaking mentor to an unfledged novice. Also in the French Department at Aberdeen in the 1970s I have to acknowledge the advice and help of †Professor Charles Chadwick and Professor J.C. Laidlaw. Dr Sarah V. Spilsbury was especially kind in allowing me to read her article on 'The Imprecatory *Ballade*' before it appeared in print, and in sharing her notes on the watermarks of BnF MSS n. a. fr. 6220-4.

Professor G.M. Roccati, Faculty of Modern Languages, University of Turin, sent me the text of his edition of Creton's *Ballades* II–IV. He kindly made helpful suggestions as to the meaning of a number of obscure lines in the *Prinse et mort* and, in the best tradition of open-handed scholarship, has always been prepared to offer stimulating encouragement. I thank him most sincerely.

Throughout the years I have worked on the *Prinse et mort* I have received courtesy and co-operation from the staff of the MSS Departments of the British Library, the Bibliothèque nationale de France, and Lambeth Palace Library; these institutions have granted permission to consult and publish the six MSS described here. I take this opportunity to thank them all.

Encouragement to seek publication came from †J.K. Hyde, Professor of Medieval History in the University of Manchester, who suggested an approach to the Royal Historical Society. Diana E. Greenway, FBA, Professor of Medieval History, Honorary Fellow, Institute of Historical Research, University of London, sometime Literary Director of the Royal Historical Society, made an equally positive assessment and suggested that an evaluation of the importance of the poem be added to the Introduction. Most of all, publication of this edition is due in no small way to the support of Andrew Spicer, Professor of Early Modern History, Oxford Brookes University, and formerly Literary Director of the Royal Historical Society. I express my warmest thanks to him.

In 1979 J.J.N. Palmer, now Professor Emeritus in the University of Hull, very kindly loaned me the typescript of his article 'The

Authorship, Date and Historical Value of the French Chronicles on the Lancastrian Revolution' before it appeared in print. His essay on the historical value of the *Prinse et mort* in the Introduction to this edition is the gracious gesture of a leading authority in the field towards an editor without a background in academic history.

It is no easy task to turn a thesis into a work worthy of publication. It could scarcely have been done without the help, support, and encouragement of my husband: *je t'en remercie.*

Lorna A. Finlay

ABBREVIATIONS

BL	British Library
BnF	Bibliothèque nationale de France
DMF	*Dictionnaire du Moyen Français (1330–1500)*, www.atilf.fr/dmf
f. fr.	*fonds français*
MidF	Middle French
ModF	Modern French
MS(S)	manuscript(s)
H	BL MS Harley 1319
L	Lambeth Palace Library MS 598
A	BnF MS f. fr. 14645
B	BnF MS n. a. fr. 6223
C	BnF MS f. fr. 1668
D	BnF MS f. fr. 1441
n. a. fr.	*nouvelles acquisitions françaises*
ODNB	*Oxford Dictionary of National Biography*
OED	*Oxford English Dictionary*
OF	Old French
WAM	Westminster Abbey Muniments

LIST OF FIGURES

I. Creton makes obeisance to Jean de Montaigu, the first owner of **H** (BL MS Harley 1319 fo. 2r.) © The British Library Board.

II. King Richard knights Henry of Monmouth (BL MS Harley 1319 fo. 5r.) © The British Library Board.

III. Three ships arrive from Dublin (BL MS Harley 1319 fo. 7v.) © The British Library Board.

IV. McMurrough gallops downhill out of the woods (BL MS Harley 1319 fo. 9r.) © The British Library Board.

V. The Archbishop of Canterbury, holding the papal bull, preaches from the pulpit (BL MS Harley 1319 fo. 12r.) © The British Library Board.

VI. Salisbury's ships arrive at Conway (BL MS Harley 1319 fo. 14v.) © The British Library Board.

VII. King Richard's fleet leaves for Wales, one of the ships bearing his sunburst badge on her sail (BL MS Harley 1319 fo. 18r.) © The British Library Board.

VIII. King Richard, in black cowl, meets Salisbury and other companions at Conway (BL MS Harley 1319 fo. 19v.) © The British Library Board.

IX. Exeter and Surrey ride out on their embassy to Lancaster (BL MS Harley 1319 fo. 25r.) © The British Library Board.

X. Exeter and Surrey make obeisance to Lancaster at Chester (BL MS Harley 1319 fo. 30v.) © The British Library Board.

XI. Northumberland makes obeisance to King Richard at Conway (BL MS Harley 1319 fo. 37v.) © The British Library Board.

XII. Northumberland kneels before the Host (BL MS Harley 1319 fo. 41v.) © The British Library Board.

XIII. King Richard is ambushed by Northumberland (BL MS Harley 1319 fo. 44r.) © The British Library Board.

XIV. Lancaster makes obeisance to King Richard at Flint (BL MS Harley 1319 fo. 50r.) © The British Library Board.

XV. Lancaster hands King Richard over to the liverymen of London (BL MS Harley 1319 fo. 53v.) © The British Library Board.

XVI. The Deposition Parliament. The empty throne, with Lords Spiritual on the left and Lords Temporal on the right (BL MS Harley 1319 fo. 57r.) © The British Library Board.

INTRODUCTION

Jehan Creton was a Frenchman and a writer, of whose work only the *Prinse et mort*[1] and the related *ballades* and epistles survive; see Figure I for his portrait. The action of his poem takes place in 1399, in England, Ireland, and Wales, during a truce in the middle years of the Hundred Years War (1337–1453). By command of Charles VI of France – whose daughter, Isabella, had been married to Richard II in 1396 – Creton joined Richard's retinue on his second Irish expedition, in 1399, and was thus by chance able to tell how a king, at the height of his powers, was left to face an overweening subject – his mortal foe – without his army. Tricked into leaving a strong castle, whence he could have escaped by sea, Richard fell into Henry Lancaster's power, was deposed and murdered. Safely back in France, Creton could relate how this happened, without fear of reprisals, and his long poem – quatrains, prose, and couplets – is thus an important corrective to the chronicles composed under the Lancastrian regime. He did not give his work a title; this has been taken from an entry in one of the duke of Berry's account books.[2]

Unlike Jehan Froissart writing rather earlier, Creton was not a chronicler and the *Prinse et mort* is not a chronicle. On the face of it, the sophisticated verse form is unsuitable. It was never popular – it was too difficult – but it was practised in France by the major literary figures of the day. Conversely it was the choice nature of the structure that made it appropriate; only the most dazzling and difficult form was a suitable vehicle for relating the downfall of an anointed king. Unlike other accounts of Richard II's capture, Creton's was designed primarily for reading aloud to an audience rather than for silent reading. This was another reason for writing in verse, which could be followed more easily by those listening.

---

[1] *Prinse* is pronounced to rhyme with English 'freeze': the *n* is not sounded. The rhymes at ll. 572–575 and 1576–1579 show this.
[2] M. Meiss, 'The bookkeeping of Robinet d'Estampes and the chronology of Jean de Berry's manuscripts', *Art Bulletin*, 53 (1971), pp. 228–229.

Description of the Manuscripts

The *Prinse et mort* has survived in five MSS from the fifteenth century and one from the sixteenth. A seventh, Bodleian Library MS Cherry 14,[3] a copy of BL MS Harley 1319 made in 1697, has been discounted for the purposes of this edition.

British Library MS Harley 1319 (hereafter **H**)

H measures 290 × 215 mm and comprises 78 vellum folios: $A^1:1-4^8$, 5^6, $6-10^8$; the fly-leaf is numbered fo. 1, and the last folio is not numbered. There are catchwords parallel to the text, which begins on fo. 2r., beneath the initial miniature. There are 28 to 30 lines to a full page, the text finishing on fo. 78v. The poem is divided into chapters of unequal length, the initial capital of each being a delicately illuminated majuscule two lines deep, outlined in gold, and decorated with pink or blue, overpainted with white. The lower right-hand corner of each folio is soiled and limp, which gives the impression that **H** was at one time a well-thumbed volume. It has a modern, but not recent, leather binding on boards.

In the top left-hand corner of fo. 1v. is *1399*, and beneath, in a late sixteenth-century hand, is the inscription: *Histoire du Roy d'Angleterre Richard traictant particulierement la rebellion de ses subjectz et prinse de sa personne etc. Composee par un gentilhomme françois de marque qui fut a la suite dudict Roy avecques permission du Roy de France.*

From an entry in an account-book kept by Robinet d'Estampes, *garde de joyaux* to John, duke of Berry, **H** can be identified as *un livre de la prinse et mort du roy Richart d'Angleterre* which the duke received as a gift from the *vidame de Laonnois* in the latter part of 1405.[4] The first words on fo. 2r. of the volume in question are *qu'il eust*. These are the opening words of **H**'s fo. 3r., but the fly-leaf of **H** is numbered fo. 1, and the *Prinse et mort* begins on fo. 2r. Thus **H**'s present fo. 3 is the second folio of the first quire and the second folio of the text.

The *vidame de Laonnois* was Jean de Montaigu, whose portrait is in Figure I; he served both Charles V and Charles VI as secretary and steward of the household respectively.[5] One of his brothers, also

---

[3] R.W. Hunt and others, *Summary Catalogue of Western Manuscripts in the Bodleian Library at Oxford*, 7 vols [in 8], (Oxford, 1895–1953), III, p. 73, no. 9788.

[4] C.E. Wright, *Fontes Harleiani: A Study of the Sources of the Harleian Collection of Manuscripts Preserved in the Department of Manuscripts in the British Museum* (London, 1972), pp. 50, 72, 242; Meiss, 'Bookkeeping', pp. 228–229.

[5] L. Merlet, 'Biographie de Jean de Montagu [*sic*], grant maître de France (1350–1409)', *Bibliothèque de l'école des chartes*, 13 (1852), pp. 274–284.

named Jean de Montaigu, was bishop of Chartres (1390–1406) and one of those charged with negotiating the return of Queen Isabella after Richard's death (*infra*, ll. 3452–3).[6] A *livre de la prise et mort de Richard II*, which Montaigu passed around the royal court, is included in a list of his books.[7] The *vidame* was executed in 1409, the bishop fell at Agincourt.

The early, pre-1405, date indicated for **H** is corroborated by the palaeographical evidence. The hand is 'a French court-hand of the first quarter of the fifteenth century.'[8] It is very similar to the hand of BL MS Additional 21247, which has been assigned to the early fifteenth century,[9] and to the first hand of BL MS Royal 19 B XVI, which bears the date 1428.[10] The hand is well formed, with a very slightly rightwards sloping duct. The ascenders and descenders, at the head and foot of the page respectively, are often exaggeratedly long and flourished.

H has over 130 corrections, made – as far as one can tell – by the same scribe, but they do not disfigure the MS. Sometimes a letter is squeezed in later, or one letter has been written over another; some corrections are made by expunction. Most, however, have been made by erasing the original lesson and writing over the erasure; this has been done in a very neat and careful way. The corrections are inconspicuous and very easy to miss; the scribe of **H** meticulously checked his MS against another exemplar (*infra*, pp. 15–16, Manuscript Tradition).

A second early MS existed. On 16 July 1402, Philip the Bold, duke of Burgundy, paid Creton *pour et en recompensacion d'un livre faisant mencion de la prinse de feu le roy Richart*.[11] It is presumed to have been a similar volume to **H** but has not survived.

Further details of the volume noted by Robinet d'Estampes in 1405 emerge from inventories of John of Berry's library made in 1413 and 1416; they strengthen the case for identifying it with **H**.[12]

---

[6] Catholic Hierarchy, *The Hierarchy of the Catholic Church, Current and Historical Information about Its Bishops and Dioces*es, www.catholic-hierarchy.org, s.v. 'Archbishop Jean de Montagu†'(accessed 25 November 2022).

[7] Quoted in M. Rey, *Les Finances royales sous Charles VI: les causes de déficit 1388–1413* (Paris, 1965), p. 38 n. 3.

[8] E.M. Thompson, 'A contemporary account of the fall of Richard the Second', *Burlington Magazine*, 5 (1904) p. 161.

[9] Alain Chartier, *Poetical Works*, ed. J.C. Laidlaw (Cambridge, 1974), pp. 66–67.

[10] A.G. Watson, *Catalogue of Dated and Datable Manuscripts c.700–1600 in the Department of Manuscripts, the British Library*, 2 vols (London, 1979), 911.402.

[11] P. Cockshaw, 'Mentions d'auteurs, de copistes, d'enlumineurs et de libraires dans les comptes généraux de l'état bourguignon (1384–1419)', *Scriptorium*, 23 (1969), p. 135, no. 50.

[12] L.V. Delisle, *Le Cabinet des manuscrits de la Bibliothèque nationale*, 4 vols (Paris, 1868–1881), I, p. 56; III, pp. 190–191. L.V. Delisle, *Recherches sur la librairie de Charles V*, 2 vols

In both these inventories we read of *un livre de la prinse et mort du roi Richard d'Angleterre, escript en françois rimé, de lettre de court et historié en plusieurs lieux, que le vidame de Laonnois donna a Monseigneur.* again fo. 2 begins *qu'il eust.* The description fits **H** exactly: it is in French verse, in a court-hand, and is an illuminated text.

H was still in the ducal library when this was inventoried on Berry's death in 1416, passing thence to Charles of Anjou. A note in a fifteenth-century hand on fo. 78v. reads: *Ce livre de la prinse du Roy Richart d'Angleterre est a monseigneur Charles d'Anjou, conte du Maine et de Mortaing et gouverneur de Languedoc*. His signature – *Charles* – follows. At the foot of fo. 1v. the late sixteenth-century hand of the inscription[13] continues: *Hors la librairie de Monsieur le Comte de Maine comme il appert folio ultimo verso de sa main propre*. This Charles – brother of the more famous René of Anjou – was great-nephew of John of Berry; his grandfather – Louis I of Anjou – and Berry were brothers, sons of John II of France. **H** must have been in his possession between 1443, when he became governor of Languedoc, and 1472 when he died.[14]

It has been suggested[15] that the *Prinse et mort* was known in England by the 1470s, inferring that either **H** or **L** was in England by then. I have found no evidence for knowledge of the *Prinse et mort* in this country before the 1570s, when **L** was used a source by John Stow and Raphael Holinshed.[16]

It is not known how **H** came to England and was acquired by the Harleys. There is, however, a possible connection between **H** and the splendid and more magnificently illustrated 'Book of the Queen' by Christine de Pizan, BL MS Harley 4431. This MS also became available in 1472 on the death of its owner, Jacquetta of Luxembourg, and was inscribed next by Louis de Bruges, earl of Winchester. Louis was known as the greatest bibliophile of his age, said to have owned a copy of every MS valued in contemporary aristocratic circles; he would surely have known of **H**'s existence and of the possibility of obtaining it. The usurpation of Richard II was of renewed interest in the period of instability during the Wars of the Roses, and especially to Louis who had sheltered Edward IV during his brief exile in Flanders in 1470–1471. The evidence is circumstantial

---

(Paris, 1907), II, pp. 263–264; J. Barrois, *Bibliothèque protypographique, ou, Librairies des fils du roy Jean: Charles V, Jean de Berri, Philippe de Bourgogne et les siens* (Paris, 1830), p. 91, no. 521.

[13] *Supra*, p. 2.

[14] Delisle, *Recherches*, I, pp. 54–56.

[15] *Chronicles of the Revolution 1397–1400: The Reign of Richard II*, ed. C. Given-Wilson (Manchester, 1993), p. 8.

[16] *Infra*, p. 5.

but there are too many coincidences to rule it out completely as an explanation of **H**'s provenance.[17]

On the upper right-hand corner of fo. 2r. is *Oxford BH*, an autograph mark of ownership of Edward Harley (1689–1741), second earl of Oxford. The Harleian Library was founded by Robert Harley (1661–1724), father of Edward; Humphrey Wanley was appointed librarian in 1704. Commitments in Robert's public life meant that from 1711 the library was the responsibility of Edward Harley, working with Wanley. From 1715 a diary was kept by Wanley, a day-to-day record of library business. The earliest MS number mentioned in the diary is Harley 1321, thus **H** was in the collection before 1715. The Harleys possessed a considerable number of MSS before the founding of the library, from as early as the late seventeenth century, and it must be presumed that **H** was amongst these.[18]

This is corroborated by the entry for MS 1319 in Wanley's *Catalogus Brevior*, published in 1759. He begins: 'A French book, written upon Parchment by a French Hand; and in the second Page of the first Spare Leaf bearing this more Modern Title'. He continues with the inscription on fo. 1v., *supra*, p. 2. 'Concerning this book, I take Leave further to Observe ... That John Stow hath taken very much from this Author, even Verbatim in a manner ... and that Raphael Hollingshead hath also borrowed some Light of Him, for which he citeth a French Pamphlet, or Poem, in the Possession of Doctor John Dee; which perhaps, may be this very Book'.[19] Wanley was wrong here; John Dee's MS was the one now in Lambeth Palace Library, described *infra*, pp. 7–9, as the ownership inscriptions indicate. Wanley clearly had not purchased **H**, it must have been among the items waiting to be catalogued when he joined the Harleys.

H contains sixteen beautiful miniatures illustrating key personalities and incidents in the *Prinse et mort*, all depicted in the separate colour section towards the end (*infra*, pp. 331–346);[20] in the 1413 and 1416 inventories of Berry's library it is described as *historié en plusieurs*

---

[17] For Harley MS 4431, see British Library, *Catalogue of Illuminated Manuscripts*, www.bl.uk/catalogues/illuminatedmanuscripts; for Louis de Bruges, see *ODNB*, s.v. 'Brugge, Lodewijk van [Louis de Bruges; Lodewijk van Gruuthuse], earl of Winchester (*c.* 1427–1492)'; also M. Vale, 'An Anglo-Burgundian nobleman and art patron: Louis de Bruges, Lord of la Gruthuyse and Earl of Winchester', in C. Barron and N. Saul (eds), *England and the Low Countries in the Late Middle Ages* (Stroud, Gloucestershire, 1995).

[18] Humphrey Wanley, *The Diary of Humphrey Wanley 1715–1726*, ed. C.E. and R.C. Wright, 2 vols (London, 1966), II, p. 475; C.E. Wright, *Fontes Harleiani*, pp. xv–xvii.

[19] [H.Wanley], *Catalogue of the Harleian Collection of Manuscripts*, 2 vols (London, 1759), I, s.v. 1319.

[20] They occur in the text immediately preceding ll. 1, 145, 273, 341, 489, 613, 805, 869, 1173, 1469, 1841, 2045, 2169, p. 102, l. 2; p. 109, l. 16, l. 2445.

lieux.²¹ Creton refers twice, in his epistle to Richard, to the account in words *and pictures* of the King's misfortunes which he has circulated in France (p. 305, l. 24; p. 309, l. 11), and there are two references in the *Prinse et mort* to illuminations. After describing McMurrough, Creton continues:

> *Sa semblance, ainsi comme il estoit*
> *Vëez pourtraite*
> *Ycy endroit.* (ll. 339–41)

Pourtraite is the last word on fo. 8v.; the top portion of fo. 9r. is occupied by Figure IV showing McMurrough and his men riding out of a wood to meet the English. The text recommences with *Ycy endroit* beneath the miniature. Again, *Aprés entra le duc ou chastel, armé de toutes pieces excepté de bacinet, comme vous povez veoir en ceste ystoire* (p. 197, ll. 20–21) comes in the middle of fo. 49v.; more than four lines of text follow. With a little juggling, there would have been room for the miniature at the foot of fo. 49v., but the scribe has chosen to leave a large blank and place Figure XIV at the head of fo. 50r. It shows the duke of Lancaster making obeisance to King Richard. Interestingly, it would seem that the author of the *Chronicque de la traïson et mort de Richart Deux roy dengleterre*,²² who lifted his account of the meeting of Lancaster and the King at Flint from the *Prinse et mort*, copied from an MS which had this miniature. Lancaster is described in the *Traïson* as *armé de toutes pieces fors du bacinet et tenoit un baston blanc en sa main*.²³ The *Prinse et mort* makes no mention of the white staff, but Lancaster is shown holding it in Figure XIV.

Clearly Creton conceived the *Prinse et mort* as an illustrated text. When we consider also that **L** has spaces left for miniatures exactly where these occur in **H**, and that BnF MS n. a. fr. 6223 marks their position with *hystoire*, we have in **H** illustrations to the text as Creton meant them to be; they have been attributed to the workshop of the Virgil Master.²⁴ **H** was loaned to the Getty Museum in Los Angeles in 2010 for an exhibition of medieval French illuminated manuscripts. The volume published to coincide with the exhibition contains an illustration²⁵ of BnF MS *fonds français* 45, Simon de Hesdin's translation of Valerius Maximus' *Faits et paroles memorables*,

---

[21] Deslisle, *Recherches*, II, pp. 263–264.

[22] J.J.N. Palmer, 'The authorship, date and historical value of the French Chronicles on the Lancastrian Revolution', *Bulletin of the John Rylands Library*, 61:1 (1978), pp. 171–178.

[23] *Chronicque de la traïson et mort de Richart Deux roy dengleterre*, ed. B. Williams, English Historical Society (London, 1846), p. 59.

[24] M. Meiss, *French Painting in the Time of Jean de Berry: The Late Fourteenth Century and the Patronage of the Duke*, 2 vols (London, 1967), I, p. 360.

[25] E. Morrison and A.D. Hedeman (eds), *Imagining the Past in France: History in Manuscript Painting* (Los Angeles, CA, 2010) fig. 34, p. 64, and nos 30a and 30b, pp. 199–200.

whose miniatures are also attributed to the Virgil Master. The resemblance to the *Prinse et mort* leaps off the page. The Master's hand is seen in two further reproductions of this MS.[26]

Except for the first illumination in **H**, which has a more elaborate, if rather crude, ivy-leaf frame, the remaining fifteen have simple strands of ivy-leaves – *des rinceaux* – trailing from them. They come towards the beginning of Creton's poem: thirteen in the quatrains, two in the prose, and one in the couplets. The suggestion that their placing reflects a moral – a country divided against itself ends up with an empty throne – is too complex.[27] Creton clearly had a hand in organizing the miniatures; the portrayal of the King in Figures VIII, XI–XV is clearly life-like, Richard's two-pointed beard is well attested.[28] Creton chose to illustrate either incidents he himself had witnessed, or at least incidents that happened while he was with Richard.[29] It may thus be assumed that the images of Montaigu and Creton himself would also be life-like, and of particular value since faithful portraits of historical figures from as early as around 1400 are not numerous.

At the end of the MS two paper folios have been inserted containing notes, dated 1767, on the miniatures; a marginal note ascribes them to Dr Thomas Percy, bishop of Dromore from 1782 to 1811.

*Lambeth Palace Library MS 598 (hereafter **L**)*

The *Prinse et mort* is bound up in a volume[30] measuring 250 × 175 mm, comprising five portions of paper and parchment arranged alternately:

9 paper fos: contents-lists, indexes
31 parchment fos: Thomas Bray's *Conquest of Irland*
31 paper fos: blank
76 parchment fos: 1–9^8, 10^4; the *Prinse et mort*
9 paper fos: coats of arms

---

[26] Ibid. nos 32a and 32b, and discussion, pp. 205–207.

[27] Ibid. p. 207. Also, A.D. Hedeman, 'Advising France through the example of England: Visual narrative in the *Livre de la prinse et mort du roy Richart* (Harl. MS. 1319)', *Electronic British Library Journal* (2011), Article 7, p. 9.

[28] J. Stratford (ed.), *Richard II and the English Royal Treasure: [An Inventory of Richard's Treasure in 1399]* (Woodbridge, Suffolk, 2012), plate 38b.

[29] S. Whittingham, 'The chronology of the portraits of Richard II', *Burlington Magazine*, 113 (1971), p. 16; also Thompson, 'A contemporary account', p. 161.

[30] See M.R. James, *A Descriptive Catalogue of the Manuscripts in the Library of Lambeth Palace*, 5 pts, continuously paginated (Cambridge, 1930–1932), p. 779.

There is a suggestion of fire-damage to the MS of the *Prinse et mort*; the long edges of fos 26–31 are scorched, fos 31–2, and especially the latter, are puckered. There are 30 lines to a full page of the *Prinse et mort*, which begins on fo. 1r. and ends on fo. 75v. There were originally catchwords parallel to the text, but these have mostly been trimmed off. **L** has a modern, but not recent, leather binding with the Carew shield and an old pressmark *B* inlaid.

The *Prinse et mort* is written in a hand very similar to the second hand of BL MS Royal 19 B XVI, dated 1428.[31] The letter forms are larger, more open and rounded than those of **H**, but can also be assigned to the first part of the fifteenth century. There are no miniatures in **L**, but spaces have been left for them exactly where they occur in **H**. The text is also divided into the same chapters as **H**, each one beginning with an illuminated capital two lines deep, written in gold, and set in a framework of blue and/or pink, overpainted with white. The initial majuscule after each blank left for a miniature is also illuminated; the letter is formed in blue or pink with white, and set in a gold frame from which ivy ascends and descends. In the blank left on fo. 1r. for the first miniature, a fifteenth-century hand has added in large red letters: *Deposicio Regis Richardi Secundi*.

The *Prinse et mort* has been glossed, and there is an autograph and date in the same hand on fo. 3r. of the first paper section of **L**: *G. Carew 1617*. The same hand continues with a list of the contents of **L**, which include, *a Parchement Manuscript in old frenche verse of the 2: jorney which K:R:2: made into Irland and of his deposition*. Thus **L** existed in its present form at least as early as 1617. There is another note in Carew's hand at the top of fo. 1r. of the section containing the *Prinse et mort*:[32] *This booke was written by a frenchman who was with K:R:2: when he was taken in flint Castel by Henry duke of Lancaster: and he was allso with the sayed K:R:2: in his voyadge into Irland*.

George Carew, earl of Totnes (1555–1629), saw military service in Ireland and was interested in things Irish. The collection of MSS and documents that he built up went on his death to Sir Thomas Stafford, and passed from him to Archbishop Laud. The archbishop placed 42 volumes of documents relating to Ireland – most probably including the *Prinse et mort* – in Lambeth Palace Library. Carew translated into English that part of the *Prinse et mort* which relates to Richard's expedition to Ireland, and it is interesting to see how a var-

---

[31] Watson, *Catalogue*, 911.402.
[32] See J.S. Brewer and W. Bullen (eds), *Calendar of the Carew Manuscripts: Preserved in the Archiepiscopal Library at Lambeth*, 6 vols (London, 1867–1873), p. 319.

iant reading in **L** has survived the process of translation.[33] Carew's rendering of l. 441 is, 'which the Duke humbly excused', **L** having *humblement* where the other MSS have *haultement*.

An earlier mark of ownership is found on fo. 75v.: *John Dee 1575*. Dr John Dee (1527–1608), mathematician and astrologer, collected a considerable library, but exchanged his *Prinse et mort* for another volume. Immediately after his signature, in the hand of John Stow (1525–1605), is written: *I gave for this boke a boke of the foundation of [blank] in Oxfordshire*.[34] As Humphrey Wanley observed (*supra*, p. 5): *John Stow hath taken very much from this Author, even Verbatim in a manner*.[35] Stow's account of the events of 1399 – from Richard's departure for Ireland until his capture by Lancaster – comes exclusively from the *Prinse et mort*.[36] His account is a summarized translation. He does not name Creton in his list of *Authours out of whom these Chronicles are collected* – **L** does not give the author – but he relates how Richard remained at Conway *in great perplexitie and with him the Earle of Salisburie, the Bishop of Carelile, Sir William Ferebe Knight, Sir Stephen Scrope[,] mine Author, and another Frenchman*.[37] This unnamed French author is Creton.

Raphael Holinshed (1529–1580) knew and used this MS while it was still in Dee's hands. Marginal notes in his chronicles tell us that Holinshed took material relating to Richard's Irish expedition *out of a French pamphlet that belongeth to master John Dee*.[38] His account of the events immediately preceding Richard's departure from Ireland, of the embassy sent to Lancaster, of the King's subsequent capture comes also *out of master Dees French booke*.[39] Holinshed's account of the 'St Albans plot' of 1397,[40] comes *Out of an old French pamphlet belonging to John Stow*;[41] this was an MS of the *Traïson*.[42] The *Prinse et mort* only begins with the Irish expedition of 1399.

---

[33] George Carew, earl of Totnes (trans.), 'The Story of King Richard the Second. His Last being in Ireland, Written by a French Gentleman, who Accompanied the King in that Voyage to His Leaving Ireland in 1399', in *Hibernica, or, Some Antient Pieces Relating to Ireland*, Part I, ed. W. Harris (Dublin, 1757; originally published 1747), p. 25.

[34] J. Roberts and A.G. Watson, *John Dee's Library Catalogue* (London, 1990), p. 171.

[35] John Stow, *Chronicles of England from Brute* (London, 1580; Text Creation Partnership), www.name.umdl.umich.edu/A13043.0001.001 (accessed 25 November 2022). Also, P. Ure, 'Shakespeare's play and the French sources of Holinshed's and Stow's account of Richard II', *Notes and Queries*, 53 (1953), pp. 428–429.

[36] Stow, *Chronicles of England*, pp. 530–541.

[37] Ibid. p. 534.

[38] Raphael Holinshed, *Chronicles of England, Scotland and Ireland*, 6 vols (London, 1807–1808), II, p. 850.

[39] Ibid. II, pp. 854, 856.

[40] Palmer, 'French Chronicles', *Bulletin of the John Rylands Library*, 61:2 (1979), pp. 400–405.

[41] Holinshed, *Chronicles*, II, p. 836.

[42] *Chronicque de la traïson et mort*, ed. Williams, pp. 3–5.

*Bibliothèque nationale de France (BnF) MS fonds français 14645 (hereafter **A**)*

A, measuring 250 × 165 mm, comprises 90 parchment folios: A^1: 1^{10}, $2-11^8$, the fly-leaf being counted as fo. 1, and the numbers running to fo. 91.[43] There are catchwords at right angles to the text, which begins on fo. 4r. and ends on fo. 86v., with 25 lines to a page. The upper part of fo. 4r. is occupied by **A**'s only miniature – *un frontispice* – which shows Richard taking leave of the Queen as he sets sail for Ireland; McMurrough and his men are seen across the sea, conducting themselves in a warlike manner. There is a fine border of fruits and leaves, with two figures – a man, on the back of a creature which is half-animal and half-man – in the centre of the lower part. The initial letter of the text is a very highly decorated capital.

A is written in a regular, classic Gothic book-hand, which cannot be dated more precisely than fifteenth-century, although it has recently been described as late fifteenth-century.[44] J.A. Buchon does not justify his opinion that **A** is the earliest of the manuscripts.[45] A summary of the contents in an eighteenth-century hand is found on fos 1v.–3v. In the lower right-hand margin of fo. 24r. is written: *Bonne Doctrine*; it is not clear whether this denotes approval of the text – which at this point describes the harassment of the deserters from Richard's army by the Welsh (*infra*, ll. 1000–7) – or whether it is an unidentified motto.

Sixteenth-century owners of **A** are named on fo. 91v.: *Ce present livre est a Marie Lefebvre demurant a Chartres, fille de Philipes Lefebvre, procureur au siege presidial a Chartres. Maitre Philipes le Fevre, procureur au baillage et siege presidial de Chartres, 1580, xxvie jour de mars. Vivent les Febvres.* At the top of fo. 4v. is an eighteenth-century *ex-libris*: *De la bibliotheque de Charles Adrien Picard 1758.*

*Bibliothèque nationale de France (BnF) MS nouvelles acquisitions françaises 6223 (hereafter **B**)*

B measures 265 × 190 mm and is made up of 36 paper folios.[46] On fo. 1r.–v. is a fragment of *Les Chroniques de France*, the *Prinse et mort* occupying fos 2r.–32v., with 68 lines to a page. It is followed by:

---

[43] See H. Omont, *Bibliothèque Nationale: Catalogue générale des manuscrits français: ancien supplément français*, 3 vols (Paris, 1895–1896), III, pp. 235–236. (**A** was originally numbered *Supplément français* 254^{30}).

[44] Morrison and Hedeman, *Imagining the Past in France*, p. 207 n. 1.

[45] Jehan Creton, 'Histoire de Richard II', ed. J.A. Buchon, in *Collection des Chroniques*, XXIV (Paris, 1826), pp. 321–346.

[46] H. Omont, *Bibliothèque Nationale: Catalogue générale des manuscrits français: nouvelles acquisitions françaises*, 4 vols (Paris, 1899–1918), II, p. 420.

Epistre faicte par ledit Creton, fos 32v.–33v.
Balade par ledit Creton, fo. 33v.
Another epistle by Creton, fo. 34r.–v.
Balade par Creton, fos 34v.–35r.
Autre balade par ledit Creton, fo. 35r.–v; this is in fact a *chant royal* (five stanzas and an *envoi*).
Autre balade par ledit Creton, fos 35v.–36r.

B is the only one of the six MSS to name the author and to give these pieces by him. The first epistle is addressed to the deposed Richard II, the second to Philip the Bold, duke of Burgundy.

MSS n. a. fr. 6220-4 were originally one volume – St Victor 275 – in the Bibliothèque Royale, before the individual items were split up and found their way into the library of the fourth earl of Ashburnham.[47] N. a. fr. 6221-3 are in the same hasty and ill-formed hand.[48] The evidence of the watermarks of the complete St Victor 275 suggests that **B** is perhaps as late as the 1430s.[49] This is supported by the fact that n. a. fr. 6221, written in the same hand as **B**, contains Alain Chartier's *Breviaire des Nobles* and *Lay de Paix*, both ascribed to the period 1416–1426.[50]

B's text of the *Prinse et mort* is not illuminated, but the position of the miniatures as they appear in **H** is marked by *hystoire*. **B** is divided into the same chapters as **H** and **L**, the first two lines of each chapter being indented and a space left for a capital that has not been added.

The scribe of **B** appears to have copied the *Prinse et mort* from one MS, but had the other items all together from a separate source. The naming of Creton in the *explicit*: composee par [blank] *Creton*, seems to be taken from the beginning of the epistle to King Richard: *je, Creton* (*infra*, p. 301, l. 12). The scribe noticed *je, Creton*; he then added to the *explicit* and gave a title to the epistle. The *explicit* originally read:

---

[47] Chartier, *Poetical Works*, p. 77.

[48] Eustache Deschamps, *Oeuvres complètes*, ed. Marquis de Queux de Saint Hilaire and G. Raynaud, 11 vols (Paris, 1878–1903), II, pp. xvii–xxii.

[49] I am grateful to Dr Spilsbury for the following details:
BnF n. a. fr. 6220: paschal lamb. Briquet, *Les Filigranes*, I. no. 15 (1439).
BnF n. a. fr. 6221: various sorts of anchor, ibid. I, nos 396–400 (1420–1464); a P surmounted by a cross, ibid. III, nos 8462–8487 (1379–1455), most similar to sub-group nos 8475–8484 (1398–1426).
BnF n. a. fr. 6222: a P surmounted by a cross, tail ending in a trefoil, ibid. III, no. 8485 (1433–1440).
BnF n. a. fr. 6223: arms of Valois Burgundy, ibid. I, no. 1649 (1406–1413).
BnF n. a. fr. 6224: bow, ibid. I, nos. 821–828 (1387–1414); cross-bow, ibid. I, nos 723–725 (1418–1441). The date 29 November 1430 is written on fo. 77.

[50] Chartier, *Poetical Works*, p. 42.

Explicit l'ystoire du Roy Richart d'Engleterre. The scribe later added *composee par* [blank] *Creton*; the letters are slightly smaller and set at an awkward angle to the preceding line. E.J. Jones,[51] who made a faintly comic attempt to prove that Creton was Bishop Trevor of Saint Asaph, unaccountably illustrated the blank as being three times longer than it is, 60 mm instead of 20 mm; there is just enough space for a Christian name to be added. The other works are in order of composition, which suggests that they came in one piece to the scribe of **B**.

The epistle to Philip the Bold of Burgundy is the only item not specifically attributed, but this does not feel significant. The scribe began this second epistle at the very top of fo. 34r., and far over to the left; saving space seems to have been a major consideration for him. He continued with *ballade* II, on fo. 34v., again without a title attributing it to Creton. However, he went back and was able to insert a heading in the left-hand margin. He had no room to do this for the epistle.

B contains the 'complete works' of Jehan Creton, as they have survived. However, it is not clear why **B** takes the form it does: an unlovely MS, hastily and untidily copied and crammed into half the space of the other MSS; and equally unclear for what purpose it was made. Since it contains more material than most readers or listeners would want, and is in a format that is more difficult to read than the other MSS, it was perhaps compiled as a work of record to be deposited in an archive. The dukes of Burgundy were pioneers in the collection of chronicles and other historical records.[52] It is one of the more useful MSS for any student of Creton's writings.

*Bibliothèque nationale de France (BnF) MS fonds français 1668 (hereafter **C**)*

This volume of 75 paper folios, measuring 290 × 200 mm is in a hand of the 1470s.[53] On fo. 1v. is written in a late sixteenth-century hand: *Histoire de Richard 2, Roy d'Angleterre par un François qui se trouvoit a Londres lors de l'emprisonnement de ce prince.* The text occupies fos 2r.–74v., with 28 lines to a page. There are no miniatures, but **C** is divided into the same chapters as **H**, **L**, and **B**.

---

[51] E.J. Jones, 'An examination of the authorship of the deposition and death of Richard II attributed to Creton', *Speculum*, 15 (1940), p. 466.
[52] R. Vaughan, *Valois Burgundy* (London, 1975), p. 33.
[53] Formerly no. 7656; see J.A. Taschereau, H. Michalant, and L. Delisle, *Bibliothèque nationale, Département des manuscrits: Catalogue des manuscrits français, Ancien fonds*, 5 vols (Paris, 1868–1902), I, p. 284.

*Bibliothèque nationale de France (BnF) MS fonds français 1441 (hereafter **D**)*

D comprises 72 paper folios and measures 265 × 180 mm;[54] it is written in a sixteenth-century hand.[55] The *Prinse et mort*, copied at a rate of 28 lines to a page, occupies fos 1r.–72r. It is not divided into chapters, and there are no miniatures, although the positions of the fourteenth and fifteenth are marked by *ystoire*. The binding bears the arms of Charles IX of France.

Manuscript Tradition and Choice of Base Manuscript

The large number of variants suggests that the extant MSS are survivors of a crowded MS tradition, with many MSS now lost. The *Prinse et mort* was written between 1399 and 1402 (*infra*, p. 27), at a time when there was great interest in the fate of Richard II. Between 1401 (the last event mentioned) and 1402 (when Philip the Bold paid for his copy) a significant number of MSS were copied but have not survived. **AD** came from a source that is not **HLBC**; likewise **LB** have a common and now vanished exemplar, and **H** was corrected from a source that was not **LABCD**. MSS of the *Prinse et mort* were never as numerous as those of the prose *Traïson*, of which almost forty remain.[56] After all, the same laws of dilapidation apply to the *Traïson* as to the *Prinse et mort*. However, the small number of remaining MSS should not be taken to indicate that the *Prinse et mort* was in less than vigorous circulation.

Examination of the variants quickly revealed that **AD** often have a common reading against the other four MSS. In a large number of cases either reading is acceptable, e.g. **HLBC** *la nous convint logier*, **AD** *1.n. vimmes 1.* (l. 29); **HLBC** *lautre avoit une borde*, **AD** *et lautre ot une b.* (l. 75); **HLBC** *a mesaise car on le me conta*, **AD** *a grant meschief on le me raconta* (l. 1043). Very exceptionally **AD**'s reading is preferable, e.g. **AD** *chevaulx guinder*, **HLC** *ch. wuidier*, **B** line omitted (l. 63); **AD** *le temps si soit passe*, **HLBC** *no si* (l. 419); **AD** *faisoit par tout*, **HLBC** *faire par tout* (l. 621). Much more frequently **AD**'s reading is corrupt, e.g. **HLBC** *la feumes nous en joie*, **AD** *la mer passa en j.* (l. 54); **HLBC** *estienne scroup*, **AD** *guillaume s.* (l. 850; p. 187, l. 17); **HLBC** *qui prenront*

---

[54] Ibid. I, p. 226; formerly no. 7532.
[55] For the date of the hand, see C. Samaran and R. Marichal, *Catalogue des manuscrits en écriture latine, portant des indications de date, de lieu ou de copiste*, 7 vols (Paris, 1959–1984), I, p. CLXI, dated 1539.
[56] *Chronicque de la traïson et mort*, ed. Williams; for an almost complete list, see Palmer, 'French Chronicles', 61:1 (1978), pp. 180–181.

asez paine, **AD** *qui pourront a. p.* (l. 1662); **HLBC** *ne que en dire,* **AD** *jen muir tout dire* (l. 1752).

AD are also set apart from the other MSS in that they neither have the miniatures nor regular reference to them, nor do they divide the text into chapters as **HLBC** do. Both **A** and **D** have separative errors, which rule out one having been copied from the other, e.g. **A** *au roy preschier,* **D** *aux gens p.* (l. 470); **A** *car dix et huit apres,* **D** *car .xviii. jours apres* (l. 795); **A** *des boys grans et menus,* **D** *des boiz et des* [*grans* superscript] *menus* (l. 173); **A** *au duc r.,* **D** *le duc r.* (l. 571). Clearly, however, **AD** have a common source, and equally clearly the tradition which they represent is inferior to that represented by **HLBC**.

Each of **HLBC** has isolated readings, e.g. **LABCD** *une ville,* **H** *en une ville* (l. 611); **LABCD** *de cuer fin,* **H** *le c. f.* (l. 2788); **HABCD** *ne se firent point veoir,* **L** *no point* (l. 125); **L** line omitted (ll. 1409, 3210); **HLACD** *.iiii. jours,* **B** *troiz j.* (l. 714); **HLACD** *le duc dexcestre,* **B** *le d. de cestre* (l. 827); **C** lines omitted (ll. 2572–2573); **HLABD** *evesques abbes qui disoient,* **C** *no abbes* (l. 2574). Thus no one of the four is the source of any of the others.

B is significantly different in that it is half the size of the other MSS. The *Prinse et mort* is copied in 31 folios in **B**, with 68 lines to a page, whereas it occupies on average 76 folios (28 lines to a page) in the others. **B** also has a considerable number of errors, e.g. lines omitted (ll. 63, 703); *avant* omitted (l. 655). This has caused difficulty in editing the epistles, *ballades,* and the *chant royal,* of which it is the sole witness. Furthermore corrections made by the scribe as he went along – by scoring out or expunction – suggest that **B** was hastily copied, e.g. *larchevesque de cantorbie fier* [*disant* scored out] (l. 471); *que trestous* [*avront* scored out] *ceulx avront* (l. 479); *tous les* [*cir* scored out] *crurent* (l. 498); *moult* [*chie* scored out] *riche et chiere* (l. 981). These three points – a text containing a large number of poor readings and omissions, cramped into half the space of the other MSS, and carelessly copied – added to the fact that the MS may be as late as mid fifteenth-century, show that **B** must be excluded from the list of candidates for base MS.

C also has a considerable number of lines missing, e.g. ll. 2824, 3471, 3484, and 3511. This, as well as being a late fifteenth-century MS, is enough to render it unsuitable as a base.

H was certainly written by 1405. **L** may be as early, but we cannot be sure; palaeographical evidence points merely to a date before 1440. What is certain is that **L** has a large number of isolated readings, e.g. *humblement* (l. 441), *nouvelles bien certaines* (l. 449), *de quoy ilz furent en leur vie entechies* (l. 481); there are also lines omitted, e.g. ll. 350–351, 1028, and 2289.

H is a more carefully copied MS, its errors being rarely more than venial, e.g. *ymberne* (l. 39); *nulz* (l. 215); *cestoit* (l. 429). It does have over 130 corrections – all given in the variants beneath the text, with an underlining beneath any letter written over an erasure – but while those in **B** point to a scribe working too quickly and carelessly, the reverse is so with **H**. Sometimes a letter has been squeezed in later, e.g. *brief* > *briefz* (l. 302); *soie* > *soiez* (l. 557); *assamble* > *assamblee* (l. 759), or one letter has been written over another, e.g. *ioyaulx* > *joyaulx* (ll. 1001, 1006); *chaccun* > *chascun* (l. 1230). The large majority of corrections have been made, however, by erasing the original lesson and writing over the erasure; the corrections were almost certainly made by the original scribe.

It is interesting to note that nearly 90 times out of more than 130, the correction in **H** coincides with an error or variant in one or more of the other five MSS, e.g. **H** *alasmes*, **C** *sen alla* (l. 393); **H** *tout*, **C** *puis* (l. 1100); **H** *tout*, **LC** *trestout* (l. 1241); **H** *pour vray*, **ACD** *certes* (l. 1284); **H** *sanc*, **B** *fait* (l. 3221). Very often **H**'s correction coincides with a hypometric reading in **LB** or **LBC**, e.g. **H** *avec*, **LB** *et* (l. 108); **H** *je vous*, **LB** no *je* (l. 220); **H** *quavoit le conte*, **LB** *quot le c.* (l. 304); **H** *moult forte et* **LBC** no *moult* (l. 612); **H** *tous le laisserent*, **LBC** no *tous* (l. 744).

Some corrections leave **H** with an isolated reading. Usually, however, there is nothing to choose between it and the lesson of **LABCD**; both are equally satisfactory as far as sense and metre are concerned, e.g. **H** *en chevauchant*, **LABCD** *ilz chevauchoient* (l. 1031); **H** *et de dueil*, **LABCD** *de douleur* (l. 1254); **H** *le grant meschief*, **LABCD** *la grant misere* (l. 1397). On one occasion, however, **H**'s correction gives a better rhyme, **H** *qui de vray cuer vouloient bien conquerre*, **LABCD** *q. d. bon c. v. aler querre* (l. 883), rhyming with *querre* (l. 881).

Once the correction supplies a word clearly omitted from the other MSS, **H** *gens* [in left margin] *parmi galles*, **LABCD** no *gens* (l. 1962). One correction is especially interesting: **H** *de le* [King Richard] *desfaire assez briefment*, **LABCD** *de le faire mourir b.* (l. 2437). Whereas *faire mourir* is unequivocal, *desfaire* is ambiguous, meaning either 'to kill' or merely 'to overthrow'. This may be a reflection of the uncertainty that existed at this early date as to whether Richard were dead or alive.

It is certain that **H** originally had these variant or hypometric readings of the other MSS, which the scribe later changed when he checked **H** from another exemplar. The separative errors in the other five MSS militate against any one of them being this second exemplar; it clearly represents a different tradition from **LABCD** and the uncorrected **H**. The corrections demonstrate the scrupulous care the scribe took with his MS. Not content with carefully copying his exemplar, he went to the trouble of checking his text against a second MS. **H** offers the best text of the *Prinse et mort*, calling for the smallest amount of editorial intervention and was therefore used as the base MS for this edition.

Previous Editions

The *Prinse et mort* has been edited twice before: in 1824 by Rev. J. Webb, with a translation and notes,[57] and in 1826 by J.A. Buchon.[58] Of the six MSS surviving, Webb knew only **H**, **L**, and **D**. He used **H** as his base MS. 'Of two [*sic*] manuscripts of this tract, one in the British Museum and the other in the Library of Lambeth Palace, the former is apparently the earliest'.[59] Webb unaccountably states that the MS in Paris which he used was **C** (BnF f. fr. 1668, formerly No. 7656);[60] examination of only a few variants, however, e.g. ll. 159, 261, 457, 514, and 675, confirms that he was using **D** (BnF f. fr. 1441, formerly No. 7532).

The text as he establishes it leaves much to be desired. Scribal errors are either not corrected: *nulz* (l. 215), *pars* (l. 437); or are corrected without the fact being noted: *communent* (l. 329), *cestoit* (l. 429), *le duc de cexcestre* (l. 1073). His transcript is extremely inaccurate; the following errors occur on p. 295 alone: *verdur* for *verdure* (l. 3), *oyseaux* for *oyseaulx* (l. 5), *laisser* for *laissier* (l. 10), *pres* for *prest* (l. 18). Many errors are more serious, including errors of omission: *en* (l. 147), *scay* (l. 257), *qui est* (l. 611), *le duc* (l. 1507); and errors of transposition: *morir beaucoup* (l. 197), *chascun sa foy* (l. 221), *fu la* (l. 343).

Webb's unfamiliarity with Middle French led him to include many nonsensical readings: *jours* for *joies* (l. 387), *la guerre* for *le querre* (l. 411), *sur savis* for *sur sains* (l. 598), *niart* for *m'ait* (l. 999), *points nulx* for *pour ce nulz* (l. 1236). He also omits variants in **L**: *le pais* (l. 107), *point* omitted (l. 125), *affin tele* (l. 160); and in **D**: *plus riens* (l. 269), *le duc* (l. 571), *bien beau cousin le scay* (l. 581). Examples of all these errors could be multiplied many times over. Furthermore, Webb ignores the chapters into which both **H** and **L** divide the text, and since his is a diplomatic edition, abbreviations are not extended, nor are modern word-divisions introduced.

---

[57] Jehan Creton, 'Translation of a French Metrical History of the Deposition of King Richard the Second ... with a Copy of the Original', ed. J. Webb, *Archaeologia*, 20 (1824), pp. 1–423.

[58] Jehan Creton, 'Histoire de Richard II'.

[59] Creton, 'Translation of a French Metrical History', p. 3.

[60] Ibid. p. 293.

INTRODUCTION 17

Buchon knew and used Webb's edition,[61] but chose **A** as his base MS: [*le manuscrit*] *que j'ai suivi est à la fois le plus ancien et le plus correct*.[62] Errors of transcription abound; the following occur on p. 324 alone: *fois* for *foiz* (l. 21), *fu* for *fut* (ll. 25, and 36), *un mains* for *ung moins* (l. 25), *chevauchant* for *chevauchans* (l. 27), *mercredi* for *mercredy* (l. 30), *avoient* for *avoyent* (l. 42), *repoz* for *repos* (l. 43). He gives no variants and corrects **A** without acknowledgement: *la feumes nous* (l. 54), *survenir* (l. 59), *par droit* (l. 105), *son bien* (l. 146).

Some extracts of Creton's account – from the time Richard heard of Lancaster's return to England until the King's leaving Chester for London in Lancaster's custody, and Creton's scepticism at the news of Richard's death – have been printed in his *Chronicles of the Revolution* by Professor Given-Wilson, in Webb's translation, substantially modernized.[63] The capture of King Richard at Flint by Henry Lancaster, in Webb's translation, is printed by H. Taylor in his *Historic Notices ... of Flint*.[64] Creton's two epistles and one *ballade* were published by P.W. Dillon in 1840; this is also a very poor transcription.[65] The remaining two *ballades* and the *chant royal* were edited by Professor Roccati in 2003.[66]

The present edition is fiercely critical of the Rev. Webb and his edition. However, it should be remembered that he was writing without the benefits and advantages of modern scholarship. It was by means of his edition that a medieval text of the first importance, and most of the colour miniatures, were made available at an early date. We owe him a debt of gratitude.

The *Prinse et mort du roy Richart d'Angleterre* and the *Chronicque de la traïson et mort de Richart Deux roy dengleterre*

There are two contemporary works in French on the deposition of Richard II: the *Prinse et mort*, in verse by Creton, and the anonymous *Traïson et mort*, in prose. It has been claimed that there is a further

[61] Creton, 'Histoire de Richard II', p. 321.
[62] Ibid. p. 322.
[63] *Chronicles of the Revolution*, ed. Given-Wilson, pp. 137–152, 243–245.
[64] H. Taylor, *Historic Notices, with Topographical and Other Gleanings Descriptive of the Borough and County-town of Flint* (London, 1883), translated extracts on pp. 71–79.
[65] Jehan Creton, 'Remarks on the Manner of the Death of King Richard the Second', ed. P.W. Dillon, *Archaeologia*, 28 (1840), pp. 75–95.
[66] Jehan Creton, 'Trois ballades politiques inédites de Jean Creton (début du XVe siècle)', ed. G.M. Roccati, in *Lingua, cultura e testo: Miscellanea di studi francesi in onore di Sergio Cigala*, ed. E. Galazzi and G. Bernardelli, 3 vols (Milan, 2003), II, pt. 2, pp. 1099–1110.

French work on the death and deposition of King Richard,[67] but Professor Palmer has demonstrated that this third chronicle is a 'pirated' version of the *Traïson*.[68]

The two works are quite independent and one cannot say either that they were interdependent or that 'Deux versions de la Chronique de Richard II existent, l'une en prose, l'autre en vers'.[69] Of the 37 surviving *Traïson* MSS, half contain incidents – e.g. Richard's capture, an alternative account of his death, the return of Isabella – using phrases which suggest that the author took them from the *Prinse et mort*. For his edition of the *Traïson* Benjamin Williams used one of these – BnF f. fr. 5624 – as his base MS. However, he folded into it a large excerpt – pp. 27–33 – relating to Richard's Irish expedition, contained in MS BnF 5624 (which he refers to as MS 10212, as formerly numbered).[70] Thus Williams presents the reader with a conflated text. Furthermore, BnF MS 5624 is the only MS of the *Traïson* with this account of Richard in Ireland, which follows very closely the *Prinse et mort*, and could certainly not have been written without it. It is a clumsy rendering of verse into prose.

It is fatally easy to miss the side-notes on pp. 27–33 announcing the change of MS, and equally easy to fail to recognize their significance. Williams' edition is unfaithful to the *Traïson* as originally written, since it has – from two different sources – all the incidents included at a later date, especially the unique account of Richard in Ireland.

Like the *Traïson* itself, the interpolations are anonymous and certainly not composed by Creton. Had he wanted to insert his own accounts into the *Traïson*, he would simply have written in prose, as he did in Chapters 30–40 (pp. 187–213) of the *Prinse et mort*. The information was all inside his own head, he had no need to borrow from his own work and thus deform it. Furthermore, it would have been an insult to King Richard and to Creton's patron, the duke of Burgundy, to have debased his own elegant work in this way.

There is a final stumbling block to a clear view of the relationship between these two independent works. In one family of MSS of Froissart's *Chronicles*, Book IV, is written:[71]

---

[67] P. Rickard, *Britain in Medieval French Literature 1100–1500* (Cambridge, 1956), p. 160; D.B. Tyson, 'Jean le Bel: Portrait of a chronicler', *Journal of Medieval History*, 12 (1986), p. 331 n. 5.

[68] Palmer, 'French Chronicles', 61:1 (1978), p. 180.

[69] P.M. De Winter, *La Bibliothèque de Philippe le Hardi, duc de Bourgogne (1364–1404)* (Paris, 1985), p. 20; also M.V. Clarke, *Fourteenth-Century Studies* (Oxford, 1937), p. 68.

[70] *Prinse et mort*, ll. 31–456; *Chronicque de la traïson et mort*, ed. Williams, pp. 27–32. My remarks on the *Traïson* MSS are based on Palmer, 'French Chronicles', 61:1 (1978), pp. 145–181.

[71] A. Varvaro, 'Jean Froissart, la déposition et la mort de Richard II: Construction du récit historique', *Romania*, 124 (2006), p. 156.

Pour ce que vous, sire Jehan Froissart ... sur vostre quart volume vous taisiez de la mort du noble roy Richart, roy d'Angleterre, en vous excusant par une maniere de dire, que au jour que vous feistes vostre dit quart volume n'estiez point infourmé de la maniere de sa mort, à celle fin ... que tous vaillans hommes se puissent mirer et exemploier ou fait douloureux de sa mort, je fais savoir à tous, ainsi que j'ay esté infourmé par [un] homme digne de foy, nommé Creton, et par escript de sa propre main, lequel pour ce temps estoit en Angleterre et ou païs, et escript ce que je diray: que le roy Richart d'Angleterre fut occis et mis à mort en la tour de Londres par ung jour des Roys, l'an mil trois cens .iiij.^{xx} et .xix., par la maniere qui s'ensuit.

Verité est, ainsi que certiffie le dit Creton ...

There follows an account of Richard being hacked to death by Sir Piers Exton, *as told in the Traïson*. At first glance this is a real obstacle, but there is a persuasive answer:[72] Froissart was not in England at this time; Creton was associated with writing about Richard, and a simple mistake was made in attributing this account to him.

It might reasonably be argued that the two works were composed for different audiences: the *Prinse et mort* in verse for reading aloud to aristocratic groups, and in *de luxe* illustrated MSS for presentation to the higher nobility; the *Traïson*, with its large number of surviving copies, a very successful work intended for private reading among government officials and civil servants, prosperous merchants, and the upper *bourgeoisie* generally.

Jehan Creton: His Life

13 August 1386	Philip the Bold pays Creton *pour un livre par lui*.[73]
26 April 1399	Creton and his companion set out for England (ll. 9–29).
? September 1399	They return to France (p. 211, l. 24–p. 213, l. 4). Shortly afterwards Creton starts work on the *Prinse et mort* (*infra*, p. 27).
After August 1401	Creton gathers information from a clerk and others who gave him news of England (ll. 2377–2390).
After August 1401– before April 1402	The *Prinse et mort*, first epistle and first *ballade* are completed (*infra*, p. 27).

---

[72] A. Gransden, *Historical Writing in England*, 2 vols (London, 1974–1982), II, p. 190 n. 193.
[73] Cockshaw, 'Mentions d'auteurs, de copistes, d'enlumineurs', p. 127, no. 20.

Before April 1402	Creton is sent to Scotland to investigate the rumour of Richard's being alive there.[74]
April–October 1402	The second epistle is written, referring to the offer to Burgundy of the regency of Brittany.[75]
16 July 1402	Philip pays Creton *pour et en recompensacion d'un livre faisant mencion de la prinse de feu le roy Richart.*[76]
1402–1403	The second and third *ballades* and the *chant royal* are written.
3 March, 17 June, 4 October 1403	Philip makes payments to Creton, his *varlet de chambre*.[77]
27 April 1404	Philip dies.[78]
late 1405	Duke of Berry receives **H** from Jean de Montaigu (*supra*, pp. 2–3).
11 November 1407	John the Fearless pays Creton for a journey to visit Richard in Scotland.[79]
29 July 1410	Charles VI pays *nostre amé varlet de chambre Jehan Creton la somme de deux cens frans* for a journey made some time ago to Scotland, to see if Richard were alive there.[80]
7 August 1410	Creton's receipt for 100 of the above 200 francs.[81]
1411, 1413	Jehan Creton nominated *clerc payeur des oeuvres du roy*.[82]
1420	Royal accounts show payment *a Jehan Creton, payeur des oeuvres du roi es vicomté ... de Paris ... pour l'aider a payer sa rançon a mgr Jacques de Bouconvillier, qui naguere l'avait pris ... 200 livres tournois.*[83]

---

[74] F. Lehoux, *Jean de France, duc de Berri: Sa vie, son action politique (1340–1416)*, 4 vols (Paris, 1966–1968), II, p. 518 n. 2; p. 473 n. 6.

[75] R. Vaughan, *Philip the Bold: The Formation of the Burgundian State* (London, 1962), p. 53.

[76] Cockshaw, 'Mentions d'auteurs, de copistes, d'enlumineurs', p. 135, no. 50.

[77] Ibid. p. 135, no. 50; p. 137, no. 61.

[78] Vaughan, *Philip the Bold*, p. 240.

[79] Cockshaw, 'Mentions d'auteurs, de copistes, d'enlumineurs', p. 138, no. 69.

[80] Creton, 'Remarks', p. 94. The reference to the document concerned, BnF Pièces originales 930, Creton, nos 1–2, is given by Palmer, 'French Chronicles', 61:1 (1978), p. 153 n. 2.

[81] Creton, 'Remarks', ed. Dillon, p. 95.

[82] M. Rey, *Le Domaine du roi et les finances extraordinaires sous Charles VI 1388–1413* (Paris, 1965), p. 157 n. 1.

[83] B.A. Pocquet du Haut-Jussé, *La France gouvernée par Jean sans Peur: Les Dépenses du receveur général du royaume* (Paris, 1949), no. 1250.

The entry for 16 July 1402 has caused considerable confusion. In his catalogue of the library of the dukes of Burgundy, Gabriel Peignot wrongly notes the one entry he found for Creton:[84] *Du 16 juillet, le Duc achepte de Jehan Creston [sic], moyennant neuf escus d'or, ung liure faisant mention de La prinse du Roy Richar.* The entry is transcribed correctly by Pierre Cockshaw: *A Jehan Creton, pour don a lui fait par mon dit seigneur de grace especial, la somme de LX escuz d'or pour et en recompensacion d'un livre faisant mencion de la prinse de feu le roy Richart, si comme il appert... par les lectres patentes... donnees a Paris le XVIe jour de juillet l'an mil CCCC et deux. ...*[85] Creton is receiving payment for the book, i.e. for his work in writing it. Incorrectly, Georges Doutrepont and Muriel J. Hughes follow Peignot, Hughes listing, 'Creston, Jehan. Bookseller. On 16 July 1401 [sic] he sold the duke a book mentioning *La Prinse du Roy Richar*'.[86] De Winter confuses the *Prinse et mort* with the *Traïson*.[87]

It should be said at the outset that the position of *valet de chambre*, either to Charles VI or to Philip the Bold, entailed no duties in the royal or ducal bedchamber. By the end of the fourteenth century the title was bestowed on writers, artists, and craftsmen: this was how they were paid for their services: *la qualification de varlet de chambre... fut conférée à des hommes que les ducs voulaient honorer.*[88] Similarly the *clerc payeur des oeuvres du roy* was held in high esteem: *l'office a souvent été tenu par des membres de la bonne bourgeoisie parisienne... c'étaient tous des personnages fort considérés.*[89]

There is no external evidence for Creton's background or life before the entry in the Burgundian accounts of 1386. He has been said to belong to 'the respectable family of Estourmel'[90] but no evidence is offered. His link to a family holding land at Moulbaix (near Ath, in Hainault) in the fifteenth century, adduced by Kervyn de Lettenhove,[91] is equally problematic. The assertion that he

---

[84] G. Peignot, *Catalogue d'une partie des livres composant la bibliothèque des ducs de Bourgogne au XVe siècle*, 2nd edn (Dijon, 1841), p. 32. Furthermore, Peignot misreads *LX escuz* (*soixante escuz*, 'sixty crowns') as *IX escus* (*neuf escus*, 'nine crowns').

[85] Cockshaw, 'Mentions d'auteurs, de copistes, d'enlumineurs', p. 135, no. 50; Vaughan, *Philip the Bold*, pp. 200–201.

[86] G. Doutrepont, *La Littérature française à la cour des ducs de Bourgogne* (Paris, 1909), p. 405; M.J. Hughes, 'The Library of Philip the Bold and Margaret of Flanders', *Journal of Medieval History*, 4 (1978), item II.3, p. 168.

[87] De Winter, La Bibliothèque de Philippe le Hardi, p. 19.

[88] Doutrepont, *La Littérature française*, pp. 470–471; Vaughan, *Valois Burgundy*, pp. 166, 180.

[89] Rey, *Le Domaine du roi*, p. 156.

[90] *Chronicque de la traïson et mort*, ed. Williams, p. viii n. 1.

[91] J. Kervyn de Lettenhove, 'Les Chroniques inédites de Gilles le Bel', *Bulletins de l'Académie royale des sciences, des lettres et des beaux-arts de Belgique*, 2nd ser., 2 (Brussels, 1857), p. 459.

was of Norman extraction has not been justified, and the Jehan Creton serving with Robert de Clermont in 1357 is of an earlier generation.[92]

The internal evidence of the *Prinse et mort* shows that he was a native of Paris or the surrounding region. The *Prinse et mort* is written in *francien*, the dialect of Paris and the Île de France, before which all other Old French dialects faded out, and which became Modern French.[93] Such few Picardisms as occur are usually scribal in origin, e.g. *biau* (ll. 520, 3702); *mangonniaulx*: *monchiaulx*: *nouviaulx* (ll. 1765–1767); *commencha* (l. 2555); *chieulx* (l. 3207).[94]

The fact that he was attached to the house of Burgundy does not mean that Creton was a Northerner.[95] Philip the Bold had been created the first Valois duke of Burgundy by his father, John the Good,[96] and although he did everything he could to increase the size and importance of his duchy, he was fundamentally a prince of the French royal house. After the death of his brother, Charles V, in 1380, and the accession of the unstable Charles VI, he was locked in bitter rivalry for influence over the new king with Louis d'Orléans, the king's brother. Hostility between these two ran at a high pitch in the early years of the fifteenth century, and only the active intervention of the queen and the dukes of Bourbon and Berry prevented France from being precipitated into civil war at the beginning of 1402.[97] Burgundy's power base was at the royal court in Paris. From the mid 1390s until his death in 1404, 'Paris was his favourite and habitual place of residence'.[98]

An educated guess can be made as to Creton's age. He could not have been such a very young man when Philip paid him in 1386 *pour un livre par lui* (*supra*, p. 19); he must have been in his early twenties at a minimum. Both Richard II and Henry Lancaster were born in 1367;[99] Creton was at least slightly older than they were, perhaps born around 1361–1363. The difficulty here is Lancaster's addressing him and his companion at Flint as *Mes enfans* (p. 197, l. 17). This is not to be taken literally; a priest might use the same expression to his congregation, i.e. someone in authority talking to people

---

[92] V. Leclerc, *Histoire littéraire de la France au quatorzième siècle*, 2 vols (Paris, 1865), II, p. 18; Creton, 'Remarks', ed. Dillon, p. 86.

[93] M.K. Pope, *From Latin to Modern French with Especial Consideration of Anglo-Norman, Phonology and Morphology*, rev. edn (Manchester, 1952), §60, pp. 33–34; §169, pp. 81–82.

[94] Ibid. §1320 Northern Region; *Phonology*: §§i, viii, pp. 486–488.

[95] D. McGettigan, *Richard II and the Irish Kings* (Dublin, 2016), pp. 21–24, 219.

[96] Vaughan, *Philip the Bold*, p. 3.

[97] Ibid. p. 56.

[98] Vaughan, *Valois Burgundy*, p. 49.

[99] N. Saul, *Richard II* (New Haven, CT, 1997), p. 12; C. Given-Wilson, *Henry IV* (New Haven, CT, 2016), p. 11.

towards whom he is well disposed, regardless of their age. Henry is speaking *de haut en bas*; *mes enfants* is translated here as 'my sons'.

Where external evidence is lacking, some modern writers have stepped in with their own view on Creton: he is variously a French nobleman; a French chronicler, a 'hanger-on ... looking for an exotic adventure'; a squire; a French valet; Richard's French adherent.[100] M.V. Clarke and V.H. Galbraith thought he was so unimportant that the earl of Salisbury left him behind at Flint Castle when he withdrew on Conway despite the fact that Creton was a royal envoy.[101] This was necessary in order for them to explain the absence of Archbishop Arundel at Conway in Creton's account.[102] Creton himself tells us that *le roy nous avoit envoié avecques le roy Richart en Irlande* (p. 197, ll. 13–14), thus Clarke and Galbraith are asking us to believe that Salisbury had simply abandoned Creton and his companion, royal envoys from France, at Flint. Richard's party – Richard, Salisbury, and some of Richard's entourage – returned that way from Conway, but it was *after* Richard had been lured from Conway by Northumberland's treachery. On retreating to Conway, Salisbury must have been thinking of escaping by sea (see map p. ii).

When Creton came to England in 1399, it should be understood that he was in his thirties at least. He says that he had been despatched by Charles VI, but given his attachment to the duke of Burgundy, and Burgundy's influence over the king, he was sent by Philip the Bold. He was specifically instructed to go to Ireland, *pour veoir le païs* (p. 197, l. 15) and does seem to have gone out of his way to see as much as possible: when the earl of Gloucester was sent to parley with McMurrough:

> *Avecques eulx alay, comme celui*
> *Qui vouloit voir*
> *L'onneur, l'estat, la force et le povoir*
> *De Maquemore. ...* (ll. 315–318)

It is too much to call Creton a spy, but he does seem to have been sent as Burgundy's eyes and ears, on a diplomatic mission of some sort.[103]

---

[100] Taylor, *Historic Notices*, p. 72; McGettigan, *Richard II*, pp. 22, 167; L. D. Duls, *Richard II in the Early Chronicles* (The Hague, 1973), p. 133 n. 51; D. Biggs, *Three Armies in Britain: The Irish Campaign of Richard II and the Usurpation of Henry IV 1397–1399* (Leiden, 2006), pp. 202, 233; P. Strohm, 'The Trouble with Richard: The reburial of Richard II and Lancastrian symbolic strategy', *Speculum*, 71 (1996), p. 88.

[101] Clarke, *Fourteenth-Century Studies*, p. 69. Chapter III, 'The Deposition of Richard II' was written in collaboration with V.H. Galbraith, and originally published in 1930.

[102] J. Sherborne, *War, Politics and Culture* (London, 1994), pp. 142–143.

[103] Vaughan, *Philip the Bold*, p. 10.

The Burgundian state was built on alliances and good relations, rather than on warfare and conquest, especially with England;[104] Philip's need for intelligence was essential for achieving his objectives. Three times in 1403 (*supra*, p. 20), Creton was paid for unspecified reasons.

Internal evidence suggests that Creton was attached to the earl of Salisbury when in England. He pronounces Salisbury a Francophile and poet (ll. 771–772, 779–781) and this is confirmed by Christine de Pizan who said of him: *icellui gracieux chevalier amast dictiez, et lui meismes fust gracieux dicteur*.[105] Jehan du Castel, Christine's son, spent some time in his service: *je consenti ... que l'ainsné de mes filz, assez abille et bien chantant enfant de l'aage de .XII. ans, alast avec lui oudit païs d'Engleterre pour estre avec ung sien filz aucques de l'aage*.[106] Salisbury and Creton could have met at the end of the previous year, when Salisbury was sent to Paris by Richard to break off the negotiations initiated by Lancaster for a marriage between himself and Mary of Berry.[107] Lancaster bore the earl a grudge for his intervention, taunting him when he had him in his power: *Conte de Salsebery, sachiez de certain que, nyent plus que vous ne daignastes parler a Monseigneur le duc de Lancastre, quant lui et vous estiez a Paris au Noël derreinerement passé, il ne parlera a vous* (p. 204, ll. 18–21).

Creton was interested in Salisbury and his family: the son of his countess by an earlier marriage is the only one of the new knights created, along with Lancaster's son, whom Creton mentions (p. 187, ll. 20–22). Although of different rank, they were both educated men with similar interests and outlook on life. When Salisbury was ordered by Richard to return before him to Wales and raise the Welshmen for the King, Creton went with him (ll. 603–609). His presence in Salisbury's entourage would account for Creton's being practically at the King's elbow from the time he met up with the army on the way to Milford Haven (ll. 50–53) until Richard fell into Lancaster's hands at Flint (p. 203, ll. 26–27).

Salisbury realized immediately the King was captured that the Frenchman might be the only one left alive to tell the tale, and was concerned that Creton should be fully aware of what was going on. To this end, he repeated to him what the Archbishop of Canterbury said to Richard at Flint, since Creton had not been able to hear for himself (p. 193, ll. 5–7), and translated from English into French the exchange between the King and Lancaster

---

[104] Vaughan, *Valois Burgundy*, p. 48.
[105] Christine de Pizan, *Le Livre de l'advision Cristine*, ed. C. Reno and L. Dulac (Paris, 2001), p. 112.
[106] Ibid.
[107] Saul, *Richard II*, pp. 405–406 n. 8.

(p. 199, ll. 17–18). This gives the lie to the dismissal of Creton's information on the proceedings of the Council when they were in Ireland;[108] Salisbury was keeping him *au fait* with what was being discussed.

Creton thought very highly of the earl, witness his panegyric when Salisbury was deserted by his troops in Wales (ll. 773–786). No other person is described in such glowing terms, Salisbury is the very model of a perfect knight.[109]

Creton returned to France in September 1399. Before April 1402 (*supra*, p. 20) he was sent to Scotland to investigate the rumour that Richard was alive there. Having been with Richard for four months, he would certainly have been able to identify an impostor. This was a large responsibility for him; on his finding rested the fate of Queen Isabella.

It was persistently alleged in the early 1400s that Richard was still alive.[110] While it was clearly in the interests of the enemies of Henry IV to put it about that Richard was not dead, the particular concern of the French lay in the legal position of Isabella. Was she Richard's wife or his widow? Was she free to remarry? An ordinance of Charles VI dating from early 1402 states that it is: *commune renommée que nostre filz Richart, jadiz roy d'Angleterre, est en vie ou royaume d'Escoce, auquel pour en savoir la verité nous avons envoié certains nos messaiges.*[111] Creton was certainly one of these messengers (*supra*, p. 20).

Creton found no reason to believe Richard alive: in his epistle to Philip the Bold, written April to October 1402 (*supra*, p. 20), he implores Burgundy to avenge the death of King Richard (p. 319, ll. 1–12). In June 1404, Isabella was betrothed to Charles d'Orléans, son of Louis, future poet and prisoner of Agincourt.[112]

Creton was nominated *clerc payeur des oeuvres du roy* in 1411 and 1413. This clerk of the king's works was not a professional, although he had the advice of a master-mason and a master-carpenter: *l'office a souvent été tenu par des membres de la bonne bourgeoisie parisienne.*[113] Civil strife raged in France at this time, and control of Paris and the king – and thus over appointments – fluctuated between Burgundians and Armagnacs/Orleanists. Burgundian influence extended from 1411 to 1413, at the end of which year they were

---

[108] D. B. Johnston, 'Richard II's departure from Ireland', *English Historical Review*, 98 (1983) p. 787.
[109] G. Mathew, *The Court of Richard II* (London, 1968), pp. 114–128.
[110] G. Lecuppre, *L'Imposture politique au Moyen Age: La Seconde Vie des rois* (Paris, 2005), pp. 63–65.
[111] Lehoux, *Jean de France*, II, p. 518 n. 2; p. 473 n. 6.
[112] See *ODNB*, s.v. 'Isabella [Isabella of France] (1389–1409)'.
[113] Rey, *Le Domaine du roi*, p. 157 n. 1.

expelled from Paris.[114] By 1418, Burgundians again ruled the capital. The entry in the royal accounts for 1420 suggests that Creton had been captured by the Armagnacs while trying to flee Paris in 1413.[115] Nothing more has been discovered about Creton; he then disappears from the world stage.

Jehan Creton: His Writings

The date by which the *Prinse et mort* was completed is easy to fix. On 16 July 1402, Philip the Bold paid Creton for his MS. While the earl of Salisbury had urged Creton to write about Richard's betrayal, it is likely that Philip commissioned the work for reading aloud at court:[116] it is noticeable that Creton refers always to listeners, not to readers (l. 164, note). The expression *com vous orrez*, 'as you will hear', or something very similar, occurs eighteen times (e.g. ll. 164–165, 461, 579). Reading aloud was commonplace in courtly circles:[117] Christine de Pizan says of Charles V: *En yver ... se occupoit souvent a ouir lire de diverses belles hystoires ... jusques a heure de souppper.*[118] She assumes that her biography of Charles V, written for Philip the Bold, will be read aloud: *Pour ce que trop longue narracion ... tourne aux oyans ... à annuy ... souffise à present la declaracion des vertus ... qui ... est la premiere partie de ce present traittié. ...*[119]

Creton uses the expression *com vous orrez* in two ways. After ll. 165, 2471, 3184, for example, he immediately tells the next part of the story. However, *com vous orrez* (l. 164); *vous orrez bien comment* (l. 791); *com vous orrez / Ici aprés* (ll. 1176–1177); *Com vous orrez ains qu'il soit gueres tart* (l. 2221) and so forth set down a marker for an episode that will be related later. Creton goes on to fulfil these promises, except on one occasion: *Et vous l'orrez* (l. 835) indicates that we will be told further about how two of the three bishops in Richard's party were not loyal to him. We hear no more of this, and when writing subsequently of Richard's companions, only the bishop of Carlisle is mentioned; the other two – Lincoln and St David's – are dropped completely. This interweaving of episodes bespeaks careful planning.

---

[114] E. Perroy, *La Guerre de Cent Ans* (Paris, 1945), pp. 197–211; Vaughan, *Valois Burgundy*, p. 153.
[115] Pocquet du Haut-Jussé, *La France gouvernée par Jean sans Peur*, no. 1250.
[116] De Winter, *La Bibliothèque de Philippe le Hardi*, p. 54.
[117] Bratu, '«Or vous dirai»: La V ocalité des récits historiques français du Moyen Age (XIIe–XVe siècles)', *Neophilologus*, 96 (2012), p. 344.
[118] Christine de Pizan, *Le Livre des fais et bonnes meurs du sage roy Charles V*, ed. S. Solente, 2 vols (Paris, 1936–1941), I, pp. 47–48.
[119] Ibid. I, pp. 103–104.

Writing for listeners demands repetition. Modern-day preachers employ the same technique when delivering a sermon. People being read to do not have the luxury of stopping the narrative and going back through the pages if they want to remind themselves of something already said; the poet has to repeat the most important episodes for them. Creton tells us (ll. 677–752) that the Welsh desert Salisbury; the earl confesses this to Richard when they meet (ll. 877–899). Creton recounts how Rutland disbanded Richard's army at Milford Haven (ll. 945–1046); a messenger reports this to the King at Conway (ll. 1261–1284). Archbishop Arundel suggests Lancaster's demands of Richard (ll. 1628–1640); Northumberland fleshes them out in the King's presence at Conway (ll. 1839–1927). Rutland's betrayal of the Epiphany Rising is touched on, *comme vous orrez cy aval* (ll. 2883–2884); his treachery is laid out (ll. 3006–3011, 3056–3106).

As well as telling the story twice, Creton seeks to keep his listeners engaged by nudging them, referring back to what they had already heard. He reminds them – *Com vous avez / Devant oÿ* (ll. 1064–1065) – that the Welsh harassed the English deserters; he does it again (p. 191, l. 28). He refers back to Northumberland's treacherous deceit (p. 201, ll. 5–6); and once more with *Comme j'ay dit ycy devant* (ll. 3699–3704). Two 'nudges' towards the end of the work go to the heart of the matter of the *Prinse et mort*: *En la forme et maniere que vous avez oÿ, prist le duc Henry le roy Richart* (p. 203, l. 3); and *Ainsi com vous avez ouÿ / ... Fu desfait le roy ancïen* (ll. 2833–2837).

Before April 1402 Creton was sent to Scotland to see whether Richard was alive there (*supra*, p. 20). In his epistle to the King announcing his intention to come to him (pp. 301–309), Creton says that the *Prinse et mort* has already been written and is in circulation: *Et saiches que tous les maulx et horribles traÿsons, qu'ilz t'ont faictes, j'ay manifestees par figures* [*et*] *par diz ou royaulme de France* (p. 305, ll. 23–25).

The last event mentioned in Creton's poem is the restitution of Queen Isabella at Leulingham on Sunday 31 July 1401 (ll. 3495–3498). Creton was not present at this ceremony himself, but took his information at second hand. He then writes of Isabella's return to Paris (ll. 3642–3643).

Clearly he did not compose the whole of the *Prinse et mort* between August 1401 and April 1402. It is a work of almost 4,000 lines plus an important prose section. He was back in France by September 1399 (p. 213, ll. 1–4); allowing for time spent in reporting back to the duke of Burgundy, and settling down to planning his work, he would have started writing in the autumn of 1399, while events were still fresh in his mind. The *Prinse et mort* was written 1399–1402.

The deposition of Richard, son-in-law to Charles VI, was an event with huge repercussions in France.[120] It happened during a truce in the Hundred Years' War, and had the potential to call into question Charles's right to the throne on account of his spells of incapacity. The large number of surviving MSS of the *Traïson*, plus Creton's account, bear witness to this. In particular, the *Traïson* must have had a very extensive readership. By contrast, the deposition of the ineffective Wenceslas IV, King of Germany, but never crowned Holy Roman Emperor, in 1400 was equally portentous but, unlike Richard's deposition, had little impact.[121]

It was common currency that Henry had had Richard murdered. Louis d'Orléans, who formed an alliance with Lancaster when he was in exile in Paris (1398–1399), accused him, in veiled terms, of regicide, in an exchange of insulting letters (1402–1403), referred to in Creton's *ballade IV* (pp. 327–329): *d'avoir entreprins encontre vostre lige et souverain seigneur le roy Richard ... ce que avez fait ... au temps que je fis ladicte aliance je n'eusse ... pensé que vous eussiez fait contre vostre roy ce qui est congneu et que chascun scet que vous avez fait ... je ne sçay se à vostre seigneur le roy Richard vous rendistes le serement de feaulté que vous aviez à luy avant que vous procédissiez contre sa personne par la manière que avez fait ... la dignité en quoy vous estes, je ne pense que la vertu divine vous y ait mis.*[122]

Eustache Deschamps stated baldly that Lancaster had captured and killed Richard,[123] and Christine de Pizan said of the marriage of Richard and Isabella of France: *duquel dit mariage fust ensuivi si grant bien ... se Fortune n'eust consenti perfaire la trahison, que fist Henri de Lancastre, qui cellui roy Richart par faulz et desloial tour prist et fist morir.*[124] Echoing these, a contemporary hand has added a marginal note to an early fifteenth-century MS of Valerius Maximus' *Facta et dicta memorabilia*; Demaratus betrayed Xerxes who gave him refuge when he was in exile: *Nota contre les François qui recepterent Henry de Lencastre qui au partir d'eulz fist mourir son seigneur le roy Richart d'Angleterre, gendre du roy de France et son alié, et fu environ les annees mil iii^c iiii^{xx} xviii, xix et les ensuivantes.*[125] Creton's views are entirely those of his contemporaries in France, which he had helped to shape.

---

[120] C. Taylor, ' "Weep thou for me in France": French views of the deposition of Richard II', in W.M. Ormrod (ed.), *Fourteenth Century England*, III (Woodbridge, Suffolk, 2004), pp. 207–214.
[121] Vaughan, *Valois Burgundy*, p. 17.
[122] Enguerran de Monstrelet, *La Chronique d'Enguerran de Monstrelet*, 6 vols (Paris, 1857–1862), I, pp. 54–55.
[123] Deschamps, *Oeuvres complètes*, VI, no. 1200, pp. 184–185.
[124] Christine de Pizan, *Le Livre des fais et bonnes meurs*, I, p. 147.
[125] John Rylands Library, Manchester, French MS. 63, fo. 56r.

The *Prinse et mort* falls into three separate sections: quatrains (ll. 1–2295), prose (pp. 186–212), and couplets (ll. 2335–3712), with an imprecatory *ballade* cursing Lancaster following the prose section (ll. 2296–2334). Each section tells a different part of the story: the first covers the events leading to Richard's capture; the middle, prose section comprises an accurate eye-witness account of the capture itself; and the final section deals with the deposition and its aftermath. The *Prinse et mort* is therefore quite unlike any of the other sources for the usurpation. Apart from Chandos Herald's *Vie du Prince Noir* and the anonymous *Voeux du Héron*,[126] it is the only account in French of a significant moment in English later medieval history made in a poetic form.

When Creton returned to France and set to work, the events described in the quatrains and prose had already happened: Richard was in prison and Parliament was going to meet to elect another King. However, Creton refers forward to the death of the earl of Salisbury (ll. 788–790), executed for his part in the failed Epiphany Rising of January 1400. Creton is actually writing about the earl being deserted by the Welshmen he had raised to fight for Richard, but inserts a panegyric on Salisbury. This reads just like a funeral eulogy, the emotion is quite raw and heart-felt; it seems as though news of the Rising had just reached Creton, and he responds to it with this outburst of feeling.

As he was writing the quatrains and prose, the events described in the couplets were still unfolding. News of the Parliament where Lancaster was elected King, his coronation and the Epiphany Rising came to Creton at second hand, he says from a French clerk who had travelled to England with Lancaster (ll. 2383–2390). In fact he was likely to have had information from various sources.

Creton wrote firmly in the tradition of the Middle French poets, although couplets, not quatrains, were the standard verse form of the period; only a highly competent writer, skilled in French verse, could accomplish a poem of this calibre. Even prolific authors such as Froissart and Chartier used the form only sparingly, and Creton himself slips into couplets in the final section.

The form he used, a system of concatenation – three decasyllabic lines rhymed together, while the four-syllable line following set the rhyme of the three ten-syllable lines coming after – was practised by leading Middle-French poets: Guillaume de Machaut, *Le Jugement du roi de Behaigne*; Jehan Froissart, *Le Dit dou bleu chevalier*; Christine de Pizan, *Le Livre du dit de Poissy*, *Le Livre des trois jugemens*,

---

[126] Chandos Herald, *La Vie du Prince Noir*, ed. D.B. Tyson (Tübingen, 1975); *The Vows of the Heron (Les Voeux du Héron): A Middle French Vowing Poem*, ed. J.L. Grigsby and N.J. Lacy, trans. N.J. Lacy (New York, 1992).

and *Le Livre du debat de deux amans*; and Alain Chartier, *Le Debat des deux fortunés d'amours*. Chartier also used this form in *Le Livre des quatre dames*, but in octosyllabics. The form may be a development of the tercets – two long lines, one short – practised by Rutebeuf in the mid thirteenth century, perhaps the inspiration also for Dante's *terza rima*.[127]

Creton sustains this complicated structure well, and the weaknesses are those to which any late Middle French writer might succumb: the second part of a decasyllable is occasionally mere padding (e.g. ll. 205, 851, 1537); the metre is awkwardly handled (ll. 1837, 1869, 2241); some rhymes are laboured (ll. 964–967, 2635–2636); there is assonance rather than rhyme in three quatrains (ll. 896–899, 1240–1243, 2144–2147); and he resorts fairly frequently to rhyming the same word with itself (ll. 81:83, 164–165, 832:835, 1312:1314, 1377–1378). One should note that *Ballades* I–IV are found only in one MS, a slovenly and hastily executed one (see, *infra*, p. 301). At first sight they display a distressing number of errors of rhyme and metre, but these are scribal in origin and easily corrected. The *Ballades* should not counter the view that Creton was an accomplished wordsmith.

Creton realized that what happened between Richard and Lancaster at Flint was of prime importance, the reason for which he was writing the *Prinse et mort*:

> *Or vous vueil dire sans plus rime querir*
> *Du roy la prinse. Et pour mieulx acomplir*
> *Les paroles qu'ilz dirent au venir*
>   *Eulx deux ensemble –*
> *Car retenues les ay bien, ce me semble –*
> *Si les diray en prose, car il semble*
> *Aucunesfoiz qu'on adjouste ou assemble*
>   *Trop de langaige*
> *A la matiere de quoy on fait ouvrage.*   (ll. 2285–2293)

Following the imprecatory *ballade*, which allows him full rein to curse Henry Lancaster, Creton picks up the narrative, this time from information received at second hand, in rhyming octosyllabic couplets. This is much less difficult to sustain, but Creton's narrative never recaptures the *élan* of the quatrains. It is as though he found it easier to write when he was drawing from his own experience. He had all the events in his memory, had lived most of them. Writing from

---

[127] L.E. Kastner, 'A neglected French poetic form', *Zeitschrift für französische Sprache und Literatur*, 28 (1905), pp. 288–292.

another person's information did not suit Creton. Although it would have been easier to write, the third section is pedestrian; recounting events he did not personally witness seems to handicap him.

It was Creton's view that the English hated the French (ll. 2391–2394, 3661), and that Richard was deposed solely because he loved his father-in-law, Charles VI, King of France (ll. 3292–3297). It is clear from the pejorative terms in which he wrote of the English, with the exception of the King and the earl of Salisbury, that Creton greatly disliked, perhaps even hated the English (ll. 2243–2244; p. 188, ll. 10–12; p. 201, ll. 8–11; p. 212, ll. 4–6; p. 111, ll. 5–7; ll. 2341, 2348–2358, 2374–2376, 2457–2459, 2650, 2929–2930, 3653–3655, 3667–3668). Creton's last word on the subject is in *Ballade* IV, in which he urges the duke of Orleans to invade England at the head of an army that will burn and devastate the country (p. 327, ll. 28–31). Creton's animosity is reflected in Henry's name always being written in the English way, whereas Richard always receives French spelling: *Richart*. The exception is l. 1157, where *Henri* makes a better rhyme for the eye with *di* : *choisi* : *failli*.

Creton is given to exaggeration, and has a poor grasp of numbers. He consistently gets distances wrong (ll. 90, 1739–1740; p. 193, ll. 12–13), and insists that Richard rode overnight from Milford Haven to Conway (ll. 865–868, 1257–1258), a distance of around 150 miles. Lancaster reduces his army to 30,000–40,000 men, which will be enough now that the King has been captured (p. 205, ll. 6–7), clearly a preposterous figure. He tries to add up three figures to make a total of 22 – the number of years that Richard has been on the throne – and gets 21 (ll. 934–935). Dates receive the same cavalier treatment (*infra*, p. 36).

The accounts of Richard's weeping should be taken as hyperbole. Creton has everyone weeping (l. 465): Salisbury and Richard when they meet up in Conway (ll. 869–872); Creton himself (ll. 1385–1387); Exeter and Surrey when Lancaster will not let them return to the King (l. 1551); Lancaster when he sees his father's tomb (p. 211, ll. 18–19); Sir Thomas Percy and the English ambassadors at the restitution of Isabella (ll. 3572–3573, 3596–3597); and Isabella herself on her return to France (p. 307, ll. 2–3). *Plourant* is an exaggerated description of an unhappy person.

Like Froissart, Creton was unfamiliar with the English parliamentary system.[128] This made it difficult for him to describe what was happening in London after Richard had returned there in Lancaster's custody. Thus problems arose in translating his terms: *la commune* (p. 207, l. 3), *les comunes* (p. 211, l. 5), *de / aux communes*

---

[128] Varvaro, 'Jean Froissart, la déposition', p. 134.

(p. 207, l. 26; p. 209, l. 15), *le commun* (ll. 2415, 2817, 3317), *le peuple commun* (l. 2671), *la communauté* (l. 2653).

Creton's knowledge of English was probably not extensive. By this time, English was the language of the court, although the nobility spoke French as well.[129] Froissart confirms that Richard could both talk and read French: *il ... regarda dedens le livre ... et y lisy, car moult bien parloit et lisoit franchois*.[130] A slight understanding of English would have served to enable Creton to travel from Paris to London, and then to Scotland in 1402, but once in England he was attached to the household of the French-speaking earl of Salisbury (*supra*, pp. 24–25) on whom he could rely to keep him *au fait* with events around him. The words spoken when Richard and Lancaster met at Flint were understood by Creton but, for avoidance of doubt, *si le mes [sic] recorda le conte de Salsebery en françoiz* (p. 199, ll. 17–18). When Creton wished to return to France, he asked Lancaster Herald to approach Lancaster for him (p. 195, ll. 30–33). The Herald obviously talked to Creton in French because, when he conversed with Lancaster, Creton states that he spoke *en langage englesch* (p. 197, l. 13). On learning that Creton and his companion were French, Lancaster addressed them in French (p. 197, ll. 16–18), and when the Frenchmen begged a safe conduct, they went directly to him since they now knew that the duke understood French (p. 211, ll. 26–28).

Creton stands accused of bad faith by trying to deceive his readers; his use of direct speech is taken as an attempt to say that he was present when he was not. For Clarke and Galbraith: 'it has been too hastily assumed that because he was an eyewitness for part of the time that he was an eyewitness all the time. This is exactly what he wanted his readers to believe'.[131] The intention to deceive is quite wrong. It should not be presumed that anything given in direct speech is to be taken as the actual words spoken.[132] Professor Ainsworth has demonstrated this by comparing an extract from Froissart's first and third redactions of Book I of his *Chronicles*: in the first he uses indirect speech, in the third direct speech; no one thought that Froissart had suddenly remembered the exact words from thirty years before.[133] Direct speech was a narrative technique

---

[129] Mathew, *Court of Richard II*, pp. 30–31; I. Short, 'On bilingualism in Anglo-Norman England', *Romance Philology*, 33 (1980), pp. 467–469.
[130] Jean Froissart, *Chroniques de France et d'Angleterre, livre quatrième*, ed. A.Varvaro (Brussels, 2015), p. 376.
[131] Clarke, *Fourteenth-Century Studies*, pp. 68–69.
[132] Johnston, 'Richard II's departure from Ireland', p. 789.
[133] P. Ainsworth, 'Style direct et peinture des personnages chez Froissart', *Romania*, 93 (1972), pp. 499–501.

to lend depth and texture to the account, giving the person reading the poem aloud the opportunity to 'act' the different speeches by varying intonation or gesture.[134]

It is important to remember that Creton was not writing a chronicle. He was the author of a literary work. This explains his opening lines; placing the action in a springtime setting was typical of Old and Middle French verse. One can mention for example Guillaume de Lorris: *Le Roman de la Rose*:

> *Que l'en ne voit buisson ne haie*
> *Qui en may parer ne se veille*
> *Et covrir de novele fuelle.*
> *Li bois recuevrent lor verdure...*
> *Mout a dur cuer qui en may n'aime,*
> *Quant il ot chanter sus la raime*
> *As oisiaus les douz chans piteus* (ll. 50–53, 81–83)

Guillaume de Machaut: *Le Jugement du roy de Behaigne*:

> *Au temps pascour que toute rien s'esgaie,*
> *Que la terre mainte coulour gaie*
> *Se cointoie...*
> *En ce doux temps, contre le mois de may, ...*
>   *Et cil oisel,*
> *Pour la douceur du joli temps nouvel,*
> *Si liement et de si grant revel*
> *Chantoient tuit...* (ll. 1–3, 9, 20–3)

Chandos Herald: *La Vie du Prince Noir*:

> *Seigniour, le temps qe je vous di,*
> *Ce fut droit par un samadi,*
> *Trois jours droit eu mois d'averille,*
> *Qe cil doulce oisselet gentille*
> *Preignent a refaire lour chantz*
> *Pres prees, per bois et per champs.*
> *En cellui temps fut, tut sanz faille,*
> *Devant Nazarz la grant bataille.* (ll. 3473–3480)

Jehan Froissart: *Le Dit dou bleu chevalier*:

> *Ce fu ou mois d'avril le deduisant,*
> *Sur le declin, pres dou may approçant,*
>   *Que cil oisiel*

---

[134] C. Muscatine, *Chaucer and the French Tradition* (Berkeley, CA, 1957), pp. 79–80.

> *Chantent moult cler pour le doulc temps nouvel,*
> *Au raverdir prendent cil arbrissiel. ...*
> *Car la chantoient et marles et mauvis*
> *Et li tres doulz rosegnols seignouris*
> *Moult doucement.*[135] (ll. 10–14, 18–20)

Froissart's most recent editor was of the opinion that the chronicler did not know the *Prinse et mort*,[136] but I venture to disagree. Froissart's account of the deposition of Richard is largely fanciful, but echoes of Creton's description of Richard's being tricked out of the safety of one of his castles are found in Froissart. He has Richard return from Ireland to Bristol, then take himself off to Flint Castle, where Lancaster comes to him *with only eleven other men* [editor's italics] and persuades him *par doulces parolles* to come to London.[137] It seems reasonable to suggest that Froissart had been present at a reading of the *Prinse et mort*; his account omits Northumberland at Conway, and condenses the action to Lancaster at Flint. This has the advantage of having the sneaking trick played on Richard carried out by Lancaster himself, rather than by his agent.

Creton's epistle to the duke of Burgundy, composed April–October 1402 (*supra*, p. 20), deserves special mention. In it he quotes from Valerius Maximus and other Classical authors. Valerius Maximus' *Facta et dicta memorabilia*, compiled in the first century AD, was a collection of 'memorable deeds and sayings' intended for the teaching of rhetoric.[138]

Considering the decline in the ability to read Latin, Charles V in 1375 commissioned Simon de Hesdin to translate Valerius into French. On Hesdin's death in 1383, partway through Book Seven (of nine), Nicolas de Gonesse completed the work in 1401. *Les Faits et dits memorables* enjoyed a huge success – more than sixty MSS survive[139] – and it is clear that Creton had unfettered access to an MS; he may even have owned one.

There are more than half-a-dozen substantial borrowings from Valerius Maximus, quoted almost word for word, either from the

---

[135] Guillaume de Lorris and Jean de Meun, *Le Roman de la Rose*, ed. F. Lecoy, 3 vols (Paris, 1965–1970), I, pp. 2–3; Guillaume de Machaut, *Le Jugement du roy de Behaigne and Remede de Fortune*, ed. J.I. Wimsatt and W.W. Kibler (Athens, GA, 1988), p. 61; Chandos Herald, *La Vie du Prince Noir*, p. 143; Jean Froissart, *Oeuvres de Froissart: Poésies*, ed. A. Scheler, 3 vols (Brussels, 1870–1872), I, p. 348.

[136] Varvaro, 'Jean Froissart, la déposition', p. 115.

[137] Froissart, *Chroniques de France et d'Angleterre, livre quatrième*, pp. 616–620.

[138] *The Oxford Classical Dictionary*, 4th edn (Oxford, 2012); https://oxfordre.com/classics, s.v. Valerius Maximus.

[139] A. Dubois, *Valère Maxime en français à la fin du Moyen Age* (Turnhout 2016), pp. 383–386.

author's text or from the translator's gloss. Also, when Creton 'quotes' from other writers, e.g. Suetonius or St Isidore of Seville, he takes his text not from them but from Valerius Maximus; there can be no doubt about this, as he quotes verbatim from Valerius. All the 'borrowed' passages have been made italic, and identified in the notes;[140] all come from the beginning of Book I. Creton does not move in a straight line through his model, but ranges to and fro. Obviously it is only in the prose epistle that it can be certain that Creton borrowed directly from Valerius Maximus. In the *ballades* it seems very likely that he had the information from Valerius, but given that he was writing in verse, and had to condense his source, the borrowing cannot be so easily verified.

This wholesale plagiarism seems underhand to us, but was not perceived that way in Middle French. At exactly the same time as Creton was composing his epistle to Philip the Bold (1402), Christine de Pizan was composing her *Chemin de long estude*, full of word-for-word borrowings from Valerius Maximus, and 'secondhand' borrowings from Valerius' sources.[141] Christine employs the same technique in her *Livre du corps de policie* (1404–1407).[142] It is certainly passing strange that two writers should be writing in the same way at the same time.

Thoughts might be entertained of Creton as an early exponent of humanism, but the Middle Ages were studded with moral tales from the Classics; they were a lesson in how to live, they were essentially practical.[143] Creton is not interested in the Classics for themselves, for the beauty of their form; his role is that of preceptor, his approach is quite medieval. The *Prinse et mort* occasionally looks backwards. Creton's use of an Old French word or expression to fulfil the needs of rhyme or metre shows the marvellous flexibility of the French language in the Middle French period.

---

[140] Valerius Maximus [Valère Maxime], *Facta et dicta memorabilia*, trans. Simon de Hesdin, Books I–III, ed. M. C. Enriello C. Di Nunzio, and A. Vitale-Brovarone (the only modern text, just available online and never printed), www.pluteus.it (accessed 25 November 2022); 'La Traduction de Valère-Maxime par Nicolas de Gonesse', ed. C. Charras, PhD thesis, McGill University, Montreal, 1982, covers Books VII (part)–IX.

[141] D. Lechat, 'L'Utilisation par Christine de Pizan de la traduction de Valère Maxime par Simon de Hesdin et Nicolas de Gonesse dans *Le Livre du chemin de long estude*', in E. Hicks (ed.), *Au champ des escriptures, IIIe Colloque international sur Christine de Pizan* (Paris, 2000), pp. 175–196.

[142] Christine de Pizan, *Le Livre du corps de policie*, ed. A.J. Kennedy (Paris, 1998), pp. xix, xxix–xxxii.

[143] J. Monfrin, 'Humanisme et traductions', *Journal des Savants* (1963), pp. 189–190; Vaughan, *Valois Burgundy*, p. 187.

Historical Value of the *Prinse et mort*. By J.J.N. Palmer

Creton was neither a chronicler nor an historian but a bystander involved by chance in events of high political drama. He was urged to recount these events by another of their victims, the earl of Salisbury, who believed that the truth would not otherwise emerge. His story is therefore largely based upon his own personal experiences and drawn from his own memory. It was almost certainly written down after an interval of some months, without the aid of documented sources, but more speedily than many of the other accounts.

Inevitably, such an account has many weaknesses, the most obvious being its chronology. Creton handles dates and figures with all the licence of a versifier. Richard, we are told, toured the castles of North Wales for 'four or six' days (l. 1393); Lancaster was accompanied by 'nine or eleven' great lords (p. 197, l. 9); an English king would reign for 'twenty to twenty-two' years (p. 199, ll. 25–26); Richard was guarded by 'ten or twelve' men (p. 205, l. 18). Impossibilities abound, his entire chronology is too 'long'. He relates that the English army left Kilkenny on 23 June and arrived in Dublin after eleven days of near-starvation and an unspecified number of days on the march. Yet the army was in Dublin by 1 July.[144] He further states that the army remained in Dublin more than eight weeks,[145] before news of Lancaster's invasion reached the King, and that Richard himself delayed in Ireland for a further eighteen days before leaving (ll. 795–797).[146] On this chronology, even the incredible feat which Creton attributes to Richard of riding the 150 or so miles from Milford Haven to Conway between midnight and daybreak would not have brought the King to Conway until weeks after the date which the poet gives for his critical meeting there with the earl of Northumberland.[147] On any reconstruction, Creton's Irish chronology is impossible.[148]

---

[144] If not some days earlier; Johnston, 'Richard II's departure from Ireland', p. 789 n. 3.

[145] More than two weeks (*quinzaine*) before Rutland's arrival (l. 405), and then a further six until news of Lancaster's invasion reached them from England. (ll. 446–450).

[146] Not eighteen days until he rejoined Salisbury, as stated by Johnston, 'Richard II's departure from Ireland', p. 789.

[147] The latest possible date for Richard's capture – and the most likely one – is the date given by Creton (Tuesday 19 August), p. 187, ll. 6–7. See Palmer, 'French Chronicles', 61:2 (1979), p. 420. Tuesday 22 August is an impossible date. In 1399, 22 August was a Friday: therefore Creton meant either Friday 22 August or Tuesday 19 August. Comparison with other sources favours Tuesday 19 August.

[148] Johnston, 'Richard II's departure from Ireland', pp. 789–790, makes a brave attempt to reconcile Creton's dates with those of other sources by resurrecting a suggestion made long ago by J.H. Ramsay (*The Genesis of Lancaster, or, The Three Reigns of Edward II, Edward III,*

Despite his imprecision, however, Creton's testimony is vital for the chronology of the events of July and August 1399; for he alone provides the information which enables us to make sense of the dates supplied by other sources. The most puzzling feature of this chronology is the delay between Lancaster's invasion and the King's reaction to it. News of Lancaster's arrival had reached Westminster by 28 June at the latest.[149] If the government reacted with the urgency we might expect, Richard should have been informed within the week. We do not know the exact date of his return to South Wales, but the earliest suggested is over three weeks later, the latest well over a month.[150] Of the various dates supplied by the English chroniclers, that of the monk of Evesham, who dates Richard's return some four weeks after Henry's arrival (c. 25 July), is probably nearest the truth.[151] Why did Richard take so long to return?

Two of the English chroniclers refer explicitly to this delay but only Walsingham attempts to explain it. But his inconsequential story of the English army embarking for Wales only to disembark in order to change ports,[152] would be utterly baffling without the aid of Creton's narrative by which to interpret it. Creton gives two reasons for the delay: the weather, and the strategic decisions taken by the King on the advice of his cousin, Edward Plantagenet, earl of Rutland and duke of Aumale. The first was in many respects the crucial factor. According to Creton, all communication between England and the army in Dublin was interrupted for several weeks

---

and *Richard II, 1307–1399*, 2 vols (Oxford, 1913), II, p. 355 n. 1) that Creton meant that Richard stayed eight (i.e. two plus six) weeks in Ireland, not in Dublin. But apart from the fact that this does nothing to resolve the other difficulties with Creton's chronology, Creton plainly says eight (i.e. two plus six) weeks in Dublin (*supra*, n. 145), and there is nothing in the text at this point to suggest that this was a slip of the pen.

[149] The sources give a variety of dates. A. Tuck, *Richard II and the English Nobility* (London, 1973), pp. 213–215, adduces record evidence which suggests a date towards the end of June. A hitherto unnoticed source confirms this deduction and lends precision: WAM, Book 1 (Liber Niger Quaternus), fo. 86v., 'In vigilia Nativitatis Sancti Johannis Baptiste [23 June] venit Henricus dux Herefordie versus Angliam. Et in vigilia Apostolorum Petri et Pauli [28 June] venerunt prima nova ad Westmonasterium de adventu ipsius. Et iiij die julij appliciut apud Pykeryng'. It may be presumed that the Council was informed no later than the Abbey of Henry's approach.

[150] Adam Usk, *The Chronicle of Adam Usk 1377–1421*, ed. C. Given-Wilson (Oxford, 1997), p. 58, gives 22 July; Thomas Walsingham, *Annales Ricardi Secundi et Henrici Quarti*, in J. de Trokelowe et Anon., *Chronica et Annales*, ed. H.T. Riley, Rolls Series (London, 1866) p. 247, *c.*1 Aug.

[151] *Historia Vitae et Regni Ricardi Secundi*, ed. G.B. Stow (Philadelphia, PA, 1977), p. 151.

[152] Walsingham, *Annales Ricardi Secundi*, p. 248. Sherborne, *War, Politics and Culture*, pp. 119–124, provides a lucid analysis of the different accounts told by the chroniclers.

by storms in the Irish Sea (ll. 446–456).[153] When they abated, news of the invasion was immediately brought to the King; but by this date, Lancaster was already in control of much of England (ll. 457–512). Creton's story appears, inexplicably, to have been all but ignored by the secondary authorities.

Richard left Dublin on 17 July,[154] but his return to England was further delayed by the decision he had taken to divide his forces, sending the earl of Salisbury directly to Conway while he himself marched south to Waterford, whence he sailed to Milford Haven. Creton, who is our only authority for this decision, also supplies the reasoning behind it. The shipping available at Dublin was adequate for only a small force. The remainder of the navy which had brought Richard to Ireland was scattered down the coast as far as Waterford. It made sense to collect these forces, and detachments of the army, at Waterford, and then cross directly to South Wales (ll. 538–557).[155]

Another factor, unknown to Creton, reinforced this reasoning. The actions of the English Council, and of Lancaster himself, very strongly suggest that it had arranged to join forces with the King near Bristol in order to confront the invader together, a sound enough strategy in view of Lancaster's line of march. The delays involved in communications and in moving the King's forces, however, meant that Lancaster was able to interpose his forces between those of the King and the Council. On 27 July, at about the moment of Richard's disembarcation in South Wales,[156] Lancaster came to terms with the Regent, the duke of York, at Berkeley; two days

---

[153] It is not clear why Sherborne states that we do not know where Richard was at this time; ibid. p. 120.

[154] The date is given by the account of the Receiver of Richard's chamber. J. Lufwyk: 'xvii die julii ... quo die predictus nuper rex cum exercitu suo recessit de Dublin ... ' (The National Archives, Kew, PRO E101/403/21). The misreading of the date in the enrolled version of this account by various authorities has caused considerable confusion, described at length by G.O. Sayles, 'Richard II in 1381 and 1399', *English Historical Review*, 94 (1979), pp. 822–826, and by Johnston, 'Richard II's departure from Ireland', pp. 790–793, who rather exaggerates Lufwyk's record. There is no reason at all to doubt his very precise statement that Richard left Dublin on 17 July. It should be noted that the particulars of Lufwyk's account cited here both confirm the enrolled version and are of superior authority.

[155] Ibid. pp. 790, 793, says that Creton is suspect on this point. While it is true that there is no direct corroboration of his statement that Richard sailed from Waterford, it makes such good sense of the events that followed that it may be accepted without reserve as true and as further evidence of Creton's value in enabling us to understand events for which no other testimony is available.

[156] Having left Dublin on 17 July, Richard can scarcely have landed more than a day or so earlier than this, given the distances involved. There is a useful illustration in Given-Wilson, *Henry IV*, Map 3, p. 128.

later he was master of Bristol and promptly executed those members of the Council who had attempted to hold the city for the King. Richard's route from South Wales into England was effectively blocked.

The ensuing events in South Wales are perhaps the most obscure of all the episodes leading to the usurpation, not least because Creton was no longer in the King's entourage, having sailed for Conway with the earl of Salisbury. We therefore have no eye-witness account of what Richard did on his arrival; how long he remained with his army; in what circumstances he left it; what caused the army to disperse; or when the King set out for Conway.[157] The widespread belief that Richard himself abandoned his army is too evidently propagated in the interests of all concerned to be taken on trust. Only Usk's story of Richard's attempt to secure troops from Glamorgan,[158] offers any reliable clue as to his activities in this area.

By contrast, Creton gives a very clear account of Salisbury's attempts to raise an army in North Wales and Cheshire, and of the circumstances in which that army too melted away before the King could join it (ll. 633–749). But for Creton, we would not even have known of Salisbury's presence in North Wales and would therefore be quite unable to make any sense of the King's decision to cross the length of Wales from Pembroke to Conway.

There is one other factor in Creton's account of the events between Richard's departure from Dublin and his arrival at Conway which deserves mention: the alleged treachery of Rutland. Creton is the principal witness against Rutland, and many historians have accepted his word and have held Rutland's treachery to have been a major factor in Richard's downfall. Without rejecting Creton's testimony, it is possible to take a different view. Creton's case against Rutland is that he was responsible for the advice to divide the army, with the disastrous consequence which ensued, and to delay his departure from Ireland (ll. 527–557, 730–736, 793–801); that he was one of the two men in charge of the royal forces in South Wales which dispersed without striking a blow for the King (ll. 945–1007; p. 191, ll. 24–30); and that when next seen by Creton, Rutland was in the company of Lancaster, wearing his badge (ll. 1053–1058). In addition Creton knew at the time he was writing that Rutland was believed responsible for

---

[157] Sherborne, *War, Politics and Culture*, pp. 122–127, reviews the conflicting accounts. To his sources, add WAM, Liber Niger Quaternus, fo.86v., 'In vigilia Sancti Petri ad Vincula [31 July] fugit Rex Ricardus a facie ducis Henrici'.
[158] Usk, *Chronicle*, ed. Given-Wilson, p. 58.

betraying to Lancaster the Epiphany Rising of January 1400 (ll. 3074–3091).[159]

In view of all this, Creton's admission (p. 191, l. 23) that appearances might possibly be deceptive, is remarkable testimony to his fair-mindedness. It is clear that he had witnessed no overt act of treachery by Rutland; nor, it should be stated, does he claim to have done so. His case against him rested upon the dire consequences of his acts, which Creton assumed to have been intentional, but which may not have been.

The most valued part of Creton's poem has long been his circumstantial story of the events surrounding the capture of the King. His account flatly contradicts the official version retailed by the Rolls of Parliament and by the majority of the English chroniclers. While they relate that Richard cheerfully resigned his crown when still a free man at Conway, Creton alleges that Richard was betrayed into surrendering himself by the promise of the earl of Northumberland – given under oath – that Lancaster's grievances were against *Ceulx qui aront fait mal, vice ne erreur / Ou traÿson* (ll.1883–1884), not the King himself, and that they should be tried in open parliament. To these terms the King agreed, and was thus:

> ...*faulsement*
> *Par traittié et par parlement*
> *Atraiz hors de ses forts chastiaulx*
> *Qui sont en Galles bons et biaulx,*
> *Du conte de Northomberlant,* (ll. 3699–3703)

who immediately broke his oath, ambushed the King, and led him captive to Flint.

It has been argued that Creton's account is not to be trusted; that he did not witness many of the events he reported; that he was wrong about a number of key facts; and that his testimony should therefore be rejected in favour of that of the Dieulacres chronicle, which tells essentially the same story, shorn of the rhetoric.[160] But Creton is in fact unusually meticulous in reporting which events he personally witnessed; his 'mistakes' may not be errors at all; and the very brief account in the anonymous Dieulacres chronicle would carry

---

[159] Johnston, 'Richard II's departure from Ireland', pp. 788–789, rather oversimplifies Creton's account of Rutland's alleged treachery, and is wrong in suggesting that Creton should have excused his late arrival in Dublin on the grounds of bad weather, since Creton, who is our only source for the state of the weather, clearly says that the storms arose after Rutland's arrival (ll. 425–465).

[160] Clarke, *Fourteenth-Century Studies*, pp. 68–75.

little weight but for the circumstantial story in Creton with which is agrees, and from which it may well be derived.[161]

For the events surrounding Richard's surrender we are therefore almost entirely dependent upon Creton, whose testimony cannot be directly verified but must be accepted or rejected on grounds of inherent plausibility and the general trustworthiness of the poem. Although Creton makes a number of mistakes, they are the kind of mistakes which might be expected from an eye-witness writing from memory some months after the events had occurred. There is nothing elsewhere in his narrative to suggest that he told deliberate lies or invented scenes which he claimed to have witnessed. When he states that he was present at the meeting of Northumberland and Richard at Conway; was there when the King was ambushed by the earl; and was told the details of Northumberland's *desloyale traïson* (l. 3687) by the earl of Salisbury, who was present when the terms of Richard's surrender were agreed; there would appear to be no good grounds for rejecting his testimony.

Creton's story of the events of June to August 1399 owes its considerable value to the fact that he personally witnessed many of the key episodes in a major political drama of which our other sources were either ignorant or were misleadingly informed by interested parties. None of this is true of the remainder of his poem. For the events of the Deposition Parliament and the Epiphany Rising, Creton relied on the report of:

> ... *un clerc que le duc Henry*
> *En avoit mené avec ly*
> *Quant il se parti de Paris* (ll. 2383–2385)

His account has all the defects of the earlier part of his poem and none of its merits. Its only possible value is the evidence it supplies as to how these events may have been viewed in Paris.

For the final section of his poem, Creton does not name his sources, the only occasion on which he fails to do so. This is unfortunate since this part of his work offers the best materials by which to judge his abilities as a reporter of current events. The subject matter – the return of Queen Isabella to France – is less contentious than earlier parts of his narrative; there are reliable materials with which his account may be compared; and we may reasonably presume that Creton was no longer constrained to depend entirely upon his own memory in reconstructing events. Whatever his sources, this final section does reveal that Creton was a fair and

---

[161] Palmer, 'French Chronicles', 61:2 (1979), pp. 413–419.

accurate reporter. The worst error of which he can be convicted is of placing 25 July on the wrong day of the week (ll. 3477–3478).[162] This part of his narrative does therefore give some assurance of his essential trustworthiness.

---

[162] For the materials for these negotiations, see J.H. Wylie, *England under Henry the Fourth*, 4 vols (London, 1884–1898), I, pp. 115, 129–130, 205–211; IV, pp. 259–264; and L. Mirot, 'Isabelle de France, reine d'Angleterre (1389–1409)', *Revue d'histoire diplomatique*, 18 (1904), pp. 481–508.

EDITORIAL PRINCIPLES

H's reading has been retained except where obviously corrupt; scribal errors have been corrected and amended readings suggested where metrical irregularities occur. The scribe has not been consistent in his treatment of word divisions, which have been regularized on the basis of the form most commonly used: thus *sique, sicomme, pour quoy, de rechief*. *Tres* is usually written as an adverbial prefix, e.g. *tresbien, tresbon*, and has been treated thus here.

Punctuation, capitals, and accents have been supplied by the editor according to usual practice.[1] Diaeresis is extensively used to indicate where two contiguous vowels should be sounded separately. Historical notes are rendered as footnotes to the translation and indicated by numerical superscripts printed only in the translation. An asterisk in the French text indicates the presence of an endnote (pp. 347–366). *Ez* usually indicates stressed final *e*, however, the scribe of **H** occasionally uses *ez* for *es* in the final position when *e* is unstressed, e.g. *moult de painez* (l. 255), *a merveillez ysnel* (l. 346), and *nous y fusmez* (l. 405). *V* and *j* have been substituted for consonant *u* and *i* respectively. Forms of the type *povez* (l. 18), *povoit* (l. 31), were preferred to *pouez, pouoit* on the analogy of the rhymes at ll. 316–319, 1296–1299, and 1640–1642.

The spelling of variants is that of the first MS quoted. Purely orthographic variants have not been given; these include alternatives of the type *fu/fut, archevesque/arcevesque, laissier/laisser*. Among the variants are included underlined readings of **H**; these indicate that they have been written over an erasure. Words supplied by the editor are given in square brackets; round brackets are used for phrases filling up a line by supplying a rhyme.

In the interests of pleasing the eye, the editor has indented the short line of the quatrains. This has the added advantage of linking the short line more closely to the three following decasyllables, with which it rhymes.

---

[1] See A. Foulet and M.B. Speer, *On Editing Old French Texts* (Lawrence, KS, 1979); M.B. Speer, 'Editing Old French texts in the eighties: Theory and practice', *Romance Philology*, 45 (1991), pp. 7–43.

The text in MSS **HLBC** is divided into chapters but the numbering has been provided by the editor, who has also written the rubrics at the head of each chapter. Further rubrics indicate the positions of the sixteen miniatures in the text. These are reproduced, for the first time in their entirety, in a section of colour plates towards the end of the work (*infra*, pp. 331–346) and are fully listed at the beginning, *supra*, pp. xiii–xiv).

Division into paragraphs in the translation, the prose section (Chapters 30–40), and in the two epistles have also been made by the editor. Italic passages in the Epistle to Philip the Bold, duke of Burgundy, indicate borrowings from Valerius Maximus, as translated by Simon de Hesdin.[2]

Henry Bolingbroke, duke of Lancaster is always called Henry Lancaster by Creton, and that nomenclature has been adopted here. Edward, earl of Rutland, and sometime duke of Aumale, is referred to as the earl of Rutland. Welsh place names in the translation have been given their anglicized spelling, on the grounds that this is closer to Creton's French.

---

[2] Valerius Maximus, *Facta et dicta memorabilia*, trans. Simon de Hesdin, Books I–III, ed. M.C. Enriello and others, www.pluteus.it.

LA PRINSE ET MORT DU ROY RICHART D'ANGLETERRE

by Jehan Creton

(composed 1399–1402)

Complete verse text plus prose section, with a facing-page translation

EPISTLES AND *BALLADES*

by Jehan Creton

with a facing-page translation

THE CAPTURE AND DEATH OF KING RICHARD OF ENGLAND

[fo. 2r.] Figure I: Creton makes obeisance to Jean de Montaigu, the first owner of H.

§1 Lines 1–68. Creton arrives in England and accompanies King Richard to Ireland.

When cold Winter has taken his leave[1] and Spring clothes the world in green again, and when bushes and flowers bloom in profusion in the fields, and birds sing sweetly for joy, you can hear the song of the nightingale which makes the hearts of lovers happy and carefree.

Five days before the first day of May,[2] when every man should cast aside sorrow and sadness, a knight[3] whom I dearly loved, said tenderly to me,

'My friend, I fondly beg that you will willingly accompany me to England; I wish to go there, and that right soon.'

[fo. 2v.] I replied,

'Sire, fear not, you may command me, I am ready to bend my will to yours.'

The knight thanked me one hundredfold, saying,

'Brother, we should certainly leave soon; for certain we should make haste.'

---

[1] Line 1. *Au departir de la froide saison.* Placing the action of a poem in a rustic setting, in springtime, is a commonplace of OF literature. *Supra*, Introduction, pp. 33–34.

[2] Lines 9, 25. *Cinq jours devant le premier jour de may ... en l'an mil quatre cens un mains.* 26 April 1399.

[3] Line 11. *Un chevalier.* In fact, Creton tells us later, p. 197, ll. 13–15, that Charles VI had sent them to accompany King Richard to Ireland. There is no merit in the unsubstantiated suggestion that the knight – a completely passive figure if he even existed – was the disputatious Pierre de Craon. See M. Bennett, *Richard II and the Revolution of 1399* (Stroud, Gloucestershire, 1999), p. 148 nn. 100, 101; also pp. 76, 136–137.

LA PRINSE ET MORT DU ROY RICHART D'ANGLETERRE

[fo. 2r.] Figure I: Creton makes obeisance to Jean de Montaigu, the first owner of H.

§1 Lines 1–68. Creton arrives in England and accompanies King Richard to Ireland.

Au departir de la froide saison,
Que printemps a fait reparacïon
De verdure,[1]* et qu'au[2] champs maint buisson
   Voit on flourir   4
Et les oyseaulx doulcement resjoïr,
Le roussignol peut on[3] chanter oïr,
Qui maint amant fait souvent devenir
   Joyeux et gay.*   8
Cinq jours devant[4] le premier jour de may –
Que chascun doit laissier dueil et esmay –
Un chevalier, que de bon cuer amay,
   Moult doulcement   12
Me dit: 'Amy, je vous pri* chierement
'Qu'en Albïon vueilliez joyeusement
'Avecques moy venir; prochainnement[5]
   'Y[6] vueil aler.'   16
[fo. 2v.] Je respondi: 'Monseigneur, commander
'Povez sur moy, je sui prest d'encliner
'Ma voulenté a vostre bon penser,[7]
   'N'en doubtez ja.'   20
Le chevalier cent foiz me mercia,
Disant: 'Frere, certes il convendra[8]
'Bien brief[9] partir, car[10] haster nous fauldra,
   'Soiez certains.'   24

---

[1] AD de la verdure
[2] LA quaux
[3] L en
[4] ACD avant
[5] AD car briefment
[6] LB gy
[7] L plaiser B ~~plaisir~~ penser
[8] L disant certes il nous convendra
[9] L briefment
[10] AD et

This was in the year fourteen hundred less one, that full of joy we left Paris, riding all day long, without delay until we came to London. There we took lodging one Wednesday, in time for our repast. Many a knight could be seen leaving the town, for good King Richard had set out with the Steward;[4] he rode hard, for his aim was to cross the salty sea,[5] on account of the troubles and vexations that his mortal foes in Ireland had caused him. They had killed many of his closest friends,[6] which meant that the King would never rest until [fo. 3r.] he had taken ample vengeance on McMurrough,[7] who calls himself king and lord of Ireland (where there is scarcely any meadow or open land).

Therefore the King urges his men to press forward, so that it can soon be reported that he is come to the port of Milford Haven which is richly provisioned. There we remained in joy and pleasure for ten whole days awaiting a north wind that we might depart. The sound of many minstrels playing trumpets day and night could be heard, men-at-arms coming from all parts to load the ships with

---

[4] Line 34. *l'estuuart*. Sir Thomas Percy; see *ODNB*, s.v. 'Percy, Thomas, earl of Worcester (*c*.1343–1403)'. Creton twice explains that he was the King's *grant maistre d'ostel*, ll. 989–990; p. 191, ll. 25–26. Sir Thomas was brother to Henry Percy, earl of Northumberland, l. 1655 ff.

[5] Lines 37–456. *il estoit de passer envïeux / la mer salee ... / ... sur le roy fu yrez / Nostre Seigneur*. Creton's account of Richard in Ireland is plagiarized by the author of the *Chronicque de la traïson et mort de Richart Deux*, ed. Williams, pp. 27–33: *La beissiez maint chlr partir ... quil nest barge ne nef qui sur la mer peust durer*. The *Traïson*'s account is a very clumsy rendering of verse into prose.

[6] Lines 41–42. *Grant quantité de ses amis parfaiz / Avoient fait mourir*. These friends included the fourth earl of March who was among those murdered at Kenlys, Leinster, in July 1398, *infra*, l. 354. This was at least one reason for Richard's second Irish expedition. See A. Steel, *Richard II* (Cambridge, 1941), p. 244.

[7] Line 46. For Art McMurrough, king of Leinster, see *ODNB*, s.v. 'Mac Murchadha, Art Caomhánach [Art Kavanagh MacMurrough]; *called* Art Mór Mac Murchadha] (d. 1416/17)'.

Ce fu en l'an mil quatre cens un mains
Que de Paris, chascun de joie plains,*
Nous partismes, chevauchant soirs et mains
   Sans atargier 28
Jusqu'a[11] Londres. La nous convint[12] logier
Un mercredi a heure[13] de mengier.
La povoit on vëoir maint chevalier
   Faire depart 32
De la ville, car le bon roy Richart
Estoit partiz avecques l'estuuart.
De chevauchier au matin et au tart
   Fu moult songneux, 36
Car il estoit de passer envïeux
La mer salee, pour les despiz et deulx
Qu'en Ymbernie[14] ses enemis morteulx*
   Li orent faiz. 40
Grant quantité* de ses amis parfaiz
Avoient fait mourir, sique jamaiz
Ne vouloit estre a repoz në a paix,
   Jusques a tant 44
[fo. 3r.] Qu'il eüst prins[15] vengence souffisant
De Maquemore, qui se dit excellant
Roy et seigneur d'Ymbernie la grant
   Et dë Illande[16] 48
(Ou gueres n'a de plainne ne de lande.)
Pour ce le roy souventesfoiz[17] commande
De s'avancier et que tantost on mande
   Qu'il vient au port 52
De Milleforde, ou il a bel apport.[18]
La feumes nous[19] en joie et en depport
Dix jours entiers atendant le vent nort
   Pour nous partir. 56
Mainte trompette y povoit[20] on oïr
De jour, de nuit menestrelz[21] retentir,
De toutes parts gendarmes survenir[22]
   Chargier vaisseaulx 60

---

[11] AB jusques a
[12] AD vimmes
[13] B a le heure
[14] H ymberne ABD ybernie
[15] B prise
[16] HLBC et dillande AD et de yrlande
[17] AD assez souvent
[18] A ou il y a bel port D ou il a bel port
[19] AD la mer passa
[20] C on y povoit
[21] AD et jour et nuit menestriers
[22] AD de venir

bread and wine, cows and calves, salt meat and many casks of water, and to hoist fine horses on board; no man failed to prepare his baggage. Good King Richard took leave of the ladies[8] and set off in fine array on the eleventh day.

§2 Lines 69–120. Richard arrives in Waterford and moves on to Kilkenny.

Then without further delay the sailors hoisted sail, with such address that within two days we could see the tower of Waterford[9] [fo. 3v.] in Ireland. The people I saw were ill-favoured and wretched; some were ragged, others girt with a rope, some lived in holes in the ground, others in hovels. They were made to carry great burdens and to wade into the water up to their waists for the speedy unloading of the barges,[10] as the King and his men were already in the town, where he was well received by the common people and the merchants.

Six days later the King and his Englishmen took to the field.[11] They rode in closed ranks, bold and unafraid, as far as Kilkenny, eighty miles[12] into the country and close to the enemy. There the

---

[8] Line 66. *aux dames*. Queen Isabella was not amongst these ladies, Richard having left her at Windsor. *Infra*, p. 307, ll. 23–24, *tu partis d'elle a Windesore pour aler en ton voyage d'Yrlande*.

[9] Line 72. *Watreforde*. Richard and his army arrived there on 1 June. See *Anglo-Norman Letters and Petitions*, ed. M.D. Legge (Oxford, 1941), no. 286.

[10] Line 79. *les barges*. In the fourteenth century barges were sea-going vessels having oars as well as masts; thus they were not dependent on the wind. Creton is using the term loosely here, as *supra* ll. 55–56 he says they waited ten days for the wind. See Sherborne, *War, Politics and Culture*, pp. 33–34, 71–76.

[11] Lines 85–445. This part of Creton's account, translated into English and in places much abbreviated, is borrowed by Raphael Holinshed 'out of a French pamphlet that belongeth to master John Dee', i.e. **L**. See Holinshed, *Chronicles*, II, pp. 850–851.

[12] Line 90. *Quatrevins mile*. Kilkenny is thirty-two miles north of Waterford.

De pain, de vin, de vaches et[23] de veaulx,
De char salee et d'eaue mains tonneaulx,
Chevaulx guinder[24]* qui furent bons et beaulx;
    Chascun pour soy   64
N'oublia pas d'apprester son arroy.
La print congié aux[25] dames le bon roy
Et se parti en graciëux conroy
    L'onziesme jour.   68

§2 Lines 69–120. Richard arrives in Waterford and moves on to Kilkenny.

Lors maronniers[26] sans plus faire sejour
Leverent hault leurs voiles, par tel tour
Qu'avant deux jours on apperceut la tour*
    De Watreforde   72
[fo. 3v.] En Irlande, ou gens vi[27] laide et orde,
L'un desciré, l'autre[28] ceint d'une corde;
L'un ot un trou, l'autre avoit[29]* une borde
    Pour demourer.   76
La leur fist on de grans fardeaulx porter,
Et dedans l'eaue jusques aux rains entrer
Pour deschargier les barges de la mer
    Hastivement,   80
Car ja le roy[30] avecques[31] de sa gent
Dedens la ville estoit, ou doulcement
Fu recuilliz[32] de la menue gent
    Et des marchans.   84
Six[33] jours aprés se mist le roy aux[34] champs
Avec[35] Angloiz, qui furent chevauchans
Serreement,[36] non pas comme meschans
    Në esbahiz,   88
A Kilkigny, bien avant ou païs
Quatrevins mile, et pres des ennemis.
La fu le roy avecques ses amis
    Quatorze jours,   92

---

[23] C *no* et
[24] HLC wuidier AD guinder B *line omitted*
[25] C des
[26] LAD mariniers
[27] L vil
[28] D et lautre
[29] AD et lautre ot
[30] A car le bon roy [bon *at line end*] D car le roy
[31] B avec de la gent
[32] LB recueilli
[33] B dix
[34] BC au
[35] AD avecques
[36] HC serrement

52   LA PRINSE ET MORT DU ROY RICHART D'ANGLETERRE

King and his friends spent fourteen days awaiting reinforcement from the earl of Rutland,[13] who henceforth led a life of evil doing and deceit.

On setting out every man was victualled as well as he could be with bread, wine and wheat. Very early in the morning of St John's Eve[14] [fo. 4r.] the King set out, heading straight for McMurrough, who refused to bend the knee to him, rather did he declare himself rightful king of Ireland and said that war would dog Richard's steps; he would defend his country with his last breath, Richard was wrong to want to wrest it from him. Thereupon the King set out to hunt him through the rocky, barren places, for he lived in the woods. He lived that way in all seasons and had with him – it was said – 3,000 men, so bold and resourceful that I never saw the like before; it seemed to me that they had very little fear of the English.

§3 Lines 121–184. Henry of Monmouth is knighted. The Irish refuse to join battle; Richard attempts to burn them out.

The king's entire army drew up in good order where the tall trees began and every man made himself ready, for at that moment they thought that they would join battle.

---

[13] Lines 93–94. *conte* ... / *De Rotelant*. Rutland was Richard's cousin and his favourite, *infra*, ll. 433–434. He was granted the office of Constable in 1397, in succession to the duke of Gloucester and created duke of Aumale, one of Gloucester's titles, in the same year; he was degraded in the first parliament of Henry IV. He died on the field of Agincourt in 1415. See *ODNB*, s.v. 'Edward [Edward of Langley, Edward of York], second duke of York (*c.*1373–1415)'. Creton consistently brands him a traitor.

[14] Line 99. 23 June, the vigil of St John the Baptist's Day. The Baptist was one of Richard's patron saints. See Saul, *Richard II*, p. 309; D. Gordon, L. Monnas, and C. Elam (eds), *The Regal Image of Richard II and the Wilton Diptych* (London, 1997), pp. 119–122. If this date is correct, subsequent details about the length of the campaign against McMurrough are inaccurate.

En atendant du conte le secours
De Rotelant, qui depuis tout son cours
En malfaisant et en estranges tours[37]
   A demené.   96
Au departir[38] chascun fu ordonné
Au mieulx qu'il pot de pain, de vin, de blé.
La veille droit de Saint Jehan d'Esté
   Tresbien matin   100
[fo. 4r.] Parti le roy, tenant le droit chemin
Vers Maquemore, qui ne voult estre enclin
N'obeïssant a lui a quelque fin,
   Ains se disoit   104
D'Ibernië estre roy et par[39] droit,
Et que de guerre jamaiz ne lui fauldroit;
Jusqu'a[40] la mort son[41] païs deffendroit
   Avec[42]* sa terre,   108
Disant que a tort la lui vouloit conquerre.
Et lors le roy fist aprester son erre
Es haulx deserts pour le trouver et querre,
   Car sa maison   112
Estoit es bois. C'est sa convercïon[43]
D'y demourer en quelconque saison,
Et la dedens avoit – ce disoit on –
   Avecques lui   116
Trois mil hommes qui furent moult hardi
Et si apers, c'onques telz gens ne vy;
D'Angloiz trop pou estoient esbahi,*
Ce me sembla.   120

§3 Lines 121–184. Henry of Monmouth is knighted. The Irish refuse to join battle; Richard attempts to burn them out.

A l'entree des haulx bois s'assembla
Tout l'ost du roy, et chascun s'ordonna
Tresbien et bel, car pour l'eure on cuida
   Bataille avoir,   124

---

[37] AD en traison en mal et en faulx tours
[38] B au [de *superscript*] partir
[39] AD a
[40] B jusques a
[41] H son LB le
[42] H avec LB et
[43] AD condicion

However, the Irish kept out of sight at this time; I know this to be true. Then the King commanded that everything round about should be burned, [fo. 4v.] the decision was taken that everything should be set alight, to lessen the grip of the Irish; many villages and houses were burned.

While this was being done, the King – who bears leopards[15] on his arms – had the men drawn up in ranks, and pennons and standards hoisted. Then with great good will and without unpleasantness he had the son of the duke of Lancaster[16] sent for; he was a fine, handsome young man. Thereupon he made him a knight,[17] saying to him,

'Fair cousin, may you henceforth be valiant and brave, for you will be of little worth if you do not fight and win.'

[fo. 5r.] Figure II: King Richard knights Henry of Monmouth.

To heap more honours on him and to increase his well-being and pleasure, in order that he might remember this day for a long time to come, the King created more knights, eight or ten of them, but as to their names,[18] I truly know nothing. I was not much concerned with them or anything about them, considering that Grief, Torment and Care had entirely taken up residence in my heart, and that Regret had robbed me of Joy; why this was, I would never say. Thus did I ride with them and watch everything they did, so that

---

[15] Lines 133–134. *le roy – qui les liepars / Porte en blason*. In heraldic terms leopards are lions passant guardant – walking, looking at the viewer – as in the royal arms of England. See E.E. Dorling, *Leopards of England and Other Papers on Heraldry* (London, 1912), pp. 1–37. In his first *ballade*, p. 311, l. 26, Creton refers to Richard himself as *le liepart*, as does Deschamps, *Oeuvres complètes*, ed. de Queux and Raynaud, V, no. 1059, p. 350, l. 5, and VII, no. 1390, p. 244, l. 15. Deschamps also refers to the English as *le liepart*, I, no. 26, p. 106, l. 9, and no, 168, p. 300 l. 20.

[16] Line 138. *Le filz au duc de Lanclastre*. Henry of Monmouth, eldest son of Henry Lancaster and the future Henry V. See *ODNB*, s.v. 'Henry V (1386–1422)'.

[17] Figure II. It can be seen under magnification that the King's face is not a portrait; he is unbearded. Cf. Figures VIII, XI–XV.

[18] Lines 149–150. *comment / Leurs nons feurent, pas ne sçay vrayement*. But Creton tells us *infra*, p. 187, ll. 20–22, and note, that one of the new knights was the son of the countess of Salisbury. It seems likely that Humphrey, son of the late duke of Gloucester, and Thomas Mowbray, earl of Nottingham, son of the duke of Norfolk, whom Richard had taken to Ireland along with Henry of Monmouth, were also knighted with him. See G.E.C. Cockayne (ed.), *Complete Peerage*, 12 vols (London, 1910–1959), s.v. 'Humphrey of Buckingham'; *ODNB*, s.v. 'Mowbray, Thomas, second earl of Nottingham (1385–1405)'.

Maiz les Yrlois ne se firent point[44] veoir
A ceste foiz, je le sçay bien de voir.
Lors commanda le roy de tout ardoir
   La environ, 128
[fo. 4v.] De feux[45] bouter fu la conclusïon
Pour amendrir la dominacïon
Des Irlandoiz; maint village et maison
   La furent ars. 132
En ce faisant le roy – qui les liepars
Porte en blason – fist rens de toutes pars
Faire, et tantost panons et estandars
   En hault lever. 136
Aprés fist il de vray cuer sans amer
Le filz au duc de Lanclastre mander,
Qui estoit bel et jeune bacheler
   Et avenant, 140
Et puis le fist chevalier, en disant:
'Mon beau cousin, soiez preu et vaillant
'Desoremaiz, car pou avez vaillant
   'Sans conquerir.' 144

[fo. 5r.] Figure II: King Richard knights Henry of Monmouth.

Et pour le plus honnorer et cherir
En accroissant son bien[46] et son plaisir,
Affin telle qu'il en eust souvenir
   Plus longuement, 148
En fist d'autres .viii. ou dix. Maiz comment
Leurs nons feurent, pas ne sçay vrayement,
Car de leur fait ne m'en[47] chaloit granment*
   Ne d'eulx aussi, 152
Veu qu'en mon cuer Dueil, Ennuy et Soussi[48]
Avoient fait, et de tous poins choisi,
Leur mensïon, et Desir* dessaisi
   M'avoit de Joie; 156
Pour quoy c'estoit jamaiz ne le diroie.[49]
En cel[50] estat avec[51] eulx chevauchoie,
Et tous leurs faiz assez je regardoie,[52]
   A la fin[53] tele 160

---

[44] L *no* point
[45] LAD feu
[46] AD beau
[47] ACD me
[48] AD veu qua mon cuer ennuy dueil et soussi
[49] AD jamais je ne diroie
[50] LABD tel
[51] D avecques
[52] D regarderoye
[53] LB affin

[fo. 5v.] in time to come I could relate what happened, and how cold-hearted high treason soon ensued, as you will hear.[19]

But before that you will hear of the victory enjoyed by the King who remained with his men, encamped in tents facing the woods. Everyone was preparing to move on, when two thousand and five hundred good men living thereabouts came to cut down the trees, both tall and low-growing, for there were no roads; no one, no matter how many bold and brave men he had, could ever get through, so dangerous are the woods. And do you know that in many places the woods are so deep that, if a man does not take care to watch where he steps, he will sink in up to his waist or be swallowed up altogether? For this reason none can catch the Irish, it is their refuge.

§4 Lines 185–320. The Irish harass the English troops who endure starvation. McMurrough's uncle pleads for mercy and the earl of Gloucester is sent to parley with McMurrough.

Thus we got through the woods cautiously, as the Irish were very afraid of our arrows. They screamed and shouted so loudly that I think

---

[19] Line 164. *Com vous orrez*, 'as you will hear'. This is the first reference to listeners, rather than readers of this work, which is peppered with similar expressions, e.g. l. 1066, *or vous diray du roy*; p. 201, l. 5–6, *comme vous avez oÿ devant*; l. 3184, *comme vous orrez cy compter*. Unlike Froissart, who wrote for readers also, Creton's work seems to have been primarily intended to be read aloud. See Bratu, '«Or vous dirai»', p. 343. Also, *supra*, Introduction, pp. 26–27.

LA PRINSE ET MORT DU ROY RICHART D'ANGLETERRE 57

[fo. 5v.] Qu'en aucun temps j'en sceüsse[54] nouvelle
Dire, et comment la traïson mortele
Bien tost aprés s'ensuÿ[55] moult cruele,
    Com vous orrez.   164
Maiz la conqueste avant dire m'orrez
Que le roy fist, qui estoit demourez
Devant les boiz, aux tentes et aux trez,[56]
    Avec[57] ses gens.   168
De deslogier fu chascun diligens
Quant les bons homs, bien .ii.^{m} et cinq cens,
Qui ou païs estoient residens,
    Furent venus   172
Pour abatre des boiz grans et menus,[58]
Car de[59] chemins adonc n'y avoit nulz;
N'oncques maiz[60] homs,* tant feust[61] de gens pourveuz,[62]
    Hardiz ne preux,   176
N'y pot passer, tant sont boiz[63] pereilleux.*
Et savez vous comment en pluseurs lieux
Fait si parfont, que[64] qui n'est bien songneux
    De regarder   180
Ou l'en[65] marche, il y fault enfondrer[66]
Jusques aux[67] rains, ou tout dedens entrer?
Et pour ce nulz ne les puet atrapper,
    C'est leur retrait.   184

§4 Lines 185–320. The Irish harass the English troops who endure starvation. McMurrough's uncle pleads for mercy and the earl of Gloucester is sent to parley with McMurrough.

Ainsi les bois passames tout a trait,
Car les Irloiz doubtoient moult le trait.
La menoient[68] tel crierie[69] et tel brait,
    Qu'a mon advis[70]   188

---

[54] AD je sceusse B jen faisse [sceusse *superscript*]
[55] A sensuivit
[56] AD es tentes et es trez
[57] AD avecques
[58] D des boiz et des [grans *superscript*] menus
[59] L des
[60] L nuls
[61] B fust C fu
[62] AD pourvus
[63] HLBC tant sont les boiz AD si sont les boiz
[64] AC car
[65] AD en [*no* le]
[66] D enfrendrer enfondrer
[67] B au
[68] H *originally read* demenoient; de *has been almost erased* L demenerent
[69] AD la demenoient tel cry BC la demenoient tel crierie
[70] B admis

[fo. 6r.] you would have heard them a good league off. They were almost beside themselves with anguish on account of the archers who were often face to face with them. The Irish made many attacks on the vanguard and dealt out so many blows with their spears that they struck right through coats of mail and plates of armour. They killed many of the English when they went foraging, without waiting for the standard to be raised,[20] for the native horses speed more swiftly over hill and vale than does a leaping stag. This is why they inflicted great harm on the King's men; his brave design was to subdue into servitude such men, who were little more than savages.

And then McMurrough's own craven uncle came one day to beg mercy from the King and to fall at his feet; he had a halter round his neck and bore a naked spear,[21] there were many others wearing this livery, naked, barefoot, unkempt and close to death. [fo. 6v.] When the King saw them he was minded to be merciful, saying,

'Friends, in short I pardon the injuries which you have done me, provided that every man swears that henceforth he will be true to me.'

Willingly they all grant his demand. When this had been done, he

---

[20] Line 199. *l'eure de l'estendart* = 'the raising of the standard' (literally = 'the time of the standard').

[21] Lines 213–215. *La hart au col, tenant nue l'espee / ... Nuz et deschaulx*. Having a halter around their necks, barefoot and stripped to their linens were symbols of defeat and submission; soldiers would also hand over their weapons. Froissart describes the capitulation of the town of Calais to Edward III in similar terms. See Jean Froissart, *Chroniques ... premier livre*, ed. G.T. Diller (Geneva, 1972), pp. 841–844. In ll. 1009–1011, *infra*, Creton describes in this way the deserters from Richard's army arriving in Lancaster's camp.

[fo. 6r.] On les eust bien[71] d'une grant lieue oÿs.
A pou de dueil n'esragoient[72]* tous[73] vifs
Pour les archiers, qui souvent viz a viz
   D'entr'eulx[74] estoient. 192
L'avangarde moult souvent assailloient,
Et de dardes si grans cops ilz[75] gettoient
Que haubergons[76] et les plates perçoient
   De part en part. 196
D'Angloiz firent beaucop morir[77] a part
Quant en fourrage aloient quelque part
Sans atendre l'eure de[78] l'estendart,
   Car[79] mons et vaulx 200
Courent plus tost du païs les chevaulx
Que cerf ne fait quant il a fait grans saulx.[80]
C'est ce par quoy ilz[81] firent foison maulx
   Et grant[82] dommage 204
Aux[83] gens du roy, qui ot[84] fier le courage,
Veu que telz gens, qui sont presque sauvage,
Vot soubzmettre du tout en[85] son servage
   Et conquerir. 208
Et de fait vint pour mercy requerir
L'oncle propre Maquemore cheïr
Aux piez du roy, car paour ot de mourir,
   Une journee 212
La hart au[86] col,* tenant nue l'espee;
D'autres y vy foison[87] de sa livree,
Nuz[88] et deschaulx comme gent diffamee
   Preste[89] de mort. 216
[fo. 6v.] Lors quant le roy les vit, il ot remort
De pacïence, disant: 'Amis,[90] au fort
'Les maulx qu'avez vers moy faiz et le tort
   'Je[91] vous pardonne, 220
'Maiz que sa foy chascun[92] me jure et donne,
'Que desoremaiz* serez vraie gent bonne.'
De tresbon cuer chascun lui abandonne
   La[93] sa demande. 224

---

[71] AD no bien
[72] D narragoient
[73] B tout
[74] LB deulx
[75] L il
[76] HBC haubergon
L haubregon
AD hauberions
[77] AD mourir beaucoup
[78] L et
[79] A par
[80] AD qun cherf ne fait quant il fait ses grans saulx
[81] C il
[82] H grant *superscript*
LB *no* grant
[83] B au
[84] L ont
[85] B a
[86] LCD ou
[87] A pluiseurs
[88] H nulz
[89] AD et pres
[90] B ainz
[91] H je vous LB *no* je
[92] ACD chascun sa foy
[93] H la sa LB *no* la

sent to McMurrough – who claimed to be king of Ireland (where there are many woods and little open land) – saying that if he were to come to him, a rope around his neck, like his uncle, he would grant him clemency and give him land and castles in another part of the country. McMurrough told the King's messengers that he would not comply, not for all the gold here or overseas, rather he would carry war and torment to him. He knew very well that the English had scarcely a thing to eat, for even if one were to go mad in the attempt, one would not have found a pennyworth of food to buy, unless one had brought it along.

The army had to remain like this for eleven days, without finding anything [fo. 7r.] except a little oats, and not much of that, for the horses, who were often bedded in the fields, frozen in the wind and rain; many died of hunger, men too, big and small. You could not begin to comprehend the suffering endured by the English, who failed to get the better of McMurrough; he made them suffer greatly again from starvation. One day I saw for certain sure that four or six men had only one loaf between them; some men ate no bread for five whole days.

Quant ce fu fait, a Maquemore mande –
Qui se disoit seigneur et roy d'Irlande
(Ou[94] maint boiz a et pou y a de lande) –
   Que s'il vouloit   228
Vers lui venir, la hart ou[95] col tout droit
Comme son oncle, a mercy le prendroit,
Et qu'assez terre et chasteaulx lui donroit
   Ailleurs que la.   232
Aux gens du roy Maquemore dit a
Que pour[96] tout l'or dela mer ne[97] deça
Ne le feroit, ains guerre lui fera
   Et encombrier.   236
Trop[98] bien savoit que gueres a mengier
N'orent Engloiz, car qui deust enragier,[99]
Trouvé n'eust pas qui[100] vaulsist un denier
   A achetter,   240
S'il[101] ne l'avoit o lui fait apporter.
En cest estat faillu l'ost sejourner
Bien .xi. jours, sans nulle riens* trouver
   Fors seulement   244
[fo. 7r.] Avoines vers un[102] pou, non pas granment,
Pour les chevaulx, qui estoient souvent
Logiez aux champs, a la pluie et au vent,
   Tous morfonduz;   248
De famine en y[103] ot maints[104] perdus,
D'ommes aussi, grans, petis et menus.
La grant paine croire ne pourroit nulz
   Ne le meschief   252
Qu'orent Angloiz, qui ne porent a chief
De Maquemore venir; ains de rechief
Leur faisoit moult de painez[105]* et de grief
   Avoir de fain.   256
Tel jour y vy – je[106] le sçay bien[107] certain –
Que quatre ou six n'avoient qu'un seul pain;
De telz y ot qui n'en mengerent grain
   Cinq jours entiers.   260

---

[94] A o
[95] A au
[96] C par
[97] L et
[98] AD car
[99] D arragier
[100] D que
[101] AD sy
[102] AD no un
[103] B no y
[104] C moult
[105] LBC paine
[106] B sy
[107] LACD de B no bien

Which men were these? Knights and squires. As for myself I would rather have been penniless in Poitiers or Paris, for in that place was no Delight or Laughter, but in their stead Hardship, Suffering and Danger; Grief took the honoured place of Joy.

The army would not have stayed there any longer for anything, but then three ships rode the waves from Dublin, where there was abundance of supplies and food.

[fo. 7v.] Figure III: Three ships arrive from Dublin.

Men fought to get hold of some of it, they jumped into the water as if it were straw. Everyone paid out his penny or his halfpenny, some on drink, others on food; everything was plundered without delay. More than a thousand men were drunk that day, seeing that the wines were from Alsace and also from Spain, a fine country; there were many punches and blows traded.

Nevertheless the King set out early the next morning directly towards Dublin, ignoring the harassment from the enemy. [fo. 8r.] Then McMurrough sent to the King a beggar, who announced that McMurrough wanted to be his friend and to plead for mercy with clasped hands;

Voire, quelz[108] gens? Chevaliers, escuiers.[109]
Quant est de moy, j'eusse bien[110] voulentiers
Voulu estre sans argent a Poitiers
   Ou a Paris, 264
Car la n'avoit Esbatement[111] ne Ris,
Maiz en ce lieu[112] Travail, Painne et Perilz;
Dueil pour Joie y estoit bien serviz
   Et honnourez. 268
Pour[113] riens ne feust la l'ost plus demourez,
Maiz cependent par la mer vint .iii. nefs[114]
De Duveline, ou il y ot assez
   Biens et vitaille. 272

[fo. 7v.] Figure III: Three ships arrive from Dublin.

Pour en avoir y ot souvent[115] bataille,
Dedens la mer entroient comme en paille.
Chascun pour soy y emploia sa maille
   Ou son denier, 276
Les uns en boire, les autres en mengier,
Tout fu rifflé sans gueres attargier.
D'ivres[116] y ot – je croy – plus d'un millier
   Celle journee, 280
Veu que d'Osoie si[117] estoit la vinee*
Et d'Espaigne, qui est bonne contree;
Par eulx fu la mainte buffe donnee
   Et maint tatin. 284
Non obstant ce, l'andemain a[118] matin
Le roy parti,[119] tenant le droit chemin
A Duveline maugré tout le hutin
   Des ennemis, 288
[fo. 8r.] Quant Maquemoire vers le roy a tramis
Un mendiant, disant que ses amis*
Vouloit[120] estre et lui crier mercis
   A jointes mains; 292

---

[108] D que
[109] B et escuiers
[110] A moult
[111] AD nesbatement
[112] L en cellui B en tel lieu
[113] D plus
[114] AD par la vint trois grans nefs
[115] C souvent y ot
[116] C divers
[117] HBC *no* si AD dosoie si L dosoie en
[118] LC au AD bien
[119] AD nous partismes
[120] L vouloient

also that the King should send to him a loyal and trustworthy lord to negotiate peace, so that their enmity, which for long had been pitiless, might be brought to an end. This news gladdened many hearts in the King's army, for everyone wanted peace. He asked his Council for their advice, and what would be the best thing to do. They quickly agreed that, considering his good name and reputation, the earl of Gloucester[22] – an honourable man – should go and should spell out to McMurrough the great injury he has done to the King and what this amounts to. Gloucester took his leave of the King and led off the reargurd, of which he was captain. There were 200 lancers – I tell you – and 1,000 archers, I never saw better. I went with them, for I wanted to see[23] [fo. 8v.] the prestige, estate, strength and power of McMurrough, and how the earl would do his duty to find peace.

§5 Lines 321–388. The meeting between Gloucester and McMurrough.

I saw McMurrough ride down the hillside between two woods, quite some way from the sea, and there were a great number of Irishmen with him, more than I can reckon.

---

[22] Lines 304–305. *le conte / De Glocestre*. Thomas Despenser, earl of Gloucester. He initially deserted Richard and threw in his lot with Lancaster, however, he was executed for his part in the Epiphany Rising of January 1400. See *ODNB*, s.v. 'Despenser, Thomas, second Lord Despenser (1373–1400)'.

[23] Lines 315–316. *Comme celui / Qui vouloit voir* = 'for I wanted to see'. See *Chrestomathie de la langue française au XVe siècle*, ed. P. Rickard (Cambridge, 1976) no. 8, p. 71, l. 65 and note.

Ou que vers lui vueille envoier[121] au mains
Aucun seigneur, qui soit[122]* vraiz et certains,[123]
Pour traittier paix, sique tout soit estains
   Le courroux d'eulx,   296
Qui longuement avoit esté crueulx.
Ces nouvelles en firent mains[124] joieux
En l'ost du roy, car chascun envïeux
   Fu de repos.   300
A son conseil demanda leur propos
Et qu'i* seroit bon de faire. A briefz[125] mos
Furent d'accort, pour[126] le bon nom et los
   Qu'avoit le conte[127]   304
De Glocestre – qui oncques n'ama honte –
Quë il iroit, maiz que bien lui raconte
Le grant oultrage et a combien ce monte
   Ce qu'il a fait.   308
Present le roy,* se parti et de fait
L'arriere garde, de quoy il estoit fait
Cappitaine, enmena[128] tout a fait
   Avecques lui.   312
Deux cens lances furent – bien vous affi –
Et mile archiers, oncques meilleurs ne vy.
Avecques eulx alay, comme celui
   Qui vouloit voir   316
[fo. 8v.] L'onneur, l'estat, la force et[129] le povoir
De Maquemore, et coment[130] son devoir
Vouloit faire pour bonne paix avoir
   Et confermer.   320

§5 Lines 321–388. The meeting between Gloucester and McMurrough.

Entre deux bois assez loing de la mer
Maquemore la montaigne avaler
Vy, et d'Irloiz – que pas ne sçay nommbrer[131] –
   Y ot foison.   324

---

[121] C envers
[122] H soient ABCD soit
[123] L aucuns seigneurs qui soient bien certains
[124] A moult
[125] C deulx
[126] AD que pour bon nom [no le]
[127] H qu<u>avoit le conte</u> LB quot le conte
[128] L amena B a̶ [en superscript] mena
[129] C *no* et
[130] C *no* et
[131] H nomm<u>brer</u> AD nommer B n̶o̶m̶m̶e̶r̶ nombrer

He had a very fine horse, with neither saddle nor pommel, which they said had cost him 400 cows, there being little money in that country; for this reason they are accustomed just to barter with animals. The horse galloped more swiftly downhill than ever did I see any hare, stag, sheep or other animal, I tell you this for certain. In McMurrough's right hand he carried a spear which was long and stout and which he could launch with telling effect; you can see his portrait painted right here, just the way he looked.[24]

[fo. 9r.] Figure IV: McMurrough gallops downhill out of the woods.

But his people were held back in front of the wood, like a look-out. The meeting between the two of them took place near a stream. There stood McMurrough, a fine-looking man: he was tall and very quick on his feet; as you can see he was strong, fierce and warlike, and a man of action. He and the earl talked about the situation; the earl said how McMurrough had several times inflicted harm and mischief on the King, and how all those had forsworn their oath who cruelly killed the noble earl of March[25] without benefit of law.

---

[24] Lines 339–340. *Sa semblance ... / Veez pourtraite*. A reference to Figure IV, at the head of fo. 9r. See also ll. 339–340, endnote.

[25] Line 354. *le conte de la Marche*. Roger Mortimer, earl of March, killed in July 1398, *supra*, ll. 41–42, note. See *ODNB*, s.v. 'Mortimer, Roger, fourth earl of March and sixth earl of Ulster (1374–1398)'.

Un cheval ot sans sele në arçon
Qui lui[132] avoit cousté – ce disoit on –
Quatre cens vaches, tant estoit bel et bon,
    Car pou d'argent   328
A ou païs; pour[133] ce communement[134]
Marchandent eulx a bestes seulement.
En descendant couroit si asprement
    Qu'a mon advis,   332
Oncques maiz jour de ma vie ne vis
Courre si tost lievre, cerf ne brebis
N'autre[135]* beste – pour certain le vous dis –
    Comme il faisoit.   336
En sa main dextre une darde portoit
Grant[136] et longue, de quoy molt bien gettoit,
Sa semblance, ainsi comme il estoit,[137]
    Vëez* pourtraite*   340

[fo. 9r.] Figure IV: McMurrough gallops downhill out of the woods.

Ycy endroit. Maiz sa gent fu retraite
Devant[138] le boiz commë[139] une escharguete,
Et d'eulx deux la fu l'assemblee faite[140]*
    Pres d'un ruissel.   344
La se maintint Maquemore assez[141] bel,
Grans homs[142] estoit, a merveillez ysnel;
A veue d'ueil sembloit fort, fier[143] et fel
    Et homs de fait.   348
Lui et le conte parlerent de leur fait,
En racontant* le mal et le mesfait
Que Maquemoire avoit vers le roy fait[144]
    Par pluseurs foiz,   352
Et comment tous parjurerent leurs foyz
Quant le conte de la Marche courtoiz
Firent mourir, sans jugement ne loiz
    A grant meschief.   356

---

[132] B que ly
[133] C par
[134] H communent
LABCD communement
[135] H nautre B autre
[136] C grande
[137] AD sa semblance tout ainsy quil estoit
[138] AD devers
[139] L les boiz sicomme
[140] HB [no et] deulx deux
L et deulx deux AD deulx
[141] H asselz
[142] L grant homme
[143] AD fier fort
[144] L lines 350–351 omitted

deux fu lassemblee la faite
C de eux deux fu la

[fo. 9v.] They then talked on and repeated what had been said, but came to no agreement; their leave-taking was short and abrupt.

They went their separate ways, and the earl went back to King Richard, for he was very impatient to tell him what he has done and his innermost thoughts: how all McMurrough wants is to treat for mercy, being assured beforehand that he will be pardoned unconditionally, without any other punishment or imprisonment, or otherwise he will never make peace for as long as he lives; and will resolve to get the upper hand, if he wants to.

These words were not pleasing to the King, whose face paled with anger, it seemed to me. In great wrath he swore by St Edward[26] that he would never leave Ireland until he captured him, dead or alive. Alas! He knew nothing of the great harm and deadly actions that were being directed against him by those from whom he expected support at all times. [fo. 10r.] And Fortune, who rules the world contrariwise, intended to cut short his course, turning his joy into grief in a very short time.

---

[26] Line 377. *Saint Edouart*. Richard had a particular veneration for Edward the Confessor. See Saul, *Richard II*, pp. 311–316; Gordon and others (eds), *Regal Image of Richard II*, pp. 115–118. During Richard's reign the Confessor rather than Edward I, came to be seen as 'the Royal Ancestor ... the dynastic counterpart of St Louis'. See Mathew, *Court of Richard II*, pp. 21, 36.

[fo. 9v.] Puis parlerent assez et de rechief,
Maiz d'accorder ne vindrent pas a chief;
Le congié fu d'eulx[145] assez prompt et brief
    Et le depart.   360
Chascun se mist en[146] son chemin a part
Et le conte devers le roy Richart
S'en[147] retourna, car moult lui estoit tart*
    De raconter   364
Trestout son fait et son subtil[148] penser:
Et comment riens ne peut[149] en lui trouver
Fors seulement qu'il veult mercy crier,
    Voire comment   368
Qu'il soit certain[150] d'avoir paix ligement[151]
Sans autre grief në emprisonnement,
Ou ja accort n'en fera autrement
    Jour de sa vie;   372
Et qu'i cuidra avoir bon, si l'envie.*
Ceste parole ne fu pas au roy lie;
La face en ot de mautalent palie,
    Ce me sembla.   376
Par grant couroux Saint Edouart jura
Que jamaiz jour ne se departira
D'Imbernie, jusqu'a[152] tant qu'il l'avra[153]
    Ou vif ou mort.   380
Las! Le grant mal ne le mortel effort
Ne savoit pas qu'i lui sourdoit a fort
Par ceulx de qui il atendoit confort
    Trestous les jours.   384
[fo. 10r.] Et Fortune, qui fait tout au rebours,
Ne volt souffrir qu'il eust plus guere cours,
Ains lui tourna ses joies en doulours
    En bien pou d'eure.   388

---

[145] L deulx fu
[146] C a
[147] AD se
[148] AD de trestout son fait et soubtilz
[149] AD pot B pust
[150] ACD certains
[151] AD ligerement
[152] B jusques a
[153] A quil ara

§6 Lines 389–624. Richard advances on Dublin. The earl of Rutland arrives. Six weeks of bad weather ensue, then news of Henry Lancaster's invasion is received. Salisbury is sent to Conway, Creton goes too.

The army struck camp without delay, for nothing worth a fig could be found to eat there at that time. Thus we marched directly to Dublin,[27] a fine town situated by the sea. There was such an abundance of goods and gear that throughout the King's army, it was said, no flesh nor fish was henceforth expensive, no bread, wheat, nor wine, nor other provision. I know full well that there were more than 30,000 men there; all their misfortunes were quite forgotten, and their great suffering also. We were there for more than two weeks, as happy as fish in water. Dublin was the foremost town in Ireland for provisions.

The King could not forget McMurrough. He had three parties of his men made up to hunt for him. He urged them [fo. 10v.] to do their utmost, saying that he would willingly give 100 marks of fine gold to whoever captures him – everyone bears this in mind, as it sounds very good – and should they be unable to catch him, Jesus granting him health, when autumn comes and the trees are stripped

---

[27] Line 393. *Duveline*. The army arrived there by 1 July. Johnston, 'Richard II's departure from Ireland', p. 789 n. 3.

§6 Lines 389–624. Richard advances on Dublin. The earl of Rutland arrives. Six weeks of bad weather ensue, then news of Henry Lancaster's invasion is received. Salisbury is sent to Conway, Creton goes too.

L'ost desloga sans plus faire demeure,
Car de mengier qui vaulsist une meure*
N'eüst on pas trouvé la a celle heure.
    Pour ce tout droit   392
A Duveline alasmes,[154] qui estoit
Bonne ville, car[155] sur la mer sëoit.
De marchandise et de biens y avoit
    Si grant foison,   396
Que par[156] tout l'ost du roy – ce disoit on –
Oncques plus chier n'en fu[157] char ne poisson,
Pain, blé ne vin[158] në autre garnison.
    Si[159] sçay je assez,   400
Que trente mile estoient ilz[160] passez
Qui furent la et entour sejournez;
Trestous leurs maulx furent tost oubliez
    Et leur grief painne.   404
Nous y fusmez assez plus de quinzaine
Aises[161] du[162] corps comme poisson en Saine;*
D'Illande estoit la ville souveraine
    Pour marchander.   408
Le roy ne pot Maquemore oublier.
De ses gens fist bien et bel[163] ordonner
Trois parties pour le querre et trouver
    Et leur pria   412
[fo. 10v.] De bien faire, disant: qui l'amenra,
Cent mars d'or fin de bon cuer lui donra –
Chascun pour soy ce mot pas[164] n'oublia,
    Car tresbien sonne –   416
Et s'on ne peut atrapper[165] sa personne,
Maiz que Jhesus bonne santé lui donne,
Et que le temps si[166] soit passé d'autonne[167]*
    Que desvestus   420

---

[154] H alasmes C sen alla
[155] AD tresbonne ville et
[156] HLB pour
[157] L ne fu pain A ne fu char
[158] L ne char ne ble AD ne pain ne vin
[159] L se AD ce
[160] ACD il
[161] AD aise
[162] A en
[163] AD bel et bien
[164] C pas ce mot
[165] AD oublier
[166] HLBC no si A le temps si soit D si *superscript*
[167] L de autompne

of leaves, the King will have all the woods, great and small, burned down; thus will McMurrough be caught – I think – and not otherwise.

On this very day[28] the false earl of Rutland arrived with his men in one hundred barges fitted out nobly for war. At this time he was Constable of England and duke of Aumale (where he has fine estates). He could ask anything he wanted of the King for – so help me God – there was no man in the world whom he loved more: brother, uncle or cousin, young or old. The King was very joyful and heartened at his coming. Several times he asked him:

'Constable, where have you tarried so long? Why have you not come to us sooner?'

[fo. 11r.] He made his excuses boldly in front of everyone. The King was happy because he was humble and gentle towards him, even although he had done the opposite of what he said he had done, which earned him many curses.

Thus[29] did we spend six weeks[30] in Dublin in transports of delight, without hearing reliable news from England, for no matter what risks were run, shipping could not make port safely. The wind was so unfavourable from all directions and the storms at sea so violent[31] that I thought Our Lord was angry with the King, for

---

[28] Line 425. *ce jour mesmes*. This would place Rutland's arrival in mid July, which is difficult to believe, since he would certainly have had information about Lancaster's invasion by this date and could scarcely have concealed it.

[29] Lines 446–744. This passage is also in Holinshed, *Chronicles*, II, p. 844, again much abbreviated. See *supra*, ll. 85–445 and note. The marginal note reads: 'out of master Dees French booke'.

[30] Line 448. *Bien six sepmaines*. This is impossible on any chronology. *Supra*, Introduction, p. 36 n. 145.

[31] Line 454. *tempeste si oultrez*. *Supra*, Introduction, pp. 38; 40 n. 159, for the importance of this detail.

Seront arbres et[168] de leurs fueilles nuz,
Ardre fera les boiz grans et menuz;
Sique – je croy – qu'ainsi[169] sera tenuz
  Non autrement.   424
Ce jour mesmes[170] arriva proprement
De Roteland le faulx[171] conte et sa gent,
A cent barges garnies grandement
  Tout pour la guerre.   428
Connestable estoit[172] lors d'Angleterre
Et duc d'Aumarle (ou il a[173] belle terre).
Tout ce qu'il vot au roy pot bien[174] requerre,
  Car[175] – se[176] m'ait* Dieux –   432
Ou monde n'ot homme qu'il amast mieulx,
Frere ne oncle, cousin jeune ne vieulx;
De sa venue ot le cuer moult joieux
  Et asseuré.   436
Par[177] pluseurs foiz lui a il demandé:
'Connestable, ou avez demouré
'Si longuement? Que n'estes arrivé
  'Plus tost a nous?'   440
[fo. 11r.] Il s'excusa haultement[178] devant tous.
Content en fu le roy, car humble[179] et doulx
Estoit vers lui, non obstant qu'a rebous[180]*
  De ce qu'ot[181] dit   444
Avoit fait, dont pluseurs[182] foiz fu maudit.
Ainsi fusmes en joie et en delit[183]
A Duveline, ou tresgracïeux fit,
  Bien six sepmaines   448
Sans point oïr de[184] nouvelles certaines[185]
D'Angleterre, car pour perilz ne[186] paines
C'on entreprinst[187] n'y[188] porent venir saines
  Barges ne nefs.   452
Tant fu le vent contraire de tous lez[189]
Et en la mer tempeste si oultrez
Qu'a mon cuider sur le roy fu yrez
  Nostre Seigneur,   456

---

[168] C no et
[169] C ainsi [no que]
[170] D meismes
[171] H faulx *superscript* LBC no faulx
[172] H cestoit
[173] B il y a
[174] AD pot bien au roy C peut
[175] AD no car
[176] L si
[177] H pars
[178] H humblement
[179] H humble [*erasure*] et
[180] A quaurebours
[181] B ~~quot~~ que ot
[182] C maintez
[183] AD deduit
[184] H de *superscript* LBC no de
[185] L oir nouvelles bien certaines
[186] L et
[187] D nentrepreist
[188] AD ne
[189] H lez

meanwhile the duke[32] captured the greater part of England so unaccountably that I never heard of anything worse in my life; you will hear the tale, provided I do not wander off the point.

A little later the sea was calmed. When it pleased the King who governs all down here, there came a barge which drew tears from many eyes. Those on board related to the King how the duke had had his Treasurer[33] executed [fo. 11v.] and how, when he first arrived on his estates, he had the noble Archbishop of Canterbury[34] preach to people, saying,

' "Good people, listen all to me. You know how the King unjustly and without cause banished[35] your lord Henry; for this reason I have won a judgement from the Holy Father, who is our benefactor: all those who help him – be certain of this – will have remission of all the sins with which they have been sullied since the time of their baptism. And here is the papal bull[36] that the Pope in the holy city of Rome has sent me for you all, good friends.

---

[32] Line 458. *le duc*. Henry, duke of Lancaster, the future Henry IV. See *ODNB*, s.v. 'Henry IV [*known as* Henry Bolingbroke](1367–1413)'; also Given-Wilson, *Henry IV*.

[33] Line 468. *Son tresorier*. William le Scrope was executed at Bristol on 29 July, by which date, Richard had certainly left Dublin and was probably back in England. William le Scrope had been Chamberlain of the Household, but resigned the post to his younger brother Stephen (*infra*, l. 850, note) on becoming Treasurer of England in 1398. See C. Given-Wilson, *The Royal Household and the King's Affinity: Service, Politics and Finance in England 1360–1413* (New Haven, CT, 1986), pp. 71–72; also *ODNB*, s.v. 'Scrope, William, earl of Wiltshire (1351?–1399)'.

[34] Line 471. *l'arcevesque de Cantorbie*. Thomas Arundel, Archbishop of Canterbury, was impeached of treason in 1397 and sentenced to exile. His brother Richard, earl of Arundel, was also imprisoned and executed (cf. *infra*, l. 1633, note). Thomas joined forces with Henry Lancaster in Paris and returned to England with him in 1399. He was definitely hostile to Richard. See *ODNB*, s.v. 'Arundel [Fitzalan], Thomas (1353–1414)', also Saul, *Richard II*, pp. 377–378.

[35] Lines 474–475. *le roy banny / A ... vostre seigneur Henry*. On 16 September 1398 Richard stopped the trial by combat which was about to take place between Henry Lancaster and Thomas Mowbray, duke of Norfolk, each accusing the other of plotting against the King. Both were banished. See Given-Wilson, *Henry IV*, pp. 114–115.

[36] Line 485. *la bulle sëellee*. No other source tells this story, which cannot be verified. John Stow copies it from Creton. See Stow, *Chronicles of England*, p. 532, 'Lancaster ... had caused Thomas Arundell, Archbishop of Canterbury, to preach againste King Richarde, who also shewed a Bull procured from Rome, promising remission of sinnes to all those whiche should ayde the sayde Henry, in conquering of his enimies, and after their death, to be placed in Paradise ... '.

Car entandiz[190] la partie greigneur
D'Engleterre prist le duc par faveur
Si estrange, oncques[191] ne vy[192] pïeur
   Jour de ma vie; 460
Et vous l'orrez, maiz que je ne devie.
Un pou aprés la mer fu apaisie.
Quant au roy pleut[193], qui[194]* tout ça jus maistrie,
   Vint arriver 464
Une barge qui mains yeulx fist[195] plourer.
Ceulx de[196] dedens vouldrent au roy compter
Comment[197] le duc avoit fait decoler
   Son tresorier, 468
[fo. 11v.] Et comment, quant il arriva premier
En son païs, il fist aux gens[198] preschier
L'arcevesque de Cantorbie fier[199]
   Disant ainsi: 472
'Mes bonnes gens, entendez tous ici.
'Vous savez bien coment le roy banny
'A a grant[200] tort vostre seigneur Henry
   'Et sans raison. 476
'Et pour ce j'ay fait impetracïon
'Au Saint Pere, qui est nostre patron:
'Que trestous ceulx avront[201] remissïon
   'De leurs pechiez, 480
'De quoy oncques ilz furent entachiez[202]
'Depuis l'eure qu'ilz furent baptisiez,
'Qui lui aideront* – tous certains en soiez –
   'Celle journee. 484
'Et ves en ci[203] la bulle sëellee[204]
'Que le Pappe de Romme la louee
'M'a envoiee[205]* et pour[206] vous tous donnee,
   'Mes bons amis. 488

---

[190] A en ce temps D en temps la diz partie
[191] ACD quoncques
[192] AD noy [no ne]
[193] L plot
[194] H que
[195] AD qui fist mains
[196] B no de
[197] L comme
[198] A au roy B aux g-gens C illec
[199] B cantorbie fier disant
[200] L moult grant [only one a in LACD]
[201] B que trestous avront ceulx avront
[202] L de quoy ilz furent en leur vie entachiez C il furent
[203] AD et veez en ycy LB et veesent cy
[204] ACD scellee
[205] HACD envoie LB envoiee
[206] C par

[fo. 12r.] Figure V: The Archbishop of Canterbury, holding the papal bull, preaches from the pulpit.

Help him then to defeat his enemies and you will be with those who are in Paradise when you die."

'Then you could have seen young and old, weak and strong, start to murmur and with one accord, with no heed to right or wrong, rise up in rebellion, thinking that what they had been told was the truth. They all believed it to be true, for such people have scarcely any sense or knowledge. The archbishop thought up this scheme because no one dared to join the rebellion, for everyone feared your anger, dear Sire. [fo. 12v.] When the sermon was finished they started fleeing to the duke, to overthrow and destroy you and ravage your country in several ways: capturing towns and castles in his name, subjecting young and old to his sway; certainly nothing that can be carried away is left for the poor. For God's sake, make haste, Sire, to thwart his criminal plans, that is my advice.'

The King's face grew pale with anger and he said:

'Come here, my friends. Good God, does this man intend to take my country from me?'

He had the young men and elders of his Council brought together to decide on the best response to these events. They agreed one

[fo. 12r.] Figure V: The Archbishop of Canterbury, holding the papal bull, preaches from the pulpit.

'Vuelliez[207] lui donc aidier ses ennemis
'A conquerre,[208] et vous en serez mis
'Avecques ceulx qui sont en Paradis
   'Aprés la mort.'   492
'Lors veïssiez* jeune, viel, feble et fort
'Murmure faire et par commun accort,
'Sans regarder ne le droit ne le tort,
   'Eulx esmouvoir,   496
'Cuidant que ce c'on leur fist assavoir
'Feust verité. Tous le crurent[209] de[210] voir,
'Car de sens n'ont gueres ne de savoir,
   'De telz y a.   500
'L'arcevesque ce conseil cy trouva
'Pour ce que nulz esmouvoir ne s'oza,
'Car un chascun le courroulx redoubta
   'De vous, chier Sire.[211]   504
[fo. 12v.] 'Ce sermon fait, commencerent a fuire
'Devers le duc pour vous confondre et nuire,
'Vostre païs en conquerant destruire
   'De plusieurs biens: 508
'Villes, chasteaulx prenant comme pour siens,
'A lui soubzmet jeunes et ancïens;
'Aux povres gens certes ne laissent[212] riens
   'C'on[213] puist porter.   512
'Pour Dieu, Sire, pensez de vous haster,
'Affin que tost lui[214] puissiez destourner
'Son emprise, qui trop fait a blasmer,
   'Ce m'est advis.'   516
Le roy en ot de maltalent le viz
Descouluré, disant: 'Vien ça, amis.
'Me veult cest homme oster de mon païs,
   'Biau* Sire[215] Dieux?'   520
Assembler fist les jeunes et les vieulx
De son conseil pour regarder le mieulx
De cest affaire. Or fu leur accort tieulx
   Un samedi,   524

---

[207] C veilles
[208] B [a in left margin] conquerre
[209] B les ~~eir~~ crurent
[210] AD pour
[211] H chier LB no chier AD de chier vous sire
[212] B laisse
[213] C com
[214] A vous D len
[215] L beaulx sires

Saturday to set sail the following Monday without any further delay. When the duke of Aumale[37] heard that they were to leave, an evil thought entered his mind: he decided secretly that if he could, he would arrange otherwise.

He came in private to the King to undo [fo. 13r.] what all the others had done, saying,

'Sire, may it please you, I have never heard such bad faith. Do not make haste to depart, it would be much better to take time to gather shipping, for we do not have a hundred barges.[38] How can we set out, considering that in the sea here are rocks like mountains, and the sea-bed is dangerous? Come, it would be much better to send the earl of Salisbury[39] over there. He will hold the field against the duke and carry battle to him; he will have all the Welsh to fight him. Meanwhile we will go by land to Waterford. There you will send for shipping from all ports, so that, weak and strong, all your army can make the crossing. You will soon see your enemies captured and killed or defeated; be assured and confident of this.'

The King believed him more than all his friends, the other advice was completely overthrown by his.

---

[37] Line 527. *le duc d'Ammarlë*. Rutland, *supra*, ll. 93–94, note.

[38] Lines 540–541. *nous n'avons / Pas cent barges*. The hundred barges with which Rutland arrive six weeks earlier, ll. 425–428, had presumably been discharged.

[39] Line 546. *De Salsebery le conte*. The earl of Salisbury was one of Richard's staunchest friends, losing his life in the Epiphany Rising. See *ODNB*, s.v. 'Montagu [Montacute] John, third earl of Salisbury (*c*.1350–1400)'.

D'entrer en mer le plus prouchain lundi
Sans atendre plus long jour ne demy.
Et quant le duc d'Ammarlë entendi
    Le partement,   528
D'un[216] malice s'advisa, coyement
Pensant: s'il peut, il fera[217] autrement.
Au roy s'en vint[218] assez secretement
    Pour tout desfaire[219]   532
[fo. 13r.] Ce que trestous avoient[220] peü faire,
Disant: 'Sire, ne vous vueille desplaire,
'Car oncques maiz n'oÿ[221] de tel affaire
    'Si bien mentir.   536
'Ne vous hastez ja si de vous partir,[222]
'Il vault trop mieulx c'on face avant venir
'Du navire trestout par[223] bon loysir,
    'Car nous n'avons   540
'Pas cent barges. Comment nous en yrons,
'Veu qu'en la mer les[224] roches par grans mons
'Sont cy endroit, s'est[225] perilleux li[226] fons?*
    'Maiz venez sa,[227]   544
'Il vault trop mieulx envoier par dela
'De Salsebery le conte, qui tenra
'Contre le duc les champs et lui fera
    'Assez de guerre;   548
'Tous les Galoiz avra pour le conquerre.
'Et entendiz[228] nous en yrons par terre
'A Watreforde. La envoierez querre
    'Par tous les pors   552
'Du navire, sique febles et fors
'Puissent passer et tout vostre ost alors.
'Voz ennemis verrez tost[229] prins et[230] mors
    'Ou desconfiz;   556
'De tout cecy soiez[231] certains et fiz.'
Le roy le crut plus que tous ses amis,
L'autre conseil fu desfait et desmis
    Tout par[232] le sien.   560

---

[216] C dune
[217] D sera
[218] B vient
[219] H tout desfaire LB no tout
[220] A si avoient
[221] A noy jamaiz D nouy [jamais *superscript*]
[222] A si de partir
[223] C pour
[224] H le
[225] HLBC et sest AD et sont
[226] LB le
[227] B ey ca
[228] D en temps [dis *superscript*]
[229] AD tous
[230] LCD ou
[231] H soie [z *added later*]
[232] AD pour

[fo. 13v.] This displeased some of the elders who loved the King sincerely. They said:

'Delay in our situation is not a good idea, dear Sire.'

Nothing that was said to him did any good, his true friends found no cause to rejoice, their hearts were full of sorrow and anger. Without further discussion the King had the earl of Salisbury sent for and said,

'Cousin, you must cross to England and challenge the duke's mad undertaking, his men must be put to death or captured. Find out how he has stirred up my country and raised it against me.'

The earl replied,

'Sire, by my faith I shall do this, so that – I believe – you will soon hear of the fighting, or I will die in the attempt.'

'This I know, cousin,' said the King. 'And I will make haste to come across as soon as I can, for I shall have no rest so long as the false traitor[40] who has played such a trick on me remains alive. [fo. 14r.] If I can hold him in my grasp, I will make him die such a death that they will talk about it as far away as Turkey[41] for years to come.'

---

[40] Line 586. *le faulx traïtour*. Henry Lancaster.

[41] Line 591. *Turquie* was probably simply chosen for the rhyme, but might be an oblique reference to the annihilation of the crusading forces led by Philip the Bold's son – John of Nevers, later John the Fearless, see below ll. 3611–3612 and note – by the Turks at Nicopolis on 25 September 1396; see J.J.N. Palmer, *England, France and Christendom* (London, 1972), pp. 204–207.

[fo. 13v.] Il en despleut[233] a aucun ancïen
Qui de vray cuer amoient le roy bien,
Disant: 'L'atendre[234] en tel cas ne vault rien
   'Certes, chier[235] Sire.'   564
Riens ne[236] valu chose qu'on[237] lui peust dire,
Ses bons amis s'en[238] tindrent bien de rire
Et en orent au cuer grant dueil et ire.
   Sans plus parler   568
De Salsebery fist le conte mander,
Disant: 'Cousin, il vous en fault aler
'En Engleterre et au[239] duc resister
   'Sa folle emprinse,   572
'Et que sa gent soit mise a mort ou prinse.*
'Et si sachiez comment ne[240] par quel[241] guise
'Il a[242] ma terre ainsi troublee[243] et mise[244]
   'Encontre moy.'   576
Le conte dist: 'Monseigneur, par ma foy
'Je le feray, telement que – je croy –
'En pou de temps vous en orrez l'effroy
   'Ou je mourray   580
'En la paine.' 'Beau cousin, bien le sçay,'[245]
Ce dit le roy: 'Et je m'avanceray
'D'oultre passer au plus tost que pourray,
   'Car jamaiz jour   584
'De ma vie n'avray bien ne sejour,
'Jusques a tant que le faulx traïtour,
'Qui maintenant m'a joué d'un tel tour,
   'Sera en vie.   588
[fo. 14r.] 'Se je le puis tenir en ma baillie,
'Par tele[246] mort lui feray perdre vie,[247]
'Qu'on en parlera* jusques en la Turquie
   Bien longuement.'   592

---

[233] A il despleut moult
D il despleut [moult *superscript*]
[234] AD lentendre
[235] H chier
[236] AD ny
[237] H quon
[238] L se
[239] D le
[240] L et
[241] A *no* quel
[242] AD ara
[243] H trouble [e *added later*]
[244] B il a ma te terre troubler mise
[245] AD bien beau cousin le scay B bien leschay [al *superscript*] le scay
[246] B tel
[247] LAD la vie

The earl soon had his men and vessels made ready to depart. He took his loyal leave of the King and begged him to follow as soon as possible. The King swore on holy relics that he would set sail within six days,[42] whatever happened. Then the earl, who was very eager to set out to fight for the cause of King Richard, begged me to cross with him to provide diversion and singing and I agreed willingly; my companion and I sailed over the sea with him.

Now it happened that the earl landed at Conway,[43] a fine strong town, I tell you;

[fo. 14v.] Figure VI: Salisbury's ships arrive at Conway.

it was in Wales. There we learned of the duke's cruel behaviour, such as was unheard of anywhere. They told us that he had already taken the greater part of England, and captured towns and castles, dismissed office-holders and made new appointments everywhere in his own name; all those who displeased him he had had killed, without granting pardon as a lord should.

---

[42] Line 599. *Ainçoiz six jours*. This would be the absolute minimum, given the time necessary for the march to Waterford.

[43] Line 610. *Corniiay*. Creton is the only source for Salisbury's activities at Conway, or indeed for his presence there.

Le conte fist appareillier sa gent
Et ses vaisseaulx pour partir promptement.[248]
Au roy congié prist bien et sagement
   Et lui pria 596
De s'avancier au plus tost qu'il pourra.
Le roy sur[249] sains lui enconvenença:[250]
Ainçoiz six jours en la mer entrera
   Coment qu'il soit. 600
Lors le conte, qui grant desir avoit
De se[251] partir pour deffendre le droit
Du roy Richart, assez prié m'avoit
   D'oultre passer 604
Avecques lui, pour rire et pour chanter,[252]
Et je m'y volz de bon cuer accorder;
Mon compaignon et moy dela la mer
   Avecques lui 608
En alasmes. Or advint[253] il ainsi
Qu'a Cornüay le conte descendi
En une[254] ville qui est – je vous affi –
   Moult forte et[255] belle; 612

[fo. 14v.] Figure VI: Salisbury's ships arrive at Conway.

En Gales fu. La oÿmes nouvelle
De l'emprise du duc, qui fu cruelle,
Oncques – je croy – on ne parla[256] de telle
   En nul païs. 616
Car on nous dist qu'il avoit ja conquis
D'Angleterre la plus grant part et pris
Villes, chasteaulx, officïers[257] desmis,
   Et en son nom 620
Faisoit[258] par tout autre institucïon;
Tous ceulx qu'il ot en[259] indignacïon
Faisoit mourir sans leur fere pardon
   Comme seigneur. 624

---

[248] L proprement
[249] L sus
[250] H enconvenca LABCD enconvenenca
[251] B soy
[252] AD pour rire et chanter
[253] B advient
[254] H en [une *superscript*] LABCD *no* en
[255] H moult forte et LBC *no* moult
[256] B parle
[257] ABCD et officiers
[258] HLBC faire AD faisoit
[259] H ot en

§7 Lines 625–76. Salisbury raises 40,000 Welshmen and men of Cheshire for the King.

When the earl heard these bad tidings, it was no surprise that he was struck with fear, [fo. 15r.] for the duke had already managed to win over most of the English nobles; we were told that he had 60,000 men eager to fight. The earl immediately called to arms the Welsh and the men of Cheshire: he said how all good men, archers and others, if they valued their life, should rally to him in support of King Richard, who loved them dearly. They were eager to do this, thinking for sure that the King had arrived at Conway. I know for certain that within four days[44] there were 40,000 men drilling and mustering in the fields; they all sincerely wanted to fight against the enemies of King Richard, who was valiant and brave all his life long.

Then the earl, filled with great grief and distress, rode out to meet them, swearing in the name of Jesus, who hung on the Cross for us, that within three days he would grasp the duke and his supporters so tightly in his power that they would no longer go around sacking the country.

---

[44] Line 642. *Avant qu'il feust .iiii. jours.* There is no way of checking this.

§7 Lines 625–676. Salisbury raises 40,000 Welshmen and men of Cheshire for the King.

Quant le conte oÿ celle douleur
Ce ne fu pas merveilles[260]* s'il ot peur[261]
Car des nobles la partie greigneur
    Dë Engleterre[262]   628
[fo. 15r.] Avoit le duc desja sceu bien[263] acquerre;
Soixante mil desirans tous la guerre
Estoient[264] bien, ce nous fist on[265] acroirre.
    Lors promptement   632
Le conte fist faire son mandement
Parmy Gales et par Cestre: comment
Tous gentilz homs, archiers et autre gent
    Tost sur leur[266] vie   636
Vinssent[267] a[268] lui pour tenir la partie
Du roy[269] Richart, qui ne les haioit mie.*
De ce faire orent tresgrant envie,
    Cuidant pour vray   640
Qu'arrivé feust* le roy a Cornüay.
Avant qu'il feust .iiii. jours – bien le sçay –
Quarante mil furent faisant assay
    Et moustre aux champs,   644
Qui de vray cuer furent tous desirans[270]
D'avoir bataille a tous les malveillans
Du roy Richart, qui fu preux et vaillans,
    Tant qu'il dura.   648
Lors le conte, qui assez endura
Paine et travail, vers eulx tous s'en ala,
Jurant: Jhesus, qui pour nous se laissa
    Pendre en la croix,   652
Avant qu'il soit acompli des jours trois,
Tendra le duc et ses gens si estrois[271]
Que plus avant[272] n'yront a celle foiz
    Gastant[273] païs.   656

---

[260] AD merveille
[261] BD paour
[262] *all mss* dengleterre
[263] AD pour bien C bien sceu
[264] H estoient estoie bien
[265] B *no* on D on *superscript*
[266] H leur LB *no* leur
[267] LB venissent
[268] AD vers
[269] H roy *superscript*
[270] A qui aussy furent tous de vray desirans D qui [ausy *superscript*] furent tous de vray desirans
[271] L destrois
[272] B *no* avant
[273] ACD gastans

[fo. 15v.] A little later the earl found his men gathered together in the fields. He addressed them, saying,

'Good people, let us take pains to avenge King Richard before he comes, that he might forever be pleased with us. As for me, I do not intend to take my ease or rest until I have done my utmost against those who are so wicked and cruel towards him. Let us leave this place and carry the fight to them. God will help us if we work hard to attack them, for our belief is that every man must maintain what is right all his life long; God expressly commands us in several places to do this.'

§8 Lines 677–708. Having learned that Richard is not at Conway, the Welsh refuse to fight.

On hearing that the King was not there, the Welsh were all disheartened and afraid and many whispered one to the other: they thought that the King had died and feared the awful cruelty of the duke of Lancaster and his men. [fo. 16r.] They were not happy with the earl, and said:

'Sire, you may be sure that we will advance no further at the present time, since the King is not here. And would you know why?

[fo. 15v.] Un pou aprés le conte ses amis
Trouva aux champs trestous ensemble mis.
A eulx parla, disant: 'Par bon advis,
   'Mes bonnes gens,   660
'Soions[274] trestous de vengier diligens
'Le roy Richart, qui est yci absens,
'Afin tele qu'il soit de nous contens
   'A tousjours maiz.   664
'Quant est de moy, je ne pense jamaiz
'A reposer në a prendre relaiz,
'Jusques a tant qu'aray fait mes essaiz
   'Encontre ceulx   668
'Qui sont vers lui si felons et crueulx.
'Partons d'ici et alons tost[275] sur eulx,
'Dieux nous aidra se nous somez songneulx
   'D'eulx assaillir,   672
'Car selon ce[276] nostre loy soustenir
'Doit un chascun le droit jusqu'au[277] mourir;
'Dieux le commande expressement[278] tenir
   'En plusieurs cas.'   676

§8 Lines 677–708. Having learned that Richard is not at Conway, the Welsh refuse to fight.

Quant les Galoiz entendirent que pas
N'estoit le roy la, ilz furent tous mas,
L'un a[279] l'autre murmurant a[280] grant[281] tas,
   Plains de frëeur,   680
Cuidant[282] le roy estre mort a douleur
Et[283] recraingnant l'orrible et grant rigeur
Du duc, qui fu de Lencastre seigneur,
   Et de sa gent.   684
[fo. 16r.] Pas ne furent du conte bien content,
Disant:[284] 'Sire, sachiez[285] certainnement
'Nous n'irons plus avant quant a present,
   'Puis que le roy   688

---

[274] L soyes
[275] C tous
[276] B ce en ce [nostre superscript] loy
[277] ACD jusqua / B jusques au
[278] D et expressement
[279] C no a
[280] AD par
[281] ACD grans
[282] LABCD cuidans
[283] A en
[284] LB disans
[285] C saches

Here is the duke who subjects all to his will. This fills us with fear and dread, for we believe that the King is dead, since he did not arrive with you. Had he been here – by fair means or foul – each one of us would have been eager to fight his enemies, but for now we will not advance with you.'

The earl almost lost his wits, so great was his wrath. He wept hot tears, it was most distressing to see his plight.

'Alas!' he said. 'What shame is mine today. Death, come to me, tarry not, strike me down; I hate my life. Alas! The King will think that I have betrayed him.'

§9 Lines 709–52. The Welsh desert Salisbury.

Lamenting thus, he said:

'My friends, may Jesus Christ forgive you, come with me – I beg you – and we will hold the field [fo. 16v.] for King Richard who will be here within four and a half days. He told me when I left Ireland that he would set sail before the end of the week; he swore this on his life.[45] Messeigneurs – I beg you – let us be diligent.'

---

[45] Lines 715–718. *Car il me dist ... / ... la sepmaine acomplie.* Creton is referring back to ll. 598–600.

'N'est pas ici, et savez vous[286] pour quoy?
'Veci[287] le duc qui soubzmet tout a soy,
'La quele chose nous est tresgrant effroy
  'Et desconfort,   692
'Car nous pensons bien que le roy soit[288] mort,
'Puis qu'avec[289] vous n'est arrivé a[290] port.
'S'il feust ici – feust a droit ou a tort –
  'Chascun de nous   696
'Fust d'assaillir ses[291] ennemis jaloux,
'Maiz nous n'irons pas ore[292] aveque vous.'
Le conte en ot au[293] cuer si grant courroux
  Qu'a pou de dueil   700
N'issi du sens, plourant, la[294] larme a l'ueil;
Grant pitié fu de vëoir son accueil.
'Helas!' dist il: 'Quel honte je recueil[295]
  'Ceste journee.   704
'Mort, vien a moy, ne fay plus demouree;
'Fay moy mourir, je hes ma destinee.
'Las! Or cuidra le roy qu'en ma pensee
  'Ait traïson.'   708

§9 Lines 709–752. The Welsh desert Salisbury.

Ce dueil faisant, disoit: 'My* compaignon,[296]
'Que[297] Jhesucrist vous face vray pardon.
'Venez o[298] moy, si serons champïon,
  'Je vous en pri,[299]   712
[fo. 16v.] 'Du roy Richart, le quel sera icy
'Avant qu'il soit .iiii.[300] jours et demy.
'Car il me dist, quant je me departi
  'Dë Ibernie[301]   716
'Qu'il enterroit en la mer sur sa vie,
'Avant qu'il feust la sepmaine acomplie;
'De nous partir, Messeigneurs, je vous prie,[302]
  'Soions songneux.'   720

---

[286] A bien
[287] LC vez ci
[288] A si soit
[289] AD quavecques
[290] A au
[291] C les
[292] ACD ores
[293] C ou
[294] D *no* la
[295] B *line omitted*
[296] A ce dueil faisant en lamentacion D ce dueil faisant amy compaignon
[297] A dist
[298] B a
[299] B empry
[300] B troiz
[301] ABD dybernie
[302] B en prie

It was to no avail. They remained faint-hearted and dejected. Many of them wanted to flee to join the duke, as they feared for their lives, but the earl kept them fourteen days in the field, awaiting the arrival of King Richard. The earl kept saying to himself:

'It seems to me, my lord, that your delay means that you will keep no part of England. God in Paradise, what can this mean? I believe you have been betrayed, since I hear no news of you in word or deed. Alas! These men are afraid, they fear the duke's enmity. They will leave me; they are an unknowing and ignorant people.'

[fo. 17r.] Thus did the good earl turn things over in his mind in the field as he rode along with these men, who very shortly all deserted him; some went directly to the duke, others returned to Wales. Thus they left the earl alone in the field with only his own men, who were fewer than one hundred, I think. He made great lamentation, saying sorrowfully,

'We should retreat, for our affairs are going very badly.'

Riens n'y[303] valu. Comme gens paoureux
Demourerent tous[304] merencolïeux.
Grant partie en y ot d'envïeux
 D'eulx en fouir   724
Devers le duc, pour paour qu'ont[305] de mourir,
Maiz le conte les fist aux champs tenir
Quatorze jours, atendant le venir
 Du roy Richart.   728
Par maintez foiz dist le bon conte a part:
'D'Angleterre arrez petite part,
'Mon[306] droit Seigneur, quant demourez si tart,
 'Ce m'est advis.   732
'Que peut ce estre, vray Dieu de Paradiz?
'Certes je croy que vous estes traÿs,
'Quant de vous n'oy, në en faiz në en diz,
 'Nouvelle vraie.   736
'Helas! Je voy que ceste gent s'esmaie
'De peur qu'ilz[307] ont que le duc ne les haie.
'Il[308] me lairont; ce ne sont que gens[309] laie
 'Et non saichans.'*   740
[fo. 17r.] Ainsi disoit a lui mesmes aux champs
Le bon conte, qui estoit chevauchans
Avecques eulx, les quelx en pou de temps
 Tous le laisserent;[310]   744
Les uns au duc tout droit si s'en alerent,
Et les autres en Gales retournerent.
Le conte ainsi enmy les champs planterent
 Seul fors sa gent,   748
Qui ne furent pas – ce cuide je[311] – un cent.
Grant dueil faisoit, disant piteusement:
'Retraions nous, car trop va malement
 'Nostrë[312] emprise.'   752

---

[303] B ne
[304] H demourerent c̶o̶m̶m̶e̶ tous A demourerent la tous
[305] L no quont
[306] D moult
[307] C quil
[308] LABD ilz
[309] LABCD gent
[310] H tous le laisserent LBC no tous
[311] L no je
[312] AD la myenne

§10 Lines 753–824. Salisbury withdraws on Conway. Richard arrives at Milford Haven; dressed as a priest he leaves his army and rides to Conway.

Thus does the earl hate himself, for he can plainly see that he has neither killed nor captured the duke's men; his heart fills with deep shame. Without further delay the enemy advanced, for they had learned that the earl had mustered his forces to attack them in strength. The duke was happy at this: he wanted nothing so much as to go to war against those who would defend or serve King Richard. He made his way as directly as he could towards the earl, who retreated on Conway, [fo. 17v.] full of grief, fear and despair. This made me very sad, for I loved him dearly, because he sincerely loved the French, and in all he did was modest, gentle and chivalrous,[46] and had the reputation of being loyal at all times and a worthy man. He dispensed generous and liberal gifts, was bold and fierce as a lion, wrote *ballades* and songs, *rondeaux* and *lais*; and yet he was a lay person. Nevertheless all his actions were so full of grace that to my mind no fellow countryman ever had so many God-given gifts as he. May his soul for ever be with the saints in Paradise, for he was thereafter

---

[46] Lines 773–786. This reads like a eulogy, a funeral oration. *Supra*, Introduction, pp. 25, 29. For a discussion of the knightly ideal in the fourteenth century, see Mathew, *Court of Richard II*, pp. 114–128.

§10 Lines 753–824. Salisbury withdraws on Conway. Richard arrives at Milford Haven; dressed as a priest he leaves his army and rides to Conway.

Le conte ainsi sa vie moult desprise,
Car il voit bien qu'il n'a ne mort ne prise
Les gens du duc; ce forment[313] li atise
    Au cuer despit.   756
Les ennemis sans plus faire respit
S'avancerent, car on leur avoit dit
Que le conte son assamblee[314] fist
    Pour encontre eulx   760
Venir a fort. Le duc en fu joyeux:
De nulle rien n'estoit[315] si desireux
Fors seulement de combatre a tous ceulx,
    Qui deffendre*   764
Le roy[316] Richart vouloient ou atendre.
Son chemin fist le plus droit qu'il pot prendre
Devers le conte, le quel s'en[317] ala rendre
    A Cornüay,   768
[fo. 17v.] Plain de doulour, de tristresse et d'esmay.
Grant mal m'en fist certes, car je l'amay
Parfaitement, pour[318] ce que de cuer vray
    Amoit Françoiz,   772
Et si estoit humble, doulz et courtoiz
En tous ses faiz, et de chascun la voiz
Avoit d'estre loyal en tous endroiz
    Et bien preudoms.   776
Moult largement donnoit et de preulx dons,
Hardi estoit et fier comme lions,
Et si faisoit balades et chançons,
    Rondeaulx et laiz   780
Tresbien et bel; si n'estoit il que homs lais.
Non obstant ce[319] estoient tous ses faiz
Si gracïeux que – je croy – que jamaiz
    De son païs   784
N'istra homme ou Dieux ait tant biens[320] mis,
Comme en celui. Son ame en Paradis
Puist estre mise avec les sains toudiz,
    Car laidement   788

---

[313] D ce forment *repeated*
[314] H assamble [e *added later*]
[315] A estoit
[316] A roy *repeated*
[317] C se
[318] C par
[319] B ey [sy *superscript*]
[320] AD de biens C de biens

foully killed,[47] suffering a martyr's death, while he loyally upheld what was righteous and true; you will hear how, if God spares me.

But before that I want to tell you about the arrival of King Richard, which was too long delayed, for he waited 18 days[48] after our departure from Ireland; [fo. 18r.] this was very great foolishness. May Jesus Christ curse in mind and body the man who contrived this,[49] for well did he show his love for the King who loved him so.

The King issued orders throughout his army for the barges and ships to be loaded up and for all men capable of bearing arms to embark.

Figure VII: King Richard's fleet leaves for Wales, one of the ships bearing his sunburst badge on her sail.

Thus King Richard crossed the sea[50] in a short time, for the weather was fine and clear and the wind favourable, so that he arrived at Milford Haven within two days. He did not linger there, in the light of the weeping and wailing of the poor people and the intense grief that everyone felt. [fo. 18v.] Then he decided that he would leave his army, at midnight without saying a word, accompanied by only a few people, for he did not want to attract attention. He dressed right there in a borrowed garment, like a poor priest;[51] he was afraid of being recognized by his enemies. Alas! He thought that the earl [of Salisbury] was still holding the field with his men; thus, sad and melancholy, he rode swiftly towards him.

---

[47] Lines 788–792. Salisbury's death is reported at ll. 3189–3197.

[48] Line 795. *.xviii. jours*. This is the sort of detail that Creton might have committed to memory. Although he considered it an impossibly long time, and therefore evidence of Rutland's treachery, it is an entirely plausible period into which to fit the march to Waterford, some activity in South Wales, and the arduous journey from Milford to Conway.

[49] Line 798. *Par qui ce fu*. Rutland is meant.

[50] *one of the ships bearing his sunburst badge*. Figure VII. Saul, *Richard II*, p. 440. Also, Gordon and others (eds), *Regal Image of Richard II*, pp. 13, 118, 177.

[51] Line 818. Comme *un prestre qui a pou de menus*. Creton, 'Translation of a French Metrical History', ed. Webb, p. 77, translates 'like a poor priest of the Minors'. However, Webb himself says, p. 77, note w, 'Franciscans wore grey cassocks and cowls', while six of the miniatures show Richard wearing a red cassock and black cowl. F. Godefroy, *Dictionnaire de l'ancienne langue française*, 10 vols (Paris, 1881–1902), s.v. '*menu*' = *petite monnaie*.

L'ont fait mourir depuis a grant tourment
Comme martir, maintenant loyaulment
Raison et droit; vous orrez bien comment
    Se Dieux me gart.   792
Maiz la venue avant du roy Richart
Vous vueil compter, quil* fu pour lui trop tart,
Car .xviii. jours aprés[321] nostre depart
    Dë Ybernie[322]   796
[fo. 18r.] Demoura il; ce fu trop grant folie.
Par qui ce fu, Jhesucrist le maudie
Et confonde du corps et de la vie,
    Car bien monstra   800
L'amour qu'il ot au roy, qui tant l'ama.
Par tout son ost de chargier[323] commanda
Barges et nefs, et d'entrer qui pourra
    Armes porter.   804

Figure VII: King Richard's fleet leaves for Wales, one of the ships bearing his sunburst badge on her sail.

Ainsi passa le roy Richart la mer
En pou de temps, car l'air fu bel et cler
Et le vent bon, qui le fist arriver
    Avant deux jours   808
A Milleforde. La ne fist pas sejours,
Veu le meschief,[324] les plaintes et les plours
Des povres gens, et les mortelz doulours
    Que chascun ot.   812
[fo. 18v.] Lors s'avisa que, sans dire nul mot,
Se partiroit a minuit[325] de son ost
A pou de gent,[326] car pour rien il ne vot
    Estre aperçus.   816
De robe estrange fu la endroit vestus
Comme un prestre qui a pou de menus,
Pour la doubte qu'il ot d'estre congneuz
    De ses nuisans.   820
Las! Il cuidoit que le conte les champs
Tenist encores avec[327] ses combatans;
Pour ce vers lui estoit fort chevauchans,
    Triste et pensis.   824

[321] A car dix et huit apres
[322] B dybernie
[323] AD deschargier
[324] AD les meschiefz
[325] HLABD mienuit C minuit
[326] LAD gens
[327] D avecques

§11 Lines 825–56. Those who rode with Richard from Milford Haven to Conway are named.

Now you should know the names of the friends who were with him as he rode: I saw there the duke of Exeter[52] – his brother – and also the good duke of Surrey[53] who was loyal and true to the end; the fearless earl of Gloucester[54] was with them.

There were three bishops, two of whom did not behave with integrity, and you will hear how; but first I want to tell you their names. One was bishop of St David's[55] and the other bishop of Carlisle; he was the least bad of them, for he never sought to flee the King or change sides, [fo. 19r.] whatever was said to him. The third was bishop of Lincoln;[56] he would not give a rotten pear for what they did, for he was brother german to the duke [of Lancaster] and thought that he could always make his peace with him.

Of laymen there were two knights, gracious and noble, well versed in arms: the first was called Stephen Scrope,[57] the other Ferriby,[58] who was young and dashing. Also with them was Janico,[59] who was said to be a first-rate soldier, undertaking great feats of arms, so people said.

---

[52] Line 827. *Le duc d'Excestre – son frere.* John Holland, duke of Exeter, was half-brother to Richard and brother-in-law to Henry Lancaster, whose sister Elizabeth was his wife. Cf. *infra*, ll. 3199–3202. He was executed after the Epiphany Rising. See *ODNB*, s.v. 'Holland, John, first earl of Huntingdon and duke of Exeter (*c.*1352–1400)'.

[53] Line 829. *le ... duc de Soudray.* Thomas Holland, duke of Surrey, was the son of Thomas Holland, brother of John Holland, duke of Exeter. He was nephew to Richard and to the duke of Exeter. He was executed after the Epiphany Rising. See *ODNB*, s.v. 'Holland [Holand], Thomas, sixth earl of Kent and duke of Surrey (*c.*1374–1400)'.

[54] Line 831. *de Clocestre le conte.* See *supra*, ll. 304–305 and note.

[55] Line 837. *evesque de Saint David et sire / De Gerlic.* Guy de Mohun remained bishop of St David's until his death in 1407. See *ODNB*, s.v. 'Mohun [Mone], Guy (d. 1407)'. For Thomas Merk, bishop of Carlisle, see *ODNB*, s.v. 'Merk [Merke], Thomas (d. 1409/10)'. The *Traïson*'s account of Merk's speech in defence of Richard at the Deposition Parliament has been described as 'fanciful'. See Palmer, 'French Chronicles', 61:2 (1979), pp. 411–412.

[56] Line 842. *evesque de Nicole.* Henry Beaufort, bishop of Lincoln, son of John of Gaunt and Katherine Swynford, was half-brother to Henry Lancaster. See *ODNB*, s.v. 'Beaufort, Henry [*called* the Cardinal of England] (1375?–1447)'.

[57] Line 850. *Estienne Scroup.* Sir Stephen le Scrope was younger brother of William, earl of Wiltshire. Cf. *supra*, l. 468, note. He went on to serve Henry IV after the deposition. Except at l. 1190, when they call him *Steven*, every time **HLBC** mention *Estienne Scroup*, **AD** call him *Guillaume*.

[58] Line 851. *Ferbric.* William Ferriby, King's Clerk, remained loyal to Richard, and was executed for his part in the Epiphany Rising. See Given-Wilson, *Royal Household*, p. 225.

[59] Line 853. *Jenico.* Janico Dartasso, a Navarrese soldier of fortune in the service of the English crown. See S. Walker, *Political Culture in Later Medieval England: Essays* (Manchester, 2006), pp. 115–135; also *ODNB*, s.v. 'Dartasso, Janico (d. 1426)'.

§11 Lines 825–856. Those who rode with Richard from Milford Haven to Conway are named.

    Or est raison que sachiez ses amis,
Qui avec[328] lui estoient aux champs mis:
Le duc d'Excestre[329] – son frere – je l'i[330] vis,
    Et s'avisay   828
Avecques lui le bon duc de Soudray,
Qui fu loyal[331] jusqu'a[332] la mort et vray;
Et de Clocestre le conte sans esmay
    Fu avec[333] eulx.   832
Trois evesques y ot, de quoy les deux
Ne firent[334] pas comme gens[335] graciëux,
Et vous l'orrez; maiz avant les noms[336] d'eulx
    Je vous vueil dire.   836
L'un fu evesque de Saint David[337] et sire
De Gerlic l'autre; ce fu d'eulx le mains pire,
Car du bon roy ne s'en[338] volt oncques fuire,[339]
    Ne pour parole   840
[fo. 19r.] Qu'on lui en[340] dist oncques n'en[341] changa colle.
Le tiers si[342] fu evesque de Nicole,
Qui n'acontoit pas une poire mole
    A tous leurs faiz,   844
Car il estoit frere germain parfaiz
Du duc, pensant que bien feroit sa paix
Tousjours a lui. La avoit de[343] gens laiz
    Deux chevaliers   848
Tresgraciëux en armes, preux et fiers:
Estienne[344] Scroup fu nommé li primiers,[345]
L'autre Ferbric, qui fu joins et ligiers.
    Et si estoit   852
Avecques eulx Jenico,[346] q'on tenoit
Pour bon routier, car il entreprenoit
De tresgrans[347] faiz, ainsi comme on[348] disoit
    Comunement.   856

---

[328] D avecques
[329] B de cestre
[330] ABCD le
[331] C qui loial fu
[332] B jusques a
[333] AD avecques
[334] B furent
[335] C gent
[336] AD le nom
[337] AD damide
[338] B *no* sen
[339] B ~~fire~~ fuire
[340] LB *no* en
[341] AD ne
[342] B *no* si
[343] LB des
[344] AD guillaume
[345] B le premiers
[346] AD jenier
[347] B *no* tres
[348] C que lon

§12 Lines 857–944. Richard and Salisbury meet at Conway, where the King learns that he has no army in Wales.

Thus the King went off that very night with just 13 companions. He rode hard for he wanted to meet up quickly with the earl of Salisbury: humiliated and ashamed, the earl considered himself worthless, because the duke overthrows all obstacles in his path, wherever he goes.

The King rode unrecognized and so hard that he arrived at Conway (where there are many slate roofs) at day-break.[60]

[fo. 19v.] Figure VIII: King Richard, in black cowl, meets Salisbury and other companions at Conway.

When the King and the earl met there was great sorrow instead of joy: tears, laments and sighs, groans and grief went on and on. It was certainly most distressing to see their faces and how they behaved when they met.

The earl's face was pale with fatigue. He told the King how badly things had gone for him, how he had mustered his troops when he landed in England,[61] and how he had immediately called up the men of Cheshire, the Manxmen and the Welsh; they all wanted to destroy their enemies. [fo. 20r.]

---

[60] Lines 866–868. *a Cornüay ... / ... arriva ... / Au point du jour*. This of course was impossible. It reveals Creton's ignorance of the geography of Wales and helps to explain why he could not understand how it took Richard so long to reach Conway. Sherborne, *War, Politics and Culture*, p. 141, estimates that Richard would have 'needed a week to reach Conway'. They could perhaps have ridden thirty miles a day. Creton insists on his own timescale, saying *infra*, l. 1257, that Richard had left his army *avant hier*, 'the day before yesterday'.

[61] Line 880. *En Engleterre*. At Conway, in Wales. *Supra*, l. 610.

§12 Lines 857–944. Richard and Salisbury meet at Conway, where the King learns that he has no army in Wales.

    Ainsi le roy s'en ala seulement
Lui quatorziesme celle nuit proprement.
Fort chevaucha desirant briefvement[349]
    Trouver le conte   860
De Salsebery, qui ne tenoit maiz conte
De sa vie pour le despit et honte
Qu'il ot du duc, qui ainsi tout[350] surmonte,
    Quel[351] part qu'il voise.*   864
Tant chevaucha le roy sans faire noise
Qu'a Cornüay (ou il a mainte ardoise
Sur[352] les maisons) arriva, qui qu'en poise,
    Au point du jour.   868

[fo. 19v.] Figure VIII: King Richard, in black cowl, meets Salisbury and other companions at Conway.

    A l'assambler du roy et du contour
En lieu de joie y ot moult grant doulour:
Pleurs, plains,[353] suspirs n'y[354] firent pas sejour,
    Gemirs ne dueil.   872
Certes c'estoit grant pitié a voir[355] d'ueil
Leur contenance[356] et leur mortel acueil.[357]
Le conte avoit la face de sonmueil[358]
    Descoulouree.   876
Au roy conta sa dure destinee
Et comment[359] fait avoit son assemblee,
Quant descendu fu de la mer sallee
    En Engleterre,   880
Et qu'il avoit tantost envoié querre
Les Cessiers, Mans et les Galoiz par terre,
Qui de vray cuer vouloient bien conquerre[360]
    Leurs annemis.   884

---

[349] L de briefment
[350] C tout ainsi
[351] AD quelque
[352] L sus
[353] C plains pleurs
[354] A ne

[355] B veue
[356] C ordonnance
[357] L *lines 873–874 transposed*
[358] B de son mireil ~~descoul~~

[359] B come
[360] H qui de <u>vray</u> cuer vouloient <u>bien</u> <u>conquerre</u> LABCD qui de bon cuer vouloient aler querre

'There were forty thousand of them gathered together. I repeated to them time and again,
 ' "Friends, let us advance. The King has sent me here to lead you. Rest assured that I will never leave you until I die."
'But I could not prevail upon them, for when he saw his chance, everyone left; some went to the duke, others came in this direction. Because they did not see you right here, they thought that you were surely dead across the surging sea. Thus I remained alone in the field where I had held them for almost two weeks. Alas! He who kept you back in Ireland has very little love for you. All is lost, unless God, who hung on the Cross, intervenes; for sure I believe that money has betrayed us.'

The King's sorrow was so great that you would not have believed a third, or a fourth, part of it, however loyal you were. His mortal suffering and his anger were no small matter, and he said over and over again:

'Sweet and glorious God – who hung on the Cross for us – if I have sinned greatly against Thee, [fo. 20v.] I clasp my hands and beg for mercy. Grant not that I lose my country and my life at the hands of these disloyal and jealous traitors who would drive me

[fo. 20r.] 'Quarante mil furent ensemble mis.
'La leur di je souvent: "Mes bons amis,
' "Alons avant, le roy m'a cy tramis
  ' "Pour vous conduire. 888
' "Sachiez de[361] vray, jusqu'a tant que je muyre
' "Ne vous laray." Maiz je ne les[362] poz duire,
'Qu'un[363] chascun, quant il vit sa queue luire,[364]*
  'Si s'en ala: 892
'Les uns au duc, les autres par deça,
'Pour ce que point ne vous virent droit la,
'Pensant[365] que mort feussiez pour vray[366] dela
  'La mer haultaine. 896
'Ainsi tout seul demouray en la plaine,[367]
'Quant je les oz tenuz pres de quinzaine
'Parmi les champs. Hellas! Trop pou vous aime*
  'Qui tant tenu 900
'En Ybernie vous a.[368] Tout est perdu
'Se Dieu n'en pense, qui en croix fu pendu;
'Certes je croy que nous sommez vendu
  'A fins[369] deniers.' 904
Le roy en ot tel dueil qu'a quart n'a tiers[370]
Ne le croiroit homme, tant soit entiers.
Son mortel mal ne fu mie ligiers
  Ne son courroux, 908
Disant souvent: 'Glorïeux Dieux et doulx –
'Qui vous laissastes crucefier pour nous –
'Se[371] par pechié ay trop mesfait vers vous,
  'Merci vous crie[372] 912
[fo. 20v.] 'A jointes mains, et ne consentez[373] mie
'Que je perde[374] mon païs ne[375] ma vie
'Par ces felons traïtres, plains[376] d'envie,
  'Qui hors bouter 916

---

[361] AD pour
[362] B le
[363] L que
[364] C queue ~~vir~~ luire
[365] L pensans
[366] C voir
[367] L paine
[368] AD vous a en ybernie
B en ybernie vous ~~ey~~ a

[369] H a fin LACD a fins
B affin
[370] L quau quart nau tiers
[371] C si
[372] B merci vous crie ~~a joinctes mains et ne consentes mie~~

[373] L ne vous consentez
[no et]
[374] D perdre
[375] LAD et
[376] L felons qui sont tresplains

out and disinherit me.

'Alas! I know not what they want of me; to the best of my ability I have supported justice and the law. I truly appeal to our sovereign King, who sits on high and sees afar, that my poor heart wants everyone who is alive now, has been, and is to come, to know what is in my mind and what I want. If I have been merciless and inflexible in maintaining the law, that is only right, for the King must be resolute and decisive and remain steadfast; he must punish wrong-doers and remain fair at all times. Alas! Because I have followed these principles to the best of my ability for three, nay eight and ten years,[62] these people persecute me. Gracious God, I promise Thee truly and respectfully that, as well as I could, I never allowed harm to be done to anyone who did not deserve it. [fo. 21r.] Have mercy on me, poor, wretched King, for I know for sure that I am undone if Thou dost not help me now.'

---

[62] Lines 934–935. *des ans troiz / Voir .viii. et .x.* Creton knew that Richard had been on the throne for twenty-two years, *infra*, l. 1771, *l'espasse de bien .xxii. ans.* An amendment has therefore been made to l. 935, changing *ou* to *et* – the numbers are a total and not alternatives – which must have been what Creton originally wrote. The numbers add up to twenty-one, which is almost twenty-two. Numbers were not Creton's strong point. *Supra*, Introduction, p. 31.

'Ainsi me vuellent et moy[377] deshireter.
'Las! Je ne sai qu'on* me veult demander;
'A mon povoir ay je voulu garder
 'Justice et droit. 920
'Le souverain* roy, qui hault siet et loing voit,
'En appelle a tesmoing cy endroit
'Si vrayement, que mon las cuer vouldroit
 'Que trestous ceulx 924
'Qui ont esté, sont et seront morteulx,
'Sceüssent bien ma pensee et mes[378] veulx.
'Se j'ay esté en droit gardant crueux,
 'Non[379] variable, 928
'Raison le veult, car fermë et estable[380]
'Doit estre roy et tenir soy[381] notable,
'Pugnir les maulx et estre veritable
 'En tous endroiz. 932
'Las! Et pour ce qu'ay ensuÿ[382] ces[383] droiz
'A mon povoir passé a des ans troiz,
'Voir[384] .viii. et .x., me tiennent si destroiz
 'Ces gens ici. 936
'Glorïeux Dieux, d'umble cuer te depri[385]
'Si vrayement, c'onques ne consenti
'Faire nul mal, qui ne l'ot deservi,
 'A mon povoir. 940
[fo. 21r.] 'Vueillez de moy, povre, las roy,[386] avoir
'Misericorde, car je sçay bien de voir
'Que perdus[387] sui, se ne me daingniez voir
 'Prouchainement.' 944

---

[377] C me
[378] C mon
[379] B nat non
[380] AD tresferme et estable L ferme et bien estable
[381] AD sens
[382] AD ensuivy B suy
[383] C les
[384] *all mss* voire .viii ou .x
[385] L cuer je te pri
[386] B povre roy las roy
[387] L perdu

§13 Lines 945–1028. Rutland engineers the defection of Richard's army from Milford Haven; the men plunder the King's treasure as they leave. The English are robbed in turn by the Welsh.

Now I will tell you how the Constable,[63] who commanded the King's army, wrongfully went off without waiting for him and took all his men with him. This was a great sin, for no one esteemed him henceforth. This is not surprising, since up until now no man of noble rank had done such a thing as wanting to overthrow his rightful lord.

As the Constable schemed to fulfil his aim, on the very night that the King left the port at midnight, disquiet and commotion arose in the ranks, and men cried out:

'The King is fleeing without saying a word.'

The Constable was overjoyed at this, for really he had not been able to find a way to leave. But when he saw that the army was in turmoil, he said loudly enough for everyone to hear:

'Let us go, we are all doomed since Monseigneur had fled to save himself.'

[fo. 21v.] He swiftly had trumpets sounded and commanded that every man should be ready to leave immediately, since he does not know if the King is coming back.

---

[63] Line 946. *le connestable*. Rutland.

§13 **Lines 945–1028. Rutland engineers the defection of Richard's army from Milford Haven; the men plunder the King's treasure as they leave. The English are robbed in turn by the Welsh.**

Or vous vueil dire la maniere comment	
Le connestable, qui gouverna sa gent,	
Sans l'atendre s'en ala laidement	
Et enmena	948
Toutes ses gens, dont trop fort mesprins a,	
Car oncques puis arme* ne le prisa.	
Et ce n'est pas merveilles, car pieça	
On ne vit faire	952
Homme tel fait, qui feust de noble affaire,	
Com de vouloir son droit seigneur desfaire.	
Lui desirant tout son vouloir[388] parfaire,	
Icelle[389] nuit	956
Que le bon roy se parti a minuit	
Du port de mer, la murmure et le[390] bruit	
Leva en l'ost, criant: 'Le roy s'en fuit	
'Sans dire mot.'	960
Le connestable alors grant joie en ot,	
Car bonnement trouver voie ne pot	
Pour s'en aler. Maiz quant il vit que l'ost	
Fu esmeüz,	964
Il dit si hault que bien fu entenduz:	
'Alons nous ent, nous sommez tous perduz,	
'Quant Monseigneur s'en est ainsi fouyus*	
'Soy garentir.'	968
[fo. 21v.] Promptement fist trompetes retentir	
Et commanda que chascun de partir	
Fust tantost prest, puis que le revenir	
Ne scet du roy.	972

[388] C desir   [389] AD la propre   [390] L *no* le

Then there was incredible uproar, ships were discharged and carts loaded; everyone soon got his baggage ready for going away. The King's treasure[64] was all carried off: gowns, jewels, fine gold and shining silver, many good horses of foreign breed, many precious stones of great worth, many splendid cloaks and many whole ermine furs, much splendid foreign cloth of gold, and many lengths of cramoisy.

Sir Thomas Percy[65] was absolute master over all these things. He was the King's Steward – in French that is *maître d'hôtel* – and had served the King for many years. The Constable and he put their heads together. A short time later they [all] went from there and headed straight through Wales, but the Welsh saw their treacherous behaviour and [fo. 22r.] accosted them in strength, one thousand here, two thousand there. They shouted out repeatedly:

'Wretched traitors, by God's will you will advance no further here and you will give up all the jewels that you are carrying off as booty, for the King did not give them to you.'

Thus were the English plundered by the Welsh. They took back the baggage and all the armour, gold and silver, jewels, precious stones and cloth of gold.

---

[64] Line 977. *L'avoir du roy*. Sumptuous clothing figures largely amongst Richard's treasure. Creton uses *maint(e)* six times in ll. 977–984, underlining the bulk of the wealth, while he also stresses its exotic nature: *d'oultre la mer, precïeuse, riche et chiere, d'estrange maniere*. See Stratford (ed.), *Richard II and the English Royal Treasure*, pp. 111–115.

[65] Line 986. *Sir Thomas de Persi. Supra*, l. 34, note.

LA PRINSE ET MORT DU ROY RICHART D'ANGLETERRE 107

La avoit il moult merveilleux desroy,
Nes estrangier et chargier[391] le charroy;
Chascun bien tost apresta son arroy[392]
    Pour s'en aler. 976
L'avoir du roy tout en firent mener:
Robes, joyaux, or fin et argent cler,
Maint bon cheval, qui fu d'oultre la mer,[393]
    Et mainte pierre 980
Precïeuse, qui fu moult riche[394] et chiere,
Maint bon mantel et mainte ermine entiere,
Maint bon drap d'or et d'estrange maniere,
    Maint cramoisi. 984
De tout ce fu gouverneur sans nul si
Un qui ot nom Sir[395] Thomas de Persi.
Estuuart[396] fu du roy, le quel servi
    L'ot[397] longuement: 988
C'est a dire en françoiz proprement
Le grant maistre d'ostel principaument.
Le connestable et lui leur parlement
    Ensemble firent. 992
Un pou aprés de la se departirent*
Et leur chemin droit[398] parmi Galles prirent,[399]
Maiz les Galoiz, qui leur traïson virent,
    Au devant d'eulx 996
[fo. 22r.] Vindrent a fort – cy un millier cy deux –
Disant[400] souvent: 'Traïttres[401] maleureux,
'Par cy avant n'irés plus – se[402] m'ait Dieux –
    'Et si lairés 1000
'Tous les joyaulx qu'en larrecin portez,
'Car le roy pas ne les vous a donnez.'[403]
Ainsi furent Engloiz tous destroussez
    Par les Galoiz: 1004
Le cariage et trestout le harnoiz,
Or et argent, joyaulx, pierres, orfroiz
Retindrent eulx. Lors furent bien destroiz
    Et courrouciez 1008

---

[391] L en trousser males et chargier AD nes deschargier et chargier
[392] L lines 974–975 transposed
[393] A qui furent doultre mer
[394] B moult chie riche
[395] all mss sire
[396] A estiware
[397] AD moult [no lot]
[398] H droit *superscript* BC *no* droit
[399] AD tindrent
[400] ACD disans
[401] C traiteres
[402] L si
[403] B ne vous les [a *superscript*] donnez

Then were the English maddened and in torment, for a thousand of them were stripped of their clothing[66] and sent to the duke wearing only their doublets, a white stick in their hands and nothing on their feet; moreover the man who was not better equipped than this had to say whence he came and where he was going, and pay his due – willy-nilly – or be killed. And if you think this is too hard to believe, it is not, for the Welsh were of one mind, having pity for the great wrong and outrage that the English had meted out to the King. Alas! What were the English thinking? God will pay them back one day, for if someone knowingly does wrong to another, [fo. 22v.] it is commonly seen that God will dole him out great punishment, for God is powerful over all who are, and have been.

§14 Lines 1029–1172. The English are harassed by the Welsh; Rutland joins Henry Lancaster. Richard sends the dukes of Exeter and Surrey from Conway to treat with Lancaster at Chester.

This is how the English were attacked by the Welsh, who showed them no mercy; they were routed and rode in groups of ten, twenty, forty or a hundred. They had to leave the treasure, for countless Welshmen emerged from the mountains, and things went very badly for them,

---

[66] Lines 1009–1011. *despoulliez*. Confirmed by *Anglo-Norman Letters and Petitions*, ed. Legge, no. 381. *En pourpoint ... / Un blanc baston en leurs mains et nuz piez*. The English deserters were robbed of their clothing and made to carry a white stick (cut from the hedgerow and peeled of its bark). See G. Di Stefano, *Dictionnaire des locutions en moyen français* (Montreal, 1991), s.v. 'baton', *le baston blanc, signe de reddition, d'humiliation*. Cf. description *supra*, ll. 213–215, of McMurrough's uncle begging for mercy.

Englez, car mil en y ot despoulliez
Qui au duc furent en pourpoint envoiez,
Un blanc baston en leurs[404] mains et nuz piez,
    Car qui n'estoit   1012
Davantaige montez, la lui failloit
Dire dont vient në ou aler vouloit,
Et son truage paier – fu tort, fu[405] droit –
    Ou estre mort.   1016
Et s'il sembloit a aucun que trop fort
Feüst a croire, non est, car d'un accort
Furent, aians pitié du tresgrant tort
    Et de l'outrage   1020
Qu'au roy firent Engloiz.[406] Las! Quel courage![407]
Dieux une foiz leur en rendra paiage,
Car qui mal fait a autruy ne dommage
    A essiant,   1024
[fo. 22v.] On voit souvent avenir que tresgrant
Pugnicïon en prent Dieux, car puissant
Est sur[408] tous ceulx[409] qui ores sont vivant
    Et ont esté.[410]   1028

§14 Lines 1029–1172. The English are harassed by the Welsh; Rutland joins Henry Lancaster. Richard sends the dukes of Exeter and Surrey from Conway to treat with Lancaster at Chester.

Vecy[411] comment[412] Engloiz furent tasté
Par les Galoiz, qui d'eulx n'orent pitié,
En chevauchant[413] comme gent[414] desrouté,
    Cy dix, cy vint,   1032
Cy quarante, cy cent. La leur convint
Laissier l'avoir,[415] car des montaignes[416] vint
De ces Galoiz sans nombre, et si advint
    Trop mal pour eulx,   1036

---

[404] D leur
[405] LC ou
[406] L quanglois firent au roy AD quau roy firent [no engloiz]
[407] AD las quel meschant courage [D meschant *superscript*]
[408] L sus
[409] C *no* ceulx
[410] L *line 1028 omitted*
[411] LC vez cy
[412] B comme
[413] H en chevauchant
LABCD ilz chevauchoient
[414] A gens
[415] H laissier lavoir
LABCD laissier leur proye
[416] C de montaigne

since out of two or three roads, they had chosen the most dangerous and the narrowest. God made them happy to go that way where there were great heaps of rocks and stones, so that they found it difficult to ride. This was told me a week later.[67]

Thus the English lost all their booty, seeing that the Welsh, who were bold, daring, strong and high-spirited men of action, followed hot on their heels; certainly to my mind this was a very good thing. I do not know where the English then retreated or made tracks to, but I tell you that [fo. 23r.] within a month I saw the Constable in duke Henry's army. The lord Percy, formerly Steward of noble King Richard, was there too, wearing the duke's badge.[68] Also I was told that they had come directly and as fast as they could to him, along with five hundred other naked men whom the Welsh had stripped to their doublets and beaten, as you have heard already, if you remember.

Now I will tell you about the King[69] who remained at Conway weeping tears of dismay. He said,

'My lords, in the name of God in Paradise, counsel me, for it is in time of need that a man often sees who his friends are.'

---

[67] Lines 1043–1044. *on le me conta / huit jours aprés*. Presumably when the messenger arrived from Milford Haven, *infra*, ll. 1261–1284.

[68] Line 1058. *l'ordre du duc*. This was likely to have been the Lancastrian collar of esses, which Richard himself had sometimes worn as a sign of affection for his uncle, John of Gaunt. See D. Fletcher, 'The Lancastrian Collar of Esses: Its origins and transformations down the centuries', in J.L. Gillespie (ed.), *The Age of Richard II* (Stroud, Gloucestershire, 1997), pp. 191–204. Also Saul, *Richard II*, p. 242.

[69] Line 1066. *Or vous diray du roy*. Chapter 14 (§14) is relatively long, comprising 36 quatrains. This seems the natural place to have started a new chapter, as the scene shifts from the army to the King at Conway.

Car des chemins[417] – ou de trois ou de deux –
Avoient pris tout le plus perilleux
Et le mains large.[418] Dieux les fist eüreux
   D'aler par la,   1040
Car de roches et de pierres y a
Grant quantité, si c'on y[419] chevaucha
A mesaise, car on le me[420] conta[421]
   Huit[422] jours aprés.   1044
Ensi perdirent tout leur pillage Anglez,
Veu que Galoiz les suïrent[423] de pres
Comme hardiz, estourdiz,* fors[424] et frez
   Et gens de fait;   1048
Certez ce fu a mon vueil trop bien[425] fait.
Je ne sçay pas ou Englez leur retrait[426]
Alors firent, në[427] ou ilz firent trait,[428]
   Maiz je vous di   1052
[fo. 23r.] Qu'avant un mois le connestable vi
En l'ost du duc c'on[429] appellë Henry.
Et si estoit li sires[430] de Persi,
   Qui estuuart[431]   1056
Avoit esté du noble roy Richart,
Portant l'ordre du duc. Et d'autre part
On me dit bien qu'au matin et au tart
   Furent venus,   1060
Tout droit a lui et des autres, tous nus
Plus de cinq cens, que Galoiz desvestus
En leurs pourpoins orent[432] et bien batus,
   Com[433] vous avez   1064
Devant oÿ, se[434] retenu l'avez.
Or vous diray du roy, qui demourez
A Cornüay estoit tous[435] esplourez
   Et esbahiz,   1068
Disant: 'Seigneurs, pour Dieu de Paradiz
'Conseillez moy selon ce[436] vostre advis,
'Car au besoing voit li homs ses amis
   'Communement.'   1072

---

[417] H chimins LABCD chemins
[418] AD et les mains larges
[419] A sy comme il B sy com il D sy com y
[420] B me le
[421] AD a grant meschief on le me raconta
[422] ACD dix
[423] AD sy les suivoyent L les suivirent
[424] B fors estourdiz
[425] ACD tresbien
[426] L attrait
[427] D no ne
[428] A furent retrait D furent trait
[429] C que len
[430] L le sire
[431] B qui estuuart avoit este
[432] B eurent
[433] AD comme
[434] C si
[435] ACD tout
[436] A cy selon D no ce

The duke of Exeter spoke first, for he was the King's brother, saying that the best thing would be to send with all speed to the duke to find out what he wants to do, or what is his wish.

'Why does he want to seize your kingdom, your person and your treasure and does he want to be [fo. 23v.] King of England and her sovereign lord, Prince of Wales and lord of Chester?'

Thus spoke the noble duke of Exeter to his brother.

'And he should be told that he was banished[70] with his father's approval, so that he should consider carefully what he is going to do. It would be a great disgrace for all time if his rightful King were overthrown by him or his actions; he would never outlive such shame all the days of his life. He should be told that all living kings, nobles and knights would hate him, and rightfully so, and that over all the world he would be called the veritable Mirror of Treason if he sought to destroy and overthrow his lord. He should follow the example of his father who all his life long was virtuous and honourable, only ever wanting to be loyal to you and abhor treachery.

---

[70] Lines 1085–1086. *par l'accort son pere / Fu hors banny.* Lancaster's banishment has already been mentioned in the archbishop's sermon, *supra*, ll. 474–475. *Son pere* = John of Gaunt.

Le duc de Excestre[437] parla premierement,
Car frere fu[438] du roy, disant: comment
Il seroit bon d'envoier promptement
    Au duc savoir 1076
Qu'il veult fere, ne[439] quel est[440] son vouloir,
'Ne a quel cause il veult prenre et avoir[441]
'Vostre royaume, vostre corps, vostre avoir,
    'Ne s'il veult estre 1080
[fo. 23v.] 'D'Engleterre[442] roy et souverain maistre,
'De Galles prince et droit sire[443] de Cestre.'
Ainsi disoit le noble duc[444] d'Excestre
    A son beau[445] frere.*
'Et c'on lui die* que par l'accort son pere
'Fu hors banny,[446] sique bien considere
'Ce[447] qu'il fera, car trop grant vitupere
    'A tousjours maiz 1088
'Seroit pour lui,[448] s'il failloit que desfaiz
'Feust son droit roy par[449] lui ne par[450] ses faiz;
'Celle honte ne recouvroit[451] jamaiz
    'Jour de sa vie. 1092
'Et comment[452] tous les roys qui sont en vie,
'Toute noblesse et chevallerie[453]
'Sur lui avroient desplaisir[454] et envie
    'Et a bon droit, 1096
'Et que par tout le monde on[455] diroit*
'De traïson le droit mirouer seroit,
'Se[456] son seigneur destruire ainsi[457] vouloit
    'Et tout[458] desfaire. 1100
'Et qu'yl prende[459] a son pere exemplaire,
'Qui son vivant fu doulz et debonnaire,
'Në oncques jour[460] ne volt penser ne faire
    'Fors loyauté 1104

---

[437] H de cexcestre LACD dexcestre B de cestre
[438] H car frere ~~frere~~ fu B *no* fu
[439] L et B *no* ne
[440] B est *superscript*
[441] H veult prenre L aussi il veult avoir B il veult orez avoir
[442] H denglenterre
[443] B sires
[444] H le noble duc L le tresbon duc ABCD le bon duc
[445] H beau LB *no* beau AD au roy son frere
[446] ACD banniz
[447] L et
[448] C *no* lui
[449] LBC pour
[450] LBC pour
[451] ABD recouverroit
[452] B come
[453] AD la chevallerie [D la *superscript*] B chevallerie [*no* et]
[454] B des plaisirs
[455] AD len
[456] C si
[457] ABD ainsy destruire
[458] H tout C puis
[459] AD preigne
[460] AD noncques nul jour

'All these things should be told him: that his family had never been accused [fo. 24r.] of any treason or violent crime – it would be a very bad thing if he disgraced his lineage by his present conduct – that God hates and despises the man who supports treachery in any form – that is our law, taught us by Holy Church – and that the duke can enter into possession of his estates again,[71] provided that he at least comes and begs mercy of you for your honour's sake. If he will not consent to come, someone who is able must give you different advice; if it pleases you, this is what he will be told. Let us consider who will go to him, for we should make haste, with no further delay, if you agree with what I have said. On the other hand if someone can offer better advice, let him give it for Our Lord God's sake, for there should be no bias amongst us; we are few in number and the duke is merciless and cruel – as you can see – and ill-disposed towards us.'

Then the King replied piteously:

'Brother you speak the truth, you have found a good solution. [fo. 24v.] As for me, I do not think we could have taken better counsel. Cousins and loyal friends, every one of you must say what he thinks,

---

[71] Line 1117. *Et que sa terre ... toute reprengne*. When John of Gaunt died, 3 February 1399, Henry being in exile, Richard extended his term of exile from ten years to life; his Lancastrian inheritance fell forfeit to the Crown. Given-Wilson, *Henry IV*, pp. 121–122.

'Encontre vous[461] et haïr[462] faulseté.
'Trestous ces faiz lui soient bien conté,
'Et c'onques[463] maiz riens ne fu reprouvé
   'A son lignage   1108
[fo. 24r.] 'Ou il eüst traïson në oultrage –
'Sique pour[464] lui seroit trop grant dommage,
'S'il fourlignoit ainsi a son parage
   'Par ceste emprise –   1112
'Et comment[465] Dieux[466] het cellui[467] et desprise
'Qui faulceté maintient en nulle guise –
'C'est[468] nostre loy, sicomme Sainte Eglise
   'Le nous ensengne –   1116
'Et que sa terre ainsi[469] toute reprengne,
'Maiz que vers vous au moins a mercy viengne[470]
'Pour vostre honneur. Et se[471] venir n'y[472] daigne,
   'Il convendra   1120
'Autre conseil adviser qui pourra;
'Se bon vous semble, ainsi on lui dira.
'Et regardons[473] qui devers lui ira,
   'Car le haster   1124
'Nous est besoing sans plus gueres tarder,
'Voire maiz que vous vueilliez accorder
'Ce que j'ay dit. Ou qui pourra[474] trouver
   'Conseil meilleur,   1128
'Si le die pour Dieu, Nostre Seigneur,
'Car entre nous ne doit avoir faveur;
'Nous sommes pou, et si est la rigueur
   'Du duc crueuse –   1132
'Comme vous veez[475]* – et pour nous perilleuse.'
Lors respondi le roy de voix piteuse:
'Vous dites voir,[476] beau frere, graciëuse
   'Voie avez quis,   1136
[fo. 24v.] 'Car quant a moy, il ne m'est pas[477] advis
'Que par nous feust nul meilleur conseil pris.
'Mes beaux cousins et mes loyaulx amis,
   'Chascun en die   1140

---

[461] L tous
[462] A hait
[463] AD oncques
[464] A par
[465] B come
[466] ACD dieu
[467] C ait cil
[468] L et
[469] AD aussy
[470] H mercy A no au moins B a ~~mercy~~ mercy viengne C a mercy en viengne
[471] C si
[472] ABD ne
[473] A or regardez
[474] H ou qui [erasure] pourra C ou quil pourra
[475] L vez
[476] AD vray
[477] B pas *superscript*

I beg you, for God's sake, as our honour and our lives are at stake. May Jesus Christ curse duke Henry who mortally hates us and does us great wrong. Now let us consider whether we are in agreement and if everyone will agree with this.'

Then they all said:

'Yes, for there is no better course of action in the world. If someone is suffering, he has to seek a cure; if he acts before the time is right, there is a danger that he will die or the suffering remain.'

Thus – as I tell you – they agreed there and then to send someone to duke Henry.

Now it came about that the duke of Exeter was chosen by them, for no better man could have been found to speak so wisely nor deal with such an important matter. The good King had his cousin – [fo. 25r] the duke of Surrey[72] – go with him. In the morning they took leave of the King, who earnestly begged them to take the shortest route and to relate to duke Henry[73] all that you have heard spoken of here, so that they can win from him submission or peace.

---

[72] Line 1165. *duc de Soudray. Supra*, l. 829, note. The English chroniclers name only Exeter. Holinshed, *Chronicles*, II, p. 856, quotes 'out of master Dee's book', i.e. **L**: 'By some writers it should seeme, not onelie the duke of Excester, but also the duke of Surrie were sent unto duke Henrie from King Richard, and that duke Henrie staied them both, and would not suffer them to returne to the King againe ... .'

[73] Line 1157. *Henri. Supra*, Introduction, p. 31.

'Son bon semblant, pour Dieu je vous en prie,[478]
'Veu qu'il touche nostre honneur et no* vie,
'Car duc[479] Henry – que[480] Jhesucrist maudie –
 'Nous het a mort,   1144
'Et si a il certes vers nous grant tort.
'Or regardons se[481] nous sommes d'accort,
'Et se[482] chascun de vous a cest accort
 'Tenir se veult.'   1148
Lors dirent tous: 'Oïl, car on ne peut
'Ou monde mieulx trouver.[483] Veu qui se deult,
'Querir lui fault remede; et s'il s'esmeut
 'Ains qu'il soit heure,   1152
'En peril est que la mort n'en enqueure,
'Ou que le blasme tout ne lui en demeure.'
Ainsi d'accort furent ilz a[484] celle heure –
 Com[485] je vous di –   1156
Pour envoier devers le duc Henri.
Or advint il que par eulx fu choisi
Le duc d'Excestre, car on eust bien failli
 La a trouver[486]   1160
Homme qui sceust si sagement parler,
Në[487] un grant fait prononcier et conter.
Avecques lui fist le bon[488] roy aler
 Son beau cousin,   1164
[fo. 25r.] Qui estoit duc[489] de Soudray. Le matin
Partirent eulx[490] du roy, le quel de fin
Cuer leur pria de abregier le[491] chemin
 Et de bien faire,   1168
Et que tresbien lui comptent tout[492] l'affaire,
Que[493] cy devant avez oÿ retraire,
Affin telle que de lui puissent[494] traire
 Accort ou paix.   1172

---

[478] B emprie
[479] AD le duc
[480] LB qui
[481] BC sy
[482] AD que C si
[483] L *no* trouver
[484] C il en
[485] AD comme
[486] B la a trouver h̶o̶m̶m̶e̶
[487] C ou
[488] A lui voult du bon
D lui voult le bon
[489] AD *no* duc
[490] AD ilz
[491] LAD leur
[492] C *no* tout
[493] AD quy
[494] B luy p̶-o̶i̶t̶ [puissent *superscript*]

Figure IX: Exeter and Surrey ride out on their embassy to Lancaster.

§15 Lines 1173–1244. Richard remains at Conway with a small retinue. Creton discourses on Fortune and her role in men's lives.

Thus they left the King, but had little opportunity to return, for duke Henry kept a tight hold of them, as you will hear [fo. 25v.] later.

Bathed in tears, the King remained at Conway, where he had with him only two or three of his closest friends;[74] they were sad, downhearted and in distress. The courtly earl of Salisbury was there and the tall and upright bishop of Carlisle, and with them was Ferriby who was not unthreatened, for the duke hated him; I do not know why, but Ferriby feared him greatly, to my mind. With them was another of their good friends, whom I heard called Sir Stephen Scrope; I often saw him with the King in those days. My companion and I were there too; we all feared greatly for our safety, as we were right to do, as you can see.[75] And I want you to know in truth that neither our number nor our strength was great,

---

[74] Line 1179. *ses amis privez*. These have all been named already in Chapter 11, ll. 825–856.

[75] Lines 1196–1199. These four lines are present only in **AD**, which do not have the miniatures. They were omitted in **HLBC** because l. 1196, *Comme on peut voir*, refers to a miniature that was not subsequently included. There are two reasons for this: the subject would have been the same as Figure VIII, and Figure IX is on the recto of this folio. Omitting l. 1196 meant leaving out the other three lines of the quatrain.

Figure IX: Exeter and Surrey ride out on their embassy to Lancaster.

§15 Lines 1173–1244. Richard remains at Conway with a small retinue. Creton discourses on Fortune and her role in men's lives.

Ainsi du roy se partirent[495] eulx, maiz
Du retourner n'orent[496] pas grant relaiz,
Car duc Henry les tint bien aux abais,
    Com[497] vous orrez   1176
[fo. 25v.] Ici aprés. Or estoit demourez
A Cornüay le roy tous[498] esplourez,
Ou il n'ot maiz de ses amis[499] privez
    Que deux ou trois   1180
Avecques lui, tristes, mas et destroiz.
Le conte y fu de Salseberi courtoiz,
Et de Guerlille l'evesque grans et droiz,
    Et si estoit[500]   1184
Avecques eulx[501] Ferbric, qui pas n'estoit
Bien asseür, car le duc le haioit;
Ne sçay pour quoy, maiz moult le[502] redoubtoit,
    Ce m'est advis.   1188
Encor y ot un[503] de leurs[504] bons amis,
Messire Estienne Scroup nommer[505] l'oÿs;
Par maintes foiz avec[506] le roy le viz
    En ce temps la.[507]   1192
Mon compaignon et moy fumes[508] droit la;
Chascun pour soy moult forment s'esmaya,
Car la raison assez s'i enclina,
    Comme on peut voir.   1196
Et si vueil bien que vous sachiez de voir
Que le nombre de nous ne le povoir
Ne fu pas grant, bien le povez[509] savoir,[510]
    Et[511] vraiement   1200

---

[495] AD departirent [D de superscript] D *no* eulx
[496] C neurent
[497] AD comme
[498] ACD tout
[499] L *no* amis B sens ses amis
[500] B sy tost estoit
[501] D ceulx
[502] B *no* le
[503] AD lun
[504] C ses
[505] AD sire steven scroup ainsy nommer
[506] B avecques
[507] B ey en ce temps la
[508] L feumes
[509] AD povoiz
[510] HLBC *lines 1196–1199 omitted; these lines are in* AD
[511] AD car

and certainly there were only sixteen of us all included, nobles and others.

Now see the distress, suffering and pain – considering his might, wealth and high standing – of King Richard, who was such a great lord. He was beset by injustice and treachery, [fo. 26r.] and by Fortune,[76] who at all times has the strength and sway to undo those whom she wants to, like a cruel and powerful ruler who is also very fickle and impetuous; for she is so merciless that she never had any wish to stop acting like this. And when she wants to work according to her nature, which is often bad for some people, one simply has to put up with it – for good or ill – as no one can resist what she wants to hand out. She makes some laugh, others sing, and then tumbles them back down into distress and anguish. Sometimes like a hypocrite she calls herself a mother, but then is cruel and malevolent; she does not consider whether a man be king or prince, it is all one to her. I reveal her to be like this, for she has allowed one of the most powerful kings in Christendom – as everyone says – to keep from among all his possessions, only a scanty measure. She sets one man up and pulls the other down; her way of working is capricious. There is nothing good in her, and thus the man

---

[76] Line 1209 *Et par Fortune*. H has a heading *Fortune* in the left margin.
ll. 1209–1244 comprise a long interjection on the mutability of Fortune, a common theme in OF to MidF literature. For Christine de Pizan's view on the role of Fortune, see C. Taylor, '"Weep thou for me in France"', pp. 213–214. For Deschamps, see G.M. Cropp and A. Hanham, 'Richard II from donkey to royal martyr: Perceptions of Eustache Deschamps and contemporary French writers', *Parergon*, 24 (2007), pp. 132–133. For Chartier, see J.M. Ferrier, 'The theme of Fortune in the writings of Alain Chartier', in F. Whitehead, A.H. Diverres, and F.E. Sutcliffe (eds), *Medieval Miscellany Presented to Eugène Vinaver* (Manchester, 1965), pp. 124–135.

Nous ne fumes que .xvi. seulement,
A compter tout, nobles et autre gent.[512]
Or regardez quel meschief, quel tourment
 Ne quel douleur,   1204
Veu la force, l'avoir[513] et la grandeur
Du roy Richart, qui fu si grant seigneur,
Lui estre ainsi demené[514]* par faveur
 Et traÿson   1208
[fo. 26r.] Et par Fortune, qui en toute saison
A la puissance et dominacïon
De desfaire ceulx qu'i lui[515] semble bon
 Comme crueuse   1212
Et maistresse puissant et orgueilleuse,
Et moult changable et moult[516] impetueuse;
Car d'arrester, tant est elle ennuieuse,
 Nul lieu n'a cure.   1216
Et quant ouvrer veult selon sa nature,
Qui est souvent pour aucunes gens dure –
Soit bien ou mal – il convient c'on l'endure,
 Car resister   1220
Ne peut nul[517] contre ce qu'elle veult donner.
Les uns fait rire, les autres fait chanter,[518]
Et puis les fait en douleurs[519] retourner
 Et en misere.   1224
Aucunesfoiz fainttement se dist mere,[520]
Maiz en[521] present est crueuse[522] et amere;
A roy n'a prince[523] en[524] riens ne considere,
 Tout lui est un.   1228
Bien la monstre, car des puissans roys l'un
Des crestïens – sicomme dit chascun* –
De tous[525] ses biens reprendre qu'un desjun[526]
 N'a elle fait.   1232
Elle fait l'un et l'autre elle desfait;
C'est un droit songe certes que de son fait.
En elle n'a nulle riens de parfait,[527]
 Et pour ce nulz,   1236

---

[512] L autrement
[513] C lavoir la force
[514] ACD demoure
[515] L de faire ceulx qui a lui B de faire ceulx qui ly AD de desfaire ceulx a qui [D a *superscript*]
[516] H moult *superscript* LABCD *no* moult
[517] ACD nulz
[518] B et les autres chanter
[519] LACD douleur
[520] B se destmere destueure
[521] A a
[522] B est ~~eu~~ crueuse
[523] B a prince
[524] LC a AD na B ne
[525] AD *no* tous
[526] B qui desum
[527] B ~~forfait~~ parfait

[fo. 26v.] who is wise and resolved to stand firm, would pay no heed to her foolish and fluctuating virtues, for we came completely naked into the world[77] – poor, wretched and quite destitute – and we will return to the earth, be we prince, king, earl or whoever.

§16 Lines 1245–1292. Richard learns of Rutland's defection and the theft of his treasure.

I do not want to talk any more about Fortune at the moment, for a wise man would only want her gifts in moderation. I want to come now to the end of the story of King Richard who, humiliated by Fortune and betrayed, was alone at Conway – as I have already said – full of sadness, grief and dismay.

He and the earl [of Salisbury] said[78] – for I know this well – that they should send to the men whom the King had left the day before yesterday[79] at the port [of Milford Haven], for them to come straight there without delay. However, by chance a messenger arrived who stopped someone going, for he told the King what the Constable[80] had done, [fo. 27r.] which did not paint him in a good light, considering that the messenger said without a lie that he appeared to be disloyal to him.

---

[77] Lines 1239–1240. *nous vinmes tous nus / En cestui monde*. Job 1:21.

[78] Lines 1255–1258. *Lui et le conte dirent … / Que d'envoier / Devers ses gens, qu'il laissa avant hier / Au port de mer, seroit tresgrant mestier*. This report of Creton's deserves credence and seems to disprove the suggestion that Richard disbanded the army himself, or ordered it to disband after his departure.

[79] Line 1257. *avant hier*. Supra, ll. 866–868, note.

[80] Lines 1263–1264. *le fait … / Du connestable*. For Rutland's desertion, supra, ll. 945–1065.

[fo. 26v.] S'il estoit sage[528] et d'endurer pourveuz,
De ses foles et muables vertus
Ne tenroit[529] compte, car nous vinmes tous nus
    En cestui[530] monde –   1240
Povres, chaitifs et de trestout[531]* bien[532] monde –
Et si convient qu'en la terre parfonde
Tous retournons, soit prince, roy[533] ou conte,
    Ou qui[534] qu'il soit.   1244

§16 Lines 1245–1292. Richard learns of Rutland's defection and the theft of his treasure.

De Fortune parler plus cy endroit[535]
Quant a present ne vueil, car qui seroit
Saiges, ses biens pas ne convoiteroit
    Fors par raison.   1248
Or vueil venir[536] a la conclusïon
Du roy Richart, qui par desrisïon
De Fortune avecques Traïson,
    A Cornüay   1252
Estoit[537] tout seul – comme devant dit ay –
Plain de tristresse et de dueil[538] et d'esmay.
Lui et le conte dirent – car bien le say –
    Que d'envoier[539]   1256
Devers ses gens, qu'il laissa avant hier
Au port de mer, seroit tresgrant mestier,
Affin telle que sans plus atargier
    Vinssent droit la.   1260
Maiz cependant d'aventure[540] arriva
Un chevaucheur qui l'aler destourna,
Car au bon roy trestout le fait compta
    Du connestable,   1264
[fo. 27r.] Qui n'estoit pas pour lui trop[541] honnorable,
Veu qu'il disoit sans mençonge ne fable
Quë il estoit[542] par semblant variable
    Par devers lui,   1268

---

[528] ABCD sages
[529] C tenoit
[530] C ce
[531] H tout LC trestout AD tout
[532] B tous biens
[533] AC retournions soit roy prince
[534] LA quel D quil

[535] H plus cy endroit C plus parler cy endroit
[536] B or vueil [venir *in left margin*]
[537] B estoit estoit *in left margin*
[538] H plain de tristresse et de dueil et desmay LABCD plain de tristresse de douleur et desmay
[539] C demourer
[540] H cependant daventure LABCD daventure cependant
[541] AD trop pour luy
[542] A nestoit

As soon as the King had left Milford Haven and the Constable had heard of this, he left there, and the Steward had no wish to stay behind.

'Rather did he have all your treasure which remained on board ship packed up, and then they [all] went away. But the Welsh, who were strong and bold, followed hot on their heels; they re-captured all your treasure and killed very many of the English. Those who escaped went straight to the duke; thus in truth it is told me, dear Sire.'

When the King had let him tell everything he had to say, you may know that he did not feel like laughing, for on all sides affliction and suffering came at him in a steady stream.

'Virgin Mary,[81] sovereign Queen, who bore Jesus without sin,' thus said the King, 'Fortune deals very severely with me.'

§17 Lines 1293–1316. Richard deplores the treachery of those who have betrayed him.

[fo. 27v.] **T**hen he said,

'Earl of Salisbury, how shall we deal with the duke and his people, who have the power to treat us so cruelly? Alas! They have failed in their duty to us if this man is telling the truth, given that we have always strived to behave well towards them all.

---

[81] Line 1289. *Vierge Marie*. Richard had a personal devotion to the Virgin Mary. See Gordon and others (eds), *Regal Image of Richard II*, pp. 123–124. Also *infra*, p. 197, l. 5 n. 137.

LA PRINSE ET MORT DU ROY RICHART D'ANGLETERRE   125

Et qu'aussi tost que le roy fu parti
De Milleforde, et qu'il en ot oÿ
Les nouvelles, de la se departi
    Pour s'en aler,   1272
Et l'estuuart ne volt pas demourer
Derriere li. 'Ains fist l'avoir trousser
'Qui encores estoit dedens la mer,
    'Et puis aprés   1276
'S'en alerent.* Maiz les Galoiz de pres
'Les suïrent,[543] qui furent fors et frez;
'Tout vostre avoir retindrent eulx et tres
    'Grant quantité   1280
'En tuerent. Maiz[544] ceulx qui eschapé
'Furent de la, tout droit s'en sont alé
'Devers le duc; ainsi m'est[545] il conté
    'Pour vray,[546] chier Sire.'   1284
Et quant le roy lui ot tout laissié dire,
Sachiez de vray qu'il n'ot[547] pas fain de rire,
Car de tous lez lui venoit[548] tire a tire
    Meschief et paine.*   1288
'Vierge Marie, roÿne souveraine,
'Qui de Jhesus enfantas pure et saine,'
Ce dist le roy: 'Fortune[549] me demaine
    Trop durement.'   1292

§17 Lines 1293–1316. Richard deplores the treachery of those who have betrayed him.

[fo. 27v.] Lors dist: 'Conte[550] de Salsebri, comment
'Chevirons nous du duc et de sa gent,
'Qui nous maine[551] si douloureusement
    'Par son povoir?   1296
'Helas! Ilz[552] n'ont pas bien fait leur devoir
'Par devers nous, se[553] cest homme dit voir,
'Veu que tousjours de force et de povoir
    'Avons bien fait   1300

---

[543] LA suivirent
[544] L et
[545] B my est
[546] H pour vray
ACD certes
[547] L na

[548] H lui venoit [erasure]
A luy venoient
[549] H fotune
[550] H dist [erasure] conte
LABCD dist au conte

[551] H nous [erasure]
maine LABCD nous
demaine
[552] C il
[553] B sy

And if their loyalty is suspect, God will see that and know how to punish the sinner's transgression; He is the true judge. For I know that when the Flood comes and He sits in judgement, evil-doers will find no protection or deliverance, rather will they reap what they have sown and will be condemned out of God's own mouth into everlasting Hell; that is our Law. Therefore we place our trust entirely in Him; it is often said that when arms speak, the laws are silent.'[82]

Then the earl said,

'By my faith, Monseigneur, you speak the truth.'

§18 Lines 1317–1388. Richard moves from Conway to Beaumaris to Caernarvon.

Then they agreed that they would remain no longer at Conway, for they were very afraid, and rightly so. [fo. 28r.] They went directly to Beaumaris,[83] which was ten miles from Conway – it is a castle that could not be taken in two years, providing always that there was enough food and also a stout garrison – one of its sides faces the fields, the other the sea; St Edward had it built, so I heard it said by the English.

The King decided not to remain long there, rather he felt that

---

[82] Line 1314. *Force n'a loy*. In the right-hand margin of **H** has been written in a contemporary hand *Inter arma silent leges*. For the source of this in Cicero's *Oratio pro Milone*, see C.T. Lewis and C. Short (eds), *Latin Dictionary* (Oxford, 1879), s.v. '*sileo*, II'. Creton quotes the proverb again, l. 2054.

[83] Lines 1321–1329. *A Beaumarey s'en alerent* ... / ... *Saint Edouart le fist* ... *fonder*. Beaumaris on Anglesey was one of ten royal castles built over twenty years from 1277 by Edward I – not the Confessor – with a view to subduing North Wales. See Colvin (ed.), *History of the King's Works*, I, p. 293. All the Welsh castles mentioned by Creton, with the exception of Holt, a lordship castle, and Chester, an earlier royal castle, were part of this castle-building programme. For a photograph of Beaumaris Castle, see Biggs, *Three Armies in Britain*, p. 162.

'A eulx trestous. Et s'ilz[554] ne sont parfait
'En loyauté, Dieux verra bien leur fait,
'Qui du pecheur scet pugnir le mesfait;
   'C'est le droit juge.   1304
'Car je sçay bien, quant le jour du deluge
'Sera venu et qu'il tendra son juge,*
'Que les mauvaiz n'aront point de reffuge
   'Ne de respit,   1308
'Ains trouveront ce qu'avront[555] fait et dit,
'Et lors seront de sa bouche maudit
'En l'infernal paine, sicomme on[556] dit;
   'C'est nostre loy.   1312
'Pour ce du tout nous atendons a soy,
'Et si dist on souvent: "Force n'a loy." '*
Lors dist le conte: 'Monseigneur, par ma foy
   'Vous[557] dites vray.'   1316

§18 Lines 1317–1388. Richard moves from Conway to Beaumaris to Caernarvon.

La furent ilz[558] d'accort qu'a Cornüay
Ne feroient[559] plus sejour[560] ne delay,
Car ilz[561] orent[562] grant peur et grant esmay
   Et a bon droit.   1320
[fo. 28r.] A Beaumarey s'en alerent tout droit,
Qui a[563] dix mille de Cornüay estoit –
C'est un chastel que prendre on ne pourroit
   Pas en deux[564] ans,   1324
Maiz qu'ilz[565] eussent vitaille pour ce temps,
Et qu'il y[566] eust aucuns bons deffendans –
L'un des costez si est assis aux champs,
   L'autre en la mer;   1328
Saint Edouart le fist faire et fonder,
Ainsi l'oÿ a[567] Engloiz recorder.
Le roy cy[568] fu qui n'y[569] volt demourer
   Pas longuement,   1332

---

[554] LACD sil B sy
[555] H quavront fait B ce quen tout fait
[556] C si com len
[557] H vou
[558] AD eulx C il
[559] C feirent
[560] B ce jour
[561] C il
[562] A eurent
[563] B qui jadix a
[564] L .x.
[565] C quil
[566] B no y
[567] H loy eust a L loy aux
[568] LACD y
[569] D ne

he and his people would be safer at Caernarvon.[84] The town and castle are very fine and well fortified; on one side there are ample woods for hunting, on the other the mighty sea. There the King stayed, his face often losing all colour as he bewailed his cruel fate and cursed the hour and the day that he ever crossed the salty sea to Ireland, repeating often,

'Gracious Virgin Mary, help me, I beg you for mercy, for never have I deserved [fo. 28v.] to be hounded thus by the duke or by my own people, who have for no reason grown to hate me and falsely betrayed me, as you can see. Alas! And when the true story is known in sweet France, certainly I hope that the heart of my father-in-law[85] will be gripped with bitter pain, for it will be a great insult to him – and to all mortal kings – on account of the outrage, torment and reduced state I am in; I am deserted by those who have always been with me. Now they have turned against me, I know not why. Alas! Such bad faith will be held against them for all time, for as long

---

[84] Line 1334. *Karnarvan*. For Caernarvon Castle, see ibid. I, pp. 369–395, especially p. 370. The detail points to Creton having accompanied Richard. Photographs of Caernarvon, Conway, Rhuddlan, and Flint Castles may be seen in G. Dodd, 'The road to Richard II's downfall', in G. Dodd (ed.), *The Reign of Richard II* (Stroud, Gloucestershire, 2000), pp. 111–114.

[85] Line 1356. Richard had married Isabella, the daughter of Charles VI of France in 1396. See Palmer, *England, France and Christendom*, pp. 168–175; also *ODNB*, s.v. 'Isabella [Isabella of France] (1389–1409)'.

Ains lui sembla que plus seürement
A Karnarvan seroit lui et sa gent –
Ville et chastel y a tresbel et gent
    Et forte place – 1336
A l'un des lez[570] foison[571] bois pour la chace,
Et d'autre part la haulte mer y passe.
La fu le roy qui ot souvent la face
    Descoulouree, 1340
En regretant sa dure destinee,
Et[572] maudissant et l'eure et la journee
C'oncques avoit passé la mer sallee
    En Ybernie, 1344
Disant souvent: 'Doulce[573] Vierge Marie,
'Secourez moy, Dame, mercy vous crie
'Si vraiement, c'oncques jour de ma vie
    'Ne deservy 1348
[fo. 28v.] 'Envers le duc de me[574] chacier ainsi
'Në a mes gens, les quelx m'ont enhaÿ
'Sans desserte et faulcement traÿ,
    'Comme on peut voir; 1352
'Chascun le scet et peut apercevoir.
'Elas! Et quant on[575] en sara le voir
'En doulce France, certainement j'espoir*
    'Que mon beau pere 1356
'Si en avra au cuer douleur amere,
'Car ce[576] sera pour lui grant vitupere –
'Voire et pour[577] tous les roiz[578] qui nez de mere
    'Sont au jour d'uy – 1360
'Veu l'oultrage et le tresgrant ennuy,[579]
'La povreté et le point ou je suy;
'Et que par ceulx[580] ainsi je me deffuy
    'Qui ont esté 1364
'Tousjours[581] a moy. Or sont ilz[582] retourné;
'Ne say pour quoy. Helas! Quel faulseté
'A tousjours maiz leur sera reprouvé,
    'Tant que le monde 1368

---

[570] AD leez
[571] C force
[572] H et *superscript* LBC *no* et A en
[573] AD glorieuse
[574] B moy
[575] C len
[576] A et sy D ce ce
[577] C par
[578] H le [s *superscript*] roiz A le roys
[579] B ennuy envy
[580] A eulx
[581] B tous les jours
[582] D il

as the world remains and the waters continue to roll; these past events count against them grievously.

'God in the Highest, who died on the Cross for us, may the beams of Thy radiant eyes shine upon me, for none other than Thou canst [fo. 29r.] help me at this pass. And if I have to lose my country or my life, I will have to take it in good part if that is the will of Dame Fortune, for everything must happen as she commands.'

Thus did King Richard repeat these words, sighing piteously, so that I shed tears more than a hundred times; there is no beating heart so hard nor so obdurate that would not have wept, considering the attacks made upon him.

§19 Lines 1389–1436. Richard returns from Caernarvon to Conway; his regrets for Queen Isabella.

Yet there was worse to come, for there were no provisions in his castles to which he had withdrawn and only straw for a bed. He slept there four or six nights, really you would not have found a halfpennyworth of food or anything else there. Certainly I dare not recount the King's great distress; he did not remain long at Caernarvon, for he had little rest there, in the light of

'Sera durant, et que la mer parfonde
'Pourra getter[583] ne[584] maree[585] në onde;
'Car ce fait cy a trop grant mal redonde
   'Pour eulx trestous.   1372
'Glorïeux Dieux, qui morustes pour nous
'Pendant en croix, de voz yeulx beaulx et doulx
'Vueilliez me[586] voir, car nul autre que vous
   'Si ne me peut   1376
[fo. 29r.] 'A ce besoing aidier. Et si m'estuet[587]
'Perdre ma terre ou[588] ma vie, il estuet
'Tout prendre en gré se[589] Fortune le veult,
   'Car autrement   1380
'Ne peut estre qu'a son commandement.'
Ainsi disoit le roy Richart souvent
En souppirant du[590] cuer piteusement,
   Tant que par m'ame*   1384
Plus de cent foiz en gettay mainte larme;
N'il[591] n'est vivant[592] si dur cuer ne si ferme
Qui n'en eüst plouré, veu le diffame
   C'on[593] lui faisoit.   1388

§19 Lines 1389–1436. Richard returns from Caernarvon to Conway; his regrets for Queen Isabella.

Encore[594]* y a trop pis, car il n'avoit
En ses[595] chasteaulx, la ou retrait s'estoit,[596]
Garnison nulle, ne couchier ne savoit
   Fors qu'en[597] la paille.   1392
Quatre ou six nuis y coucha il sans faille,
Car vrayement qui vaulsist une maille
Ne eüst[598] on pas la trouvé[599] de vitaille
   Ne d'autre chose.   1396
Le grant meschief[600] certes dire je n'ose
Que le roy ot, qui ne fu[601] pas[602] grant pose
A Karnavan, car[603] petit y repose,
   Consideré   1400

---

[583] A sus getter
[584] AD *no* ne
[585] L riviere
[586] L moy
[587] C me sieut
[588] AD et ou
[589] C si
[590] L de
[591] A il [*no* ne]

[592] H vivant LABCD ou monde
[593] C com
[594] HBC encores L encor AD encore
[595] B ces
[596] B ou il retrait estoit C ou il se retraoit
[597] L en A que

[598] ABD neust
[599] AD pas trouve la B la pas trouve C ~~trompe~~ on trouve la pas
[600] H le grant meschief LABCD la grant misere
[601] LC fit
[602] B *no* pas
[603] A *no* car

his suffering and penury.

He returned to Conway. He missed his wife greatly, saying,

'My beloved [fo. 29v.] wife,[86] may Jesus Christ curse the man who has separated us so shamefully; he has no love for us. I expire with grief, my fair sister, my bride and my heart's desire, when I cannot feast my eyes on you. There is such pain and grief in my heart that I am often near to despair. Alas! Isabella, virtuous daughter of France, you were wont to be my joy, my hope and my comfort.

'Now I can see that through the work of Fortune, who has killed many a man, I must part from you to our great disadvantage. Thus my heart grieves with such intense pain that I am in danger of expiring at any moment – and this is not surprising considering that I have fallen so low from so great a height – and of losing my joy, my comfort and my wife. I can see that no one hesitates to wound or betray me. Alas! Everyone attacks or abuses me. God, [fo. 30r.] who is in His Heaven above, be praised.'

Thus said the King, weeping piteously, for he could do no more at that time.

---

[86] Lines 1404–1416. *M'amie* ... / ... *Et mon confort*. Queen Isabella is a little girl of not quite ten years. On her marriage to Richard in 1396, her trousseau included not only the costly jewels and plate appropriate for a queen, but also *les pouppees de ladicte dame*, the child-bride's dolls. See Stratford (ed.), *Richard II and the English Royal Treasure*, p. 396, J 27. Creton has the King address her thus again, *infra* ll. 2233–2234.

Le mal qu'il ot et la grant povreté.
A Cornüay s'en est il[604] retourné,
Ou[605] il a moult sa femme regreté,
  Disant: 'M'amie 1404
[fo. 29v.] 'Et ma compaigne, Jhesucrist le maudie
'Qui de nous deux fait telle departie
'Et si honteuse; il ne nous aime mie.
  'J'en muir[606] de dueil,[607] 1408
'Ma belle suer, ma dame et tout[608] mon vueil,[609]
'Quant voir ne puis vostre plaisant accueil.
'Dedens mon cuer tant de douleur recueil
  'Et de grevance 1412
'Que souvent sui pres de desesperance.[610]
'Las! Ysabel, droite fille de France,
'Vous souliez estre ma joie et[611] m'esperance
  'Et mon confort. 1416
'Or voy je bien que par le grant effort
'De Fortune, qui a maint homme mort,
'M'estuet de vous eslongier[612] a grant tort,
  'Par quoy j'endure 1420
'Au cuer souvent une douleur si dure,
'Que jour et nuit je sui en aventure
'De recevoir la mort amere et sure –
  'Et ce n'est pas 1424
'De merveilles, consideré le cas
'De moy, qui sui cheut de si hault si bas –
'Et de perdre ma joie et mon soulas
  'Et ma compaigne. 1428
'Et si voy bien qu'il[613] n'est nul qui se faigne
'De me[614] faire desplaisir et engaigne.
'Elas! Chascun me mort ou[615] me dehaigne.
  'Or en soit Dieux 1432
[fo. 30r.] 'Loé, qui est la sus en ses sains[616] cieulx.'
Ainsi disoit[617] le roy plourant des yeulx
Piteusement, car il ne povoit mieulx
  En ce temps la. 1436

---

[604] B il *superscript*
[605] C la ou
[606] C meurs
[607] B de ~~deul~~ dueil
[608] H tout *superscript* B *no* tout
[609] L *line 1409 omitted*
[610] L desperance B ~~desp~~ desesperance
[611] AD *no* et
[612] AD aloingnier
[613] H bien quil
[614] LB moy
[615] C et
[616] C haulz
[617] B disant

§20 Lines 1437–1512. Exeter delivers Richard's message to Lancaster at Chester.

Now I shall tell you how the duke dealt with the King's brother, who went to him along with the duke of Surrey, who loved King Richard steadfastly, so much so that he endured great suffering and met an ignoble death hereafter,[87] as you will soon hear, if God spares me.

The two dukes rode all day long until they came to Chester, which the duke [of Lancaster] had captured without fighting, through his skill and judgement; they both entered. They were accompanied by very many people, who thought that they were unwilling to serve the King, and had come to beg mercy of Henry, duke of Lancaster; but it was great folly to think so, for they would not have abandoned the King for all the gold in England.

They were led swiftly to duke Henry, directly to the castle (which was skilfully built); he had great joy and gladness in his heart when he saw them. [fo. 30v.] He pretended[88] to give them a very warm welcome, and then said to the duke of Exeter:

'Now, brother-in-law,[89] without demur, I beg you, give me your news.'

'Brother-in-law, the news is not good for Monseigneur; it is bad and uncertain, which makes me anguished and despondent.'

---

[87] Lines 1441–1442. *laidement / En reçut mort depuis.* Surrey's death is reported *infra*, ll. 3185–3192.

[88] Line 1461. *par semblance.* Hypocrisy is one of the charges Creton lays against Henry Lancaster. See also *infra*, l. 3256.

[89] Line 1463. Exeter was Lancaster's brother-in-law, *supra*, l. 827, note.

§20 Lines 1437–1512. Exeter delivers Richard's message to Lancaster at Chester.

Or vous diray[618] comment[619] le duc ouvra
Du frere au roy, qui devers lui ala
Avec le duc de Soudray, qui ama
    Tresloyaument   1440
Le roy Richart, et tant que laidement
En reçut mort depuis a grant tourment,
Com[620] vous orrez assez prouchainement,
    Se Dieux me gart.   1444
Tant chevaucherent les deux ducs main et tart
Qu'a Cestre vindrent, que le duc de sa part
Avoit prise[621] sans assault, par[622] son art
    Et par son sens;   1448
Ilz entrerent entrë eulx deux dedens.[623]
Avecques eulx y ot grant foison gens,[624]
Cuidant[625] qu'ilz feussent de servir le roy lens,
    Et qu'a Henry,   1452
Duc de Lancastre, vinssent[626] crier mercy;
Maiz grant follie[627] les[628] fist penser ainsi,
Car pour tout l'or d'Engleterre guerpi
    Ne l'eussent pas.   1456
Au duc Henry furent menez le pas,
Droit ou[629] chastel (qui fu fait a[630] compas;)
Au cuer en ot grant joie et grant soulas,
    Quant il les vit.   1460
[fo. 30v.] Tresbonne chiere par semblance leur fist[631]
Et puis aprés au duc d'Excestre[632]* dit:
'Or ça, beau frere, sans plus de contredit,
    'De voz nouvelles,   1464
'Je vous suppli, que vous me diez[633] quelles
'Ilz[634] sont.' 'Beau frere, y[635] ne sont pas* trop belles
'Pour Monseigneur; ains sont laidez[636] et felles,
    'Dont moult doulant   1468

---

[618] H diray LBC vueil dire
[619] B come
[620] AD comme
[621] L avoit ja prise
[622] AD de
[623] B ilz entre [rent superscript] eulx deux dedens [erent in left margin. Beginning of word lost in binding]
[624] AB de gens
[625] LB cuidans
[626] LABD venissent
[627] D no follie, cross in left margin
[628] A le
[629] CD au
[630] A par C au
[631] B chiere leur fist par semblance leur fist
[632] H duc de [x superscript] cestre LABCD duc dexcestre
[633] A dictes
[634] AD y
[635] LA ilz
[636] H laide [z added later]

Figure X: Exeter and Surrey make obeisance to Lancaster at Chester.

Then he told him most seriously all that you have heard already when they left the King: [fo. 31r.] that it will be a very great wrong if he betrays his loyalty to his lord in this manner, and that he was banished at the request and with the consent of his own father – he should think carefully about all these things – and how all mortal kings will be shamed and insulted by his behaviour, and that he will be hated by his friends; that all who love honour, loyalty, virtue and worthy deeds will be his enemies. He will bring great shame on his lineage for all time to come if he commits such an outrage, considering that he ought to be a wise and moderate lord: but if it happens that his rightful King is disinherited – either by his resignation or by use of force – he will be compared to Ganelon,[90] who in his day committed many acts of treason, which led to the deaths of many good knights; he should therefore for God's sake beware of this comparison. He will get back his estates and his wealth, provided that he henceforth does his duty, and the King will gladly pardon

---

[90] Line 1492. *Guenelon*. Ganelon was the traitor of the *Chanson de Roland*, who betrayed Charlemagne's army to the Saracens, leading to the death of Roland and his companions.

Figure X: Exeter and Surrey make obeisance to Lancaster at Chester.

'Sui et marry.' Et lors lui va comptant*
Tressagement tout ce qu'icy[637] devant
Avez oÿ, quant ilz furent partant
    D'avec[638] le roy: 1472
[fo. 31r.] Et que[639] pour lui sera trop grant desroy,
S'a son seigneur ainsi faulse sa foy,
Et[640]* que banniz par le vueil et ottroy[641]
    De son bon[642] pere   1476
Fu – sique bien tout ce[643] fait considere –
Et comment[644] a tous les roiz nez de mere
Fera grant honte et tresgrant[645]* vitupere,
    Et que haïz   1480
Sera de ceulx qui sont ses bons amis;
Et que tous ceulx seront ses ennemis
Qui aymeront honneur, loyauté, pris[646]
    Et vasselaige.   1484
Et qu'il fera grant honte a son lignage
A tousjours maiz, s'il fait un tel oultrage,
Veu qu'il doit estre un grant seigneur et saige
    Et attrempé: 1488
Maiz s'ainsi est que de sa voulenté
Ou de force, par lui[647] desherité
Soit son droit roy, il sera[648] comparé
    A Guenelon,   1492
Qui a[649] son temps fist mainte traïson,
Par quoy moururent maint chevalier et bon;
Sique pour Dieu ceste[650] comparaison[651]
    Ne vueille avoir.   1496
Et qu'il avra[652] sa terre et son avoir,
Maiz qu'il face desoremaiz son devoir,
Et que le roy de bon cuer et vouloir
    Lui pardonra   1500

---

[637] C tout que cy
[638] B avec
[639] AD sique
[640] H et
[641] L lottroy
[642] A no bon
[643] C le
[644] B comme

[645] H tresgrant L moult grant ABD grant C tresgrant
[646] A honneur et loyaulte et pris B loyaulte honneur pris D honneur loyaulte et pris
[647] C par force de luy

[648] D se sera
[649] ABD en
[650] AD telle
[651] B comparacion
[652] A qui ara

[fo. 31v.] all the wrongs that he has done him.

Thus did the duke of Exeter tell him what he had to say and dared to talk quite boldly to him, for he had married Lancaster's sister and thus was of his family. The noble duke of Exeter added:

'I beg you, brother-in-law, grant us your swift response, wholly or in part, for Monseigneur awaits us, and he is not in a good situation.'

§21 Lines 1513–1544. Lancaster refuses to let Exeter and Surrey return to Richard.

Then said duke Henry:

'You have explained everything to me very well, but you will not go back today, nor yet in a week's time, if Christ grants me health and joy. It would not be sensible for me to send you straight back, you are not paid messengers,[91] and Monseigneur was not wise in sending you here. Could he not find other messengers apart from the two of you? It is not very clever to send here men of such eminent rank.'

Thus did the duke stand in their way, but his brother-in-law kept urging him to grant them leave to go, [fo. 32r.] saying,

'Sire, the King may think that it is treason that keeps us here; we will never in our lives be able to survive such shame.

---

[91] Lines 1517–1524. Creton was not present to witness the dukes' reception by Lancaster. These words attributed to him might well reflect the poet's own opinion.

[fo. 31v.] Trestout l'outraige et ce que fait lui a.*
Ainsi le duc d'Excestre[653] lui compta
Tresbien et bel son fait, et si osa
    Bien hardiment[654]   1504
Parler a lui, car sa suer proprement[655]
Ot espousee et si fu son parent.
Encor lui dist le duc d'Excestre gent:
    'Je vous supplie,   1508
'Mon beau[656] frere, que promptement baillie
'Nous soit response du tout ou en partie,
'Car Monseigneur nous attent, qui n'est mie
    'En tresbon point.'[657]   1512

§21 Lines 1513–1544. Lancaster refuses to let Exeter and Surrey return to Richard.

Lors dist le duc Henry: 'Moult[658] bien a point
'Le m'avez dit, maiz meshuy[659] n'irez point
'Ne de sepmaine, se Jhesucrist me doint*
    'Santé et joie.   1516
'Raison n'est pas[660] que si tost vous renvoie.[661]
'Vous n'estes pas messagiers pour monnoie,
'Et Monseigneur, qui icy vous[662] envoie,
    'N'est pas bien saige.   1520
'Ne povoit il trouver autre messaige
'Que de vous deux? C'est petit vasselage
'De gens qui sont de si treshault parage
    'Cy envoier.'   1524
Ainsi les volt[663] le duc contralier,
Maiz son beau frere ne cessoit de prier
Qu'il leur voulsist le congié ottroyer
    Pour en aler,   1528
[fo. 32r.] Disant: 'Sire, le roy pourra penser
'Que traïson nous fait cy demourer;
'Celle[664] honte ne[665] pourrons recouvrer
    'Jamaiz nul jour.   1532

---

[653] H duc de [x added later] cestre
[654] H hardement L hardiment ABCD hardiement
[655] B ~~promptement~~ proprement
[656] C bon
[657] C no point
[658] AD trop
[659] B huy
[660] H pas LBC mie
[661] AC envoye
[662] H qu [i added later] cy vous B qui vous cy
[663] C veult
[664] A telle
[665] C nous

Therefore, in God's name, we beg you with true love, brother-in-law, let us go, for honour's sake, lest disgrace attach itself to us.'

Then said the duke (who was as bold as a lion):

'Do not speak any more of this, brother-in-law; when the time is right we will send you back to the King. And keep away from me, for I swear to you by my faith that however much you bother me, you will not escape from me within a month.'

§22 Lines 1545–1764. The castle of Holt is surrendered to Lancaster. The Archbishop of Canterbury suggests a ruse to capture Richard and the earl of Northumberland is sent to Conway to carry it out; the castles of Flint and Rhuddlan surrender to him. Richard suspects that Exeter has met with trouble.

Thus did the two dukes remain with sorrow in their hearts, considering that duke Henry was angry with them at that time. They wanted to be with the King, who remains alone with no one to help him. Thus they both often weep, but they just had to put up with everything, heartache and joy. Duke Henry made them separate: he made his brother-in-law – the duke of Exeter – stay with him, [fo. 32v.] and he had the good duke of Surrey imprisoned in Chester Castle (where there are many fine windows and many high walls.

'Sique pour Dieu, beau frere, et[666] pour honnour,
'Afin tele que n'ayons deshonnour,
'Laissiez nous ent aler, par[667] vraie amour
    'Vous en prions.'   1536
Lors dist le duc (qui fu fiers com[668] lions):
'N'en parlez[669] plus, beau frere; quant saisons
'Il en sera, bien vous renvoierons[670]
    'Devers le roy.   1540
'Et ne vous veez* plus ycy[671] devant moy,
'Car je vous jure[672] et promet par ma foy
'Que de[673] cest[674] mois premier pour[675] quelque ennoy[676]
    'Ne m'eschaprez.'[677]   1544

§22 Lines 1545–1764. The castle of Holt is surrendered to Lancaster. The Archbishop of Canterbury suggests a ruse to capture Richard and the earl of Northumberland is sent to Conway to carry it out; the castles of Flint and Rhuddlan surrender to him. Richard suspects that Exeter has met with trouble.

Ainsi furent les deux ducs demourez,
Qui au cuer orent[678] du desplaisir assez,
Considerant[679] que le duc fu yrez
    A eulx pour l'eure,   1548
Et[680] regretant le roy qui seul demeure
Sans ame avoir qui l'aidë[681] ou[682] sequeure.
Ainsi chascun des deux ducs souvent pleure,
    Maiz tout souffrir   1552
Leur convenoit plaisir et[683] desplaisir.
Le duc Henry les fist en deux partir:
Avec[684] lui fist son beau frere tenir,
    Le duc d'Excestre,   1556
[fo. 32v.] Et le bon duc de Souldray fist il[685] mettre
Et enfermer ens ou chastel de Cestre[686]
(Ou il y a mainte belle[687] fenestre
    Et maint hault mur.   1560

[666] L no et
[667] C pour
[668] AD comme
[669] H parelez
[670] L vous en remenrons B vous envoierons
[671] L vez plus ycy B veez ey plus ycy C voiez plus yci
[672] A no jure
[673] C no de
[674] AD ce
[675] C par
[676] L esmoy
[677] L neschapperez D ne meschappez
[678] C eurent
[679] LACD considerans
[680] AD en
[681] AD luy aide
[682] L et
[683] AD ou
[684] B avecques
[685] A il fist
[686] AD dexcestre
[687] AD bonne

It reminded me of the castle of Namur[92] when I saw it, it is so high and forbidding); the duke did not feel very safe there, and rightly so.

Six miles from the town there was another castle called Holt,[93] perched high on a rock. The duke of Lancaster approached it at the head of his army. The people inside were so afraid that they did not know what to do, even although they knew for sure that the duke could not lay a finger on them, for the castle is so strong and solid that I do not think it could have been taken by force in ten years, considering the rock on which it was sited and that there was a very stout garrison of good men. There were a hundred choice men-of-arms installed within by King Richard, but they failed [fo. 33r.] to guard the narrow entrance passage where one had to ascend carefully, step by step. Wretched and afraid, they surrendered it to the duke, who was very happy to enter, for there were more than one hundred thousand marks sterling in gold which King Richard had amassed in that place. There was also a great store of other precious things: by St Mor, I heard it said

---

[92] Line 1561. It was only in 1421 that Namur became part of the duchy of Burgundy, when Philip the Good – grandson of Philip the Bold – purchased the county. See Vaughan, *Valois Burgundy*, p. 18. Creton probably chose Namur – which has no bearing on his account – simply for the rhyme.

[93] Line 1566. *Hoult*. Holt, ten miles upstream of Chester on the Dee, and belonging to the earls of Arundel, fell forfeit to the Crown on the execution of the fourth earl in 1397. See Colvin (ed.), *History of the King's Works*, I, pp. 334–345. Richard housed there the treasury of his new principality of Chester. See R.R. Davies, 'Richard II and the principality of Chester', in F.R.H. du Boulay and C.M. Barron (eds), *The Reign of Richard II: Essays in Honour of May McKisack* (London, 1971), pp. 270–272. Also *infra*, l. 1633, note.

Il me souvint[688] du chastel de Namur,
Quant je le vi, tant est il hault et dur;)
La ne fu pas le bon duc trop asseur,
    Et a bon droit.   1564
A .vi. mile de la ville y avoit
Un autre fort, que Hoult[689] on appelloit,
Sur[690] une roche moult hault assis estoit.
    En cependent[691]*   1568
Ala le duc a tout son ost devant.
Ceulx de[692] dedens orent pour si tresgrant[693]
Qu'il[694] ne sorent[695] que faire, non obstant
    Que pour certain   1572
Savoient bien que le duc un seul grain
Ne les povoit grever ne soir ne main,
Car le chastel est si fort et si sain
    Qu'a mon advis   1576
On ne l'eust pas par force en dix ans prins*
Veu la montaigne ou il estoit assis,
Et si estoit tresgrandement garnis
    De bonnes gens.   1580
Cent hommes d'armes y[696] avoit il dedens,
Voire d'eslite et garnis de grant[697] sens
De par le roy Richart, maiz diligens
    Ne furent pas   1584
[fo. 33r.] De bien garder l'entree ne[698] le pas,
Qui est estroite, et si faut pas pour pas
Aler a pié amont.[699] Maiz comme las
    Et pouereux   1588
Le rendirent au duc, qui fu soigneux
D'entrer dedens plus c'onques maiz joyeux,
Car il y ot cent mile mars[700] et mieulx
    D'esterlins d'or,   1592
Que le bon roy Richart la en tresor
Faisoit garder. Et si avoit encor
D'autres joyaulx grant foison: par Saint Mor
    J'oÿ conter   1596

---

[688] LBC souvient
[689] B que h [ou *written over other letters*] lt [hoult *also at line end*]
[690] L sus
[691] ACD et ce pendant
[692] LBD *no* de
[693] LA paour si grant B pour sy [tres *superscript*] grant
[694] LAB quilz
[695] A noserent B ne sceurent D ne sorerent
[696] B *no* y
[697] ACD grans
[698] H <u>ne</u>
[699] AD amont a pie
[700] H mar [s *added later*]

that the total there was worth an estimated two hundred thousand marks in gold; duke Henry had it all taken away with him.

Thus was Holt surrendered – as I tell you – and all King Richard's treasure stolen, and yet there were artillery pieces defending it, and provisions – bread, wine, sweet water and cattle – enough for six years. Such people were not worth a straw, for without joining battle or putting up a defence they immediately gave it up to duke Henry; please God that he would have had them all hanged.

He did not want to linger there, but rather returned [fo. 33v.] directly to Chester, where he summoned all the members of his Council and asked each man to say what seemed to be the best way to proceed.

The Archbishop of Canterbury replied before anyone else and said:

'My lords, King Richard has retreated to Wales, where there are many perilous mountains, which waggons and baggage cannot traverse. On the other side is the sea (where many sardines[94] can be caught); you cannot get your army near him. You should send someone to him to swear and promise that you want lasting peace between you, provided that he pledges to call a Parliament where the

---

[94] Lines 1623–1624. *ou maintez ales / Peut on peschier*. It is unlikely that sardines were caught off the coast of North Wales. Creton needed a rhyme ending in *-ales*.

Qu'a deux cens mille mars d'or estimer[701]
Povoit on bien, ce[702] qu'on pot la trouver;
Le duc Henry en[703] fist tout enmener[704]
    Avecques lui.   1600
Ainsi fu Hoult rendus[705] – com[706] je vous di –
Et tout l'avoir du roy Richart saisi,
Si estoit il d'artillerie* garny
    Et de vitaille: 1604
De pain, de vin, d'eaue doulce et d'aumaille,[707]
Bien pour six ans. Telz[708] gens pas une paille[709]
Ne valent mie,[710] car sans faire bataille
    Në eulx deffendre   1608
Au duc Henry tantost le[711] voldrent rendre;
Pleust ore[712] a Dieu qu'il les eust tous faiz[713] pendre.
La ne volt il pas longuement atendre,[714]
    Ains retourna   1612
[fo. 33v.] Tout droit a Cestre, ou trestous ceulx manda[715]
De son conseil,[716] et lors il[717] leur pria
Que chascun die ce qu'il lui semblera
    Bon estre fait.   1616
L'archevesque[718] de Cantorbie a fait
Par devant tous la response, et[719] de fait
Dist: 'Beaux Seigneurs, le roy Richart retrait[720]
    'Si est[721] en Gales,   1620
'Ou il y a maintes montaignes males,
'Par ou ne peut passer charroy ne males.
'D'autre part est la mer (ou[722] maintez ales
    'Peut on peschier;)   1624
'De lui vostre ost ne pourrez[723] aprouchier.
'Maiz il convient devers lui envoier
'Et li jurer et enconvenancier
    'Que bonne paix   1628
'Voulez avoir a[724] lui a tousjours maiz,
'Maiz qu'il vueille jurer que par lui faiz
'Un Parlement sera, ou les mauvaiz
    'Seront pugnis –   1632

[701] L a estimer
[702] B lor
[703] B le
[704] LB amener
[705] L rendu
[706] A comme
[707] C doulce et aimable
[708] AD telles
[709] LAD maille
[710] AD pas
[711] B trestout [le superscript]
[712] ACD ores
[713] ABCD fait
[714] B longuement ainz retourna actendre
[715] B demanda
[716] H consil
[717] AD moult
[718] AD lors larchevesque
[719] AD no et
[720] B le [mark of omission] richart retrait [roy at line end]
[721] L si sest
[722] A en
[723] LB pourroit
[724] B o

malefactors – those who had his uncles[95] put to death – will be punished; thus you will be henceforth good friends and you will humbly beg mercy of him. And he should set a suitable date in some place where everyone – clerk or lay, knight, priest or nun – can see him. [fo. 34r.] Otherwise you will not be able to capture him, since whatever we do he can set sail at any time to escape, for I have heard it said that he has had shipping impressed at Conway. Thus my advice is that you need to reflect on this; now say what you think, Messeigneurs and friends.'

Then everyone said:

'By God in Paradise, I never heard better advice than his.'

Then duke Henry said:

'The old earl of Northumberland[96] – my cousin – will be a good mediator and accomplish this. I command him to set out very early tomorrow[97] morning and not to return for whatever reason until he brings the King, by fair means or foul. He should have with him 400 lancers and one thousand archers, who will do their job well, for more than anything else I wish to capture him.'

Then he said to the earl:

'Cousin, have a care to depart and accomplish your task, for you can give me no greater pleasure

---

[95] Line 1633. *ses oncles*. Thomas of Woodstock, duke of Gloucester, and Richard Fitzalan, earl of Arundel, of whom only Gloucester was Richard's uncle. Creton is more exact at ll. 1875–1876. For Gloucester, see *ODNB*, s.v. 'Thomas [Thomas of Woodstock], duke of Gloucester (1355–1397)'; for Arundel, *ODNB*, s.v. 'Fitzalan, Richard, fourth earl of Arundel, and ninth earl of Surrey (1346–1397)'. Creton is referring to the arrest of the two peers on charges of treason in 1397, Gloucester dying while imprisoned in Calais, and Arundel being executed after a summary trial. See Saul, *Richard II*, pp. 377–379. Their sons are mentioned *infra*, p. 203, ll. 13–16.

[96] Line 1655. *Northomberlant*. See *ODNB*, s.v. 'Percy, Henry, first earl of Northumberland (1341–1408)'. Northumberland was 57 years old – *ancien* – at this time. The Figures XI, XII and XIII show him as a jaunty figure with white hair and beard. Although Creton was not in Lancaster's camp when Northumberland alone was sent to parley with Richard, he was with Richard at Conway when the earl arrived. Creton contradicts the official *Record and Process*, which states that Archbishop Arundel went with Northumberland. The archbishop was known to be hostile to Richard, *supra*, l. 471, note, and thus was a most unlikely messenger for Lancaster to have sent to protest his good intentions. See Sherborne, *War, Politics and Culture*, pp. 142–143; also Introduction, *supra*, p. 23.

[97] Line 1657. *demain* = 'tomorrow'. Usk, an eye-witness, dates this 14 August. See Usk, *Chronicle*, ed. Given-Wilson, p. 58.

'Par qui ses oncles furent a la mort mis –
'Ainsi serez desoremaiz bons amis,
'Et lui crirez[725] treshumblement mercis.[726]
   'Et qu'il ordonne   1636
'Telle journee qui lui semblera bonne
'Et en tel lieu, que chascune personne,
'Soit clerc ou lay, chevalier, prestre[727] ou monne,[728]*
   'Le[729] puisse voir.   1640
[fo. 34r.] 'Car autrement ne le[730] povez avoir,
'Veu qu'il a[731] bien maugré nous[732] le povoir
'D'entrer en mer au matin et au soir[733]
   'Pour s'en aler,   1644
'Car il a fait du[734] navire arrester
'A Cornüay – je l'ay ouÿ compter –
'Siqu'il vous fault sur ce fait aviser,
   'Ce m'est advis;   1648
'Or en ditez,[735] Messeigneurs et amis.'
Lors[736] dit chascun: 'Oncques[737] maiz je n'oÿs
'Meilleur conseil par Dieu de Paradis
   'Comme le sien.'[738]   1652
Le duc Henry dist lors: 'Tresbel et bien
'Fera le fait et sera bon moyen
'Northomberlant, le conté ancïien,
   'Mon beau cousin.   1656
'Je lo qu'il parte demain au plus matin
'Sans retourner[739] jamaiz a quelque fin,
'Jusques a tant que[740] par paix ou hutin[741]
   'Le roy amaine.   1660
'Et qu'avec[742]* lui .iiii.^c lances maine[743]
'Et mil archiers qui prenront[744] asez paine,
'Car je[745] desir plus que chose mondaine
   'A le tenir.'   1664
Lors dist au conte: 'Beau cousin, de partir
'Soiez songneux et de bien acomplir
'Vostre emprise, car nul plus grant plaisir
   'Ne me povez   1668

---

[725] C cries
[726] HLB *line 1635 omitted*
[727] AD prestre chevalier
[728] LABD moine
[729] L la
[730] L les
[731] B a *superscript*
[732] B vous
[733] C le matin et le soir
[734] A le D de
[735] D dees
[736] C or
[737] H oncques C quonques
[738] B comme les le sien
[739] A arrester D no retourner
[740] B no que
[741] B ou par hutin
[742] HB et avecques L et aveuc AD et quavec C et que avecques
[743] A deux cens lances il maine D deux cens lances maine
[744] AD pourront
[745] A jay

[fo. 34v.] in the world. In the name of God, make haste, and I shall stay at Chester until you return or I hear news of you that makes my heart swell with joy.'

'God grant that my news may be such,' said the earl. 'By sound judgement or trick, I shall bring him.'

Thus the earl left without delay. He took the most direct route to Conway, worrying how he can capture the King. He and his men rode hard until they arrived at a very strong castle called Flint.[98] He demanded that those within surrender it to him in the name of duke Henry, or they will all be killed without clemency or pardon. Fearing for their lives, they opened the gate to him; he had King Richard's people ejected and set a large portion of his own men to guard it. It was in this castle called Flint that the King was captured, as you will hear tell later.

Now Northumberland had his men make haste, and went directly from there to Rhuddlan,[99] where he found the going rough and difficult, with many hills and large boulders. [fo. 35r.] He passed through them as well as he could, to his great satisfaction. He sent to the constable[100] of the castle, who was an old knight, to tell

---

[98] Line 1683. *Flint*. The castle, fifteen miles from Chester, was built on a rocky outcrop rising from the marshes of the River Dee. The sea has receded now, but in the Middle Ages the river rose at high tide to lap the castle walls. See Colvin (ed.), *History of the King's Works*, I, pp. 308–318.

[99] Line 1697. *Rothelant*. Rhuddlan Castle is a further eighteen miles on from Flint, and built on the canalized River Clwyd. It is almost three miles from the sea, so that when Creton says that *la mer salee / Vient es fossez*, ll. 1719–1720, he means that the river flooded the moat at high tide. Colvin (ed.), *History of the King's Works*, I, pp. 318–327.

[100] Line 1703. *chastellain*. Messham, 'Henry Coneway, Knight', p. 36, is of the opinion that Creton is too harsh in calling the constable a coward – *couart*, l. 1726: nothing would have been served by defending Rhuddlan for the King, since Northumberland would have called up reinforcements from Lancaster's army at Chester. However this might be, it remains true that Coneway served his own interests and not those of his sovereign to whom he owed allegiance. Messham gives the impression that Creton has the Archbishop of Canterbury accompany Northumberland, but Creton does not say that.

[fo. 34v.] 'Faire ou[746] monde. Pour Dieu or vous hastez,
'Et je seray a Cestre demourez,
'Jusques a tant que vous retournerez,[747]
 'Ou que nouvelle   1672
'Aie de vous, qui mon cuer renouvelle
'En plaisance.' 'Dieux doint qu'elle soit telle,'
Dist le conte. 'Par sens ou par cautelle
 'Je l'amenray.'   1676
Ainsi parti le conte sans delay.
Tout au plus droit qu'il pot a Cornüay
Prist son chemin, pensant et plain d'esmay
 Comment pourra   1680
Le roi avoir. Ainsi fort chevaucha
Lui et ses gens,[748] tant quë il arriva[749]
A un[750] chastel, que[751] Flint on appella,
 Qui est moult fort.   1684
Dedens manda c'on lui rendist le fort
De par le duc Henry, ou tous a mort
Seront livrez sans leur[752] faire deport
 Ne nul respit.   1688
Ainsi la porte par paour on ly[753] ouvrit;[754]
Les gens du roy Richart hors bouter[755] fist
Et de ses gens grant partie y commist[756]
 Pour le garder.   1692
En ce chastel, que Flint m'öez nommer,
Fu prins le roy, com[757] vous orrez compter
Yci aprés. Or fist ses gens haster
 Northomberlant,   1696
De la tout droit ala a Rothelant,
Ou il trouva chemin fort et pesant,[758]
Mainte montaigne et mainte roche grant.
 A entredeux   1700
[fo. 35r.] Oultre passa, le plus bel et le mieulx
Qu'il onques[759] pot; alors[760] fu moult joieux.
Il envoia au chastellain, qui vieulx
 Chevalier fu,   1704

---

[746] H ou LABCD en ce
[747] C que seres retournez
[748] H gens *superscript*
[749] A fist tant quil arriva
[750] AB en ung
[751] B qui
[752] L eulx
[753] B *no* ly
[754] H ouvrit LB rendit
[755] C gecter
[756] D line 1691 is in right margin
[757] AD comme
[758] C poisant
[759] A que oncques B quil conques
[760] AD adont

him that the castle should immediately be surrendered to him in the duke's name, or he will be hanged without mercy along with all the others there: truly they will not escape the sting of death, not for all the treasure in the kingdom, if they do not yield the castle. Thus does the earl threaten the constable of the castle, whose face was pale with fright, for he had held the castle and its entrance in the King's name for many a day. It is very strongly defended, considering that the salty sea comes up into the ditches, and also it is perched very high on a rock; the walls are stout and wide and fortified with fat towers.[101] But the old keeper was so afraid that he handed over the keys like a coward; and yet King Richard had begged him most courteously [fo. 35v.] to defend it, since it was very richly supplied with wine and wheat, for he had been there recently, and I with him.[102] Thereupon the constable of the castle pledged to the earl that he would surrender it to him, in the name of duke Henry, on condition that he remain governor for life; the earl agreed.

Now it was just ten miles[103] of quite straight road to Conway

---

[101] Line 1723. *De grosses tours*. Even in their present dilapidated state, the round towers in the walls of Rhuddlan Castle – especially the twin towers of the two gatehouses – are louring and menacing.

[102] Lines 1731–1732. *il y ot esté prouchainnement / Et moy o lui*. Creton is saying that Richard made a sortie from Conway to Rhuddlan, before retreating to Conway. Strangely, the *Prinse et mort* does not recount this.

[103] Lines 1739–1740. *dix mile ... / A Corniiay*. Rhuddlan is almost seventeen miles from Conway.

Dire que tost le fort lui fu[761]* rendu
Ou nom du duc, ou il sera pendu –
Lui et tous ceulx qui y[762] seront tenu –
    Sans en avoir[763]   1708
Nulle pitié: non pas pour tout l'avoir
Du[764] royaulme n'eschapperont[765] pour voir,
Que de la mort le morsel recevoir
    Ne[766] leur en face,   1712
S'il[767] ne rendent le chastel et la place.
Le conte ainsi le chastelain menace,
Le quel en ot de peur toute la face
    Descoulouree,   1716
Car il avoit[768] gardé mainte journee
Ou nom de roy le chastel et l'entree,
Qui est moult fort, veu que la mer salee
    Vient es fossez,   1720
Et d'autre part est il moult hault troussez
Sur une roche, et les murs fors et lez;
De grosses tours est il bien reparez.
    Maiz le viellart   1724
Ot si grant paour au matin et au tart
Qu'il lui rendi les clefs comme couart;
Et si lui ot prié le roy Richart
    Moult doulcement   1728
[fo. 35v.] Qu'il le gardast,[769] veu que tresgrandement
Estoit garnis de vin et de froument,
Car il y ot esté prouchainnement,
    Et moy o lui.   1732
Le chastelain au conte la[770] plevy:
Ou[771] nom du duc, qu'on appellë Henry,
Desoremaiz lui rendi,[772] par tel sy
    Qu'il demourroit   1736
Toute sa vie chastelain la endroit;
Le conte en fu d'accort. Or n'y avoit
Que dix mile de chemin assez droit
    A Cornüay,   1740

---

[761] L fust AD feust
[762] B *no* y
[763] B sans en [en *superscript*] avoir
[764] LABD de ce C de tout ce
[765] AB neschapperoit
[766] C ni
[767] LBD silz
[768] LC lavoit
[769] H quil regardast LACD quil le gardast B quil re [le *superscript*] gardast
[770] L le
[771] AD quou
[772] HC lui tendi LB lui rendi AD le tenroit

where the King remained in sorrow and dismay. He knew nothing about the earl's approach, but repeated to himself:

'I know not what this means; glorious God, creator of my life, what can have happened to my brother Exeter? A week ago he went to Chester to reconcile the duke and me; now he has not been able to come back. In truth I believe that they have met with trouble and distress. I know not what to think or say.'

Thus did the King suffer greatly, considering the misfortunes that came upon him thick and fast; nevertheless [fo. 36r.] he rendered thanks to Almighty God.

Now it is right that you know the truth about Northumberland and how he schemed to capture King Richard, for he knew perfectly well that if the King guesses that he has come in strength, he will absolutely refuse to leave his castles.

§23 Lines 1765–1916. Northumberland leaves most of his men behind as an ambush to capture the King and goes forward with a small party to outline Lancaster's terms to Richard.

He had his men split into two groups behind some boulders, bristling with catapults. They were keen and willing

Ou le roy fu en dueil et en esmay.
De la venue au conte riens de vray
Ne savoit il, maiz souvent dist: 'Ne say[773]
 'Que ce peut[774] estre;   1744
'Glor̃ieux Dieux, qui me feïstes[775]* nestre,
'Que peut avoir mon beau frere d'Excestre?
'.viii.[776] jours y a qu'il est alé[777] a Cestre
 'Pour accorder   1748
'Le duc et moy; or ne scet retourner.
'Certes je croy qu'ilz[778] ont a endurer
'Paine ou[779] meschief. Je n'en say[780] que[781] penser
 'Ne quë en dire.'[782]*   1752
Ainsi le roy estoit a grant martire,
Veu le meschief qui sur lui tire a tire
Venoit a fort pour le plus desconfire;
 Maiz non obstant   1756
[fo. 36r.] Graces rendoit a Dieu[783] le tout puissant.
Or est raison que de Northomberlant
Sachiez le[784] vray, et ce qu'ala[785] pensant*
 Pour mieulx avoir   1760
Le roy Richart, car il sot bien de voir
Que, së il scet sa force et son povoir,
Pour nulle rien ne se vouldra[786] mouvoir
 De ses chasteaulx.   1764

§23 Lines 1765–1916. Northumberland leaves most of his men behind as an ambush to capture the King and goes forward with a small party to outline Lancaster's terms to Richard.

Soubz une roche, qui de grans mangonniaulx
Est[787] roide* et haulte, fist faire .ii. monchiaulx
De ses gens, qui furent frez et nouviaulx*
 Et desirans   1768

---

[773] A sy ne savoit mais dist comme je scay D ne savoit mes dit ne scay B maiz souvent dist ne fay scay
[774] A peut ce
[775] HB fistes LACD feistes
[776] B .xx.
[777] C quil a este
[778] C quil
[779] B et
[780] BC je ne sces
[781] C quen
[782] HLBC ne quen dire AD jen muir tout dire
[783] C a dieu rendoit
[784] A de
[785] C le voir et que aloit
[786] C vouldroit
[787] L et

to capture the King as though he were a treacherous tyrant. Alas! Such people! What were they thinking of, when they had held him in great esteem as their rightful lord for twenty-two years, and now wanted to depose and ruin him? It is my view that this is such a cardinal error that they should, for all time, be considered most wicked, and fresh chronicles should be written so that people could see, in greater detail, what they had done and how unworthy they were. Then the earl, who was wise and astute, said to his men:

'Guard well this pass, and I will go across the river with five others, [fo. 36v.] and please God, before tomorrow morning I will say such things to the King – in prose or rhyme – that unless he is a man of steel, I think he will be flushed out; but on pain of death do not move until you see the King or me[104] returning.'

Thus they arranged themselves in good order and the earl went off quietly to Conway to fulfil his pledge.

There is an arm of the sea in front of the town[105] and when the earl got there he sent a herald to King Richard to ask if it were his pleasure that he be granted safe-conduct to come across to tell him how the duke wants to be reconciled with him.

---

[104] Line 1792. *Le roy ou moy*. **ACD** have *le roy o moy*. Either reading is acceptable: 'the King or me', i.e. they did not travel together, or 'the King with me'.

[105] Line 1797. *Devant la ville un bras de mer y a*. Approaching Conway Castle from the east, Northumberland would have had to cross the estuary of the River Conway, which is very wide where the river flows into Conway Bay. See Colvin (ed.), *History of the King's Works*, I, p. 337.

D'avoir le roy comme felons tirans.
Hellas! Quelz gens! Qu'estoient ilz pensans,
Quant par[788] l'espasse de bien .xxii. ans
   Pour droit seigneur   1772
L'orent tenu par grant joie et honneur
Et puis aprés le desfaire a douleur?
Il m'est advis que c'est si grant erreur,[789]
   Qu'a tousjours maiz   1776
On les devroit tenir pour tresmauvaiz,
Et que croniques nouviaulx en feussent faiz,*
Afin qu'on vist plus longuement leurs faiz
   Et vasselage.   1780
Le conte alors, qui fu soubtil et saige,
Dist a ses gens: 'Gardez bien ce passaige,
'Et je m'en voiz par dessus le rivage
   'Moy le sisisme,[790]*   1784
[fo. 36v.] 'Et se[791] Dieu plaist, ains qu'il soit demain prime,
'Au roy diray – ou par prose ou par rime –
'Telles nouvelles, s'il n'est plus dur que lime
   'De fin acier,   1788
'Je[792] le feray – ce croy je – deslogier;
'Maiz gardez vous sur[793] la mort[794] de bougier,
'Jusques a tant que[795] verrez repairier
   'Le roy ou[796] moy.'   1792
Ainsi se mirent en gracïeux conroy,[797]
Et le conte sans faire nul effroy
A Cornüay pour acquittier sa foy
   Si s'en ala.   1796
Devant la ville un bras de mer y a,
Maiz quant le conte par devant arriva,
Au roy Richart un herault envoya
   Pour demander   1800
S'il lui plaisoit qu'il peust oultre passer
Par[798] saufconduit pour lui dire et conter
Comment le duc veult a lui accorder.
   Lors le herault   1804

---

[788] C pour
[789] C crueur
[790] all mss moy sixiesme
[791] C si
[792] B et
[793] L sus
[794] AD mais bien gardez sur la mort [D bien superscript]
[795] AD a ce que [D ad ce superscript]
[796] ACD o
[797] B ainsi se misent mirent en gracieux arroy conroy
[798] C pour

Then the herald crossed the water and found the King in the castle on high,[106] engulfed in sadness. He said eagerly to him:

'Sire, the honourable earl of Northumberland has sent me here, to tell you how duke Henry wants to have a genuine and speedy peace between you. [fo. 37r.] For the true state of affairs to emerge you will grant him, if you please, safe-conduct and permission to come here, for otherwise he will not dare to set out.'

Then Salisbury, who was there, told King Richard that it would be a good plan to have the earl come there on his own. Then the King said out loud to the herald[107] in his own tongue, that he willingly grants passage to the earl of Northumberland (who was wise and astute). The herald rendered thanks one hundredfold to the King. He descended from the lofty castle, and crossed the water to where the earl had awaited him impatiently. He related to him how King Richard granted him safe-conduct kindly and willingly and begged him to make haste.

Then the earl climbed into a boat and crossed the water. He found King Richard in the castle, the earl of Salisbury and the bishop of Carlisle with him also. He said to the King,

'Sire, duke Henry has sent me here

---

[106] Lines 1805–1806. *ou chastel en hault / Trouva le roy* ... No other source reports this.

[107] Line 1820. *messaige* = 'messenger'. He is obviously the same person called *un herault*, *supra*, ll. 1799, 1804, and has been translated as 'herald'.

LA PRINSE ET MORT DU ROY RICHART D'ANGLETERRE 157

L'eaue passa[799] et ou chastel en hault
Trouva le roy, qui ot maint[800] dur assault
Par[801] tristresse. Lors[802] lui dist de cuer bault:[803]
 'Sire, le conte   1808
'De Northomberlant,* qui oncques n'ama honte,
'M'a cy tramis, afin que je vous conte
'Comment[804] le duc Henry paix bonne[805] et prompte
 'A vous avoir   1812
[fo. 37r.] 'Veult. S'il vous plaist, pour le vray mieulx savoir
'Vous lui donrez saufconduit et povoir
'De[806] venir ça, car autrement mouvoir
 'Ne s'ozeroit.'   1816
Salsebery alors, qui la estoit,
Au roy Richart dist que tresbon seroit
De le fere venir[807] seul[808] la endroit.
 Lors au messaige   1820
Dist tout en[809] hault le roy en son langage:
De tresbon cuer ottroye[810] le passaige
Au conte de Northomberlant, (qui saige
 Et soubtil fu.)   1824
Graces au roy .c. foiz en a rendu.
Du hault chastel est en bas[811] descendu,
L'eaue passa, ou le conte atendu
 L'ot longuement.   1828
La lui[812] conta la maniere comment
Le roy Richart tresamoureusement
Lui ottroya[813] saufconduit bonnement,
 Et lui pria   1832
De se[814] haster. Lors le conte monta
En un vaissel[815] et l'eaue oultre passa.
Le roy Richart ens ou chastel trouva,
 Et avec[816] lui   1836
Trouva le conte de Salsebery
Et l'esvesque de Kerlille autresi.[817]*
La[818] dist au roy: 'Sire, le duc Henry
 'M'a cy tramis,   1840

---

[799] B ~~trouva le roy~~ leaue passa
[800] B moult
[801] C de
[802] AD la
[803] L hault
[804] B come
[805] L *no* bonne
[806] C *no* de
[807] H de le fere [*erasure*] venir
[808] C feal
[809] AD *no* en
[810] B lottroie
[811] C en bas est
[812] B ja ly
[813] AD ottroye
[814] B soy
[815] AD un vaisseau [D ung *superscript*]
[816] C avecque
[817] LBC aussi
[818] AD lors

[fo. 37v.] Figure XI: Northumberland makes obeisance to King Richard at Conway.

so that there may be peace between the two of you, and that you be henceforth good friends. If it please you, Sire, and if I may be heard, I will tell you what he asks and will tell no lie: that you will be a true judge and have all those whom I shall name here come on the appointed day to Westminster, in the name of justice, to attend the Parliament that you two will cause to be held in good faith: [fo. 38r.] and that the duke will be reinstated as High Steward,[108] as the duke his father had been and all his kin, for more than 100 years. I will name those who will await judgement; it is time, if you please, Sire.'

'Yes, for I wish to know who they are.'

'Sire, know in truth that your brother[109] is the first. The second has not done his duty, it is the duke of Surrey who is in fact imprisoned and locked up in the castle of Chester; I know not how he has offended duke Henry. The others are the earl of Salisbury and the bishop of Carlisle. The fifth – as I understood – I have heard named

---

[108] Line 1853. *grant juge* (also *juge greigneur*, l. 1881). The office of High Steward (or Seneschal) of England was hereditary in the earls of Leicester, one of John of Gaunt's titles, in right of his first wife. See Armitage-Smith, *John of Gaunt*, pp. 20–21.

[109] Line 1862. *vostre frere*. Exeter.

[fo. 37v.] Figure XI: Northumberland makes obeisance to King Richard at Conway.

'Afin qu'acort entre vous deux[819] soit mis,
'Et que soiez desoremaiz bons amis.
'S'il vous plaist, Sire, et que je soie oÿs,
   'Je vous diray 1844
'Ce[820] qu'il vous mande, et[821] riens n'en[822] mentiray:
'Se vous voulez estre bon juge et vray
'Et trestous ceulx, qu'icy vous nommeray,
   'Faire venir 1848
'A certain jour pour justice acomplir
'A Wesmoustre[823] le Parlement ouïr,[824]
'Que vous ferez entre vous deux tenir
   'Par[825] loyaulté: 1852
[fo. 38r.] 'Et que grant juge soit il restitué
'D'Engleterre, comme l'avoit esté
'Le duc son pere et tout son parenté
   'Plus de cent ans. 1856
'Le nom[826] de ceulx qui seront atendans
'Le jugement vueil dire;[827] il en est temps,
'S'il vous plaist, Sire.' 'Oïl,[828] car desirans[829]
   'Suy de savoir 1860
'Les quelx ce sont.' 'Sire,[830] sachiez de voir
'Que vostre frere, je vous fay assavoir,
'Est[831] le premier. Le second son devoir
   'N'a pas bien fait, 1864
'C'est de Soudray le duc, qui est de fait[832]
'Mis en prison et ou[833] chastel[834] retrait
'De Cestre; pas ne sçay qu'il a mesfait
   'Au duc Henry. 1868
'L'autre est le conte de Salsebery
'Et l'evesque de Kerlille autresi.[835]
'Le .v.ᵉ – sicom[836] je l'entendi –
   'Oÿ nommer 1872

---

[819] AD vous et luy
[820] D et
[821] H ne [et *superscript*] LBCD ne A nen
[822] B ne
[823] LB wemoustier AD westomoustier
[824] B oyr ovrir
[825] C pour
[826] L le[s *superscript*] nom [s *superscript*]
[827] AD le jugement diray
[828] AD *no* oil C oir
[829] AD bien fort desirans [D bien fort *superscript*]
[830] B ce sont f r e sire
[831] D et
[832] B deffait D deffait
[833] B au
[834] C ou chastel et en prison
[835] *all mss* aussi
[836] LAD si comme

Monseigneur Maudelyn.[110] These men conspired to advise you to have your uncle[111] killed most treacherously. If they deny this, they must await the judgement of your Parliament, where you will be crowned King and lord in high estate, [fo. 38v.] and duke Henry will be there impartially as High Steward.[112] Those who have sinned or been traitors will be punished; this is what Monseigneur has decided. Certainly, dear Sire, he has no wish to inflict suffering except for good reason.

'I want to say something else to you: you should swiftly name a day, for well do I know that that is the duke's greatest wish. He wants only his estates and what is his, he wants nothing of yours, for you are his sole and rightful King, and he reproaches himself for the great wrong he has done you through the evil counsel of the Enemy,[113] who never rests or sleeps. Rather is he ever on the watch to place temptation in Man's way; he put him up to all this. Thus for the sake of God – who suffered the supreme agony on the Cross for us – show kindness to Monseigneur, who is downcast and in distress, and spare him your wrath this time,

---

[110] Line 1873. *Monseigneur Madelien*. Richard Maudelyn, one of the King's clerks. Creton, who had seen him in Ireland, said that he resembled Richard very closely, *infra*, ll. 3147–3158, 3274–3279. He was executed for his part in the Epiphany Rising. See Given-Wilson, *Royal Household*, pp. 179–181.

[111] Line 1875. *vostre oncle*. The duke of Gloucester, *supra*, l. 1633, note.

[112] Line 1881. *juge greigneur*. *Supra*, l. 1853, note.

[113] Line 1899. *l'ennemi*. The Devil.

'A Monseigneur Madelien. Accorder
'Vorent ceulx cy et[837] vous conseil[838] donner
'De vostre oncle faire mort endurer
    'Tresfaulcement.   1876
'Et s'ilz[839] dïent que non, le jugement
'En atendant* de vostre Parlement,
'Ou vous serez couronnez[840] haultement
    'Roy et seigneur,   1880
[fo. 38v.] 'Et la[841] sera comme juge greigneur
'Le duc Henry sans penser a faveur.
'Ceulx qui aront fait mal,[842] vice ne erreur
    'Ou traÿson   1884
'Seront[843] pugniz;[844] c'est la conclusïon
'De Monseigneur. Autre[845] desrisïon
'Ne veult faire que[846] par bonne raison,
    'Certes, chier Sire.[847]   1888
'Encor vous vueil une autre chose dire:
'Que promptement vueilliez[848] journee eslire,
'Car[849] c'est la chose qu'ou[850] monde plus desire,
    'Je le say bien.   1892
'Et si ne veult que sa terre et le sien,
'Ne du vostre ne veult il avoir rien,
'Car vous estes son droit roy sans moyen,
    'Et se remort   1896
'En conscïence du grant mal et du tort
'Qu'il vous a fait par le mauvaiz enort
'De l'ennemi, qui nulle heure ne dort
    'Ne ne sommeille.   1900
'Ains pour tenter corps humains toudiz[851] veille;
'Trestout ce fait lui a mis en l'oreille.
'Sique pour Dieu – qui la mort nonpareille
    'Pendant en croix   1904
'Souffry pour nous – vueilliez estre courtoiz
'A Monseigneur, qui est mas et destroiz,
'Et lui vueilliez pardonner une foiz
    'Vostre courroux,   1908

---

[837] AD vorent cecy et
[838] C conseil vous
[839] AD sil
[840] LACD couronne
[841] C no la
[842] C no mal
[843] H seron
[844] L puny
[845] A nautre
[846] C ne
[847] H chier sire LBC no chier
[848] C veilles
[849] L no car
[850] ACD quau
[851] AC tousjours

[fo. 39r.] and he will most humbly beg mercy of you, on his knees. After this, you will make your way together to London, peacefully like men of the cloth, or if you want to make your own way, you will do so; and then Parliament will be summoned throughout the land.

§24 Lines 1917–2004. Northumberland withdraws and Richard tells his companions that he will pretend to agree to Lancaster's terms.

'You can be certain sure of this. I will swear on the body of our Lord Jesus Christ, consecrated by priestly hand, that duke Henry will most willingly observe everything that I have said, for he pledged it to me on the Host[114] when I took my leave of him lately. Now consider, Sire, what you would do, for I have tarried long.'

Then King Richard said carefully to him:

'Northumberland, just step aside and before long you will have our reply, so that you can leave soon.'

Then you could have seen Northumberland's party draw away from them. The King and his companions discussed in detail what they had heard the earl recount; at length the King

---

[114] Lines 1922–1923. *il le me plevy / Sur le corps Dieu.* There is no mention in Creton's account of Lancaster swearing on the Host when he gave Northumberland his instructions. *Supra,* ll. 1653–1674.

[fo. 39r.] 'Et il vendra a mercy devant[852] vous
'Treshumblement, a terre les genoulx.
'Ce fait,* aprés comme beguins[853] et doulx
  'Vous en yrez   1912
'Ensemble a Londres, ou se[854] tenir voulez
'Autre chemin que li, vous le prendrez;
'Et lors sera[855] le Parlement criez[856]
  'Par le païs.   1916

§24 Lines 1917–2004. Northumberland withdraws and Richard tells his companions that he will pretend to agree to Lancaster's terms.

'**D**e tout cecy soiez certains[857] et fis.
'J'en jureray[858] sur[859] le corps Jhesucris
'De main de prestre sacré que tous mes dis
  'Et tout – ainsi   1920
'Comme j'ay dit – tenra[860] le duc Henry
'Tresloyaument, car il le[861] me plevy
'Sur[862] le corps Dieu, quant je me departi;[863]
  'Derreinement[864]   1924
'D'avecques[865] lui. Or regardez comment
'Vous voulez faire, Sire, car longuement
'Ay demouré.' Lors lui dit sagement
  Le roy Richart: 1928
'Northomberlant, or vous tirez a part,
'Et vous arez, ains qu'il soit guerez tart,
'De nous responce, afin que le depart
  'Puissiez tost faire.'   1932
Lors[866] veïssiez* les gens ensus[867] d'eulx traire.
La parlerent longuement de l'affaire,
Qu'il[868] avoient au conte oÿ retraire,
  Tant que le roy   1936

---

[852] C devers
[853] AD beguin BC benigns
[854] C si
[855] C fera
[856] C crier
[857] B certain
[858] D jurray
[859] L sus
[860] C sera
[861] B no le
[862] L sus
[863] L quant de lui me parti
[864] C derrierement D derrenierement
[865] B avecques, no de
[866] A la
[867] AD en sur
[868] LAD quilz

[fo. 39v.] said:

'Messeigneurs, we will give him what he wants, for upon my soul I can see no other way out. All is lost, you can see that as well as I, but I swear to you that the duke will meet a painful and certain death for this, whatever I promise him, considering the outrage and affront that he has caused us. And assuredly no Parliament will be held at Westminster to discuss his demands, for I love you with such a tender heart that were I to die for it, I would not let you appear in Parliament for the duke to have his way with you. For well do I know that he would make you suffer great torment and you would be in mortal danger, considering that some men are spreading false charges against you. Have no fear, despite them you will always be my closest friends, for I have found you loyal and true, without malice.

'I tell you furthermore that I will enlist the Welshmen and have them gather in secret so that we can find them when we want them, [fo. 40r.] after we have talked to duke Henry. Then we will make our way through Wales, and if he asks why, we will tell him

[fo. 39v.] Dist: 'Beaux Seigneurs, nous lui ferons ottroy,
'Car autre tour par m'ame je n'y voy.[869]
'Tout est perdu, vous le veez[870]* comme moy,
   'Maiz je vous jure   1940
'Qu'il en mourra de mort amere et sure,
'Quelque chose que je lui asseüre,
'Consideré l'oultragë[871] et l'injure[872]
   'Qu'il nous a fait.   1944
'Et ne doubtez que ja Parlement fait
'A Wemoustier[873] ne sera de ce fait,
'Car je vous ains[874]* de cuer si tresparfait,
   'Que pour mourir[875]   1948
'Ne vous lairoie en Parlement venir
'Contre le duc pour son vueil acomplir.
'Car je sçay bien[876] qu'il vous feroit souffrir
   'Paine moult dure,   1952
'Et si seriez en trop grant aventure
'De recevoir la mort amere et sure,
'Veu que plusieurs font[877] contre vous murmure.
   'Maiz ne doubtez   1956
'Que maugré eulx a tousjours maiz serez
'Mes bons amis, de moy les plus privez,
'Car je vous ay bons et loyaulx trouvez
   'Sans mal penser.   1960
'Encor vous di que je vouldray[878] mander
'Gens[879] parmi Galles et les faire assembler
'Secretement, et qu'a un jour trouver
   'Nous les puissons,   1964
[fo. 40r.] 'Maiz que parlé au duc Henry aions.
'Lors le chemin parmi Galles prenrons,[880]
'Et s'il demande pour quoy, nous li dirons
   'Que de vitaille[881]   1968

---

[869] A par maniere ny voy
[870] L vez
[871] L et loutrage
[872] AD et grant injure B linjure quil nous a fait
[873] ABD westmonstier
[874] L aim ACD aime
[875] B que pour mourir ne vous lairoie en parlement venir
[876] H bien *superscript* B no bien
[877] AD ont [D ont *superscript*]
[878] A encore vous dy que se vouloye H vouldray LBD vouldroye
[879] H gens *in left margin* LABCD *no* gens
[880] AD tenrons C prennons
[881] B que de vitaille na

that there is not a halfpenny worth of provisions out there; his troops have laid waste the country. "In order that[115] we do not run out of food, let us go that way, if you give your assent." This is what we will say to him and I think that he will easily agree; the earl has told us so.

'And when we have come upon our men, we will unfurl our banners in the wind and attack the duke with all speed and with all our strength. For I swear on my life that when they see my colours, they will be filled with such remorse – considering the wrong they have done me – that half of those who have gone over to him will abandon him and come to us, since a noble heart cannot be found lacking. They will remember that they should hold me as their rightful lord as long as I live; then you will see them come straight to us. [fo. 40v.] You know that we are in the right; God will help us, if we all believe. If we are not as many on our side as they, they will then – please God – be keen to join battle, and if it turns out that they are defeated, they will be put to death; I shall have some of them flayed alive. I would not spare them for all the gold in the land, if it pleases God that I stay alive and keep my health.'

---

[115] Lines 1971–1973. "*Et affin tele qu[e]* ... / *Se bon vous semble.*" This is direct speech within direct speech. Richard is rehearsing what he will say to Lancaster.

'N'a par dela[882] valissent une maille;
'Tout ont gasté ses gens[883] et sa bataille.
'"Et affin tele qu'a[884] garnison ne faille,
　'"Alons par la,   1972
'"Se bon vous semble." Ainsi on lui dira,
'Et je croy bien qu'il s'i[885] accordera
'De tresbon cuer; le conte le nous a
　'Dit ensement.   1976
'Et quant trouvé ensemble arons[886] no[887] gent,*
'Nous desploirons noz banieres au vent,
'Et devers lui yrons hastivement
　'Et par effort.   1980
'Car je sçay bien de certain sur ma mort,
'Quant ilz verront mes armes, tel remort
'Aront au cuer – considerant[888] le tort
　'Qu'il[889] m'aront[890] fait[891] –   1984
'Que la moittié de ceulx, qui se sont trait
'Avecques lui, le lairont et de fait
'Venront a nous, car bon cuer et parfait
　'Ne peut mentir.   1988
'Et Nature les fera souvenir
'Qu'ilz[892] me doivent pour[893] droit[894] seigneur tenir
'Tout mon vivant; lors les[895] verrez venir
　'A nous tout droit.   1992
[fo. 40v.] 'Et vous savez que nous avons bon droit;
'Dieux nous aidra, se chascun bien le croit.
'Se nous ne sommes autant[896] en nostre endroit[897]
　'Comme ilz seront,   1996
'Ja pour cela – se Dieu plaist – ne lairont
'Que la[898] bataille n'aient, et se ilz[899] sont
'Aucunement desconfiz, ilz[900] seront
　'A la mort mis;   2000
'De telz y a feray[901]* escorchier tous vifs.
'Je n'en prendroi tout[902] l'or de ce[903] païs,
'S'il plaist a Dieu que je demeure vis
　'Et en santé.'   2004

[882] B na par la dela
[883] AC sa gent
[884] LB que
[885] B se
[886] C aions
[887] AD noz
[888] L considerans
[889] LAD quilz
[890] C naront
[891] B quil maront fait que la moitie de ceulx
[892] C quil
[893] C par
[894] AD vray
[895] B no les
[896] AD tant
[897] LD droit
[898] AD no la
[899] B et silz C et si ilz
[900] C il
[901] L fray
[902] H prendroi [erasure] tout
[903] L cest

§25 Lines 2005–2076. Northumberland swears on the Host that Lancaster's terms are as they have been related to Richard.

This is what the King said to them, and the others all agreed, saying,

'Sire, let the earl of Northumberland be sent for, and let us have him swear right away the oath as he offered before; if he does so, we will go along with everything he has said.'

Thus without more ado, the earl was summoned and the King said to him:

'Northumberland, the duke sent you here to make peace between the two of us. If you swear on the Host, which we will have consecrated, that everything you have said is true, [fo. 41r.] with no falsehood about it, and that the duke will honour our agreement as a noble lord should, then we will agree to your terms. For well do I know that you are an honourable man, and would not perjure yourself for the sake of finery, jewels or gifts, for the man who wittingly breaks his oath will know only shame and affront as long as he lives; and at the last he will die in great torment.'

Then the earl replied:

'Monseigneur, have the Host consecrated, and I will swear that there is no falsehood here,

§25 Lines 2005–2076. Northumberland swears on the Host that Lancaster's terms are as they have been related to Richard.

Ainsi le roy leur a dit et conté,	
Et les autres s'i sont tous[904] accordé,	
Disant: 'Sire, le conte soit mandé,	
'De Northomberlant,*	2008
'Et qu'on lui face faire tout maintenant	
'Le serement, comme il a dit devant;	
'S'ainsi le fait, nous serons accordant	
'Trestout[905] son dit.'	2012
Lors le conte sans plus de contredit	
Fu appellez,[906] et le roy lui a dit:	
'Northomberlant, le duc cy vous tramist[907]	
'Pour accorder	2016
'Nous[908] deux ensemble. Se[909] vous voulez jurer	
'Sur le corps Dieu, que nous ferons sacrer,	
'Que tout le fait, qu'avez voulu compter,	
'Est veritable	2020
[fo. 41r.] 'Sans y avoir pensee favorable	
'Nulle quelconques,[910] maiz fermë et estable[911]	
'Tenir l'accort comme seigneur notable,	
'Nous le ferons.	2024
'Car je sçay bien que vous estes preudons,	
'Ne pour avoir robes, joyaux ne dons	
'Ne vous[912] vouldriez parjurer, car li homs	
'Qui se parjure	2028
'A escïant, que hontë et injure	
'Ne peut avoir tous le[913] temps quë il dure,	
'Et si convient au derrain qu'il en mure[914]*	
'A grant douleur.'	2032
Lors respondi le conte:[915] 'Monseigneur,	
'Faites sacrer le corps Nostre Seigneur.	
'Je jureray qu'il n'a point de faveur	
'En ce fait cy,[916]	2036

---

[904] L tout
[905] H trostout
[906] L appelle
[907] B vous a transmis
[908] B noz
[909] C si
[910] ABCD quelconque
[911] L et bien estable
[912] B no vous
[913] LBC tout le AD tous les
[914] HL au derrain quil en muire AD quau derrenier il en muire B au derrain qui sen meure C au derrain il en meure
[915] B no le conte
[916] B ycy

and that the duke will honour our agreement, as you have heard me say.'

All of them devoutly heard Mass. Then the earl, without offering any objection, swore on the Host. Alas! His blood ought to have boiled, for he knew the opposite

[fo. 41v.] Figure XII: Northumberland kneels before the Host.

to be true. Nevertheless he swore the oath – as you have heard me say – to fulfil his own wish and keep his promise to the duke who had sent him to the King. Thus did the two of them agree: one laid a wicked scheme, and the other was even worse. But the King did the lesser wrong, for it is often said,'When arms speak, the laws are silent',[116] and he did not swear an oath as the earl did: [fo. 42r.] he will die in supreme disgrace, unless he repents before God, for what he did is worse than all other sins, it seems to me; to my mind, what he did is like nothing else you can ever hear of. And therefore, the man who treads a straight path lives and reigns in great prosperity and peace until Death comes, whom we all expect at any time;

---

[116] Line 2054. *Force n'a loy. Supra*, l. 1314, note.

'Et que le duc le tenra,[917] tout ensi
'Que le m'avez oÿ compter icy.'
Chascun d'eulx la[918] devotement oÿ
    La messe dire.   2040
Le conte alors sans plus riens contredire
Fist le serement* sur le corps Nostre Sire.[919]
Elas! Le sanc lui devoit bien defrire,
    Car le[920] contraire   2044

[fo. 41v.] Figure XII: Northumberland kneels before the Host.

Savoit il bien. Non obstant volt il faire[921]
Le serement – tel que m'oez[922] retraire –
Pour acomplir son vouloir et parfaire
    Ce que promis   20
Avoit au duc, qui l'ot au roy tramis.
Ainsi firent entr'eulx leur compromis;
L'un pensoit mal et l'autre encores pis.
    Mais quant au roy,   2052
Il ne fist pas si grant mal ne desroy,
Car on dist bien souvent: 'Force n'a loy,'
Et si ne fist serement në ottroy
    Comme le conte: 2056
[fo. 42r.] Il en mourra une foiz a grant honte,
S'a Dieu[923] n'en rent par contriccïon[924] conte,
Car ce qu'il fist tous autres maulx surmonte,
    Comme il me semble;[925]   2060
A ce fait ci[926] nul autre ne ressemble,
Quant vous l'arez oÿ trestout[927] ensemble,
Ce m'est advis. Et pour[928] ce, qui[929] bien amble
    Droit et avant,   2064
Il regne et vit[930] en prosperité grant
Et dominë en paix,[931] jusques a tant
Que la mort vient, que chascun atendant
    Est[932] a toute heure,   2068

[917] B le duc tendra
[918] A sy a
[919] B n̄re nostresire
[920] B de
[921] C voulsit faire
[922] B que vous moes
[923] C si a dieu
[924] AD nen fait par confession
[925] H il me semble LBC [*no* comme] ce me semble
[926] B *no* ci
[927] AC trestous
[928] C par
[929] L que
[930] C il vit en regne
[931] B et [donne *contraction mark above*] en paix [demeure *at line end*]
[932] C et

the great are undone and the poor gobbled up. Nothing can withstand his blows, he leaves a very bad taste in one's mouth. Now please God that Death carries us off in such a way that in Heaven we may see His face and His beaming eyes, and may He be benevolent and well disposed towards us on the Last Day.

§26 Lines 2077–2136. Richard leaves Conway for Rhuddlan.

To return to our main story: the earl begged the King to make haste, saying,

'Sire, let us ride, I beg you, for well do I know that the duke is most anxious to learn that we have peace.'

Alas! The King had no inkling of the harm or the earl's wish [fo. 42v.] to deceive him in the manner laid out before you here. The King said to him:

'It is time to set out, whenever you will, but I command you to go on ahead to Rhuddlan, and have dinner prepared there.'

'It is as you wish,' the earl replied, and set off; King Richard followed soon after him.

The earl rode hard until he caught sight of all his men behind the boulders,[117] and then he was well pleased, for he could see that they were taking care to guard the defile. He told them

---

[117] Lines 2096–2097. *Toutes ses gens / Soubz la montaigne. Supra*, ll. 1765–1767.

Qui defait grans et petis tout[933] deveure.
Devant ses cops[934] nulle riens ne demeure,
C'est un morsel qui trop mauvaiz saveure.
   Or vueille Dieux   2072
Qu'elle nous preigne en tel[935] point, qu'es[936] sains cieulx
Puissons vëoir sa face et ses doulx yeulx,
Et que[937] vers[938] nous vueille estre doulz et pieulx[939]
   Au jour darnier.[940]   2076

§26 Lines 2077–2136. Richard leaves Conway for Rhuddlan.

Pour revenir a nostre fait primier:
Le conte au roy pria de s'avanchier,
Disant: 'Sire, pensons de chevauchier,
   'Je vous en prie,[941]   2080
'Car je sçay bien que le duc grant envie
'A de savoir se la paix est bastie.'
Elas! Le roy le mal ne savoit mie
   Ne le vouloir   2084
[fo .42v.] Qu'avoit le conte, qui le volt decevoir
En la maniere que cy[942] poez vëoir.[943]
Le roy lui dist: 'Il[944] est temps de mouvoir,
   'Quant vous vouldrez,   2088
'Maiz je[945] lo bien[946] que devant en alez
'A Rotelant, et que la aprestez
'Soit le disner.' 'Ainsi que vous vouldrez,'
   Lui respondi   2092
Alors le conte, et de la se parti;
Le roy Richart assez tost le sivy.[947]
Fort chevaucha le conte, tant[948] qu'il vy
   Toutes ses gens   2096
Soubz la montaigne, et lors fu il contens,
Car il vit bien qu'ilz[949] furent diligens
Du[950] pas garder* par[951] bon conroy et sens.
   Si leur conta   2100

---

[933] CD tous
[934] L corps B *no* cops
[935] B *no* tel
[936] D que
[937] B *no* que
[938] AD lors
[939] AD piteux

[940] AD derreiner
[941] D je vous emprie
[942] AD ycy
[943] L *no* veoir
[944] C *no* il
[945] B *no* je
[946] AD *no* bien

[947] LABD suivi C suy
[948] D tant *superscript*
[949] C quil
[950] C le
[951] B car

all that had happened and how he had schemed, and that the King will soon be upon them. They were all full of joy at this, for their desire to capture their lord was very great.

Then the King left Conway to go to Rhuddlan. He crossed the broad stretch of water then rode four miles further on until he ascended the boulders[118] where the earl [and his men] were hidden. [fo. 43r.] The King was astounded when he saw them, saying,

'I am betrayed! What can this mean? God in Paradise, help me.'

Then they were recognized by their pennons which were seen fluttering, and the King said,

'I think it is the earl, who got us to agree by swearing an oath.'

Then were they all plunged into bitter fear: I would rather have been in France, for I saw them close to despair, and rightly so. It was no surprise that they were all in anguish, for even had they fled, none could have escaped there, but would have been taken or captured.

If you listen to me, I will tell you how the King had come so close to Northumberland's men that it was much further to return to the town than to descend the boulders; the sea beat upon them and on the other side the way was impassable due to the rocky ground.

---

[118] Lines 2111–2136. *la roche ... la rochaille.* Sherborne, *War, Politics and Culture*, p. 148, is of the opinion that Creton's description of the site of the ambush paints it as being much wilder than it was.

Trestout le fait et comment[952] exploita,
Et que le roy tantost[953] a eulx vendra.
Un chascun d'eulx grant joie en demena,
   Car le desir 2104
Qu'ilz[954] avoient de leur seigneur tenir
Estoit moult grant. Aprés se volt partir
De Cornüay le roy et s'en venir[955]
   A Rotelant. 2108
L'eaue passa, qui fu moult large[956] et grant,
Puis chevaucha .iiii. miles avant,
Tant qu'a[957]* la roche, ou le conte au pendant
   Estoit tapis, 2112
[fo. 43r.] Monta le roy, qui fu moult[958] esbahis
Quant il les vit, disant: 'Je suy traÿs!
'Que puet ce estre? Vray Dieu de Paradis,
   'Vueilliez me aidier.'[959] 2116
Lors aux panons qu'on vëoit balloier
Furent congneuz, disant: 'A mon cuidier
'C'est le conte, qui nous a fait traittier
   'Sur sa fiance.' 2120
Lors[960] furent tous en amere doubtance:
J'eusse voulu bien alors estre[961] en France,
Car je les vy pres de desesperance
   Et a bon droit. 2124
On ne doit[962] estre esbahis se[963] destroit
Estoient tous, car nulz d'eulx ne povoit
Pour bien fouir eschapper la endroit,
   Que retenus 2128
Ne feust[964] ou prins. Mais que soie entendus,
Je vous diray comment[965] le roy venus
Fu si pres d'eulx, qu'il y avoit trop plus
   A retourner 2132
Jusqu'a[966]* la ville que[967] la roche avaler,
A la quelle batoit la haulte mer;
D'autre costé on ne povoit passer
   Pour la rochaille. 2136

---

[952] B come
[953] C tantost le roy
[954] B quil
[955] C de cornuay et tantost sen venir
[956] B moult lairg large C laide
[957] LAC que BD que a
[958] AD moult fu [D fu superscript]
[959] AD vueilliez moy aidier B veuilles moy adier C veilles maider
[960] AD la
[961] AD bien voulu estre lors
[962] C disoit
[963] L sa A sen C si
[964] B fussent
[965] B come
[966] B jusques a
[967] L qua

§27 Lines 2137–2204. Richard falls into Northumberland's ambush and is brought by him to Rhuddlan.

Thus they had to carry on, come what may, or be killed amongst the press of the earl's men who were wearing chain-mail, as you can see.[119] [fo. 43v.] Then the King gave way to such grief that I felt sorry for his plight. He kept saying:
'Blessed God, what distress and affliction come upon me! Now I can see clearly that this man is taking me to the duke, who has little love for us. Virgin Mary, sovereign Queen, pity me, for in truth I know that I am lost if you do not keep me safe.'

Thus spoke the King, who had no power there, for we numbered only twenty or twenty-two, it seemed to me.

Everyone descended the steep boulders; this displeased the King greatly, and he kept saying to Salisbury:[120]

'Now I can see that I am dead and done for, since duke Henry hates me very much. Alas! Why did we believe the earl's word? Certainly it was very foolish of us. But it is too late; may Jesus – in whom I believe – help us.'

As he spoke we had to come within a bowshot of Northumberland's men. Then the earl came and kneeled down,[121]

---

[119] Line 2140. *A veue d'ueil* = 'as you can see'. Refers to Figure XIII, top of fo. 44r., although the reference is at the top of fo. 43v. *A veue d'ueil*, l. 347, refers to Figure IV. The subject of Figure XIII is Northumberland addressing the King, ll. 2167–2173. Despite being singular, *qui fu armé de maille* refers to Northumberland's *gens*, plural, and not to the earl himself. He is wearing a surcoat so that only his legs are visible, whereas the miniature is crammed on both sides with soldiers in armour. Creton is using *gens* (plural) as if it were *gent* (singular), *supra*, ll. 73–75, endnote. *Des gens* (two syllables) gives the correct syllable count, *de la gent* (three syllables) does not.

[120] Lines 2156–2164. *Et a Salsebery / Disoit ... Jhesus ... / Nous vueille aidier*. This is AD's reading, HLBC read *Et Salsbery / lui dist*. This speech belongs to Richard: it feels quite shocking to introduce the thoughts of a person of lower rank at this critical point; Salisbury's feelings find their place, *infra*, p. 201, ll. 22–23. The switch may have been made because in AD's reading *Salsebery* has to be swallowed in two syllables. *Supra*, l. 222, endnote.

[121] Lines 2167–2168. *agenouillier / Trestout a terre*. But Figure XIII shows Northumberland on his feet, addressing the King freely, not kneeling in a position of submission.

§27 Lines 2137–2204. Richard falls into Northumberland's ambush and is brought by him to Rhuddlan.

Ainsi convint passer, vaille que vaille,
Ou estre mort tout parmy la bataille
Des gens* du conte, qui fu armé de maille
    A veue d'ueil.   2140
[fo. 43v.] La demenoit le roy si tresgrant dueil
Que pitié fu de vëoir son accueil,
Disant souvent: 'Vray Dieu, que je[968] recueil
    'Meschief et paine.*   2144
'Or voy je bien que cest homme m'enmaine
'Devers le duc, qui guerres ne nous aime.
'Vierge Marie, roÿne souveraine,
    'Vueilliez[969] avoir   2148
'De moy pitié, car je sçay bien de voir
'Que perdus[970] sui, se ne me daigniez voir.'
Ainsi disoit le roy, qui nul povoir
    N'avoit droit la,   2152
Car nous ne fumes[971] que vint – ce me sembla –
Ou vint et deux.[972] Chascun si[973] devala
La haulte roche, qui au roy moult[974] greva,
    Et a Salsebery[975]   2156
Disoit[976] souvent, comme tout[977] esbahi:
'Or voy je bien que mort sui sans nul si,
'Car trop me het certes le duc Henry.
    'Elas! Pour quoy   2160
'Avons nous cru le conte sur[978] sa foy?
'Certes pour nous a esté grant desroy.
'Maiz c'est trop tart;[979] Jhesus[980] – en qui je croy –
    'Nous vueille aidier.'   2164
Ainsi parlant,* nous convint aprochier
D'eulx sicomme au trait[981] d'un bon archier.
Lors le conte se vint[982] agenoillier
    Trestout a terre,   2168

---

[968] B *no* je
[969] B vueilles
[970] L perdu
[971] L nous nestiens
[972] L .xxii.
[973] LABCD se
[974] C qui moult le roy
[975] HLBC et salsebery
[976] HLBC lui dist
[977] B tous
[978] L sus
[979] D *no* tart
[980] H jehesus
[981] B a tout au trait
[982] B vient

[fo. 44r.] Figure XIII: King Richard is ambushed by Northumberland.

saying to the King:

'Be not displeased, my rightful Lord, I was coming to fetch you for your better safety, since the countryside is unsettled because of the fighting, as you know.'

Then said the King:

'I would have gone without all the men whom you have brought here; it seems to me that this is not what you promised me. You told me that you had been sent with five others. In the name of God in Paradise, you have behaved very badly, [fo. 44v.] considering the oath that you swore. It seems that you, who have made this move here, are lacking in loyalty. Know you that I shall return to Conway, which I left today.'

Then the earl said:

'Monseigneur, you accuse me of dishonour, but I swear to you on the body of Jesus who died on the Cross for all of us, since you are held here by me, I shall take you to duke Henry as directly as I can, for I want you to know that I promised him ten days ago that I would bring you.'

Then he had bread and wine brought and offered them himself to the King, who dared not refuse the earl's commands, considering his strong position. Then they remounted and made their way directly to Rhuddlan; they dined excellently in that strong castle.

LA PRINSE ET MORT DU ROY RICHART D'ANGLETERRE 179

[fo. 44r.] Figure XIII: King Richard is ambushed by Northumberland.

Disant au roy: 'Je vous aloie querre,
'Mon droit Seigneur – ne vous vueille desplere –
'Car le paÿs est esmeu pour la guerre –
　'Com[983] vous savez –　　　　　　　　　　　　　2172
'Affin que mieulx soiez asseürez.'
Lors dist le roy: 'Je feusse bien alez
'Sans tant de gens[984] qu'icy[985] mandé avez;
　'Il m'est advis　　　　　　　　　　　　　　　　2176
'Que ce n'est pas ce[986] que m'avez promis.
'Vous me deïstes[987] qu'on vous avoit tramis
'Vous sixiesme. Par Dieu de Paradis
　'C'est tresmal fait,　　　　　　　　　　　　　2180
[fo. 44v.] 'Consideré le serement[988] qu'avez[989] fait.
'Il semble advis que n'estes[990] pas parfait
'En loyaulté, qui avez tel retrait
　'Fait cy entour.　　　　　　　　　　　　　　　2184
'Sachiez de vray que je feray retour
'A Cornüay, dont sui parti[991] ce jour.'
Lors dist le conte: 'Monseigneur, deshonnour[992]*
　'Me mettez sus,　　　　　　　　　　　　　　　2188
'Maiz je vous jure par le corps de Jhesus,
'Qui pour nous tous[993] fu en la croix pendus:
'Puis que de moy estes icy tenus,
　'Je vous menray[994]　　　　　　　　　　　　　2192
'Au duc Henry le[995] plus droit que pourray,
'Car je vueil bien que vous sachiez de vray
'Qu'il a dix jours qu'ainsi promis li ay.'
　Lors apporter　　　　　　　　　　　　　　　　2196
Fist pain et vin; lui mesmes presenter
Le volt au roy, qui n'osa refuser
Ce que le conte voloit[996] la commander,[997]
　Consideré　　　　　　　　　　　　　　　　　　2200
Sa puissance. Aprés sont remonté,
A Rotelant tout droit s'en sont alé;
Ou fort chastel furent ilz[998] bien disné
　Et grandement.　　　　　　　　　　　　　　　2204

[983] AD comme
[984] AD no de gens
[985] B cy
[986] B no ce
[987] AD vous nous disiez
[988] L serement
[989] B que vous avez
[990] AD ne soyez
[991] B donc parti suy
　　D dont je suis parti
[992] H deshonneur
　　LABCD deshonnour
[993] B no tous
[994] B je vous m. au duc
[995] B au
[996] B volut
[997] AD ce quil vouloit la endroit commander
[998] AD fusmes nous
　　B furent il

§28 Lines 2205–2268. Northumberland takes Richard to Flint. The King apostrophizes Queen Isabella and her father, Charles VI of France.

After dinner Northumberland (who was most assiduous) ordered a man to ride straight to Chester, [fo. 45r.] for duke Henry was there, awaiting the earl amidst the throng of his men. He was greatly apprehensive about the long delay, for he knew nothing about what the earl had done: that he and his men were bringing the King from Rhuddlan.

Immediately after dinner, without further delay, we dropped down to Flint, which had been surrendered to the duke without a fight. It was in this castle that he came the next day to capture King Richard and all those who were with him, as you will hear in a very short time. Alas! You can well imagine the King's lamentations that night when he was alone, for he had plenty to lament about, considering that he could see his enemies on all sides eager to deal him a tyrant's death. That night he loudly grieved for his wife – the daughter of the King of France – saying:

'My sweetheart,[122] my sister, I bid you farewell. It is on account of my love for you that I have come to this pass, for never did I deserve to be so foully undone

---

[122] Lines 2233–2234. *Mon tresdoulz cuer.* Supra, l. 1404–1416, note.

LA PRINSE ET MORT DU ROY RICHART D'ANGLETERRE 181

§28 Lines 2205–2268. Northumberland takes Richard to Flint. The King apostrophizes Queen Isabella and her father, Charles VI of France.

Aprés disner fist ordonner[999] sa gent
Northomberlant (qui fu moult diligent)
De chevauchier a Cestre droitement,
 Car la estoit   2208
[fo. 45r.] Le duc Henry, qui le conte atendoit
Avec ses gens, dont grant foison avoit.
De sa demeure moult fort[1000] s'esbaïssoit,
 Car riens ne sçot   2212
De la besongne que le conte fait ot:
Comment[1001] le roy[1002] amenoit en[1003] son ost
De Rotelant. Aprés disner tantost
 Sans plus atendre   2216
Nous en vinmes[1004] tout droit a Flint descendre,
Qui au duc fu rendus[1005] sans le deffendre,
Ou quel chastel vint[1006] il l'endemain prendre
 Le roy Richart –   2220
Com[1007] vous orrez ains qu'il soit gueres tart –
Et trestous[1008] ceulx qui furent de sa part.
Helas! Le dueil qu'il fist la nuit a part
 Trop bien pourrez[1009]   2224
Considerer, car il avoit assez
De quoy le faire, veu que de tous costez
Ses ennemis vëoit tous aprestez
 Et desirans   2228
De le faire mourir comme tirans.
Ceste nuit la fu forment regretans
Sa compaigne – la fille au roy des Frans –
 Disant ainsi: 2232
'Mon tresdoulz cuer, ma suer, adieu[1010] vous[1011] di,
'Pour vostre amour suy demourez[1012] ainsi,
'Car a mes gens oncques ne deservy
 'De me[1013] destruire   2236

---

[999] AD appareillier
[1000] B no fort
[1001] B come
[1002] C le roy superscript
[1003] L a partially erased [no en]
[1004] B venismes
[1005] L rendu
[1006] B vient
[1007] AD comme
[1008] A et a trestous D et de trestous
[1009] LAD povez
[1010] A ainsy a dieu [no ma suer]
[1011] H vou
[1012] ACD demene
[1013] B moy

[fo. 45v.] by my subjects. But if it be Christ's pleasure that I should die, may He lead my soul into Paradise, for I can no longer escape or flee.

'Alas! Father-in-law – King of France – I shall never see you again. I leave you your daughter amongst these wicked and dishonest people; this almost fills me with despair, for she was my joy and my delight. Please God that you will swiftly seek revenge once you know what has happened, lest reproaches be heaped upon you. The matter concerns you; may you attend to it soon. Alas! I have no ships, men or money to enable me to send a messenger to you just now. Were I still at Conway I would go to you. Now it is too late. Alas! Why did we believe Northumberland who has handed us over to the wolves? I fear that we will all die, for these people are pitiless; may God confound them, body and soul.'

Thus spoke King Richard to Salisbury, [fo. 46r.] who expressed great sorrow – I never saw greater – and the bishop of Carlisle also. None of the others slept at all that night.

[fo. 45v.] 'Si laidement. Maiz s'il plaist que je[1014] muire
'A Jhesucrist, m'ame vueille conduire
'En Paradiz, car eschapper ne fuire
   'Je ne puis maiz. 2240
'Elas! Beau pere de France, jamaiz
'Ne vous verray. Vostre fille vous laiz
'Entre ces[1015] gens,[1016] qui sont faulx et mauvaiz
   'Et sans fiance, 2244
'Par quoy je sui pres de desesperance,
'Car elle estoit ma joieuse plaisance.[1017]
'Or vueille Dieux q'une foiz la vengence
   'En vueilliez prendre, 2248
'Sceü[1018] le fait,* sans longuement atendre,
'Afin que nulz ne[1019] vous en puist reprendre.
'Le fait vous touche; or y vueilliez[1020] entendre
   'Prouchainnement. 2252
'Elas! Je n'ay vaisseaulx, gens në argent
'Pour envoier devers vous en present,
'S'a Cornüay feusse encor vrayement[1021]
   'J'alaisse a vous. 2256
'Or[1022] est trop tart. Las![1023] Pour quoy creumes nous
'Northomberlant, qui en la main des loups
'Nous a livrez? Je me doubte que tous
   'Ne soions mors, 2260
'Car ces gens[1024] cy n'ont en eulx nul remors;
'Dieux leur confonde les ames et les corps.'[1025]
Ainsi disoit le roy Richart alors
   A Salsebery, 2264
[fo. 46r.] Qui faisoit dueil – onques greigneur ne vy –
Et l'evesque de Kerlille autresi.[1026]*
Tous les autres chascun pas ne dormy
   Celle nuit la. 2268

[1014] B jen
[1015] AD telz
[1016] B *no* gens
[1017] AD ma seule souffisance C majoieuse esperance [plaisance *superscript*]
[1018] B selon
[1019] L nul de
[1020] B vueilles
[1021] B vrayment
[1022] L il
[1023] C et
[1024] H cels gens LACD ces gens B telz gent
[1025] H les corps C cop corps
[1026] LBC quierlille aussi

§29 Lines 2269–2295. Northumberland apprises Lancaster of Richard's presence at Flint. Creton informs his readers that he will now change to writing in prose.

Overnight Northumberland reported to duke Henry that he was bringing the King; the messenger arrived at Chester just as day broke. He told duke Henry all that had happened with King Richard, who was presently at Flint. The duke's heart leapt with joy at the news, and rightly so, for that was what he wanted most in the whole world. His army was camped out all over the fields around Chester. Then he had it announced that each man should immediately make ready to go where he led; the English had many trumpets sounded.

Now, I will tell you about the King's capture, without having to find words that rhyme. And in order better to render the words spoken when the two of them met – for I recall them perfectly well, it seems to me – I will convey them in prose, for it seems that sometimes we add too many words [fo. 46v.] to what we are writing about. Now may it please God, who made us in His likeness, to punish all those who committed this outrage.

§29 Lines 2269–2295. Northumberland apprises Lancaster of Richard's presence at Flint. Creton informs his readers that he will now change to writing in prose.

Northomberlant au duc Henry manda
Trestoute* nuit que le roy amena;
Le chevaucheur[1027] droit[1028] a Cestre arriva
 Au point du jour.   2272
Au duc Henry compta trestout le tour
Du roy Richart,[1029] qui a Flint fist sejour.
Au cuer en ot grant joie et grant baudour
 Et a bon droit,   2276
Car[1030] en ce monde[1031] plus riens ne desiroit.
Autour de Cestre[1032] trestout son ost estoit
Logié aux[1033] champs qui grant païs tenoit.
 Lors fist crier   2280
Q'un[1034] chascun feust tantost prest pour aler[1035]
Avecques lui, ou les vouldra[1036] mener;
Mainte trompete firent Englés sonner
 Et retentir.   2284
Or vous vueil dire sans plus rime querir
Du roy la prinse. Et pour mieulx acomplir
Les paroles qu'ilz dirent au[1037] venir
 Eulx deux ensemble –   2288
Car retenues les ay bien, ce me semble[1038] –
Si les diray en prose, car il semble
Aucunesfoiz qu'on adjouste ou assemble
 Trop de langaige   2292
[fo. 46v.] A la matiere de[1039] quoy on fait ouvrage.[1040]
Or vueille Dieux, qui nous fist a s'image,
 Pugnir tous ceulx qui firent tel[1041] oultrage. 2295

[1027] AD chevalier
[1028] H droit *superscript* ABCD *no* droit
[1029] B du roy ~~rch~~ richart
[1030] L *no* car
[1031] H en [*erasure*] monde LABCD en ce monde
[1032] H autour [*erasure*] cestre LABCD autour de cestre
[1033] C au
[1034] L que
[1035] B pour en aler
[1036] AD vouldroit
[1037] B a
[1038] L *line 2289 omitted*
[1039] AD par
[1040] AD oultrage
[1041] LCD cel

§30 Lancaster leaves Chester and descends on Flint with his army.

In this part [you will hear of] the sorrow and suffering endured by King Richard, who was in the castle of Flint awaiting the arrival of the duke of Lancaster.

He left Chester on Tuesday 22 August 1399[123] with all his army, estimated by several knights and squires at more than 100,000 men, arrayed for battle and riding along the seashore,[124] full of joy and pleasure and eager for the capture of their natural and rightful lord, King Richard.

On the said Tuesday he got up early, attended by suffering, sadness and sorrow: by lamentations, tears and groans. He heard Mass very devoutly, as a good Christian should, with his true friends the earl of Salisbury, the bishop of Carlisle, Sir Stephen Scrope and one other knight named Ferriby; they all refused to abandon or desert the King, whatever hardship or ill fortune befell him. Also with them was the son of the countess of Salisbury[125] whom King Richard had knighted in Ireland along with the eldest son of the duke of Lancaster and several others, as I have told you in the first part of this work.

There too was Janico,[126] a Gascon squire, who certainly demonstrated the true love [fo. 47r.] he bore King Richard, for despite threats from knights or squires, or any request whatever, he would not take off the badge of his lord the King – the hart[127] – saying:

---

[123] Page 187, lines 6–7. *le mardi .xxii.ᵉ jour d'aoust*. An impossible date in 1399, see Palmer, 'French Chronicles', 61:2 (1979), p. 420. Perhaps Creton's date here should be Friday 15 August; this would fit with Richard celebrating the feast of the Assumption, 15 August, at Flint on that day, *infra*, p. 197, l. 5, and note. To the known sources for the date of Richard's capture should be added: WAM, Book 1 (Liber Niger Quaternus), fo. 86v.: 'in vigilia assumptionis Beate Marie [14 August] captus est et se submisit ordinacioni prelatorum et procerum Anglie'. Richard seems already to have been in Chester on 16–17 August, see Clarke, *Fourteenth-Century Studies*, p. 71 n. 1.

[124] Page 187, line 10. *parmi la greve de la mer*. Flint is about fifteen miles from the sea. Henry's army is riding along the marshes of the River Dee, which are several miles wide at this point.

[125] Page 187, line 20–21. *un qui fu filz de la contesse de Salsebery*. Salisbury had married before 1383 Maud Francis, widow of 1. John Aubrey, and 2. Sir Alan Buxhull. By the latter she had a posthumous son, Alan. See *ODNB*, s.v. 'Buxhull, Sir Alan (1323?–1381)', and 'Montagu [*née* Raunceys], Maud, countess of Salisbury (d.1424)'. See supra, ll. 149–150.

[126] Page 187, line 24. *Genico*. Supra, l. 853, note.

[127] Page 187, lines 27–28. *la devise ... le roy ... le cerf*. Richard's badge of the white hart, first distributed by him at Smithfield in 1390, is thought to have been derived from his mother, Princess Joan of Kent. See Gordon and others (eds), *Regal Image of Richard II*, pp. 100–102, 169; Saul, *Richard II*, p. 440.

§30 Lancaster leaves Chester and descends on Flint with his army.

En ceste partie, des affliccions et douleurs esquelles le roy Richart estoit ou chastel de Flint atendant la venue du duc de Lancastre.

Le quel se parti de la ville de Cestre le mardi .xxii.^{e} jour d'aoust en l'an de l'incarnacion NostreSeigneur mil .ccc iiii^{xx}.xix.,[1042] a toute sa puissance, la quele j'oÿ estimer[1043] a plusieurs chevaliers et escuiers a cent mille hommes[1044] passez, ordonnez comme pour entrer en bataille,[1045] chevauchant[1046] parmi la greve de la mer a grant joie et a[1047] grant dillectacion de plaisir, et[1048] aussi desirant[1049] la prinse de leur droit et naturel seigneur, le roy Richart.

Le quel se leva le dit mardi bien matin acompaignié de douleurs, de tristresses, d'affliccions: de plains, de pleurs et de gemissemens, oÿ la messe moult[1050] devotement comme vray[1051] catholique* avecques ses bons amis,[1052] le conte de Salsebery, l'evesque de Kerlille, Messire Estienne Scroup[1053] et un[1054] autre chevalier appellé Ferbric; les quelx, pour adversité nulle ne pour[1055] fortune quelconques que le dit roy eust, ne le vouldrent laissier ne relenquir. Encores avoit avecques eulx un[1056] qui fu filz de la contesse de Salsebery, le quel le roy Richart avoit fait nouvel[1057] chevalier en Irlande avecques le filz ainsné du duc de Lancastre et avec plusieurs autres, comme je vous ay dit es premieres parties de ceste matiere.

Et si estoit[1058] Genico, un[1059] escuier gascon, le quel monstra bien la vraie amour [fo. 47r.] qu'il avoit au roy Richart, car oncques, pour[1060] menaces de chevaliers ne escuiers[1061] ne pour priere nulle quelconques, ne volt oster la devise de son seigneur le roy – c'est assavoir le cerf – disant:

[1042] LC mil .ccc iiii^{xx} et xix.
[1043] B laquelle ja royestimoit [joy superscript] estimer
[1044] H homme C no hommes
[1045] C comme a entre en bataille
[1046] L chevauchans
[1047] L no a
[1048] L no et
[1049] H aussi disirant L ainsi desirans
[1050] C no moult
[1051] C bon
[1052] B bons ar amis
[1053] AD guillaume seroup
[1054] D une
[1055] B par
[1056] A ung avec eulx B avecques [eulx superscript] ung
[1057] L no nouvel
[1058] L et si y estoit
[1059] A genier
[1060] BC par
[1061] LBC descuiers

'God forbid that for any man I take off the badge of my rightful lord, unless he himself tells me to.'

And so it was that the duke of Lancaster heard about it and had him taken in shame and disgrace to Chester Castle, where he expected from day to day to lose his head, for that was what people were generally saying. And yet he did not die – as I heard since – but I can assure you that he was the last man in England wearing the badge of King Richard. Thus did he truly show that he would not change sides lightly, nor was he of the English race.

As for their race and character,[128] they do change sides lightly, always ranging themselves with the strongest and most powerful, without regard to right, law, reason or justice. And this is not only nowadays, but they have deposed and killed their king and lord several times,[129] as you can learn from various chronicles and histories.

In order not to digress too much from the matter I am discussing, I do not wish to write further about their character and condition for now, but to return to King Richard. Having heard Mass, he climbed up onto the castle walls, which are wide and broad, and watched the duke of Lancaster coming along the seashore[130] with all his men, wonderfully great in number, expressing such joy and satisfaction that you could hear within the castle the sound of their instruments: [fo. 47v.] horns, bugles and trumpets. And then the King commended himself to the blessed protection of Our Lord and all the saints in Paradise, saying:

§31 Richard foresees his coming death.

'Alas! Now I can see that the end of my days draws near, since I must be delivered into the hands of my enemies, who mortally hate me, without my deserving it.

---

[128] Page 189, line 10. *la generacion et nature d'eulx*. **D** has a heading in a contemporary hand in the left-hand margin: *la condicion des Angloiz*.

[129] Page 189, lines 13. *plusieurs foiz ont ilz ... destruit leur roy*. An exaggeration; the parallel is with the deposition of Edward II in 1327. See M. McKisack, *The Fourteenth Century 1307–1399* (Oxford, 1959), pp. 88–96.

[130] Page 189, line 19. *la greve de la mer*. In fact the Dee marshes. *Supra*, l. 1683, note.

'Ja Dieu ne plaise que pour homme mortel je oste l'ordre de mon droit[1062] seigneur, se li[1063] propre ne le commande.'[1064]

Et tant que le duc de Lanclastre le sçot, le quel le fist mener[1065] honteusement et vilainement ou chastel de Cestre, atendant de jour en jour que on lui trenchast la teste, car c'estoit la commune renommee du peuple. Et toutesvoies il n'en moru pas – sicomme j'ay oÿ[1066] dire depuis – maiz je vous sçay[1067] bien a dire que il[1068] fu le derrenier portant l'ordre du[1069] roy Richart en Engleterre. Et la monstra il bien qu'il n'estoit pas favorable de legier ne de leur generacion extrait.

Et[1070] quant est de la generacion et nature d'eulx, ilz sont favorables de legier, eulx tenant[1071] tousjours au plus fort[1072] et[1073] au mieulx[1074] parant[1075] sans garder droit,[1076] loy, raison ne justice. Et ce n'est pas de[1077] maintenant, car plusieurs foiz ont ilz deffait et destruit[1078] leur roy et seigneur, comme on le peut savoir par plusieurs ystoires[1079] et croniques.

Et affin que je ne m'alongne[1080] pas trop de la matiere que j'ay ouverte, de leur nature ne de leur condicion, ne vueil plus parler pour le present, maiz retourner au roy Richart.[1081] Le quel, la messe oïe, monta sur[1082] les murs du dit chastel, qui sont[1083] grans et larges par dedens, regardant venir parmy la greve de la mer le duc de Lancastre a tout son ost qui estoit merveilleusement grant, demenant tele[1084] joie et consolacion, que jusques au dit chastel on ouoit le son et bruit[1085] de leurs instrumens: [fo. 47v.] cors, buisines[1086] et trompetes. Et lors se recommanda[1087] en la[1088] sainte garde de[1089] Nostre Seigneur et de tous les[1090] sains de Paradis, disant en telle maniere:

§31 Richard foresees his coming death.

'Helas! Or voy je bien que la fin de mes jours aproche, puis qu'il fault que je soie livrez[1091] es[1092] mains de mes ennemis, les quelz me heent[1093] a mort, et sans l'avoir desservi.

[1062] B mon ~~seigneur~~ droit
[1063] B se ~~loy~~ ly
[1064] AD ne le me commande
[1065] B lequel ~~fist~~ le fist mettre
[1066] AD joy
[1067] C fay
[1068] AD se
[1069] D lordre ~~richart en eng~~ du
[1070] AD car
[1071] LABCD tenans
[1072] B fors
[1073] C *no* et
[1074] L plus
[1075] AD au plus parant et au plus fort B apparent
[1076] B sans garder ~~loy~~ droit
[1077] B nest [pas *superscript*] de
[1078] C *no* et destruit
[1079] H ystoieres
[1080] LA mesloingne
[1081] B *no* richart
[1082] L sus
[1083] AD la messe ouye ou dit chastel de flint monta sur les murs qui sont B qui ~~soie~~ sont
[1084] B *no* tele
[1085] AD bruyt et son
[1086] B cors et buisines
[1087] C commanda
[1088] AB a la C en sa
[1089] L *no* de
[1090] C ses
[1091] L livre
[1092] C entre les [*no* livrez es]
[1093] C heet

Earl of Northumberland, you should certainly be hugely afraid that Our Lord God will take revenge for the sin you committed when you so shamefully forswore Him to draw us from Conway, where we were completely safe. May God now repay you for this.'

§32 Lancaster takes Richard into his custody at Flint. He guarantees the safety of Creton and his companion.

Thus spoke King Richard to the earl of Salisbury, the bishop of Carlisle and the two knights – Sir Stephen Scrope and Ferriby – weeping softly on the castle walls and giving vent to great sorrow; certainly I believe that no one in this mortal world – be he Jew or Saracen – having seen the five of them together, would not have been filled with pity and compassion.

Lamenting thus, they saw a great number of men leaving duke Henry's army and spurring on towards the castle to find out what King Richard was doing. In this first party were the Archbishop of Canterbury, Sir Thomas Percy and the earl of Rutland,[131] from whom duke Henry had taken the office of Constable of England and the duchy of Aumale, which he had previously held of King Richard. But I firmly believe that he did this under a pretext and to throw sand in people's eyes, lest they think Rutland knew anything about the affair or the betrayal, rather than otherwise.

And yet I know not whether he did have any inkling of it, but [fo. 48r.] I do know for sure that he and Sir Thomas Percy, who had been the King's Steward – that is to say in French *grant maistre d'ostel* – left the port of Milford Haven and took with them the King's men and his treasure, of which they were robbed in Wales, as I told you previously.[132] They joined the duke – as it appears – for they were among the first coming to the castle of Flint, wearing duke Henry's badge,[133] not the hart.

---

[131] Page 191, lines 17–22. *le conte de Rotelant ... du fait ne de la träyson*. Another Constable was appointed (*infra*, ll. 2709–2711, 2759–2772) after Lancaster was elected as the new King. Rutland was deprived of his ducal title in the first parliament of Henry IV. See Given-Wilson, *Henry IV*, pp. 159–160, and n. 9. These two events happened before the Epiphany Rising, thus a wish to blind the country to Rutland's role in betraying it – *du fait ne de la träyson*, p. 191, ll. 22 – could not have been Lancaster's motive for the degradation.

[132] Page 191, line 28. *comme je vous ay dit devant*. *Supra*, ll. 945–1065.

[133] Page 191, lines 30. *l'ordre du duc Henry*. Probably the Lancasterian collar of esses. *Supra*, l. 1058, note.

Certe, conte de Northomberlant, vous devez avoir grant peur et freeur[1094] au cuer que Nostre Sire[1095] Dieux ne preingne vengence du pechié que vous feistes, quant vous le parjurastes ainsi villainement pour nous attraire hors de Cornüay, ou nous estions bien asseur. Or vous en vueille Dieux rendre[1096] le guerredon!'

§32 Lancaster takes Richard into his custody at Flint. He guarantees the safety of Creton and his companion.

Ainsi disoit le roy Richart au conte de Salsebery, a l'evesque de Kerlille et aux deux chevaliers – Sire Estienne Scroup[1097] et Ferbric – plourant moult[1098] tendrement et demenant grant dueil sur[1099] les diz murs du chastel; et tel que[1100] certes je croy qu'en ce mortel monde n'a creature quelconque[1101] – soit Juif ou Sarrasin – les avoir[1102] veuz eulx cinq ensemble, qui n'en eust eu[1103] grant pitié et compacion au cuer.

Ce dueil faisant, virent departir de l'ost du duc Henry grant quantité de gens chevauchant[1104] a force d'esperons devers le chastel pour savoir que le roy Richart[1105] faisoit. En ceste premiere compaignie estoit l'arcevesque de Cantorbie, Messire Thomas de Persi et le conte de Rotelant, au quel le duc Henry avoit osté la possession de la connestablie d'Engleterre et la duchie d'Aumarle, qu'il tenoit par avant de par le roy Richart. Maiz je croy[1106] fermement qu'il lui osta plus par ficcion et pour aveugler le monde, afin telle c'on ne cuidast mie qu'il sceut riens du fait ne de la traÿson que autrement.[1107]

Et toutesvoies ne say je[1108] pas s'il en[1109] savoit riens, maiz [fo. 48r.] je say bien[1110] tout certain[1111] que lui et Messire Thomas de Persi, le quel avoit esté estuuart du roy – c'est a dire en françoiz grant maistre d'ostel – se partirent du port de Mileforde et enmenerent[1112] ses gens et son avoir, par quoy ilz[1113] furent destroussez en Galles, comme je vous ay dit[1114] devant. Et s'en alerent devers le duc[1115] – comme il appert – car ilz[1116] vindrent ou[1117] chastel de Flint tous des[1118] premiers, portant l'ordre[1119] du duc Henry, non pas le[1120] cerf.

[1094] AD et grant freeur
[1095] LACD nostreseigneur
[1096] A donner D no rendre
[1097] AD guillaume seroup
[1098] H moul
[1099] L sus
[1100] B no que
[1101] L quelconques
[1102] L avoit
[1103] B quil en eust [eu superscript]
[1104] LABCD chevauchans
[1105] AD no richart
[1106] AD cuide
[1107] AD no que autrement
[1108] AD je ne scay
[1109] B ne
[1110] B no bien
[1111] H je say bien tout certain que A de certain
[1112] B amenerent
[1113] C pourquoy ils
[1114] H no ay
[1115] C le duc henry
[1116] C il
[1117] B au
[1118] A les
[1119] LB portans C portant ordre
[1120] A de

The archbishop entered first and the others after him; they climbed up to the keep. Then the King came down from the walls and they made most humble obeisance, kneeling before him. The King made them rise to their feet and drew the archbishop aside; they spoke together for a long time. I know not what they said, but the earl of Salisbury told me later that the archbishop had comforted the King most tenderly, saying that he should not be afraid and that no bodily harm would befall him. At this point the earl of Rutland spoke no word to the King, rather kept as far from him as he could, as though he were ashamed to be seen in his presence.

The party remounted and returned to duke Henry, who was coming up fast, for between the town of Chester and the castle of Flint there are only ten short miles[134] – round about five French leagues, or so – and there is no hedge or bush between the two, but merely the seashore[135] and the high rocks and boulders on the other side. And know for sure that they made a fine sight, for they were very well arrayed and so great in number, that it seems to me I had never seen so many men together. The principal commander of duke Henry's army was Sir Henry Percy[136] [fo. 48v.] whom they say is the foremost knight of England.

The King climbed back up onto the walls and saw that the army was only two bowshots from the castle. Then he lamented loudly again – and the others with him – uttering many heart-rending regrets for his wife, Isabella of France. He praised Our Lord Jesus Christ, saying,

'Dear Lord God, I commend myself to Thy blessed protection and beg that Thou wilt forgive me all my sins, since it is Thy pleasure that I be delivered into the hands of mine enemies. If they kill me, I will accept my death with meekness, as Thou didst for the sake of us all.'

---

[134] Page 193, line 13. *dix mille petites*. Flint is almost fifteen miles from Chester.

[135] Page 193, lines 15–16. *la greve de la mer ... et les haultes roches ... d'autre costé*. Looking upstream towards Chester, Richard and his party had the broad estuary on their left hand and the mountainous interior on their right.

[136] Page 193, line 19–20. *Messire Henry de Persi*. Hotspur, son of the earl of Northumberland. He ultimately rebelled against Henry IV and was killed at the Battle of Shrewsbury, 1403. See *ODNB*, s.v. 'Percy, Sir Henry [*called* Henry Hotspur] (1364–1403)'.

L'arcevesque entra le premier et[1121] les autres aprés; ilz monterent ou donjon. Lors le roy descendi des murs, au quel ilz[1122] firent tres-grant[1123] reverence agenoilliez a terre. Le roy les fist lever et tira l'archevesque a part, et parlerent moult longuement ensemble. Qu'ilz[1124] dirent je ne sçay pas, maiz le conte de Salsebery me dist aprés qu'il l'avoit[1125] reconforté moult doulcement, disant qu'il ne[1126] feust esbahis[1127] et qu'il n'aroit nul mal de son corps. Le conte de Rotelant ne parla point[1128] a celle heure au roy, ains[1129] s'alongnoit[1130] de lui[1131] le plus qu'il povoit, ainsi comme[1132] s'il[1133] eust esté honteux de se[1134] voir devant lui.[1135]

Ilz remonterent a cheval et s'en retournerent[1136] au devant du duc Henry, le quel aprochoit fort, car entre la ville de Cestre et le chastel n'a que dix mille petites[1137] – qui valent cinq lieues françoises ou environ – et n'y a haie ne[1138] buisson nul entredeux, fors la greve de[1139] la mer seulement et les haultes roches et montaignes d'autre costé. Et sachiez de certain qu'il les faisoit bel voir venir, car ilz estoient tres-bien ordonnez et si grant quantité que – tant qu'a[1140] moy – je ne vis oncques tant de gens[1141] ensemble, ce m'est advis. De tout l'ost du duc estoit principal capitaine Messire Henry de Persi, qu'ilz[1142] [fo. 48v.] tiennent pour le meilleur chevalier d'Engleterre.

Le roy remonta sur[1143] les murs et vit que l'ost estoit a deux trais d'arc pres[1144] du chastel. Alors demena grant dueil de rechief[1145] – et les autres qui estoient avecques lui – faisant[1146] moult de piteux regrés de sa compaigne, Ysabel de France, et loua[1147] Nostre Seigneur Jhesucrist, disant:

'Beau Sire Dieux,[1148] je me recommande en[1149] ta sainte garde, et te crie mercy que tu me vueilles pardonner tous mes[1150] pechiez, puis qu'il te plaist que je[1151] soie livrez[1152] es[1153] mains de mes ennemis. Et s'il[1154] me font morir, je prendray la mort en pasience, comme tu le[1155] prins* pour nous tous.'

[1121] ACD le premier dedans et
[1122] C il
[1123] C grant
[1124] C quil
[1125] H quil lavoit B quilz lavoient
[1126] H quil ne
[1127] L esbahy
[1128] L pas
[1129] L mais
[1130] LB sesloingnoit
[1131] B ly
[1132] A que
[1133] B no sil
[1134] B soy
[1135] B ly
[1136] C et allerent [no sen]
[1137] L .x. milles bien petites
[1138] L no ne
[1139] L et
[1140] A quant a
[1141] D oncques tout [tant superscript]
[1142] C quil
[1143] L sus
[1144] AD no pres
[1145] C no de rechief
[1146] C faisoient
[1147] C voua
[1148] H dieux superscript L no dieux B beaux sire pere
[1149] L a
[1150] B mes superscript
[1151] B no je
[1152] L livre
[1153] C entre les
[1154] LD silz
[1155] AD no le BC la

As he thus spoke, the army approached the castle and surrounded it in fine array, as far as the waters permitted. Then the earl of Northumberland went up to duke Henry, who was assembled with his men at the foot of the castle rock. They conferred for a considerable time and decided that the duke would not enter the castle until the King had dined, because he was fasting; thus the earl returned to the castle. When the table was prepared, the King sat down to dinner and had the bishop of Carlisle, the earl of Salisbury and the two knights – Sir Stephen Scrope and Ferriby – sit down, saying thus:

'My good, true and loyal friends, since you are in mortal danger for being loyal, be seated with me.'

Meanwhile a great number of knights, squires and archers detached themselves from duke Henry's army and came to the castle, eager to see their King, not for any good that they wished him, but on account of their great desire to put him to death. They went to see him dine and gave it to be understood [fo. 49r.] throughout the castle that, as soon as the duke came, all those who were with the King – bar none – would lose their heads; and they said furthermore that they knew not whether the King would be spared or not.

When this news was heard, fear struck into everyone's heart, for Nature teaches every creature to fear death above all things. As for me, I do not think that I was ever so afraid as I was then, considering the utter contempt they showed and their total disregard for law, right or loyalty. And because Nature compelled me to fear death, my companion and I approached Lancaster Herald, who had come to the castle along with a great number of men to see the King. I begged him that for the love of Our Lord he would help us save our lives, and that he would please take us to duke Henry, his master; he replied that he would do so most willingly.

Ainsi disant, aproucha l'ost du chastel et l'environna tout jusques a la mer par tresbelle[1156] ordonnance. Lors ala le conte de Northomberlant devers le duc Henry, le quel estoit rengié avecques ses gens au pié des montaignes. Ilz parlerent assez longuement ensemble et conclurrent qu'il[1157] n'entreroit[1158] point ou[1159] chastel, jusques a tant que le roy eust disné, pour la cause de ce[1160] qu'il jeunoit;[1161] ainsi le conte retourna ou[1162] dit chastel. La table mise, le roy s'assist au disner et fist asseoir l'evesque de Kerlille, le conte[1163] de Salsebery et les deux chevaliers – Sire Estienne Scroup[1164] et Ferbric – disant en telle maniere:

'Mes bons, vrais et[1165] loyaulx* amis, estant[1166] en peril de mort pour loyaulté maintenir,[1167] sëez vous avecques moy.'

Cependent se departirent grant quantité de chevaliers, d'escuiers et d'archiers[1168] de l'ost du duc Henry et vindrent ou dit chastel, desirans[1169] a[1170] veoir leur roy,[1171] non pas[1172] pour bien qu'ilz lui voulsissent, maiz pour[1173] la grant ardeur qu'ilz avoient de le destruire et faire morir. Ilz l'alerent voir disner et publierent [fo. 49r.] par tout le chastel que, tantost que le duc seroit venus, tous ceulx qui estoient avecques luy[1174] – sans nul excepter – avroient les[1175] testes tranchees; et encores disoient ilz que on ne savoit[1176] mie se[1177] le roy eschaperoit[1178] ou non.

Ces nouvelles oÿes, un chascun pour soy ot grant paour et grant freeur au cuer, car Nature ensengne a toute creature craindre et redoubter[1179] la mort plus que nule autre chose. Et[1180] tant qu'a moy, je[1181] ne cuide mie que jamaiz j'aie[1182] si grant paour comme j'euz pour l'eure, consideré la grant desrision d'eulx et le non voloir[1183] entendre droit, raison ne loyaulté.[1184] Et pour ce que Nature me contraingnoit d'avoir freeur de la mort, mon compaignon et moy advisames Lancastre le herault, le quel avec[1185] grant quantité de gens estoit venu[1186] ou[1187] dit chastel devers le roy. Si lui priay que pour l'amour de Nostre Seigneur il nous aidast a sauver la vie, et qu'il lui pleust de[1188] nous mener devers le duc Henry, son maistre; lors nous respondi qu'il le feroit tresvolentiers.

[1156] C *no* tres
[1157] D quilz
[1158] B nentreroient
[1159] C au
[1160] AD *no* de ce
[1161] H jeunoit
[1162] ABD au
[1163] AD et le conte
[1164] AD messire guillaume seroup
[1165] B *no* et
[1166] LACD estans
[1167] B *no* maintenir
[1168] L et escuriers et archiers
[1169] C desirant
[1170] L de C *no* a
[1171] L *no* leur roy
[1172] AD mye
[1173] AD par
[1174] L avecques le roy
[1175] B aroient le
[1176] C quilz ne savoient
[1177] C si
[1178] L en eschaperoit
[1179] C *no* et redoubter
[1180] L en
[1181] AD certes je
[1182] A je aye eu D je aye plus
[1183] L et non voulans
[1184] AD loyaute ne raison
[1185] C avoit
[1186] ACD venus
[1187] AD au
[1188] C *no* de

The King sat a very long time at table, not that he ate much, but because he knew well that as soon as he had eaten, the duke would come to fetch him to take him away or to have him killed; also he was left a long time at table because he was fasting for Our Lady.[137] After he had dined, the Archbishop of Canterbury and the earl of Northumberland went to fetch the duke of Lancaster, who left his men splendidly arrayed in front of the castle and came to the King, with nine or eleven of the greatest lords who were of his company.

[fo. 49v.] At the entrance to the castle, Lancaster Herald took us to the duke. Kneeling before him, the said herald told him in English that we were French, that the King [of France] had sent us to Ireland with King Richard, as a diversion and to see the country, and that for God's sake he wished to have our lives spared. Then replied the duke to us in French:

'Be not afraid of anything you see, my sons,[138] but stay close to me and I will keep you safe.'

This reply fell most joyfully on our ears.

Then the duke entered the castle, wearing all his armour except for his helmet, as you can see in this picture.[139] Then the King, who had dined in the keep, was made to come down and meet duke Henry who, as soon as he caught sight of him, bowed low to the ground; as they approached one another he bowed a second time, with his hat in his hand. And then the King took off his cowl and spoke first, addressing the duke thus:

---

[137] Page 197, line 5. *il jeunoit les marseces*. *Marseche(s)* is commonly attested as meaning 'feast of the Annunciation'. But Lady Day is 25 March and this is August. Creton probably means the feast of the Assumption, 15 August. Richard had an especial veneration for the Virgin Mary, and would naturally celebrate this day. See Sherborne, *War, Politics and Culture*, p. 149 n. 57.

[138] Page 197, line 17. *Mes enfans. Supra*, Introduction, p. 27.

[139] Page 197, line 21. *comme vous povez veoir en ceste ystoire*. A reference to Figure XIV, at the head of fo. 50r., showing Lancaster making obeisance to Richard.

Le roy fu a table moult longuement, non mie[1189] pour chose qu'il mengast gueres, maiz pour ce qu'il savoit bien que, tantost qu'il avroit disné, le duc[1190] le venroit[1191] querre pour l'enmener[1192] ou pour le faire mourir; et aussi[1193] ilz[1194] le laisserent longuement a table, pour la cause de ce qu'il[1195] jeunoit les marseces.[1196] Aprés ce qu'il ot disné, l'archevesque de Cantorbie et le conte de Northomberlant alerent querre[1197] le duc de Lancastre, le quel se parti d'avecques ses gens, qui estoient rengez par tresbelle ordonnance devant le chastel, et s'en vint, lui .x.ᵉ ou lui .xii.ᵉ[1198] des plus grans seigneurs qui estoient avecques lui, devers le roy.

[fo. 49v.] A l'entree[1199] du chastel nous mena Lancastre le herault devant le duc.[1200] Agenoilliez a terre lui dist[1201]* le dit herault en langage englesch que nous estions de France, et que le roy nous avoit envoié[1202] avecques le roy Richart en Irlande pour esbatre et pour veoir le païs, et que pour Dieu il nous voulsist sauver la vie. Et lors nous respondi le duc en françoiz:

'Mes enfans, n'aiez paour ne freeur de chose que vous voiez, et vous tenez pres de moy, et je vous garantiray la vie.'

Ceste response nous fu[1203] moult joieuse a oÿr.[1204]

Aprés entra le duc ou chastel, armé de toutes pieces excepté de bacinet, comme[1205] vous povez veoir en ceste ystoire.[1206] Lors fist on descendre le roy, qui avoit[1207] disné ou dongon, et venir a l'encontre du duc Henry le quel, de si loing qu'il l'avisa,[1208] s'enclina assez bas a tere;[1209] et en aprouchant l'un de l'autre, il s'enclina la seconde foiz, son chapel en sa[1210] main. Et lors le roy osta son chapperon et parla premier,[1211] disant en telle maniere:

[1189] H mie *superscript* LB *no* mie
[1190] C que le duc
[1191] C viendroit
[1192] B lamener
[1193] AD ainsy
[1194] B *no* ilz
[1195] A pour cause de quil B pour ce quil D pour cause de ce quil
[1196] H marseces AD marseches B marchesses
[1197] C querir
[1198] B ly disieme ou ly .xi.ᵉ
[1199] B lentre
[1200] AD le duc henry
[1201] *all mss* et lui dist
[1202] LACD envoyes
[1203] B fust
[1204] B a joye [*no* oyr]
[1205] C ainsi comme
[1206] A *no* comme vous povez veoir en ceste ystoire
[1207] C ot
[1208] B quil advisa
[1209] B *no* a tere
[1210] LBC la
[1211] L premiers AD le premier

[fo. 50r.] Figure XIV: Lancaster makes obeisance to King Richard at Flint.

§33 Lancaster meets the King at Flint; their exact words are reported.

'Fair cousin of Lancaster, you are most welcome.'

Then duke Henry replied, bowing low to the ground:

'Monseigneur, I have come sooner than you asked; I will tell you the reason why. Your people regularly say that for twenty or twenty-two years you have ruled them very badly and with an iron hand, such that they are not happy. But please God I will help you to govern them better than they have been ruled in the past.'

Then King Richard replied:

'Fair cousin of Lancaster, since that is your wish, it is our wish too.'

And know for sure [fo. 50v.] that these are the very words that they exchanged with nothing taken out or added, for I heard them quite clearly. Also the earl of Salisbury repeated them to me in French, along with another old knight – one of duke Henry's councillors – who told me as we were riding to Chester that Merlin and Bede[140] had foretold in their lifetime the capture and death of the King; were I in his castle he would show me their prophecy as I had seen it happening. He said:

§34 The prophecy of Merlin and Bede.

'There will be a king in England who will reign between 20 and 22 years in great majesty and power. He will be allied and connected to the people of France; the said king will be undone in the north of the country, in a three-cornered place.'

The knight told me that thus it was written in a book of his.

---

[140] Page 199, lines 20–21. *avoient Merlin et Bede prophecisé*. Creton is typical of his time in invoking their joint testimony. Cf Christine de Pizan, *Ditié de Jehanne d'Arc*, ed. A.J. Kennedy and K. Varty (Oxford, 1977), p. 34, ll. 241–248. Also Deschamps, *Oeuvres complètes*, ed. de Queux and Raynaud, I, no. 26, p. 106, l. 6; VI, no. 1200, p. 185, l. 18; and Cropp and Hanham, 'Richard II from donkey to royal martyr', pp. 111–117. Like most prophecies, those in the *Prinse et mort* came to light after the event. See Strohm, *England's Empty Throne*, pp. 6–8.

[fo. 50r.] Figure XIV: Lancaster makes obeisance to King Richard at Flint.

§33 Lancaster meets the King at Flint; their exact words are reported.

'Beau cousin de Lancastre, vous soiez le tresbienvenu.'[1212] Lors respondi le duc Henry, encliné assés bas a terre:[1213] 'Monseigneur, je sui venu[1214] plus tost que vous[1215] ne m'avez mandé; la raison pour quoy, je le vous diray. La commune renommee de vostre peuple si est telle: que vous[1216] les avez par l'espace de .xx. ou .xxii.[1217] ans tresmauvaisement et tresrigoreusement gouvernez, et tant qu'ilz n'en sont pas bien content.[1218] Maiz s'il plaist a Nostre Seigneur, je le[1219] vous aideray a gouverner mieulx[1220] qu'il n'a[1221] esté gouverné[1222] le[1223] temps passé.'
  Le roy Richart lui respondi alors:
'Beau cousin de Lancastre, puis qu'il vous plaist, il nous plaist bien.'[1224]
  Et sachiez de certain[1225] [fo. 50v.] que ce sont les propres paroles qu'ilz dirent eulx deux ensemble, sans y riens prendre ne adjouster, car je les oÿ et entendi assez bien. Et si le mes[1226]* recorda le conte de Salsebery en françoiz et un autre ancien chevalier,[1227] qui estoit des conseilliers du duc Henry, le quel me dist en chevauchant a Cestre que la prise du roy et la destruccion avoient[1228] Merlin et Bede prophecisé[1229] des leur vivant; et que se j'estoie en son chastel, il le[1230] me monsterroit en la forme et maniere[1231] comme je l'avoie veu advenir, disant ainsi:

§34 The prophecy of Merlin and Bede.

'Il aura un roy en Albie,* le quel regnera l'espace de[1232] .xx. a[1233] .xxii. ans en grant honneur et en grant puissance. Et sera alié et adjoint[1234] avecques ceulx de Gaule; le quel roy sera desfait es parties du nort en une place triangle.'
  Ainsi me[1235] dist le chevalier qu'il estoit escript[1236] en un sien[1237] livre.

[1212] ACD tres bienvenus
[1213] AD a la terre
[1214] ACD venus
[1215] B *no* vous
[1216] AD *no* vous
[1217] BCD ou de .xxii.
[1218] LB comptens
[1219] AD desormais je les
[1220] C mielx a gouverner
[1221] A quilz nont
[1222] LACD gouvernez
[1223] L du
[1224] B *no* il nous plaist bien
[1225] C *no* de certain
[1226] LACD les me B me les
[1227] B chevalier ancien
[1228] B avoit
[1229] L prophetie
[1230] B *no* le
[1231] AD *no* et maniere B et la maniere
[1232] C *no* lespace de
[1233] ABC ou D ou de
[1234] ACD aliez et ajoins
[1235] A ainsy le me
[1236] C estoit ainsi escript
[1237] C son

He identified the three-cornered place as the town of Conway, and in this he was right, for I can tell you that it is triangular, as if it had been measured exactly. The King was completely undone in the said town of Conway, for the earl of Northumberland drew him out – as you have already heard – by means of the agreement that he made with him; since then the King was powerless.

Thus did the said knight hold this prophecy to be true and lent it great credence, for their character is such in their country that they believe wholeheartedly in prophecies, ghosts and spells and have great recourse to them. But it seems to me that this is not a good thing, but is rather a great lapse of faith.

§35 Richard leaves Flint in Lancaster's custody.

[fo. 51r.] As you have heard, duke Henry came to the castle and spoke to the King, to the bishop of Carlisle and to the two knights – Sir Stephen Scrope and Ferriby – but he did not speak to the earl of Salisbury. Rather did he have a knight say to him:

'Earl of Salisbury,[141] you can be sure that, for as much as you would not consent to speak to Monseigneur the duke of Lancaster when he and you were in Paris last Christmas, he will not speak to you.'

Then the earl of Salisbury was very afraid and his heart filled with dread, for he could see[142] that the duke mortally hated him.

Duke Henry said in a fierce and merciless voice:

'Bring the King's horses.'

And then two sorry nags, scarcely worth 40 francs, were brought to him. The King mounted on one and the earl of Salisbury on the other. Everyone got on horseback and we left the castle of Flint around two hours after midday.

---

[141] Page 201, line 18. *Conte de Salsebery*. *Supra*, Introduction, pp. 24–25.

[142] Page 201, line 23. il *vëoit bien que le duc le haioit mortelement*. This was Salisbury's realization that he was in poor standing with Lancaster. *Supra*, ll. 2156–2164 and note.

LA PRINSE ET MORT DU ROY RICHART D'ANGLETERRE   201

La place triangle, il l'aproprioit[1238] a la ville de Cornüay, et de ce avoit il[1239] tresbonne raison, car je vous say[1240] bien a dire qu'elle est en triangle, comme[1241] se[1242] elle eust esté[1243] ainsi[1244] compassee par vraie et[1245] juste mesure. En la dicte ville de Cornüay fu le roy assez desfait, car le conte de Northomberlant le tira hors[1246] – comme vous avez oÿ devant – par le traittié qu'il fist a lui; et depuis n'ot nulle puissance.

Ainsi tenoit le dit chevalier ceste prophecie vraie et y adjoustoit grant foy,[1247] car il[1248] sont* de telle nature en leur pays que en prophecies,[1249] en fanthomes[1250] et[1251] sorceries croient tresparfaitement et en usent tresvolentiers.[1252] Maiz il m'est advis que ce n'est pas bien fait, ains est[1253] grant faulte de creance.

§35 Richard leaves Flint in Lancaster's custody.

[fo. 51r.] **A**insi comme vous avez oÿ, vint le duc Henry ou chastel et parla au roy, a l'evesque de Kerlille et aux deux[1254] chevaliers – Sire Estienne Scroup[1255] et Ferbric – maiz au conte de Salsebery ne parla il point. Ains lui fist dire par[1256] un chevalier en telle maniere:

'Conte de Salsebery, sachiez de certain que, nyent plus que vous ne[1257] daignastes parler a Monseigneur le duc[1258] de Lancastre, quant lui et vous[1259] estiez a Paris au Noël derreinerement passé, il ne parlera a vous.'

Lors fu le conte moult[1260] esbahi et ot[1261] grant paour et[1262] freeur au cuer, car il veoit bien que le duc le haioit mortelement.

Le quel duc Henry dist moult hault d'une[1263] voix fiere et crueuse:

'Amenez les chevaulx du roy.'

Et lors on lui admena deux petis chevaulx, qui[1264] ne valoient mie .xl. frans. Le roy monta sur l'un, et le conte de Salsebery[1265] sur l'autre. Chascun monta a cheval, et partismes du dit chastel de Flint environ deux heures aprés[1266] midi.

[1238] ABD approprioit
[1239] L *no* il
[1240] C fay
[1241] H conme
[1242] C si
[1243] C estee
[1244] L *no* ainsi
[1245] B *no* et
[1246] AD dehors
[1247] ABD foy et creance C foy et certaine
[1248] ABD ilz
[1249] L et aussi ceulx du pays en fanthomes et sorceries croient tres parfaitement [*no* car … prophecies]
[1250] H en fanthoimes A et fanthomes
[1251] AD et en
[1252] AD voulentiers
[1253] B *no* est
[1254] C *no* deux
[1255] AD guillaume seroup C estienne de scroup
[1256] C pour
[1257] L *no* ne
[1258] AD *no* le duc
[1259] C vous et lui
[1260] AD bien
[1261] A et en ot
[1262] L *no* paour et
[1263] AD et dune
[1264] AD les quieulx
[1265] H sasebery
[1266] C empres

§36 Richard is taken to Chester by Lancaster. From now on Creton is forbidden to speak to him.

Duke Henry captured King Richard, his lord – in the way that you have heard – and brought him with great rejoicing to Chester, whence he had set off that morning. And you should know that you could scarcely have heard the voice of God thundering, on account of the great noise and crashing sounds made by their instruments – horns, bugles and trumpets – so much so that they made the whole seashore resound.

Thus did the duke enter the town of Chester and the common people bowed down low before him, praising Our Lord; they called after their King, as if to mock him. The duke took him straight to the castle, which is very fine and strong, and made him take up his quarters in the keep. Then he handed him into the custody of the sons of the duke of Gloucester[143] [fo. 51v.] and the earl of Arundel, who hated him more than any man alive, for King Richard had had their fathers killed. There the King saw his brother – the duke of Exeter – but neither dared nor was able to speak to him.

Soon afterwards the duke sat down to dinner and had the Archbishop of Canterbury sit above him; below him at some distance were seated the duke of Exeter – brother to King Richard – the earl of Westmorland,[144] the earl of Rutland, the earl of Northumberland and Sir Thomas Percy. All these were seated at duke Henry's table, and the King remained in the tower with his close friends, the earl of Salisbury, the bishop of Carlisle and the two knights. And from that time onwards we were not able to see him, except out in the country as we rode. And we were forbidden to speak to him any more or to any of the others.

---

[143] Page 203, lines 13–14. *au filz du duc de Clocestre et au filz au conte d'Arondel*. Supra, l. 1633, note. Humphrey Plantagenet, earl of Buckingham, only son of Thomas of Woodstock, duke of Gloucester. His triumph over Richard was short-lived, as he died on the march to London and was buried at Waltham Abbey, Essex. See Cockayne (ed.), *Complete Peerage*, s.v. 'Humphrey of Buckingham'. For Arundel's son, see *ODNB*, s.v. 'Fitzalan, Thomas, fifth earl of Arundel and tenth earl of Surrey (1381–1415)'.

[144] Page 203, lines 20–21. *le conte de Westmerland*. See *ODNB*, s.v. 'Neville, Ralph, first earl of Westmorland (c.1364–1425)'.

§36 Richard is taken to Chester by Lancaster. From now on Creton is forbidden to speak to him.

En la forme et maniere que vous avez oÿ, prist le duc Henry le roy Richart – son seigneur[1267] – et l'enmena[1268] a Cestre, dont il estoit partis[1269] le matin, a grant joie et a grant consolacion. Et sachiez que a grant paine eust on[1270] oÿ Dieu tonnant,[1271] pour le grant bruit et son de leurs instrumens – cors, buisines et trompetes – et tant qu'ilz[1272] en faisoient retentir toute la greve de la mer.

Ainsi entra le duc dedens la ville de Cestre, au quel le commun peuple[1273] fist tresgrant reverence, en[1274] loant Nostre Seigneur[1275] et criant aprés leur roy ainsi comme[1276] par mocquerie. Le duc l'enmena tout droit ou chastel, le quel est moult bel et moult fort, et le fist logier ou dongon. Et lors le bailla en garde au filz du[1277] duc de Clocestre et au [fo. 51v.] filz au[1278] conte d'Arondel, les quelx le haioient[1279] plus que tous les hommes du monde, car le roy Richart avoit fait morir leurs peres. La vit il son frere, le duc d'Excestre, maiz il n'osa ne ne pot parler a lui.

Tantost aprés s'assist le duc au disner et[1280] fist asseoir au dessus[1281] de lui l'archevesque de Cantorbie et au dessoubz assez loing[1282] le duc d'Excestre – frere du roy Richart – le conte de Westmerland,[1283] le conte de Rotelant, le conte de Northomberland et Messire Thomas de Persi. Tous ceulx furent assiz a la table du duc Henry, et le roy demoura en la tour avecques ses bons amis, le conte de Salsebery, l'evesque de Kerllille et les deux chevaliers. Et de la en avant nous ne le poions voir, se ce[1284] n'estoit aux champs en chevauchant. Et nous fist on[1285] deffendre que nous ne parlissons plus[1286] a lui ne a nulz[1287] des autres.

[1267] L *no* son seigneur
[1268] L lamena
[1269] L parti
[1270] AB on *superscript*
[1271] B tonner
[1272] C quil
[1273] B le peuple
[1274] A et
[1275] B nostresire
[1276] H comme *superscript* LB *no* comme
[1277] D au
[1278] B du
[1279] C hairent
[1280] L seoir C *no* et fist asseoir
[1281] C au dessoubz
[1282] L et au dessoubz de la assez loing AC et au dessoubz et assez loing de luy D et au dessoubz assez loingn de luy
[1283] AD merland
[1284] L *no* ce
[1285] B nous en fist [on *superscript*]
[1286] B *no* plus
[1287] L nul

§37 Lancaster sets off from Chester to take Richard to London. At Lichfield Richard attempts unsuccessfully to escape.

Duke Henry remained three days at Chester and held a great Council. They decided that since the King had been captured he had too many men, and thirty to forty thousand men[145] would be enough to take the King to London; otherwise the country would be quite devastated, since it had been extensively despoiled when they came. Thus the duke had most of his men withdraw, and left Chester on the fourth day after the King's capture, and took the direct road to London.

He arrived at Lichfield[146] – a very pretty little town – and there poor King Richard attempted to escape from them by night; he slid down into a garden through the window of a stout tower where he had been lodged. But I think that it was not Our Lord's will [fo. 52r.] that he escape, for he was seen and very roughly cast back into the tower. And from then on – at all hours of the night – ten or twelve armed men guarded him without sleeping.

§38 A deputation from London demands that Richard be summarily executed. He and Lancaster continue via Coventry and St Albans. Near London, Lancaster hands the King over to the mayor and a large number of liverymen.

Now it came about that the citizens of London[147] heard the news of the capture of their rightful lord – King Richard – and set out in most prestigious company; that is to say that five or six of the greatest merchants – governors of the city – rode out as fast as they could to meet duke Henry.

---

[145] Page 205, lines 6–7. *trente a quarante mille hommes*. An impossibly large number for a much reduced portion of Lancaster's army.

[146] Page 205, line 12. *Liceflit*. John Pallays and John Seymour, esquires of the household, tried to rescue Richard at Lichfield. See Given-Wilson, *Royal Household*, p. 225.

[147] Page 205, line 25. *ceulx de Londres*. For the role of the citizens of London in the deposition of Richard, see M. McKisack, 'London and the succession to the Crown during the Middle Ages', in R.W. Hunt, W.A. Pantin, and R.W. Southern (eds), *Studies in Medieval History Presented to F.M. Powicke* (Oxford, 1948), pp. 84–85.

§37 Lancaster sets off from Chester to take Richard to London. At Lichfield Richard attempts unsuccessfully to escape.

Le duc Henry demoura .iii. jours a Cestre et tint moult[1288] grant conseil. Ilz[1289] conclurent[1290] qu'il[1291] avoit trop grant quantité de gens, puis que le roy estoit pris, et que ce seroit assez de trente a quarante mille hommes pour mener le dit roy[1292] a Londres, et que autrement[1293] le païs seroit trop grevé, veu que[1294] tresgrandement avoit esté gasté au venir. Ainsi fist[1295] le duc retraire la plus grant partie de ses gens,[1296] et parti de la ville de Cestre le .iiii.ᵉ jour aprés la prise, et prist le droit chemin a Londres.

Il arriva a Liceflit[1297] – une tresbelle petite ville[1298] – et la leur cuida le povre roy Richart[1299] eschaper par nuit, et se laissa couler en un jardinage[1300] parmy une fenestre d'une grosse tour, ou ilz l'avoient logié. Maiz je croy qu'il ne plaisoit pas [fo. 52r.] a Nostre Seigneur qu'il eschapast, car il fu aperceuz[1301] et fu moult vilainement reboutez[1302] dedens la tour. Et de la en avant – a toutes les heures de la nuit – il avoit .x. ou .xii. hommes armez, qui le gardoient sans point dormir.

§38 A deputation from London demands that Richard be summarily executed. He and Lancaster continue via Coventry and St Albans. Near London, Lancaster hands the King over to the mayor and a large number of liverymen.

Or advint il ainsi que ceulx de Londres oÿrent les nouvelles de la prinse de leur droit seigneur – le roy Richart – les quelx se partirent a tresbelle compaignie: c'est assavoir .v. ou .vi.[1303] des plus grans bourgois – gouverneurs[1304] de la dicte ville – vindrent[1305] a force d'esperon a l'encontre du duc[1306] Henry.

[1288] AD *no* moult
[1289] D il
[1290] H concluirent
[1291] D quilz
[1292] AD pour le mener
B pour mener le roy
[1293] C et ou que le pais
[1294] B *que* superscript
[1295] B le fist
[1296] LC sa gent
[1297] HL lueflit
[1298] AD une petite ville tresbelle
[1299] AD *no* richart
[1300] AD couler a terre en gardinage
[1301] LB apparceu
[1302] LACD reboute
[1303] AD cinq ou six cens
[1304] A *no* gouverneurs
C bourgeois de gouverneurs
[1305] D ilz vindrent
[1306] L du dit henry

And you may know that I heard it said by several knights and squires that, as soon as they met the duke they demanded on behalf of the citizens of London that King Richard – their rightful lord – and all those who were captured with him should be beheaded, without being taken on any further. Duke Henry would not grant this request and excused himself as reasonably as he could, saying,

'Messeigneurs, we would be in deep disgrace for all time if we put the King to death like that. But we will take him to London and there he will be judged by Parliament.'

The duke left Lichfield and rode on with all his army until he came to Coventry, which is a very fair town. But before they could arrive there, the Welsh[148] inflicted great injury and mischief on him, killing and robbing many of his men. Sometimes they set the English quarters on fire; certainly this filled me with great joy. The English were not able to capture any of them, except by chance. And when they could catch [fo. 52v.] any of them, they tied them with ropes to the tails of their horses and dragged them along the rough and stony roads; thus did they inflict a cruel and painful death on them.

The duke crossed their hills as quickly and as best he could; he reached the town of Coventry and stayed two days there. Then he moved on to St Albans, a very fine town with a beautiful abbey, and thence straight to London.[149] When he was about five or six miles from the city, the mayor accompanied by a very great number of liverymen[150] – each trade arrayed in their particular striped garments, and bearing arms – came to meet duke Henry, with great numbers of instruments and trumpets playing, and manifesting great joy and pleasure; a sword was borne in front of the mayor, as before the King.

---

[148] Page 207, line 12. *les Galoiz*. If this were true, the Welsh were some way from home.

[149] Page 207, line 24. *de la tout droit a Londres*. The detailed itinerary provided by the Monk of Evesham is to be preferred, although Creton has correctly given the main halting-places on the route to London. See *Chronicles of the Revolution*, ed. Given-Wilson, p. 130; for further information, see ibid. p. 40 and n. 58.

[150] Page 207, lines 26–27. *communes – ordonnez et vestus chascun mestier par soy de divers draps royez*. The striped garments are livery. In Figure XV, an attempt has been made to portray their gowns as striped, although they should have been of two colours. See G. Unwin, *The Gilds and Companies of London*, 4th edn (London, 1963; originally published 1908), p. 191. *Communes* has been translated here as 'liverymen', as it was the prosperous employer groups of a craft who wore the distinctive livery. See C.M. Barron, *London in the Later Middle Ages: Government and People 1200–1500* (Oxford, 2004), p. 214.

Et sachiez que j'oÿ recorder a plusieurs chevaliers et escuiers que, tantost qu'ilz furent arrivés devers le duc, ilz lui requirent de par la commune[1307] de Londres que a leur droit seigneur – le roy Richart – on tranchast la teste, et a[1308] tous ceulx qui estoient pris avecques lui, sans le[1309] mener plus avant. La quelle requeste le duc[1310] Henry ne vost faire ne accorder, et s'excusa le plus sagement qu'il pot, disant:[1311] 'Beaux Seigneurs, ce seroit trop grant vitupere a tousjours maiz[1312] pour nous, se[1313] nous le faisions ainsi mourir. Maiz nous le menrons a Londres, et la sera jugié par le[1314] Parlement.'

Le duc se parti de Liceflit[1315] et chevaucha tant a[1316] tout son ost qu'il arriva a Covimtry, qui est tresbonne ville. Maiz ains qu'ilz[1317] y[1318] peussent[1319] venir, lui[1320] firent les Galoiz moult de dommaiges et de despit,[1321] et tuerent[1322] grant quantité de sa gent[1323] et destrousserent. Aucunesfoiz venoient ilz bouter[1324] le feu ou les Anglois estoient logiez, et certes j'en avoie tresgrant[1325] joie. Et si[1326] n'estoit pas en la puissance des Engloiz d'en prendre nulz[1327] se[1328] d'aventure non. Et quant ilz en povoient aucuns [fo. 52v.] atraper, ilz les lioient[1329] de cordes a la queue[1330] de leurs chevaulx et les traynoient parmy les chemins plains de pierres;[1331] ainsi les faisoient mourir mauvaisement et a grant paine.

Le duc passa leurs montaignes au plus tost et au de mieulx qu'il pot, et arriva en[1332] la dicte[1333] ville Covimtry, et y[1334] sejourna deux jours. Aprés s'en ala a Saint Alban, ou il a tresbonne ville et belle abbaie, et[1335] de la[1336] tout droit a Londres. Quant il aproucha a .v. ou a[1337] .vi. mile pres de la dicte ville, le maire acompaignié de tresgrant quantité de communes – ordonnez[1338] et vestus chascun mestier[1339] par[1340] soy de divers draps royez, et armez – vindrent a l'encontre du duc[1341] Henry, a grant quantité d'instrumens et de trompetes, demenant[1342] grant joie et grant[1343] consolacion; et la portoit on l'espee devant le dit maire comme devant le roy.

[1307] B le commun AD *no* de par la commune de londres
[1308] D *no* a
[1309] LACD les
[1310] B la quelle le duc requeste le duc
[1311] C en disant
[1312] L *no* maiz
[1313] C si
[1314] AD *no* le
[1315] AD lireflit
[1316] L o
[1317] AD quil

[1318] B *no* y
[1319] AD peust C puissent
[1320] C leur
[1321] C et grant despit
[1322] H tue<u>r</u>ent
[1323] AD ses gens
[1324] B ilz et boutoient
[1325] C grant
[1326] C *no* si
[1327] C un
[1328] C si
[1329] B *no* les D lyent
[1330] L aux queues
[1331] A plains despines

[1332] L a
[1333] C *no* dicte
[1334] AD la
[1335] B *no* et
[1336] B la *superscript*
[1337] D *no* a
[1338] B ordonnee
[1339] B *no* mestier
[1340] C pour
[1341] ACD du dit duc
[1342] L demenans
[1343] B *no* grant

When they met, they greeted the King and then duke Henry; they made much greater reverence to him than to the King, shouting out in their own tongue in an awesome voice:

'Long live the good duke of Lancaster!'

And they said one to the other that God had revealed a miracle to them when He sent them the said duke, and how he had conquered all of England in less than a month; and that the man who could prevail like that ought to be King. And for this they most devoutly praised and thanked Our Lord, saying that it was His will, for otherwise the duke could not have done it. These foolish and credulous men also said that he would conquer a large part of [fo. 53r.] the world, and were already comparing him to Alexander the Great.[151]

As they thus talked and cast their minds forward, they came to within two miles of the city, and there the whole company stopped, all together. Then said duke Henry to the liverymen of London in a ringing voice:

'Messeigneurs, here is your King. Make up your minds what you want to do with him.'

And they replied loudly:

'We want him to be taken to Westminster.'

Thus he handed him over to them. At that point the duke reminded me of Pilate,[152] who had Our Lord Jesus Christ scourged at the stake and then led before the multitude of the Jews, saying,

'Messeigneurs, here is your King.'

And they replied:

'Let Him be crucified.'

Then did Pilate wash his hands and say:

'I am innocent of the blood of this just man' and handed Our Lord over to them. In the same way did duke Henry behave when he handed over his rightful lord to the liverymen of London so that, should they have him killed, he could say:

'I am innocent of this deed.'

---

[151] Page 209, line 12. *Alixandre le Grant.* One of the Nine Worthies. *Infra*, p. 327, ll. 4–6, note.

[152] Page 209, lines 19–20. *me souvint il de Pilate.* Matthew 27:22–24, 26.

LA PRINSE ET MORT DU ROY RICHART D'ANGLETERRE 209

A l'assambler le saluerent et le duc Henry aprés, au quel ilz firent trop plus grant reverence qu'ilz n'avoient fait au roy,[1344] criant[1345] en leur langaige d'une haulte voix et espoventable: 'Vive le bon duc de Lancastre!'

Et disoient[1346] l'un a l'autre que Dieux leur avoit monstré[1347] beau miracle,[1348] quant il[1349] leur avoit envoié le dit duc,[1350] et comment[1351] il avoit conquis tout le royaume d'Engleterre en[1352] moins d'un moys; et que bien devoit estre roy, qui ainsi savoit conquerir. Et en looient et gracioient[1353] Nostre Seigneur moult devotement, disant que c'estoit sa voulenté, et que autrement ne l'eust il peu avoir fait.[1354] Encores disoient les foles et incredules[1355] gens qu'il conquerroit une des grans[1356] parties du [fo. 53r.] monde, et le[1357] comparoient desja a Alixandre le Grant.

Ainsi disant et monopolant, aprouchèrent de la ville sicomme a deux mile,[1358] et la s'arresta[1359] tout l'ost d'une partie et d'autre. Lors dist le duc Henry moult hault aux communes[1360] de la dicte[1361] ville:

'Beaux Seigneurs, vecy vostre roy. Regardez que vous en volez faire.'[1362]

Et[1363] ilz respondirent a haute voix:

'Nous voulons[1364] qu'il soit mené a Wemoustre.'[1365]

Et ainsi il[1366] [le] leur delivra. A celle heure me souvint il[1367] de Pilate, le quel fist batre Nostre Seigneur[1368] Jhesucrist a l'estache, et aprés le fist mener devant le turbe[1369] des Juifs, disant: 'Beaux Seigneurs, vecy vostre roy.'

Les quelx respondirent:

'Nous voulons qu'il soit crucifié.'

Alors Pilate en lava ses mains, disant:

'Je sui innocent du sanc juste.'

Et ainsi leur delivra[1370] Nostre Seigneur. Assez semblablement fist le duc Henry, quant son droit seigneur livra au turbe[1371] de Londres, afin telle que, s'ilz[1372] le faisoient mourir, qu'il peust[1373] dire:

'Je sui innocent de ce fait icy.'[1374]

[1344] AD a leur roy
[1345] L crians
[1346] B disant
[1347] A avoit fait monstre
[1348] AD beaux miracles
[1349] C ilz
[1350] L le dit duc henry
[1351] B et communement comment
[1352] D a
[1353] L loerent et gracierent C loirent H gracioent
[1354] AD neust il peu faire ne avoit fait

[1355] AD les foles et mauvaises et incredules
[1356] AD plus grandes
[1357] A la
[1358] B lieues mille
[1359] B et la s se arresta C et dela sarresta
[1360] AD aux dictes communes
[1361] AD no dicte
[1362] A or regardez que vous en ferez ne voulez faire D or regardez que vous en ferez ou voulez faire
[1363] AD no et

[1364] B nous vous voulons
[1365] L wemoustier ABD westmoustier
[1366] B no il
[1367] A no il
[1368] C saulveur
[1369] AD le cure
[1370] B et ainsi delcivra delivra
[1371] AD aux turbes B livra a [au superscript] turbe
[1372] D sil
[1373] B puist
[1374] C cy

[fo. 53v.] Figure XV: Lancaster hands King Richard over to the liverymen of London.

§39 King Richard is taken to Westminster. Lancaster goes to St Paul's and then to St John's Priory, Clerkenwell.

Thus did the liverymen of London take their King to Westminster.[153] The duke went round the city to enter by the main gate, in order to pass along their great thoroughfare called Cheapside. He entered the city at the hour of Vespers and came directly to St Paul's. The people shouted after him in the streets: 'Long live the good duke of Lancaster!'

And they called blessings down upon him in their own tongue, expressing such great joy and exultation that I believe they would not have voiced greater had Our Lord God descended amongst them.

The duke dismounted at St Paul's and went to pray, fully armed, at the high altar. Then he turned away to his father's tomb,[154] which is quite near the said altar; you should know that it is a very richly ornamented sepulchre. There he wept most bitterly, as he had not seen it since [fo. 54r.] his father had been laid in it.

He remained five or six days at St Paul's, then left and went to St John's Priory,[155] a hospice of the Knights' Templar, which is outside the city of London.

§40 Creton and his companion return to France.

When we had seen and thought about these things, which filled my heart with grief and pain, and also since I was eager to leave their country, my companion and I went to duke Henry and begged him to grant us safe-conduct to come back to France; this he did right willingly.

---

[153] Page 211, lines 5–6. *Ainsi enmenerent les comunes ... leur roy a Wemoustre*. Professor Strohm writes of 'a variant version of Creton's account of Richard's humiliation at the hands of Henry IV in London', *England's Empty Throne*, pp. 23–24 n. 52. This is the *Chronicque de la traïson et mort*, ed. Williams, pp. 63–64, 215; see also Palmer, 'French Chronicles', 61:1 (1978), p. 181, no. 33.

[154] Page 211, line 16. *le tumbel de son pere. Supra*, l. 1117, note.

[155] Page 211, line 21. *Saint Jehan de Jherusalem – hospital de Templiers*. St John's Priory, Clerkenwell was the chief house in England of the Knights Hospitaller. See *Victoria History of the Counties of England: Middlesex*, I, pp. 193 ff.

[fo. 53v.] Figure XV: Lancaster hands King Richard over to the liverymen of London.

§39 King Richard is taken to Westminster. Lancaster goes to St Paul's and then to St John's Priory, Clerkenwell.

Ainsi enmenerent les comunes et le turbe de Londres leur roy a Wemoustre.[1375] Et le duc[1376] tourna[1377]* autour de[1378] la ville pour entrer par la maistre porte de Londres, affin telle qu'il passast par la grant rue qu'ilz appellent la Chipstrate.[1379] Il entra dedens la ville a heure de vespres et s'en vint tout droit a Saint Pol. La crioit le peuple aprés lui par les rues:

'Vive le bon duc de Lencastre!'[1380] Et le benissoient en leur langaige, demenant[1381] grant joie et consolacion, et telle que je croy que se Nostre Sire[1382] Dieux feust descenduz[1383] entre eulx,[1384] ilz ne l'eussent[1385] pas fait plus grant.

Il descendi a Saint Pol et ala tout armé[1386] devant le maistre autel faire ses oroisons. Aprés retourna par le tumbel de son pere, qui est[1387] assez pres du dit autel; et sachiez que c'est une tresriche sepulture.[1388] La ploura il moult fort, car il ne l'avoit veue[1389] depuis que [fo. 54r.] son pere y avoit esté mis.

Il demoura a Saint Pol .v. ou .vi. jours. Aprés se parti[1390] et s'en ala a Saint Jehan de Jherusalem – hospital de Templiers – qui est hors de la ville[1391] de Londres.

§40 Creton and his companion return to France.

Ces choses veues et considerees, les quelles me faisoient moult de mal et de douleur au cuer, et aussi moy desirant estre hors de leur païs, alasmes devers le dit duc Henry[1392] mon compaignon et moy, en lui suppliant qu'il nous voulsist ottroier saufconduit pour revenir en France, le quel le[1393] nous ottroya voulentiers.

[1375] L wemoustier ABD westmoustier
[1376] B no et C et le roy
[1377] H tourna̱ ACD tournoya̱
[1378] C no de
[1379] HL la thipstrate AD le choystrate B le tipstrate C chipstrate
[1380] H dalencastre LABCD de lencastre
[1381] L demenans
[1382] AD se nostreseigneur C si nostre sire
[1383] L descendu
[1384] B encontre entre eulx C fu desetuz mortelz entreux
[1385] B neussent
[1386] AD tout droit arme
[1387] B est *superscript*
[1388] H sepulture LB sepulcre
[1389] H lavovoit veue LABCD lavoit veu
[1390] C et puis party
[1391] AD la dicte ville
[1392] B le [dit *superscript*] duc [henry *superscript*]
[1393] L il B *no* le

Thus we left duke Henry and rode until we came to Dover. We crossed the sea and arrived at Calais, where we scarcely lingered, for I was most anxious to reach France.

And then shortly afterwards, considering their rebellions, wickedness, betrayals and mockery of their rightful lord – King Richard – I wrote a *ballade*, which begins thus:

§41 Lines 2296–2334. Imprecatory *ballade*, cursing Lancaster.

Oh, Henry, who for the present are the ruler of the land of King Richard, who was so powerful, whom you cast aside and expelled and whose treasure you stole and took for yourself, who are the image of treachery. Now everyone knows that never was man so falsely betrayed as you betrayed your King; you cannot hide this. You had him condemned in an arbitrary ruling; for this, on the Last Day you will forfeit body and soul.

For falsely and furtively, being banished, [fo. 54v.] you stole his country without issuing a challenge. It certainly seems to me that this was not a worthy thing for you to do, considering that he was abroad fighting his enemies in Ireland, where he received many painful blows from the Irish, who are as fierce as lions. He knighted your eldest son.[156] Alas! You forgot to reward him. This is a great sin of which the whole world holds you guilty; for this, on the Last Day you will forfeit body and soul.

---

[156] Line 2314. *Ton filz ainsné y fist chevalier.* Creton is going over events so far: the campaign in Ireland, *supra*, ll. 69–609, 793–809; Henry of Monmouth being knighted, *supra*, ll. 137–144; and Northumberland tricking Richard, *supra*, ll. 1653–2120.

Ainsi partismes nous du duc Henry et chevauchasmes tant que nous vinmes a Douvre. Nous passasmes la mer et arrivasmes a Calais, en la quelle ville nous n'arrestames gueres, car quant a moy, j'avoye grant desir d'estre en France.[1394]*

Et lors[1395] un pou aprés,[1396] consideré les rebellions, les maulx, les traÿsons et derisions[1397] qu'ilz avoient fait a leur droit seigneur – le roy Richart – j'en fiz une[1398] balade, la quelle se commence en tele maniere:

§41 Lines 2296–2334. Imprecatory *ballade*, cursing Lancaster.*

    O tu, Henry, qui as en gouvernance   2296
    Pour le present la terre et le païs
    Du roy Richart, qui tant ot[1399] de puissance,
    Le quel tu as hors bouté[1400] et demis
    Et tous ses biens apropriez et mis[1401]*   2300
    A toy, qui es[1402] mirouer de[1403] traïsons.
    Or scet chascun c'onques maiz trahis[1404] homs
    Si faulcement ne fu, comme tu as
    Trahi ton roy; celer ne le peus pas.   2304
    Jugier l'as[1405] fait par jugement infame;
    Tu en perdras en la fin corps et ame.

    Car faulcement, sans mander deffiance,
    En larrecin, toy estant fourbanis,   2308
    [fo. 54v.] Luy as emblé sa terre. Grant vaillance
    N'est pas a toy – certes ce m'est advis –
    Veu qu'il estoit hors sur ses ennemis
    En Irlande, ou mains durs horïons   2312
    Receut d'Irlois,[1406] qui sont fiers[1407] com lions.
    Ton filz ainsné y fist[1408] chevalier. Las!
    Le guerredon a lui rendre oublias.[1409]
    C'est grant pechié, tout le monde t'en blasme;   2316
    Tu en perdras en[1410] la fin corps et ame.

[1394] HLBC *no* ainsi partismes...en france [paragraph wholly missing]
[1395] AD *no* et lors
[1396] C apres moy revenu en france [*no* et lors un pou apres]
[1397] AD et les derisions
[1398] B *no* une
[1399] AD ot tant
[1400] AD boute hors
[1401] C *line 2300 omitted*
[1402] H es
[1403] D et
[1404] H trahis
[1405] B la
[1406] C du bois
[1407] C ~~durs~~ fiers
[1408] B ~~est~~ fust
[1409] C oublie as
[1410] BC a

For you did not keep faith with him, as you had sworn and promised to do, when treacherously and in the name of reconciliation you sent to him Northumberland, who swore on the Host that you would be his friend. Therefore before the time was right the King left his castles and quietly made his way towards you. Alas! You carried him off in shame and humiliation; for this, on the Last Day you will forfeit body and soul.

Princes and kings, knights and barons, French, Flemings, Germans and Bretons ought to attack you immediately, for you have committed the most horrid crime of any man: this is an ignoble distinction for you; for this, on the Last Day you will forfeit body and soul.

§42 Lines 2335–2361. Creton rails against the English.

[fo. 55r.] **W**hen I had finished my *ballade* I was no longer so very sick as I had been, and angry at the great injury that I had seen the English do: overthrowing their lord like traitors and usurpers; please God, may every tyrant work swiftly for their destruction. I think this would win salvation for all those who quickly and eagerly attacked them. For they are so steeped in evil, in falsehood and in wrong – in

Car a ly n'as tenu foy n'aliance,
Comme juré l'avoies[1411] et promis,
Quant faintement et[1412] en nom d'asseurance   2320
Northomberlant par toy lui fu tramis,
En promettant sur le[1413] corps Dieu qu'amis[1414]
Tu lui seroies, et que c'estoit raisons.
Ainsi le roy, ains qu'il en feust saisons,   2324
De ses chasteaulx wida, et hault et bas
Vers toy s'en vint treshumblement. Helas!
Honteusement l'enmenas[1415] a diffame;
Tu en perdras en la fin corps et ame.   2328

Princes et roys, chevaliers et barons,
Françoiz, Flamencs, Alemans et Bretons
Deveroient* courre sur[1416] toy plus que le pas,
Car tu as fait le plus orrible cas   2332
C'onques fist homs: c'est pour toy laide fame;
Tu en perdras en la fin corps et ame.

§42 Lines 2235–2361. Creton rails against the English.

[fo. 55r.] **Q**uant j'oz[1417] achevé ma balade,
Je ne fui maiz[1418] si tresmalade   2336
Que j'avoie esté par devant
De courroux, et pour[1419] le mal grant
Que je leur avoie veu faire:
De leur seigneur ainsi defaire   2340
Comme traïtres et tirans;
Plust a Dieu que chascun tirans
Fust brief a leur destrucïon.
Ce seroit la salvacïon –   2344
Ce cuide je[1420] – pour[1421] trestous ceulx,
Qui de bon cuer courir sur[1422] eulx
Yroient et de voulenté.
Car ilz sont en mal si enté,   2348

[1411] B avoies
[1412] AD *no* et
[1413] B *no* le C par le
[1414] B que ~~enemis~~ amis
[1415] L lamenas
[1416] L sus
[1417] B je oyz
[1418] L pas
[1419] C par
[1420] A cuidroy je
D cuidoye [*no* je]
[1421] C par
[1422] L sus

word and deed – that I firmly believe that there is no race beneath the heavens that is like theirs, considering their actions, which are not worthy or virtuous according to law and justice. But if I err in saying this, forgive me, for I have seen the evil in them that makes me speak so.

§43 Lines 2362–2376. Back in France, Creton expresses a wish to know how events concluded.

[fo. 55v.] **A**s you have heard, I had returned from their country quite short of money and finery, and I often thought that – at whatever cost – I needed to know the end of the business that they had started, concerning their King whom they were holding in shameful imprisonment at Westminster; this redounded to their discredit, and always will, for as long as they live. Certainly they will never have any honour, at least among faithful people, considering their very many acts of wrongdoing.

En faulceté et en oultrage –
En fait, en dit et en langage –
Que certes je croy fermement
Qu'il n'a desoubz le fiermament[1423] 2352
Generacïon qui resemble
A la leur – sicomme il me semble –
Voire consideré leur fais,
Qui ne sont loyaulx ne parfais 2356
Selon droit, raison et justice,
Ce[1424] m'est advis. Maiz se je visce[1425]*
A le[1426] dire, pardonnez le[1427] moy,
Car j'ay veu[1428] en eulx le desroy, 2360
Qui m'en[1429] fait si avant parler.

§43 Lines 2362-2376. Back in France, Creton expresses a wish to know how events concluded.

[fo. 55v] Ainsi qu'avez oÿ compter,[1430]
Fui[1431] de leur païs revenus,[1432]
D'argent et de robe assez nus,[1433] 2364
Et pensay[1434] souvent en mon cuer
Qu'il me failloit – a quelque fuer –
Savoir la fin de leur afaire,
Et comment il[1435] vorent[1436] parfaire 2368
Ce qu'il[1437] avoient entrepris
De leur roy, qu'ilz tenoient pris
A Wemoustre[1438] commë imfame;
Ce fu pour eulx moult laide fame 2372
Et sera, tant qu'ilz viveront.[1439]
Certes jamaiz honneur n'aront,
Au moins entre les gens loyaulx,
Consideré leurs tresgrans maulx. 2376

[1423] B firammement
[1424] B que ce *superscript*
[1425] L se jay vice AD se vice [*no* je] B se je veisce C si je veisce vice
[1426] A a a le dire
[1427] LA pardonnez moy
[1428] H je veu LACD jay veu B je vy
[1429] C me
[1430] C oy parler compter
[1431] ABD suis
[1432] L revenu
[1433] L nu
[1434] B pense
[1435] LABCD ilz
[1436] LB vouldrent
[1437] LABD ce quilz
[1438] LC wemoustier ABD westmonstier
[1439] BCD vivront

§44 Lines 2377–2412. Creton meets a clerk returned from England, who takes up Richard's story.

Thus I remained a long time in Paris, ignorant of what they were doing with their lord and King, whom they held imprisoned in shame and suffering for many a long day – this was a great crime – until a clerk whom duke Henry had taken with him when he left Paris, returned, sad and dejected, on account of the great wickedness he had witnessed there. He had remembered it all quite clearly, for he related it to me when he came back from there, [fo. 56r.] saying that he would not accept all the wealth in England, were he obliged to spend his life there in return, so great is the English hatred of the French.

Then he told me how they had most wrongfully imprisoned their King at Westminster, when duke Henry arrived latterly in London. The duke went directly to St Paul's and then to St John's, a Templar hospice a short way outside the walls. It was his pleasure to remain there a full two weeks,[157] without leaving; then he went off to his estates in the county of Hereford. This is what the clerk told me; he was there and could observe all their disloyal deeds and conduct.

---

[157] Line 2405. *Quinze jours*. Creton says that Lancaster stayed five or six days at St Paul's, *supra*, p. 211, l. 20, but gives no indication of how long he remained at St John's Priory, *supra*, p. 211, ll. 21.

§44 Lines 2377–2412. Creton meets a clerk returned from England, who takes up Richard's story.

Ainsi demouray longuement	
A Paris, sans savoir comment	
Ilz firent du roy, leur seigneur,	
Qu'ilz tindrent a honte et douleur	2380
Moult longuement en leur prison –	
Dont ilz firent grant mesprison –	
Tant q'un clerc, que le duc Henry	
En avoit mené avec ly,	2384
Quant il se parti de Paris,	
Retourna tristes et maris	
Pour le grant mal qu'il y ot veu.	
Le quel assez bien retenu	2388
L'avoit, car il le[1440] me compta,[1441]	
Quant retournez fu par deça,	
[fo. 56r.] Disant qu'il ne voroit[1442] avoir	
D'Engleterre pas[1443] tout l'avoir,	2392
Et qu'il y dust user sa vie,	
Tant ont ilz sur Françoiz envie.	
Aprés me dist comment[1444] le roy	
Avoient mis par grant desroy	2396
A Wemoustre[1445] et enfermé,	
Quant le duc Henry arivé	
Fu a Londres nouvellement.	
A Saint Pol ala droitement	2400
Et puis a Saint Jehan aprés,	
Qui est hors des murs assez pres:	
Un[1446] hospital des Templiers.	
La fu le duc moult voulentiers	2404
Quinze jours tous plains sans partir;	
Aprés s'en volt il departir	
Et s'en ala en[1447] sa conté	
De Harford. Tout ainsi conté	2408
Le m'a le clerc qui y estoit,	
Et qui asez bien regardoit	
Trestous leurs faiz et leur covine,	
Qui n'estoient pas en plevine.[1448]	2412

[1440] L *no* le
[1441] L recompta
[1442] L vaulroit
[1443] C *no* pas
[1444] LBC comme
[1445] LC wemoustier ABD westmonstier
[1446] *all mss* cest un
[1447] LC a
[1448] B en leur plevine

§45 Lines 2413–2424. The date is to be set for the Deposition Parliament.

The duke remained in the said county for three weeks and then came back to London, for the commons had summoned him. Then he was told that the date for Parliament should be set. This pleased [fo. 56v.] duke Henry greatly and he readily agreed; it was his dearest wish, for he knew perfectly well that the King would be deposed and that he would be made King.

§46 Lines 2425–2444. The Deposition Parliament meets.

Duke Henry had his men called to attend, and they were swift to obey. I am profoundly amazed that God could suffer the evil that was in their thoughts.

As I heard it, it was on the first Wednesday of October[158] that they all gathered. Alas! King Richard had few friends in that company, for they all wanted to depose him without delay. So they did, but I truly believe that they will pay dearly for it, as the righteous Judge in Heaven above, familiar with their words and deeds, will punish them in time, even if they meet with no other punishment.

---

[158] Lines 2431–2432. *le premier mercredi / D'ottobre*. The correct date is Monday 6 October. See Saul, *Richard II*, p. 423.

§45 Lines 2413–2424. The date is to be set for the Deposition Parliament.

  En[1449] la ditte conté se tint
  Trois sepmaines et puis revint
  A Londres, car le commun mandé
  L'avoit.[1450] La ly fu commandé[1451]   2416
  Que la journee fust eslitte
  Du Parlement. Ce moult delitte
  [fo. 56v.] Le duc Henry, et sans atendre
  Il y vot de bon cuer entendre,   2420
  Car c'estoit son plus grant plaisir,
  Pour ce qu'il sçot bien sans mentir
  Que le roy y seroit desfait,
  Et quë il[1452] y seroit roy fait.   2424

§46 Lines 2425–2444. The Deposition Parliament meets.

  Ainsi fist asambler ses gens,
  Qui furent asez diligens
  A son mandement et conseil.
  Certes trop fort je me merveil[1453]   2428
  Comment[1454] Dieux souffrir leur povoit
  Le mal que chascun la pensoit.
  Ce fu le premier mercredi
  D'ottobre – sicomme l'entendi[1455] –   2432
  Qu'ilz[1456] furent tous ensemble mis.
  Las![1457] Le roy Richart pou d'amis
  Avoit en celle compaignie,
  Car ilz avoient tous envie   2436
  De le desfaire* assez[1458] briefment.
  Si firent il,[1459] maiz vraiement
  Je croy qu'ilz le comparront chier,
  Car le juste[1460] et vray justichier,   2440
  Qui est la sus en Paradis
  Connoisant leurs faiz et leurs dis,*
  Une foiz les en pugnira,
  S'autre pugnissïon n'y a.   2444

[1449] B et en
[1450] AD *no* lavoit
[1451] A la et luy a commande
[1452] B et quil
[1453] A je mesmerveil
[1454] B come
[1455] HABCD je lentendi L *no* je
[1456] AD qui BC quil
[1457] L lors BC la
[1458] H desfaire assez
LABCD de le faire mourir
[1459] LABCD ilz
[1460] BC ~~vray~~ juste

[fo. 57r.] Figure XVI: The Deposition Parliament. The empty throne, with Lords Spiritual on the left and Lords Temporal on the right.

§47 Lines 2445–2478. Those present at the Deposition Parliament.

Thus there gathered on an evil day at Westminster, outside the city of London – this was no lie – firstly all the prelates: archbishops and bishops. Alas! What were they thinking? What was in their hearts? They must have been mad to agree to such a Parliament.

After the dukes in the first rank were marquesses, earls and knights: squires, archers and several degrees of men, who were neither great-hearted nor high-minded, [fo. 57v.] but false and disloyal traitors; there were so many of them that I hardly dare tell you. First to enter the hall were leading citizens who had previously – as I heard – had the throne made ready in magnificent state, for they hoped to elect another King; this they did, to their shame, as you will hear later.

[fo. 57r.] Figure XVI: The Deposition Parliament. The empty throne, with Lords Spiritual on the left and Lords Temporal on the right.

§47 Lines 2445–2478. Those present at the Deposition Parliament.

>Ainsi firent leur asamblee,
Qui estoit[1461] de mal[1462] enpensee,
A Wemoustre,[1463] hors de[1464] la ville
De Londres – ce ne fu[1465] pas guille* –   2448
Premierement tous les[1466] prelas:
Archevesques, evesques. Las!
Quelle[1467] pensee? Quel courage?
Bien avoient au cuer la rage   2452
De consentir tel Parlement.
Aprés les ducs premierement
Marquis, contes et chevaliers:
Escuiers, varlés et archiers   2456
Et plusieurs manieres de gens,
Qui n'estoient nobles ne gens
[fo. 57v.] Mais traïtres faulx et felons;
La estoient par si grans mons   2460
Qu'a paine l'oseroie dire.[1468]
En la sale sans contredire
Entrerent les maieurs devant,
Les quelx avoient[1469] par avant   2464
Fait – sicomme j'ouÿ compter –
Le siege royal aprester
Par tresgracïeuse ordonnance,
Car ilz[1470] avoient esperance   2468
D'eslire la un autre roy;
Si firent ilz par grant desroy,
Comme vous orrez cy aprés.

[1461] AD est [D *cross in left margin*]
[1462] A de tout mal
[1463] L wemoustier ABD westmoustier
[1464] HLBCD *no* de A hors de
[1465] *all mss* ce nest
[1466] B le
[1467] HABCD quel L quelle
[1468] B le saroie je dire
[1469] B avoient avoie
[1470] B car il

Seated round the throne and near to it were the prelates, more than six in number. On the other side all the lords – of high, middle and lesser rank – were seated in fine order; never did I hear tell of such.

§48 Lines 2479–2528. Creton names the peers present at the Deposition Parliament

Duke Henry was seated foremost, and nearest to him the duke of York,[159] his cousin – who was not well disposed towards his nephew, King Richard. Next on the same side sat the duke of Aumale[160] – son of the duke of York – [fo. 58r.] and then the good duke of Surrey,[161] who remained loyal and true. Next to him sat the duke of Exeter, who could not have been happy, since he could see in front of him the means of deposing the King, his brother german; this was the will of everyone there that day.

Also on this side was one named the Marquess[162] – he was lord of extensive lands – and then the earl of Arundel[163] (who was young and fleet of foot.) The earl of Norfolk[164] was not left out of the tally, neither was the earl of March.[165] From another region came

---

[159] Line 2481. *Le duc dë Iorc – son beau cousin*. The duke of York was uncle to both Richard and Lancaster. See *ODNB*, s.v. 'Edmund [Edmund of Langley], first duke of York (1341–1402)'.

[160] Line 2485. *Le duc d'Aumarle*. The earl of Rutland, *supra*, ll. 93–94, note.

[161] Lines 2487–2489. *Le ... duc de Souldray / ... le duc d'Excestre*. *Supra*, ll. 829, 827, notes. They had been separated from Richard after Lancaster detained them in Chester.

[162] Line 2497. *le Marquis*. John Beaufort was half-brother to Henry Lancaster. See *ODNB*, s.v. 'Beaufort, John, marquess of Dorset and marquess of Somerset (*c*.1371–1410)'.

[163] Line 2499. *le conte d'Arondel*. For the fifth earl of Arundel whom Lancaster had guard the King at Chester, *supra*, p. 203, l. 14, note.

[164] Line 2501. *de Norevic le conte*. Thomas Mowbray, elder son of Thomas, duke of Norfolk, did not succeed to the dukedom. His father had been banished along with Henry Lancaster in 1398, and had died in exile in the previous month, *supra*, ll. 474–475, note. See *ODNB*, s.v. 'Mowbray, Thomas, first duke of Norfolk (1366–1399)'. Young Thomas was taken to Ireland by Richard and was probably knighted along with Henry of Monmouth, *supra*, ll. 149–150. See *ODNB*, s.v. 'Mowbray, Thomas, second earl of Nottingham (1385–1405)'.

[165] Line 2503. *[le conte] de la Marche*. This is unlikely, as he was just a child (b. 1391). See *ODNB*, s.v. 'Mortimer, Edmund, fifth earl of March and seventh earl of Ulster (1391–1425)'. He was the son of the earl of March mentioned *supra*, l. 354.

LA PRINSE ET MORT DU ROY RICHART D'ANGLETERRE 225

Entour le dit siege asez pres 2472
Estoient les prelas assis,
De quoy il y avoit plus de sis.
D'autre costé tous les seigneurs –
Grans, moyens, petiz et meneurs[1471] – 2476
Assiz par ordonnance belle;
Oncques n'oÿ parler de telle.

§48 Lines 2479–2528. Creton names the peers present at the Deposition Parliament.

Premiers sëoit le duc Henry,
Et puis tout au plus pres de ly 2480
Le duc dë Iorc[1472] – son beau cousin –
Qui n'avoit pas le cuer trop fin
Vers son nepveu, le roy Richart.[1473]
Aprés de ceste mesme part 2484
Le duc d'Aumarle se sëoit,
Qui filz au duc dë Iorc[1474] estoit,
[fo. 58r.] Et puis le bon duc de Souldray,
Qui fu tousjours loyal et vray. 2488
Aprés sëoit le duc d'Excestre,
Qui ne devoit pas joyeux estre,
Car il vëoit[1475] devant ly faire
L'apareil pour le roy desfaire, 2492
Qui estoit son frere germain;
De ce faire au soir et au main
Avoient tous grant voulenté.
Aprés estoit de ce costé 2496
Un autre qui ot non le Marquis –
Seigneur estoit de grant païs –
Et puis le conte d'Arondel,
Qui est[1476] asez jeune et ysnel. 2500
Aprés de Norevic[1477]* le conte
Ne fu pas oublié ou[1478] compte,
Aussi ne fu cil[1479] de la Marche.
Aprés y ot d'une autre marche 2504

[1471] C menuz
[1472] *all mss* diorc
[1473] B le [*mark of omission*] richart [roy *at line end*]
[1474] *all mss* diorc
[1475] A voyoit
[1476] B estoit
[1477] *all mss* norvic
[1478] A au
[1479] B *no* cil

one who was the earl of Stafford,[166] who did not like being at peace with his lord, King Richard. Also seated on this side was a peer whom I heard called earl and baron Pembroke,[167] and right near him sat the earl of Salisbury, who remained loyal to the end, so much did he bear a tender love for the King; [fo. 58v.] the earl of Umestat[168] was there, so I heard.

All the other earls, lords and the greatest of the land were of that assembly, all wishing and planning to elect another King: in fine array were the earls of Northumberland and Westmorland,[169] on their feet all day, and for the better accomplishment of the part they had to play, they often fell to their knees; I know not why.

§49 Lines 2529–2549. The Archbishop of Canterbury's sermon.

Then the Archbishop of Canterbury[170] stood up and preached before the people in Latin: *Habuit Jacob benedictionem a patre suo*,[171] how Jacob had received the blessing instead of Esau, even though Esau was the elder son of Isaac; that is true.

---

[166] Line 2505. *le conte de Stanforde*. Thomas, earl of Stafford, died at the Battle of Shrewsbury in 1403. See Given-Wilson, *Henry IV*, pp. 225–227.

[167] Line 2510. *Conte de Panebroc*. There was no earl of Pembroke in 1399.

[168] Line 2515. *le conte d'Umestat*. Creton, 'Translation of a French Metrical History', ed. Webb, p. 194 n. i., suggests Edward de Courtenay, earl of Devon (1377–1419), called 'the blind earl'. See Cockayne (ed.), *Complete Peerage*, s.v. 'Edward (de Courtenay), Earl of Devon'.

[169] Lines 2524–2525. *le conte de Westmerland*. Supra, p. 203, ll. 20–21, note.

[170] Lines 2529–2530. *L'archevesque ... / De Cantorbie*. Supra, l. 471, note.

[171] Lines 2532–2536. *Habuit Jacob benedictionem a patre suo ... Filz dë Isaac*. Genesis 27:27–29. This text bears no relationship to the theme of the archbishop's sermon reported in the Rolls of Parliament and by the chroniclers.

LA PRINSE ET MORT DU ROY RICHART D'ANGLETERRE 227

Un qui fu[1480] conte de Stanforde,[1481]
Le quel n'aimoit[1482] pas la concorde
De son seigneur, le roy Richart.
Encor[1483] sëoit de ceste part   2508
Un que j'ouÿ asés nommer
Conte de Panebroc et ber,
Et tout au plus pres de cely[1484]
Sist le conte de Salsebery[1485]   2512
Qui fu loyal jusqu'a[1486] la fin,*
Tant ama le roy de cuer fin;
[fo. 58v.] Le conte d'Umestat y fu,
Sicomme je l'ay entendu.   2516
Tous[1487] autres contes et seigneurs,
Et du royaume les greigneurs,
Estoient a celle assamblee,
Aians voulenté et pensee   2520
D'eslire la un autre roy:
La estoient[1488] par bel aroy
Le conte de Northomberlant
Et le conte de Westmerland   2524
Toute jour* en estant sans soir,
Et pour mieulx faire leur devoir
S'agenoilloient moult souvent;
Je ne say pour quoy ne comment.   2528

§49 Lines 2529–2549. The Archbishop of Canterbury's sermon.

L'archevesque aprés se leva
De Cantorbie et sermonna[1489]
Devant tout le peuple en latin,
Et pourposa jusqu'en[1490] la fin   2532
Habuit Jacob benedictionem a patre suo:[1491]
Comment[1492] Jacob avoit eü
Benison en lieu d'Esaü,
Non obstant qu'il estoit l'aisné
Filz dë Isaac;[1493]* c'est[1494] verité.   2536

[1480] C *no* fu
[1481] AD scaforde
[1482] C navoit
[1483] A encore
[1484] LABD cellui C li
[1485] C salsbery
[1486] AB jusques a
D jusques en
[1487] B tou [s *written over* t]
es
[1488] L et la estoit
[1489] H sermonna
[1490] B jusques en C
jusqua [*no* en] D jusqua en
[1491] A *no* suo
[1492] B comme
[1493] HLB disant
ACD disaac
[1494] B ceste

Alas! What a text for a sermon! He preached it in order to demonstrate, in conclusion, that King Richard should have no share [fo. 59r.] in the kingdom of England, and that the prince[172] should have had the realm and the land. These people had completely forgotten that they had all – great and small – acknowledged King Richard as their rightful King and lord for twenty-two years; subsequently in an arbitrary judgement they deposed him by common accord.

§50 Lines 2550–2578. A document is read out which claims that Richard has resigned the throne.

When the archbishop had finished his sermon in Latin, a lawyer[173] who was also a notary and a very learned scholar got up and asked for silence. He began to read aloud a document which said that Richard – formerly King of England – had in another place, confessed, freely and without use of force, that he was neither capable nor worthy: wise, circumspect nor benevolent enough to rule; he wanted to relinquish the crown into the hands of another worthy man who was nobler and wiser than he. This is what they agreed to have been said – rightly or wrongly – [fo. 59v.] by King Richard, unlawfully imprisoned in London.

---

[172] Line 2543. *le prince.* Henry Lancaster.
[173] Line 2552. *Un juriste.* Sir William Thirning. See Tuck, *Richard II and the English Nobility*, p. 222; H.G. Richardson, 'Richard II's last Parliament', *English Historical Review*, 52 (1937), pp. 40, 42–43.

Elas! Quel tiexste de sermon!
Pour monstrer en conclusïon
Le faisoit que le roy Richart
Ne devoit avoir nulle part 2540
[fo. 59r.] A la couronne* d'Engleterre,
Et que le royaume et la terre
Deüst le prince avoir eüue.
Ceste gent[1495] bien desconneüue 2544
Estoit, quant par[1496] vint et deux ans
L'avoient tous – petiz et grans –
Tenu pour droit roy et seigneur;
Et puis aprés[1497] par grant erreur 2548
L'ont par commun accort desfait.

§50 Lines 2550–2578. A document is read out which claims that Richard has resigned the throne.

Quant l'archevesque ot parfait
Son sermon en latin langaige,
Un juriste, qui fu moult saige 2552
Docteur et si estoit notaire,
Se leva et fist les gens taire.
Car il commencha haultement
A lire la un instrument, 2556
Qui contenoit comment[1498] Richart –
Jadiz roy d'Engleterre – a part
Avoit coneu et confessé
Sans force, de[1499] sa voulenté 2560
Qu'il n'estoit ydoine ne digne:
Saige ne[1500] prudent ne benigne
Pour la couronne gouverner,
Et qu'il la vouloit resiner 2564
En la main d'un autre preudomme,
Qui fust noble et plus sage homme
Qu'il n'estoit. Ainsi par accort
Firent dire – fust droit ou[1501] tort – 2568
[fo. 59v.] Au roy Richart en la prison
De Londres par grant mesprison.

[1495] B *no* gent
[1496] A *no* par
[1497] C empres
[1498] BC comme
[1499] ACD et de
[1500] C *no* ne
[1501] AD fust

And then in this said Parliament the document was read before them all; the witnesses were bishops and abbots who swore – I know this well – that the document was completely genuine. Now look here! What testimony! No man ever heard such dishonesty.

§51 Lines 2579–2642. Lancaster is elected as the new King.

After the reading of the document all were silent. Then the archbishop got to his feet and continued his sermon, basing it on the aforesaid document; he spoke so loudly that he could be heard clearly:

'Since King Richard – formerly King of England – in his own words and of his own free will has admitted and confessed that he is not fit, suitable nor wise enough to rule his kingdom, we should take thought and elect another King.'

Alas! Messeigneurs, what madness! [fo. 60r.] They were judge and one side of the argument. This was done neither legally nor loyally, for there were only three or four men there on the side of the former King; they would not have dared for anything to contradict what the others did and said.

Et puis en ce[1502] dit Parlement
Lurent devant tous l'instrument,   2572
De quoy les tesmoings si[1503]* estoient[1504]
Evesques, abbés,[1505] qui disoient
Et tesmoingnoient – bien le say –
Que l'instrument estoit tout vray.   2576
Or regardez! Quel tesmongnage!
Oncques n'ouÿ homs tel oultrage.

§51 Lines 2579–2642. Lancaster is elected as the new King.

Aprés la lecture parfaitte
De l'instrument, sillence faitte   2580
Fu par tout. Et puis se leva
L'archevesque et repris a
Son sermon, prenant fondement
Sur le devant dit instrument,   2584
Disant si hault que bien l'ouÿ
Le peuple: 'Puis qu'il est ensi,
'Et que le roy Richart – jadiz
'Roy d'Engleterre – par ses diz   2588
'Et de sa bonne voulenté
'A reconnu et confessé
'Qu'il n'est pas asés souffisant,
'Convenable ne bien saichant   2592
'Pour le royaume gouverner,
'Il seroit tresbon d'aviser
'Et d'eslire un autre roy.'
Elas! Beaux Seigneurs, quel desroy!   2596
[fo. 60r.] Ilz furent la juge et partie.
Ce n'estoit[1506] pas chose partie
Justement ne de loyal[1507] droit,
Car il n'y avoit la endroit   2600
Homme pour[1508] le roy ansïen
Que trois ou quatre, qui[1509] pour rien
N'eüssent osé contredire
Tout ce qu'ilz[1510] vouldrent faire et dire.   2604

[1502] B ce *superscript*
[1503] HLABD *no* si
[1504] C *lines 2572–2573 omitted*
[1505] C *no* abbes
[1506] C nest
[1507] A leal
[1508] B par
[1509] C que
[1510] C quil

This was completely wrong, for they all concluded – great and small, without being of two or three opinions – that they wanted another King, who could do his duty better than King Richard had done.

When the archbishop had finished explaining in English what he wanted and what was in his heart, and the people had replied to what they had heard, he began to ask one by one:[174]

'Do you want the duke of York to be your King?'

They all replied:

'No indeed.'

'Would you then have his elder son, the duke of Aumale?'

'Let no one talk to us any more of him,' they replied in a loud voice.

Once again he asked: [fo. 60v.]

'Do you want to have his younger son?'[175]

'Indeed no, in truth,' they said.

He asked them about many others, but the people did not grasp at any of those he named. Then the archbishop stopped and was silent for a long time. Then he asked in a loud voice:

'Do you want the duke of Lancaster?'

'Yes! We want none other,' they all replied, so loudly that – as it was told to me – it seemed a wonder to relate.

Afterwards they praised Jesus Christ, as it is contained in Holy Writ.

---

[174] Line 2617. *Il commencha imterroger*. Creton made this up and most of what follows.

[175] Lines 2627–2628. *son filz* ... / *Maisné*. Richard of York, executed in 1415 for his part in a plot against Henry V. See *ODNB*, s.v. 'Richard [Richard of Conisborough], earl of Cambridge (1385–1415)'.

LA PRINSE ET MORT DU ROY RICHART D'ANGLETERRE

Ce fu moult grant desrisïon,[1511]
Car ilz[1512] firent conclusïon
Tous ensemble – grans et petiz,
Sans estre en deux n'en[1513] trois partiz –   2608
Qu'ilz[1514] vouloient[1515] un roy avoir,
Qui seut mieulx faire son devoir[1516]
Que le roy Richart n'avoit fait.
Et quant l'archevesque ot parfait   2612
Et pardit en englés langaige
Sa voulenté et son couraige,
Et le peuple ot respondu
Selon ce qu'orent entendu,   2616
Il commencha imterroger[1517]*
Et chascun par soy demander:
'Voulez vous que[1518] soit vostre roy
'Le duc dë Iorc[1519] par bon aroy?'   2620
Ilz[1520] respondirent tous: 'Nenil!'
'Voulez vous donc avoir son fil
'Ainsné, qui est duc dë Aumarle?'[1521]
'De cely[1522] plus nulz ne nous parle,'   2624
Respondirent a haute voix.
Encor[1523] demanda une fois:
[fo. 60v.] 'Voulez vous[1524] donc son filz avoir
'Maisné?' Ilz dirent:[1525] 'Nenil, voir!'   2628
D'autres asez leur demanda,
Maiz le peuple ne s'ajecta[1526]
A nul de ceulx qu'il ot nommés.
Et lors l'archevesque arestés   2632
Est[1527] sans parler moult[1528] longuement.
Aprés demanda haultement:
'Voulez vous[1529] le duc de Lencastre?'
'Ouïl! Nous ne voulons nul autre,'   2636
Respondirent eulx[1530] tous ensemble
De si haulte voix qu'il me semble –
Selon ce que j'ouÿ compter –
Grant merveilles a recorder.[1531]   2640
Aprés louerent[1532] Jhesucrist,
Sicomme contient leur escript.

[1511] C desasion
[1512] C il
[1513] B ou en
[1514] BC quil
[1515] C voldrent
[1516] C no devoir
[1517] AD a interroguer
[1518] B voules [vous superscript] quil
[1519] all mss diorc
[1520] C il
[1521] all mss daumarle
[1522] LABCD cellui
[1523] LA encore
[1524] B no vous
[1525] L no ilz dirent
[1526] LABD sarresta
[1527] AD fu
[1528] C trop
[1529] D no vous
[1530] A ilz
[1531] C raconter
[1532] AD louoyent

§52 Lines 2643–2660. The election of the new King is confirmed.

When the bishops and prelates, who omitted to do the right thing, along with the foremost lords – who forfeited their honour on the day of that election – heard the questions answered without dispute, they then like false and frenzied traitors, along with the others: knights, squires, villeins, archers and the whole body of the commons, said implacably [fo. 61r.] that the man who did not agree with them deserved to die.

And thus the spurious, false and wicked questions were asked three times; it will be held against them for ever as an evil sin.

§53 Lines 2661–2682. Lancaster accepts the crown.

Then they wrote these things down in documents: letters, charters and deeds, in the presence of all those in the hall, which was neither squalid nor dirty but very richly decorated in a fitting manner. The archbishops[176] rose together – it seemed to me – and went directly to the duke, who had now been elected by all the Commons. They both fell to their knees and said:

---

[176] Line 2668. *Les archevesques*. Creton has only mentioned Canterbury so far. The Archbishop of York was Richard Scrope, executed in 1405 for rebelling against Henry IV. See Given-Wilson, *Henry IV*, pp. 267–270.

§52 Lines 2643–2660. The election of the new King is confirmed.

   Quant les evesques et prelas,
   Qui de bien fere furent las,   2644
   Avecques des[1533] plus grans seigneurs –
   Les quelx perdirent moult d'onneurs
   Le jour de ceste elexïon –
   Orent l'interrogasïon*   2648
   Accordee sans contredire,
   Comme felons faulx et plains d'ire,
   Et tous les autres: chevaliers,
   Escuiers, villains et archiers,   2652
   Et toute la communauté,
   Ilz dirent tous par cruauté
[fo. 61r.] Qu'il estoit bien digne de mort
   Cellui qui n'yert[1534]* de cest accort.   2656
   Et ensi par trois foiz fu faite
   L'interrogasion contrefaite,
   Faulce et plaine de malice;
   A tousjours leur sera lait vice.*   2660

§53 Lines 2661–2682. Lancaster accepts the crown.

   Aprés en firent instrumens:
   Lettres, chartres, burlles, presens
   Tous ceulx* qui furent en la[1535] salle,
   Qui n'estoit villaine ne salle,   2664
   Ains fu moult richement paree
   Par maniere bien ordonnee.
   Se leverent tous deux ensemble
   Les archevesques – ce me semble –   2668
   Et alerent au duc tout droit,
   Qui ja roy[1536] esleü estoit
   De par tout le peuple commun.
   A genoulx se mirent chascun   2672

[1533] C les
[1534] AD est [no ne]
[1535] AD sa
[1536] B qui [a *superscript*]

'The great lords who are here, and also the prelates, in good order elect you and nominate you as King. Decide whether you accept.'

Then duke Henry who was on his knees at that moment, with sound judgement got up and said to them all that he accepted the crown, since it was God's will.

§54 Lines 2683–2748. Ceremonial of making Lancaster King. He ascends the throne.

[fo. 61v.] Then he himself questioned everyone[177] and asked if it was their will. They replied:

'Yes, in truth,' tremendously loudly.

This stirred him so much that he immediately accepted the crown of England.

The archbishops, both kneeling on the ground, took great pains to read aloud the rite and everything the new King was bound to observe. With many ceremonies and cultish practices they placed a cross upon his head and over his whole body, as the custom is there. Both archbishops kissed him and they then picked up the magnificent ring[178] worn by their Kings,

---

[177] Lines 2683–2748. The coronation ceremony is described in Given-Wilson, *Henry IV*, pp. 147–154. A contemporary account is given in Creton, 'Translation of a French Metrical History', ed. Webb, pp. 275–281.

[178] Lines 2703–2704. *l'anel / Du royaume*. Richard is said to have given his signet to Henry in token of his wish for him to succeed him. See Bennett, *Richard II*, pp. 178–179. It was given to Lancaster at his coronation; Given-Wilson, *Henry IV*, p. 151.

Ambedeulx[1537] en disant[1538] ainsi:*
'Les souvrains prinches qui sont cy
'Et les prelas par bel aroy
'T'eslisent et t'appellent roy; 2676
'Regarde se tu t'y consens.'
Lors le duc Henry par grant sens,
Qui estoit pour l'eure[1539] a genoulx,
Se leva et dist devant tous 2680
Qu'il aceptoit la royauté,*
Puis que Dieux l'avoit ordonné.

§54 Lines 2683–2748. Ceremonial of making Lancaster King. He ascends the throne.

[fo. 61v.] Aprés tous les interroga
Ly mesmes et leur demanda 2684
Se c'estoit ainsi[1540] leur vouloir.
Ilz respondirent: 'Ouïl, voir!'
Si hault que ce fu grant merveille.
Ce ly mist la pusse en l'oreille,* 2688
Telement que sans plus atendre
Il volt acepter et entendre[1541]
A la couronne d'Engleterre.
Les archevesques, qui a terre 2692
Furent agenoilliez tous deux,
De lire[1542] estoient[1543]* moult soigneux
Le mistere et tout ce a quoy
Estoit tenu le nouvel roy. 2696
Et par maintes serymonies,
Ofices et ydolatries
Ly metoient croix sur la[1544] teste
Et sur tout le corps par grant feste, 2700
Comme ilz[1545] ont[1546] acoustumé la.[1547]
Lors les archevesques baisa*
Tous deux, et puis prindrent l'anel
Du royaume,[1548] qui est bon et bel, 2704

[1537] HBC deulx L deulx humblement A ambedeulx D [ambe *in left margin*] deulx
[1538] L disans
[1539] A pour lors C par leure
[1540] AD aussy
[1541] H entendre L atendre B accepter et actendre al[tresi] entendre
[1542] D deslire
[1543] H estoient ACD furent
[1544] AD sa
[1545] B il
[1546] CD *no* ont
[1547] A comme la coustume est la
[1548] B l̶a̶n̶e̶l̶ du royaulme

with which it is their custom to marry their Kings; they say that this is the law. They both carried it to the Constable – Lord Percy,[179] a noble knight – [fo. 62r.] and when he had possession of the ring he showed it round to those present; then he kneeled down and placed the ring in marriage on the King's finger. But I would not give a farthing for this rite, since it was performed without law or justice; I am not saying that this would not be an honourable ceremony had it been done as it should be done. The Constable kissed the King on the lips as a proper conclusion to what they were doing; I know not what this means.

The two archbishops immediately came back to the King, who was splendidly attired, and led him by the arms to the richly decorated throne which stood near there. The King kneeled before it and prayed. Then like a second Solomon he addressed everyone there, most particularly the prelates [fo. 62v.] and then the great lords, in Latin and English.

---

[179] Lines 2709–2711. *connestable ... le sire de Persi*. The earl of Northumberland, *supra*, l. 1655, note. It seems likely that Creton did not realize that this was Northumberland.

De quoy ilz ont acoustumé
Que leurs roys[1549] soient[1550] espousé,
Qui est – ce dïent – propre droit.
Entr'eulx le porterent tout[1551] droit 2708
A cellui qui fu connestable,
Qu'ilz[1552] tiennent chevalier notable –
[fo. 62r.] Ce fu le sire de Persi –
Et quant de l'anel fu saisi, 2712
Il le monstra generaument
A ceulx[1553] qui furent la present;
Et puis aprés s'agenoilla
Et ou doit du roy imposa[1554] 2716
Le dit anel par espousaille.
Maiz je n'en donrroie une maille,
Puis que sans droit et sans justice
Est fait et formé tel office; 2720
Je ne dy[1555] pas que ce ne soit[1556]
Digne chose, qui le[1557] feroit
Ainsi c'on[1558] doit tel chose faire.
Et pour[1559] leur euvre mieulx parfaire 2724
Le roy baisa parmi la[1560] bouche
Le connestable;* a[1561] quoy touche[1562]
Ce mistere je ne say[1563] pas.
Les deux archevesques le pas 2728
Revindrent par devers le roy,
Qui estoit en tresbel aroy,
Et l'ont[1564] droit par les[1565] bras mené[1566]
Au siege royal qui paré 2732
Estoit richement pres de la.
Le roy devant s'agenoilla
Et fist dedens ses oroisons.
Aprés comme tressaiges homs 2736
Parla a tous en general,
Aux prelas par especial
[fo. 62v.] Et aux plus grans seigneurs aprés
En latin langage et englés. 2740

[1549] A leur roy
[1550] A sy soit D soit
[1551] AD *no* tout
[1552] B quil
[1553] B a tous ceulx
[1554] L si posa
[1555] B je ne dy ne dy pas
[1556] AD que ne seroit
[1557] D ne
[1558] BCD com
[1559] C par
[1560] AD sa
[1561] L et a
[1562] H touce
[1563] H fay LABCD say
[1564] L *no* lont
[1565] ABD le
[1566] L lont mene

When he had finished what he had to say, with no dissenting voice raised, he took his seat on the throne. Alas! King Richard was deprived of it for good, so much did they hate him; but please God, they will do the same to the one whom they have placed on it.

§55 Lines 2749–2772. The new Constable is confirmed in office.

He sat on the throne without speaking for a long time and made no sound, for everyone there was praying devoutly for the prosperity, authority, peace and health of the new King whom they had elected.

When everyone there had finished praying, the Constable, who was not yet established or confirmed in his office – where there should be no sin – was summoned publicly; he kneeled humbly before Henry and the lords. He was there elected [fo. 63r.] Constable by the greatest in the land without opposition, and then Henry gave into his hands the golden staff, which should incline him to worthy deeds at all times, if he intends to do his duty.

LA PRINSE ET MORT DU ROY RICHART D'ANGLETERRE 241

Maiz quant il ot finé son dit
Sans ce[1567] que nulz ly contredit,
Ou royal siege s'est assis.[1568]
Las! Le roy Richart desaisis 2744
En fu la pour toute sa vie,
Tant avoient sur ly envie;
Maiz se[1569] Dieu plaist, ainsi feront
De cellui qu'inposé[1570] y[1571] ont. 2748

§55 Lines 2749–2772. The new Constable is confirmed in office.

Ou dit siege moult longuement
Fu assis sans nul parlement
Faire et sans noise nesune,
Car entandis[1572] estoit chascune 2752
Personne la en oroyson,
Priant par grant devosïon
Pour la bonne prosperité,
Gouvernement, paix et santé 2756
Du roy nouvel qu'i[1573] orent fait.
Et quant chascun la ot parfait
Ses oroisons, le connestable,
Qui n'estoit pas encore estable 2760
Ne ferme ou devant dit office –
Au[1574] quel ne doit avoir nul vice –
Fu appellé generaument;
A genoulx se mist humblement 2764
Devant Henry et les seigneurs.
La fu esleü des greigneurs[1575]
[fo. 63r.] Connestable sans contredit,
Et lors Henry au devant dit 2768
Connestable bailla en sa[1576] main
Le baston d'or,[1577] qui soir et main
Le doit a prouesce esmouvoir,
S'il veult bien faire son devoir. 2772

[1567] B *no* ce
[1568] BD ou royal [*mark of omission*] sest assis [siege *at line end*]
[1569] C si
[1570] L qui pose D qui impose
[1571] C *no* y
[1572] D en temps dis
[1573] LA quilz
[1574] AD ou
[1575] AD seigneurs
[1576] C la
[1577] AD *no* dor

§56 Lines 2773–2794. High officers of state are elected.

Afterwards everyone there elected a new Marshal[180] and then they all in good form swore allegiance to Henry and paid homage to him. Afterwards they elected a very wise man as Chancellor,[181] and having done this they installed the Keeper of the Privy Seal;[182] they ended by filling a great number of other offices.

Next the archbishop rose to his feet and recited several Latin rites, urging them to pray loyally for the prosperity of the King and of his kingdom; he repeated this in English. When he finished what he had to say, they all of high and low degree sat down as one man.

§57 Lines 2795–2832. Lancaster's eldest son is made Prince of Wales. 13 October is set for the coronation of the new King.

[fo. 63v.] Then duke Henry got to his feet. His eldest son kneeled down humbly in front of him; he created him Prince of Wales[183] in the presence of everyone there, and granted him the land. But I think he will have to fight for it if he wants to possess it, for the Welsh would not recognize him as their lord at any price – I think – on account of the pain,

---

[180] Line 2774. *nouvel mareschal.* Ralph Neville, earl of Westmorland. *Supra*, p. 203, ll. 20–21, note.

[181] Line 2779. *chancelier.* John Scarle, Chancellor and Keeper of the Great Seal under Richard II, continued in his office under Henry IV. See *ODNB*, s.v. 'Scarle, John (d. 1403)'. Also, S. Walker, *The Lancastrian Affinity, 1361–1399* (Oxford, 1990), p. 145.

[182] Lines 2782–2784. *La garde du sëel privé; / D'autres offices ... / Firent eulx.* Richard Clifford, Keeper of the Privy Seal, also served both Richard and Henry. See *ODNB*, s.v. 'Clifford, Richard (d. 1421)'. The other office-holders are listed in Creton, 'Translation of a French Metrical History', ed. Webb, p. 204 n. v.

[183] Lines 2796–2799. *Son filz aisné ... / Prince de Galles.* Henry of Monmouth, the future Henry V. *Supra*, l. 138, note. He was created both Prince of Wales and duke of Lancaster.

§56 Lines 2773–2794. High officers of state are elected.

  Aprés trestous en general
  Eslurent[1578] nouvel mareschal,
  Et puis par tresbelle ordonnance
  Jurerent ferme foy, fiance[1579]   2776
  A Henry en faisant hommage.
  Et lors esleurent[1580] un tressage
  Homme, qui chancelier fu fait,
  Et quant ilz[1581] orent ce parfait,   2780
  Encor ont ilz institué[1582]
  La garde du sëel[1583] privé;
  D'autres offices grant foisson
  Firent eulx en conclusïon.   2784
  L'archevesque aprés se leva
  Et a tous haultement dit a
  Plusieurs misteres en latin,
  Eulx esmouvant[1584] que[1585] de[1586] cuer fin*   2788
  Prient pour la prosperité
  Du roy et de sa royaulté;*
  En englés aprés[1587] leur a dit.
  Et quant il ot parfait[1588] son dit,   2792
  Tous en general sont assis,
  Uns et autres, grans et petiz.

§57 Lines 2795–2832. Lancaster's eldest son is made Prince of Wales. 13 October is set for the coronation of the new King.

  [fo. 63v.] Lors se leva le duc Henry.
  Son filz aisné par devant ly   2796
  Se mist humblement a genoulx;
  Prince de Galles devant tous
  Le fist et ly donna la terre.
  Maiz je cuide bien que conquerre   2800
  Ly[1589] fauldra, s'il le[1590] veult avoir,
  Car les Galloiz[1591] pour nul avoir
  Ne le tenroient a seigneur –
  Ce cuide je – pour la douleur,   2804

[1578] AD eslirent
[1579] L et fiance
[1580] AD eslirent
[1581] B il
[1582] B il constitue
[1583] L seau
[1584] B esmouvans
[1585] C no que
[1586] H le LABCD de
[1587] C empres
[1588] AD parfait ot
[1589] C le
[1590] LAC la
[1591] AD car certes gales

the grief and the great disgrace that the English under his father had heaped on King Richard. Then everyone individually swore allegiance, loyalty, help and comfort to the said prince, as they had to the duke. He made his second son duke of Lancaster[184] unconditionally; everyone was very happy at that.

Afterwards all the prelates, dukes, princes, earls – it seems to me – and the whole body of the Commons bowed their heads before the duke with most profound reverence, as a sign of their submission to him. And then by common accord and without dispute – as I heard it said – [fo. 64r.] they chose as duke Henry's coronation day St Edward's day, 13 October; they were very impatient at such a long delay.

They did nothing else that day, except to say that anyone who does not greatly rejoice over the election will perhaps lose his head.

---

[184] Lines 2812–2813. *Son second filz* … / *Duc de Lencastre*. This is not correct, *supra*, ll. 2796–2799, note. See *ODNB*, s.v. 'Thomas [Thomas of Lancaster], duke of Clarence (1387–1421)'.

Le mal et le[1592] grant vittupere,
Que les Englois avec[1593] son pere
Avoient fait au roy Richart.
La jurerent chascun a part   2808
Au dit prince foy, loyauté,
Aide, confort et[1594] féaulté,*
Comme ilz avoient au duc fait.
Son second filz fist il de fait   2812
Duc de Lencastre ligement;[1595]
Chascun en fu asés content.
Aprés tous les prelas ensemble,
Ducs, princes, contes[1596] – ce[1597] me semble –   2816
Et tout le commun[1598] en la fin
Saluerent[1599] de chief enclin
Le duc par tresgrant reverence,
Monstrant[1600] signe d'obedïence.[1601]   2820
Et puis tous par commun accort
Eslurent[1602] sans point de discort
Pour le duc Henry couronner –
Sicomme j'ay oÿ compter[1603] –   2824
[fo. 64r.] Le propre jour Saint Edouuart,
.xiii.ᵉ d'octobre;[1604] moult tart
Leur estoit de si long[1605] sejour.*
Autre rien ne firent ce jour,   2828
Fors tant qu'en[1606] la conclusïon
Dirent: qui[1607] de l'elexsïon[1608]*
Au[1609] fort ne se resjouira,
Espoir decapitez sera.   2832

[1592] L la
[1593] B angloiz ont avec
[1594] HLACD no et B et superscript
[1595] AD ligierement
[1596] C contes princes
[1597] C si
[1598] C et dont le commun
[1599] H salurent LABCD saluerent
[1600] L monstrans
[1601] H dobedïence C dobeissance
[1602] ACD eslirent
[1603] C line 2824 omitted
[1604] L .xiii.ᵉ jour doctobre
[1605] LC loing
[1606] LB que
[1607] L que
[1608] H lelexsion L lelection A qui delection de lelection B qui de [le superscript] lection D qui delection delelexsion
[1609] AD a

246   LA PRINSE ET MORT DU ROY RICHART D' ANGLETERRE

§58 Lines 2833–2932. Lancaster creates forty-five new knights. He is crowned and a feast follows.

As you have heard – and as he who heard the whole affair and what Parliament did related to me – the former King was deposed without justification, unlawfully and with no half measures; it will be held against them for ever as an evil sin.

When they had done the deed and deposed good King Richard and shut him up in their prison – and this was a great wrong – very early on the following Sunday nearest the coronation Henry summoned the greatest lords of England to come to the Court in London. And in order to win for himself praise and honour he dubbed a great number of knights in the presence of them all. Thus was it told me by him who was there, and who gave the number as [fo. 64v.] forty-five, neither more nor less; you can be sure – as he said – that his younger son[185] was the first. Then he had a mind to ride through London on this very day, without staying any longer at Court, and the new knights, well arrayed, all rode together with him.

Thus did that day pass and the Wednesday arrived when – as I told you before – he was to be crowned. So he was, and in order

---

[185] Line 2856. *Son filz maisné*. As well as Thomas of Lancaster, his other two younger sons were among the new knights. Some of these are named in Given-Wilson, *Henry IV*, p. 148 n. 42.

§58 Lines 2833–2932. Lancaster creates forty-five new knights. He is crowned and a feast follows.

    Ainsi com[1610]* vous avez ouÿ –
Et que[1611] cellui, qui tout[1612] ouÿ
Le fait et le Parlement faire,
M'a voulu compter* et retraire –   2836
Fu desfait le roy ancïen
Sans droit, sans loy et sans moyen,
Sans raison, sans[1613] vraie justice;
A tousjours leur sera lait vice.   2840
Et quant ilz[1614] orent ce parfait
Et le bon roy Richart desfait
Et enfermé en leur prison –
Dont ilz firent grant mesprison –   2844
Le dimenche aprés plus prouchain
Du couronnement asés main,
A la court de Londres mander
Fist Henry et la assembler   2848
Les plus grans seigneurs d'Engleterre.
Et pour los et honneur aquerre
Fist devant tous[1615] grant quantité
De chevaliers. Ainsi compté   2852
Le m'a cellui qui y estoit,
Et qui pour le nombre afermoit
[fo. 64v.] Quarente et cinq, ne plus ne mains;
Son filz maisné – soiez certains   2856
Sicomme il dist – fu le premier.
Aprés s'en volt il chevauchier
Parmi Londres ce propre jour
Sans faire a la court plus sejour,   2860
Et estoit en sa compaignie
La nouvelle chevalerie
Tout ensamble, bien ordonnee.
Ainsi passa ceste journee,   2864
Tant que ce vint le mercredi –
Qu'isi[1616] devant pieça vous di –
Qu'il[1617] devoit couronne porter.
Si fist il, et pour deporter   2868

[1610] HABCD comme L com
[1611] C qui
[1612] C tant
[1613] L et
[1614] D et quilz
[1615] B fist [devant superscript] tous
[1616] L que cy
[1617] L no il

to celebrate the coronation more fully, four dukes ritually carried above his head a rich pall of cloth of gold. The duke of York was first and then the good duke of Surrey, who did not do it sincerely, for he loved King Richard and was always of his party, whatever they made him do. To complete their work of destruction, the duke of Aumale[186] was the third, who carried out the task willingly, for he was not loyal, as you will hear below; [fo. 65r.] the fourth knew what he was doing and was called the duke of Gloucester.[187] These four dukes – rightly or wrongly – by common assent bore the pall above their King, who was handsomely accoutred.

And when he was crowned King they returned to the Court where dinner was very richly prepared; this is how it was. After duke Henry the Archbishop of Canterbury was seated first at the royal table, have no fear of that. The duke occupied the very middle of the table which was conspicuously raised up two and a half feet higher than the two ends, as he who was present told me; he said that the middle part of the table was two arms' lengths[188] long or more. Furthermore he told me that several new bishops, neither true nor loyal

---

[186] Lines 2881–2884. *Le duc d'Aumarle ... / ... n'estoit pas bien loyal / Comme vous orrez cy aval.* Creton usually calls him earl of Rutland; *supra*, ll. 93–94. He is referring forward here to Rutland's supposed betrayal of the Epiphany Rising, *infra*, ll. 3052–3106.

[187] Line 2886. *duc de Clocestre*. There was no duke of Gloucester at this time. Thomas of Woodstock had died at Calais in 1397, and his son, Humphrey, died on the march from Chester to London. Henry IV's fourth son, Humphrey, became duke of Gloucester, but only under his brother in 1414. Creton might have meant Thomas Despenser, earl of Gloucester, who was with Richard in Ireland; *supra*, ll. 304–305, note.

[188] Line 2905. *braces*. *OED*, s.v. 'brace' = the distance between the fingertips with arms extended. For a man almost 6 feet tall, this is roughly 5 feet 9 inches (175 centimetres).

Et honnourer plus haultement
Le devant dit couronnement
Li porterent dessus sa teste
Quatre ducs par mistere et feste   2872
Un riche paille a or batu.
Le duc dë Iorc[1618] le premier fu
Et puis le bon duc de[1619] Souldray,[1620]
Qui ne le fist pas de cuer vray,   2876
Car il amoit le roy Richart
Et si fu tousjours de sa part,
Quelque chose c'on li fist faire.
Et[1621] pour leur masacre parfaire   2880
Le duc d'Aumarle fu le tiers,
Qui l'euvre faisoit voulentiers,
Car il n'estoit pas bien loyal,[1622]
Comme vous orrez cy aval;   2884
[fo. 65r.] Le quatriesme sot bien son estre
Et fu nommé duc de Clocestre.
Ces quatre ducs – fust droit ou tort –
Porterent par commun accort   2888
Le paille par dessus leur[1623] roy,
Qui estoit en tresbel aroy.
Et quant il fu roy couronné
A la court s'en sont retourné,   2892
Ou le disner moult richement
Fu apresté; vecy[1624] comment.
L'archevesque de Cantorbie
Fu le premier – n'en doubtez mie –   2896
A la table royale assis
Aprés le duc Henry. Saisis[1625]
Fu droit du[1626] milieu de la table,
Qui estoit par feste* notable   2900
Plus haulte deux piez et demi
Que les deux bous – comme celi
Le me dit qui present estoit;
La longueur – sicomme[1627] il disoit –   2904
Estoit de deux braces ou plus.
Encor me dist il du[1628] surplus
Que pluseurs evesques nouviaulx,
Qui n'estoient vrais ne loyaulx,   2908

[1618] *all mss* diorc
[1619] C *no* de
[1620] D *line 2875 repeated then scored out*
[1621] B *no* et
[1622] H loyal L loyl
[1623] AD le
[1624] L veez cy
[1625] H saisis L assis B sassis C cest sis
[1626] LA ou
[1627] AD comme [*no* si]
[1628] B de

but unjustly appointed, were also sitting at the King's table.

His elder son, in fine array, who was made Prince of Wales, was holding in his hand [fo. 65v.] a sword for jousting; but I heard no man say what this means. He was on his father's right hand, and next to him was a knight who was holding the sceptre capped with a cross. To the left – as I believe – was the new Constable who displayed the Constable's sword in front of the table; it was meant for administering justice. But at that time neither the Constable nor his sword were functioning as they should, for without restraint and with neither rhyme nor reason, but full of wickedness, evil and disloyalty, they persisted in their behaviour, as their actions reveal.

§59 Lines 2933–2984. The feast continues and homage is paid to Henry. The King's Champion enters.

The new Marshal was there, standing in front of Henry and holding the royal sceptre; he was the earl of Westmorland. Next the earl of Warwick,[189] whom they hold in very high esteem, was bread-bearer for the day. The great cup-bearer

---

[189] Line 2937. *de Werewic le conte*. Thomas Beauchamp, twelfth earl of Warwick. Along with Gloucester and Arundel, Warwick was one of the Lords Appellant of 1388, accused of treason in 1397. Having confessed, Warwick was pardoned and exiled to the Isle of Man, whence he was recalled after Richard's deposition. See *ODNB*, s.v. 'Beauchamp, Thomas, twelfth earl of Warwick (1337 × 1339–1401)'.

Maiz faiz sans droit et sans raison,
Estoient en conclusïon
Assis a la table du roy.
Son filz aisné par[1629] bel aroy,   2912
Qui prince de Galles fu fait,
Tenoit la en sa main de fait
[fo. 65v.] Une espee pour le tournoy;
Maiz a nul homme[1630] dire n'oy   2916
Que senefie ce mistere.
A la destre estoit de son pere,
Et tout au plus pres de celi
Un chevallier y avoit qui   2920
Tenoit le ceptre de la croix.
A senestre – comme[1631] je le[1632] croix –
Estoit le nouvel connestable,
Et tenoit la devant la[1633] table   2924
L'espee de connestablie,[1634]
Qui fu pour justice establie.
Maiz pour lors në[1635] ouvrerent pas,
Car[1636] sans mesure et sans compas   2928
Comme gens plains d'iniquité,
De mal et de desloyaulté
Persevererent en leur euvre,
Comme la l'euvre[1637] le[1638] descuevre.   2932

§59 Lines 2933–2984. The feast continues and homage is paid to Henry. The King's Champion enters.

La fu le nouvel mareschal,
Qui tenoit le ceptre royal
Par devant Henry en estant;
Contë estoit de Westmerlant.   2936
Aprés de Werewic[1639]* le conte,
De quoy ilz tiennent moult grant compte,
Fu ce propre jour panetier.
Et si estoit grant bouteillier   2940

[1629] C pour
[1630] L a nulluy
[1631] L com
[1632] ACD *no* le
[1633] L le
[1634] B connestable
[1635] LACD nen
[1636] L mais
[1637] LAD comme la veue
B comme leur oevre
[1638] AD *no* le
[1639] *all mss* werwic

was the earl of Arundel[190] (who is young and fleet of foot). The Marquis carved at dinner; that was how they arranged things.

[fo. 66r.] The duke of Aumale served him with wine, but before the duke's table was cleared, the Steward,[191] the Marshal and the Constable rode into the hall; they remained there in front of the table until it was cleared. And to honour the duke even more, a knight called Thomas Dymock[192] entered the hall on a mailed horse, well armed and ready for battle, and said: if there be any man – of high or low degree – who maintained that King Henry was not lord and rightful King of all England, then he challenged him to fight to the death. No man reacted to this. He rode three or four times around the hall, offering himself for combat, as he had said.

After dinner the greatest lords of England, without demur, together paid homage to duke Henry. But some there were who did not act [fo. 66v.] with a sincere heart, rather had they already plotted

---

[190] Line 2941. *conte d'Arondel*. For Thomas Fitzalan, fifth earl of Arundel, *supra*, p. 203, ll. 13–14, note.

[191] Lines 2948–2949. *le seneschal / Le mareschal, le connestable*. Thomas Percy, earl of Worcester; Ralph Neville, earl of Westmorland; Henry Percy, earl of Northumberland.

[192] Line 2954. *Thommas de Noth*. Sir Thomas Dymoke. See *ODNB*, s.v. 'Dymoke [Dymmok] family (*per. c.*1340–*c.*1580)'. In **L**, a contemporary cursive hand has written in the left margin: *dymmoc*.

Un qui fu conte d'Arondel,
(Qui est[1640] assez jeune et ysnel.)
Le Marquis trancha[1641] au[1642] disner;
Ainsi le voldrent ordonner.   2944
[fo. 66r.] Le duc d'Aumarle le servi
De vin, maiz ains[1643] que deservi
Fust le duc, vindrent a cheval
En la sale le seneschal,   2948
Le mareschal, le connestable;
La se tindrent devant la table,
Jusqu'a[1644] tant c'on volt deservir.
Et pour le mieulx a gré servir[1645]   2952
Un chevalier, qui fu nommé
Thommas de Noth,[1646] tresbien armé
Comme pour combatre en bataille,
Sur un cheval, armé de maille,   2956
Entra en la sale disant:
S'il estoit nul – petit ne grant –
Qui voulsist maintenir ne dire
Que le roy[1647] Henry ne fust sire   2960
Et droit roy de toute Engleterre,
Qu'il le vouloit d'armes requerre;
Voire quelles? Tout a oultrance.
La n'ot[1648] nul homme qui a ce*   2964
Respondist ne mot ne demy.
Ainsi chevaucha tout parmy
La sale bien[1649] trois tours ou quatre
Desirant se[1650] vouloir combatre,   2968
Comme il demonstroit par son dit.
Aprés disner sans contredit
Les plus grans seigneurs tous ensemble
D'Engleterre – comme il me semble –   2972
Firent au duc Henry hommaige.
Maiz les aucuns de bon courage
[fo. 66v.] Ne le[1651] firent pas vrayement,
Ains avoient secretement   2976

[1640] L fu
[1641] H tranch
[1642] C a
[1643] A no ains
[1644] B jusques a
[1645] L line 2952 et apres veissics venir
[1646] L dymmoc in left margin
[1647] C duc
[1648] C no not
[1649] AC no bien C pour trois
[1650] A de C le
[1651] AD les

to kill him, since he had this day had himself wrongly crowned by force of arms. They planned to have a great feast day arranged this coming Christmas at Windsor Castle (which is very strong and fine).

§60 Lines 2985–3050. The plot to kill Henry.

Thus was the feast day arranged, but those who schemed to carry out their plot planned to joust against all-comers, of high and low degree: there was the good duke of Surrey, who was always loyal and true to his lord, King Richard; Salisbury was on his side. Those two organized the jousting against all-comers – and I esteem them much for this – so that under cover of the feast day they could bring in there many men-at-arms to achieve their ends: their dearest wish was to kill duke Henry as they had undertaken to do. But subsequently they were captured [fo. 67r.] and shamefully put to death, for the treacherous duke of Aumale[193] betrayed them, in which he did great wrong: he was of their party

---

[193] Line 3006. *duc d'Aumarlle* (also at ll. 3063, 3074, 3102). He was earl of Rutland only at this date. *Supra*, p. 191, ll. 17–22, note.

Ja pieça maciné sa mort,
Pour ce que[1652] par[1653] force et a tort[1654]
S'estoit fait ce jour couronner.
La voldrent ensemble ordonner 2980
Q'une grant[1655] feste se feroit
Au Noël prouchain qui venoit
A Windesore le chastel
(Qui est molt fort et si est bel.) 2984

§60 Lines 2985–3050. The plot to kill Henry.

Ainsi fu la feste ordonnee,
Mais ceulx, qui avoient pensee
D'achever leur euvre et parfaire,
Vorent[1656] la une emprise faire 2988
De jouster contre tous venans,
Uns et autres, petiz et grans:
Ce fu le bon duc de Souldray,
Qui fu tousjours loyal et vray 2992
A son seigneur, le roy Richart;
Salsebery[1657] fu de sa part.
Ces deux firent[1658] de jouste[1659] enprise
Contre tous – dont moult je les prise – 2996
Afin telle que desoubz l'ombre
De la feste[1660] peüssent nombre
De gens d'armes la amener[1661]
Pour mieulx leur vouloir[1662] achever: 3000
Car c'estoit leur plus grant desir
Du duc Henry* faire mourir,
Comme ilz avoient entrepris.[1663]
Maiz ilz en furent depuis pris 3004
[fo. 67r.] Et mis a mort villainement,
Car duc[1664] d'Aumarlle faulcement
Les trahi, dont il ot grant tort:
Si estoit il[1665] de leur accort 3008

[1652] C parce que
[1653] AD a
[1654] B a tors tort
[1655] AD qune tres grant
[1656] LB vouldrent
[1657] C salsbery
[1658] L furent
[1659] AD jouster
[1660] L de lemprise
[1661] AD enmener
[1662] AD couvine [no leur vouloir] [D couvine superscript]
[1663] AD avoient fait entrepris B lavoient
[1664] A car le duc
[1665] A estoyent ilz

and had sworn faith and loyalty to them and that he would help in any way to make their plot succeed. The duke of Exeter also knew all about their plans and was in league with them; he had reason to be, as he was brother german to good King Richard, the former King whom they had unanimously deposed and deprived of the fair crown of England. Therefore no one should be surprised that they wanted to do their duty to place King Richard – who ought to be King of England for all of his life – back in possession of his kingdom and of his lands.

You will hear how the duke of Surrey and the earl of Salisbury, in order better to carry out their scheme in secret, laid their plans to ensure the success of their plot. They had big carts made and planned to place many men inside, [fo. 67v.] well equipped and well armed, who would be driven there covered up, as if they were suits of armour for the tourney, in order that they might more easily enter Windsor Castle, where the duke was said still to be. The men were commanded and told that as soon as they saw their masters, they should do their duty

Et avoit juré avecque[1666]* eulx
Foy, loyaulté et qu'en[1667] tous lieux
Aideroit ceste euvre parfaire.[1668]
Encor[1669] savoit tout cest affaire   3012
Et estoit de leur aliance
Le duc d'Excestre, qui a ce
Faire avoit[1670] cause soir et main,
Car il estoit frere germain   3016
Du bon roy Richart ancïen,
Qu'il[1671] avoient[1672]* sans nul moyen
Desfait et osté la couronne
D'Engleterre, qui est moult bonne.   3020
Et pour ce nulz ne doit avoir
Merveilles, se iceulx[1673] leur devoir
Vouloient faire de remettre
Le roy Richart – qui devoit estre   3024
Tout son vivant roy d'Engleterre –
En son royaume et en sa terre.
Maiz pour faire secretement
Mieulx leur fait,[1674] vous orrez[1675] comment   3028
Le duc[1676] de Souldray et le conte
De Salsebery[1677]* firent leur conte
D'achever ceste[1678] euvre et parfaire.
Ilz firent grans charrettes faire   3032
Et pourpenserent que dedens
Mettroient grant foison de gens
[fo. 67v.] Bien abilliés et bien armés,
Qui seroient couvers menés[1679]   3036
En lieu de harnoiz a jouster,
Afin qu'ilz peusent mieulx[1680] entrer
Ens ou chastel de Windesore,
Ou le duc devoit estre encore.   3040
Leur estoit commandé et dit
Que tantost, sans nul contredit,
Qu'ilz[1681] pourroient aperchevoir
Leurs seigneurs, chascun son[1682] devoir   3044

[1666] HACD avecques LB aveuc
[1667] L en [no que]
[1668] LA a parfaire
[1669] A encore
[1670] C no avoit
[1671] LABCD quilz
[1672] H avoient
[1673] L si ceulx B se iceulx ceulx de
[1674] B leur vous fait
[1675] H vous [orrez superscript] LAD diray B no orrez C dire
[1676] B [que in left margin] le duc
[1677] C salsbery
[1678] L leur [no ceste]
[1679] L couvers et menez
[1680] B quil mielx y peussent
[1681] B quil
[1682] B no son C leur

by killing those who were guarding the doors; and while they were doing that, their masters would hasten towards duke Henry and put him to death, without showing him any mercy.

§61 Lines 3051–3100. Rutland betrays the plot.

Their scheme was suspended at this point while Christmas approached, when the duke went to stay at Windsor to judge at the festivities that were going to take place. And then the duke of Surrey and the earl of Salisbury wrote a letter[194] which dealt solely with carrying out the plot. They had it taken to London by a trustworthy man, straight to the earl of Rutland,[195] (who was duke of Aumale at that time): begging him [fo. 68r.] to be ready to come to them to carry out their plot as they had vowed together; and that he bring all his men with him, so that should there be anyone ready to oppose them, they can kill them or capture and put them to death without delay.

But when the duke of Aumale saw in the letter the commands to which he was held

---

[194] Line 3056. *une lettre*. One letter, singular, becomes plural, *les firent porter*, l. 3060; *Des lettres*, ll. 3076, 3093; and *les lettres*, l. 3085. It reverts to one letter, *sa lettre*, l. 3105. It has been translated as one letter throughout. The whole story of how the conspiracy was revealed bears a general resemblance to the account in the *Traïson*, although the *Traïson* does not rely on the *Prinse et mort* at this point. It is presumably the story that had currency in France at the time. See *Chronicque de la traïson et mort*, ed. Williams, pp. 80–82.

[195] Line 3062. *conte de Rotellant,* / (*Qui estoit duc d'Aumarlle lors*). L. 3063 is an unfortunate way of filling up the couplet, as Rutland was no longer duke of Aumale at this time. *Supra*, p. 191, ll. 17–22, and note.

LA PRINSE ET MORT DU ROY RICHART D'ANGLETERRE 259

 Feïst de tuer les portiers,
 Qui les fors gardoient[1683] entiers;[1684]
 Et ainsi celle euvre faisant,
 Yroient leurs seigneurs courant   3048
 Au[1685] duc Henry pour mettre a mort
 Sans li faire plus long[1686] deport.

§61 Lines 3051–3100. Rutland betrays the plot.

 En ce point leur fait s'arresta,
 Tant que le[1687] Noël aproucha,   3052
 Que le duc s'en ala logier
 A Windesore pour jugier
 De[1688] la feste qui devoit[1689] estre.
 Et lors escriprent une lettre   3056
 Le duc de Souldray et le conte
 De Salsebery, qui ne tint[1690] compte
 De riens fors de[1691] l'euvre achever.
 A Londres les[1692] firent porter   3060
 Par un homme qui fu saichant,
 Droit au conte de Rotellant,
 (Qui estoit duc d'Aumarlle lors):
 En ly suppliant que ses corps*   3064
 [fo. 68r.] Fust tout prest de venir vers eulx
 Pour acomplir l'euvre et les[1693] veulx
 Qu'ilz avoient promis ensemble;
 Et que toutes ses gens ensemble   3068
 Face venir avecques lui,
 Afin que, s'il y a nulluy[1694]
 Qui se vueille contre eulx deffendre,
 Qu'ilz[1695] les puissent[1696] tuer ou prendre   3072
 Et mettre a mort sans nul respit.
 Maiz quant le duc d'Aumarle vit
 Le mandement et contenu
 Des lettres, ou il fu tenu   3076

[1683] L le fort gardent
[1684] H tous entiers LB tous entiers ACD no tous
[1685] C a
[1686] LAD loing
[1687] B no le
[1688] B se
[1689] L doit
[1690] B tient
[1691] B no de
[1692] A la D le
[1693] C le
[1694] B nulle envy
[1695] B qui C quil
[1696] B puisse

by his promise and by his pledged word, he pretended to be very eager to set off at top speed to obey the summons that the lords had sent him. Alas! He was not without blame: he never will be, for he does not appear so, since he carried the lords' letter to the old duke of York – his father – sparing the lords nothing. He knew for sure that the duke – his father – did not love them or King Richard; rather was he of duke Henry's party having sworn liege homage to him.

When the duke of York saw what was in the letter and what its aim was, he frowned angrily [fo. 68v.] and had a great number of men brought to him, saying,

'Take my son to the King, so that he can relate to him the great crime that is planned against him; it was thought up in an evil hour.'

§62 Lines 3101–3130. Henry escapes.

The duke of Aumale left his father and went down hastily to Windsor; he gave his letter to duke Henry and revealed the whole plot to him. But the duke did not believe him, until that very day the mayor came with all speed from London and confirmed the plot from beginning to end.

Par sa prommesse et foy baillie,[1697]
Faintement monstra grant envie
De partir bien hastivement
Pour obeir au mandement, 3080
Que les seigneurs ly orent fait.
Elas! Il n'estoit pas parfait:
Jamaiz ne[1698] sera, qu'i[1699] n'y pere,*
Car au viel duc dë Iorc[1700] – son pere – 3084
Les lettres des seigneurs porta,
Ne de riens ne les deporta.
Si savoit il bien pour[1701] certain
Que le duc – son pere – un seul grain 3088
N'amoit eulx ne le roy Richart;
Ains estoit de l'accort et part
Du duc Henry par lige hommage.
Et quant il ot veu le langage 3092
Des lettres et toute la maniere,
Par mautalent fronsa la[1702] chiere
[fo. 68v.] Et fist asambler foison gens,
Disant: 'Soiez tost[1703] diligens 3096
'De mener mon filz vers[1704] le roy
'Pour ly compter le grant desroy,
'Qui est contre ly pourpensé;
'Mal orent le fait enpensé!'[1705] 3100

§62 Lines 3101–3130. Henry escapes.

De son pere se desparti
Le duc d'Aumarle, en tel parti
Quë hastivement sans atendre
A Windesore ala descendre; 3104
Sa lettre au duc Henry bailla
Et tout le fait ly aferma.
Maiz le duc ne le crëoit[1706] pas,
Quant de Londres plus que le pas 3108
Vint le maire ce propre jour
Sans gueres faire[1707] de sejour,
Qui lui aferma de rechief[1708]
Trestout le fait de chief en chief. 3112

[1697] L bailliee A baillee
[1698] H ne BC ny [B y written over e]
[1699] AB quil
[1700] *all mss* diorc
[1701] AD de
[1702] AD froissa sa
[1703] L tous
[1704] C *no* vers
[1705] L pourpense
[1706] L crut D croit
[1707] B faire gueres
[1708] B afferma de p derrechief

When Henry heard this, he would not have waited there longer at any price. He quickly mounted on horseback for fear that he would be overthrown that day by his enemies. He set out on the road to London, he and the mayor with his men. They made great haste, but before they could arrive in London, those who wanted to kill him were already inside [fo. 69r.] Windsor Castle to carry out their plot. But when they discovered that the duke had left, they were very unhappy that they had not captured him and that he had thus escaped.

§63 Lines 3131–3158. The rebel lords move to Cirencester. They put it about that King Richard is free; his chaplain Maudelyn is to impersonate him.

They retreated from Windsor and went to Cirencester – a town that is quite near there – where they had a very large force of their men-at-arms: they all wanted to use their bodies and their weapons to restore King Richard, who in justice should be King for all of his life. They drew their men up in good order for riding; with them were many archers and they said that good King Richard had escaped from prison and was there with them.

LA PRINSE ET MORT DU ROY RICHART D'ANGLETERRE   263

>Et quant Henry l'a entendu,[1709]
>Pour riens n'eust[1710] plus la[1711] atendu.[1712]
>A cheval bien tost est monté,
>De peur qu'il ne fust surmonté   3116
>Ce jour la de ses ennemis.
>Ou[1713] chemin de Londres s'est mis,
>Lui et le maire avec ses gens.
>D'eulx haster furent deligens,   3120
>Maiz ains qu'ilz[1714] peüssent venir
>A Londres, ceulx qui grant desir
>Avoient de le[1715] mettre a mort,
>Estoient ja dedens le fort   3124
>[fo. 69r.] De[1716] Windesore bien avant
>Pour acomplir leur fait. Maiz quant
>Ilz sorent[1717] que le duc estoit
>Partiz, ilz furent moult destroit,   3128
>Quant ne l'avoient atrapé,
>Et qu'ensi estoit eschappé.

§63 Lines 3131–3158. The rebel lords move to Cirencester. They put it about that King Richard is free; his chaplain Maudelyn is to impersonate him.

>De Windesore sont retrais
>Et a Surestre se sont trais –   3132
>Une ville qui[1718] est asés pres
>De la – ou ilz avoient tres
>Grant quantité de leur[1719] gens d'armes:
>Desirant[1720] tous de corps et d'armes   3136
>A remettre en possesïon
>Le roy Richart, qui par raison
>Devoit estre[1721] son vivant roy.
>Leur[1722] gens firent mettre en conroy   3140
>Tresbien[1723] et bel pour chevauchier;
>Avec eulx avoit maint archier,
>Disant[1724] que le bon roy Richart
>Avoit fait de prison depart,   3144

[1709] A attendu
[1710] C no neust
[1711] A la plus B no plus
[1712] D entendu
[1713] AD au
[1714] C quil
[1715] B no le C les
[1716] C a
[1717] B sceurent
[1718] B une [ville in left margin] qui
[1719] LABCD leurs
[1720] ABCD desirans
[1721] B estre *superscript*
[1722] LABCD leurs
[1723] C tresbon
[1724] L disans

To make this more believable they took along a chaplain, who resembled good King Richard so closely in face, body, actions and words that anyone seeing him would have testified that he was the former King; he was called Maudelyn.[196] [fo. 69v.] I saw him often in Ireland riding through woods and plains with King Richard, his master; never did I see such a handsome priest.

§64 Lines 3159–3222. The rebel lords attempt to rally the country for King Richard but are defeated in battle. Exeter, Surrey and Salisbury are executed.

They had the above-named Maudelyn dressed in kingly armour with his helmet sumptuously crowned, so that people would really think that the King was out of prison. They then intended to ride around the country to rally all the friends and allies of King Richard. Alas! They were too late, for without delay duke Henry, who wanted them dead, swiftly sent there so many men, that none of those whom he wished to capture escaped.

---

[196] Line 3154. *Appellé estoit Madelien. Supra*, l. 1873, note.

Et qu'il estoit la avec eulx.
Et pour le faire acroire mieulx
Avoient pris un chappellain,
Qui resembloit si de certain   3148
Au bon roy Richart de visage,
De[1725] corps, de fait et de langage,
Qu'il n'est homme qui le veïst,[1726]
Qui ne certifiast et dist   3152
Que ce fust le roy ancïien;
Appellé estoit Madelien.
[fo. 69v.] Maintesfoiz le vy en Irllande
Chevauchier par bois et par lande   3156
Avec le roy Richart, son maistre;
Pieça je[1727] ne vy plus[1728] bel prestre.

§64 Lines 3159–3222. The rebel lords attempt to rally the country for King Richard but are defeated in battle. Exeter, Surrey and Salisbury are executed.

Le dessus dit firent armer
Comme roy, et puis couronner   3160
Son hëaulme moult richement,
Afin c'on cuidast vraiement
Que le roy fust hors de prison.
La avoient entensïon   3164
De chevauchier par le païs
Pour assembler tous les amis
Et aliez du roy Richart.
Elas! Ilz le firent trop tart,   3168
Car le duc Henry sans atendre,
Qui vouloit a leur mort entendre,
Hastivement y[1729] envoia
Tant de gens, c'oncquez n'eschapa   3172
Nulz[1730] de ceulx qu'il[1731] voldrent avoir.

[1725] C que
[1726] B home quil ne [le *superscript*] vist
[1727] AD *no* je
[1728] L si
[1729] B il
[1730] LB nul
[1731] LC quilz

They did their bounden duty to fight them off for a long time, but there were a hundred or more men against ten, as I heard. Those fought like false and frenzied traitors until they gained the upper hand and captured all the rebel lords by force, which was a great shame, for they had to suffer bitter death, as you will hear tell. [fo. 70r.] First of all they beheaded the duke of Exeter, next the good duke of Surrey, who was always loyal and true, and then the earl of Salisbury was not forgotten in this tally; they had these three put to death shamefully and unlawfully.

Afterwards the heads were carried to London amid great rejoicing. They were nailed up on lances on London Bridge, high enough for them to be easily seen. But to tell you the truth, they did not leave the duke of Exeter's head there long; it only stayed there a day and a night, because he was married to duke Henry's sister.[197]

---

[197] Line 3202. *La suer du duc. Supra*, l. 827, note.

Si[1732] firent ilz[1733] bien[1734] leur devoir
D'eulx deffendre moult longuement,
Maiz contre dix estoient cent   3176
Ou plus,[1735] sicomme j'ouÿ dire.
Comme felons faulx[1736] et plains d'ire
Firent, tant qu'ilz orent la force
Et qu'il[1737] les prindrent tous a force,   3180
Dont ce fu pitié et dommage,
Car la leur convint le passage
De la mort amere endurer,
Comme vous orrez cy compter.   3184
[fo. 70r.] Au duc d'Excestre tout premier
Firent eulx[1738] la teste trancher,
Aprés au bon duc de Souldray,
Qui fu tousjours loyal et vray,   3188
Et puis de Salsebery le conte
N'oublierent[1739] pas en ce compte;
Ces[1740] trois firent eulx[1741] mettre a mort
Villainement et a grant tort.[1742]   3192
Aprés firent porter les testes
A Londres, ou on[1743] en fist grans festes.
La furent mises sur[1744] le pont
A[1745] lances clouuees[1746] amont,   3196
Si hault c'on les[1747] puet[1748]* assez voir.
Maiz pour vous en dire le voir,
Celle qui fu du duc d'Excestre
N'y laisserent[1749] pas longtemps estre;   3200
Pour ce qu'il avoit espousee
La suer du[1750] duc, q'une[1751] journee[1752]
Et une nuit n'y demoura.

[1732] B sil
[1733] BD *no* ilz [B il *in left margin*]
[1734] A *no* bien
[1735] L *no* plus
[1736] C faulx felons
[1737] LABCD quilz
[1738] L ilz
[1739] H nouiblierent
[1740] C les
[1741] C ilz
[1742] D et mettre a mort [*no* a grant tort]
[1743] AD *no* on
[1744] L sus
[1745] ACD en
[1746] LB clouees
ACD cloues
[1747] D le
[1748] ABCD peust
[1749] L ne laissierent
[1750] L au
[1751] C *no* que
[1752] A *lines 3201–3202 transposed*

Now may God, who suffered death to redeem sinners from the infernal agonies of hell, preserve their souls in heaven, for at all times they were worthy men, loyal and bold, in word, thought and deed; so much so that one could not find three such knights in all England today, for they remained faithful [fo. 70v.] and devoted unto death. But if they were mindful of God and His holy Passion, I understand and believe that they are in Paradise above, for their blood was shed as martyrs[198] loyally defending what was right in all respects.

§65 Lines 3223–3234. Richard is told the bad news.

Shortly afterwards good King Richard was told the whole truth of the sorrowful affair, which was distressing for him to hear, and that was no surprise. Weeping he then said,

'Death, get ready to attack me, no one can help me any longer, since I have lost my friends. Sweetest God, who was hung on the Cross, have mercy on me, for I can live no longer like this.'

---

[198] Lines 3220–3221. *comme martirs espandus / Fu leur sanc.* Creton has already compared Salisbury to a martyr, *supra*, ll. 788–792.

LA PRINSE ET MORT DU ROY RICHART D'ANGLETERRE 269

    Or vueille[1753] Dieux, qui endura   3204
    La mort pour pecheurs rachetter
    Des infernaulx paines d'enfer,
    Avoir leurs[1754] ames es sains chieulx.
    Car ilz estoient en tous lieux   3208
    Loyaulx preudommes et hardis,
    En fait, en pensee et en dis;[1755]
    Et tant qu'en trestoute[1756] Engleterre
    On ne saroit trouver ne querre   3212
    Au jour d'uy telz trois chevalliers,
    Car ilz demourerent entiers
    [fo. 70v.] Et loyaulx jusques a la mort.
    Maiz s'il[1757] orent de Dieu remort[1758]   3216
    Et de sa[1759] sainte passïon,
    Je croy selon m'entenssïon[1760]
    Qu'ilz sont en Paradis la sus,
    Car comme martirs espandus   3220
    Fu leur sanc[1761] pour maintenir droit
    Et loyaulté en tout endroit.

§65 Lines 3223–3234. Richard is told the bad news.

    Un pou aprés firent savoir
    Au bon roy Richart tout le voir   3224
    De la besoingne douloureuse,
    Qui ly fu a ouïr[1762] piteuse,
    Dont ce ne fu pas grant[1763] merveille.
    En plourant dit lors: 'Appereille   3228
    'Toy, Mort, et me viens sus courir;[1764]
    'Nulz[1765] ne me puet plus secourir,
    'Puis que j'ay perdu mes amis.
    'Tresdoulx Dieux, qui en croix fu mis,   3232
    'Vueillez avoir de moy merchi,
    'Car vivre ne puis plus ainsi.'

[1753] H vueilliez LABC vueille D vueillie
[1754] C les
[1755] L line 3210 omitted
[1756] BC no tres
[1757] LABCD silz
[1758] H dieu [erasure] remort
[1759] A no sa
[1760] H selon [erasure] mentenssion
[1761] H sanc B fait [no sanc]
[1762] C loir
[1763] L no grant
[1764] A secourir
[1765] L nul B nulz nulz

§66 Lines 3235–3266. Richard refuses to eat and dies.

When the King received this bad news, his heart filled so much with anger that, from that time onwards, he neither ate not drank, and thus it was that he died, so they say. But really I do not believe that this was so, since some men say that for sure he is still alive and well and [fo. 71r.] shut up in their prison – which is a great crime on their part – even although they had a dead man carried openly through London – this was no lie – with all the honour and ceremony due to a deceased King, saying that it was the body of King Richard, who had died.

Duke Henry made a pretence[199] of mourning, holding in front of him the pall covering the coffin. Behind him walked his kinsmen, in good array; they had no knowledge of King Richard or the crimes that they had committed against him. This will weigh on them in the presence of God on the Last Day, when He will condemn the wicked into the flames of hell which burn for ever.

---

[199] Line 3256. *par semblance. Supra*, l. 1461, note.

§66 Lines 3235–3266. Richard refuses to eat and dies.

Aprés le roy de ces nouvelles,
Qui ne furent bonnes[1766] ne[1767] belles, 3236
En son cuer print de[1768] courroux tant
Que depuis celle[1769] heure en avant
Oncques ne menga ne ne[1770] but,
Ains convint que la mort reçut, 3240
Comme ilz[1771] dïent.[1772] Maiz vrayement
Je ne le croy pas ensement,
Car aucuns dïent pour certain
Qu'il est encore[1773] vif et sain, 3244
[fo. 71r.] Enfermé dedens leur prison –
C'est pour eulx grande[1774] mesprison –
Non obstant que tout en apert
Firent eulx porter descouvert 3248
Un homme mort parmi la ville
De Londres – ce ne fu[1775]* pas guille –
A telle honneur et[1776] a tel feste
Que pour roy mort doit estre faite, 3252
En[1777] disant que c'estoit le corps
Du roy Richart, qui estoit mors.
La faisoit dueil le duc Henry[1778]
Par semblance, droit devant ly 3256
Tenant le paille du[1779] sarceulx.
Aprés ly aloient tous ceulx
De son sanc par belle ordonnance,
Sans avoir de ly connoissance 3260
Ne des maulx qu'ilz ly[1780] orent faiz.
Devant Dieu leur[1781] sera grant[1782] faiz,
Quant[1783] ce vendra[1784] au jour derrenier,*
Qu'il vouldra les mauvaiz jugier 3264
En la flame perpetuelle
D'enfer, qui sera inmortelle.

[1766] L ne bonnes
[1767] C et
[1768] C des
[1769] C telle
[1770] D *no* ne
[1771] C il
[1772] L ilz le dient
[1773] B encor
[1774] C grant
[1775] H fu
[1776] B *no* et
[1777] C *no* en
[1778] B le roy henry [duc *at line end*]
[1779] D de
[1780] LB qui lui
[1781] B len changed to leur [*dots beneath* n, ur *contraction above*]
[1782] LB grans
[1783] D que
[1784] L quant venra [*no* ce]

§67 Lines 3267–3312. Richard's funeral.

As you hear tell, they carried the body directly to St Paul's in London, honourably and fittingly, as was appropriate for a King. But certainly I do not believe that it was the former King, rather do I believe that it was his chaplain Maudelyn, who resembled him so closely in appearance, breadth, height and build [fo. 71v.] that everyone firmly thought that it was good King Richard.

And if it was him, I pray earnestly and continually to our merciful and benevolent God that He may receive his soul in heaven above, for he hated all vice and evil, as I believe. I saw in him nothing but goodness and his Christian faith; I served him for seven[200] months to the best of my ability, in order that I might in some way merit the gifts he had promised me.

Certainly he was only deposed and betrayed because he faithfully loved the King of France – his father-in-law – with a true heart, as much as any man alive. This was the root of their hatred, even although they alleged that in

---

[200] Line 3288. *sept mois*. Creton was with Richard from May to August 1399, four months. A palaeographical error is in play here. The original reading would have been *.iiii.* (= *quatre*), the four minims easily mistaken for *.vii.*. *Sept* is repeated, *infra*, l. 3678. Similarly **A**'s *ung* (= *un*, four minims)is a misreading of *.iiii.*.

§67 Lines 3267–3312. Richard's funeral.

Ainsi com[1785] vous ouez compter,
Voldrent le corps mort enporter   3268
A Saint Pol de Londres tout droit,
Honnorablement et a droit,
Comme il appertenoit a[1786] roy.
Maiz certainement pas ne croy   3272
Que ce[1787] fust le roy anciïen,
Ains croy que c'estoit[1788] Madelien,
Son chappellain, qui de visage,
De grandeur, de long, de corsage[1789]   3276
[fo. 71v.] Le resembloit* si justement,
Que chascun cuidoit fermement
Que ce fust le bon roy Richart.
Et se[1790] c'estoit il,[1791] main et tart   3280
Prie je de vray cuer a Dieu –
Qui est misericors et pieu –
Qu'il vueille es sains chieulx avoir l'ame
De ly, car il haioit tout blasme   3284
Et tout vice, par[1792] mon advis.
N'oncques en li riens je ne vis
Fors foy[1793] cathollique et justice;
Si ly[1794] fi je sept[1795] mois service   3288
De ce que[1796] je[1797] povoy[1798] servir,
Pour aucunement deservir
Les biens quë il[1799] m'avoit promis.
Et certes il[1800] ne fu demis   3292
Ne trahy, fors tant seulement
Pour ce qu'il amoit loyaument
Le roy de France – son beau pere –
De vraie amour et singuliere,[1801]   3296
Autant qu'omme qui fut[1802] en vie.
Ce fu la rachine de[1803] l'envie,*
Non obstant qu'ilz ly[1804] mirent sus
Qu'il avoit fait mourir[1805] les ducs – 3300

[1785] HABCD comme L com
[1786] A au
[1787] B ce *superscript*
[1788] L feust [*no* ce]
[1789] B de coupsaige ce corpsage
[1790] C si
[1791] H il *superscript* B *no* il C lui
[1792] H par LABCD selon
[1793] B foy *in left margin*
[1794] A luy
[1795] A ung
[1796] B de que ce que C *no* ce
[1797] L *no* je
[1798] LABCD povoye
[1799] B quil
[1800] H et certes il LAB et je croy quil C et croy je quil D et se croy quil
[1801] L singulere B singliere
[1802] L soit
[1803] *all mss* et
[1804] C le
[1805] B quil avoit [fait *in left margin*] mourir

his folly he had had the dukes – his uncles[201] – foully murdered, and that he was neither wise nor capable enough to rule the kingdom. I could tell you plenty of other things that they say, but certainly I think I have told you [fo. 72r.] the truth as I understand it. If I had to surrender my soul, I would continue to think in this way; being a wicked and capricious race, they have a mortal hatred of the French, if only they dared to show it.

§68 Lines 3313–3405. Henry sends ambassadors to Charles VI: amongst other things he wants a marriage between Queen Isabella and the Prince of Wales.

The Commons crowned duke Henry after he had accomplished the greater part of what he wanted and deposed good King Richard. Then he appointed his official ambassadors and messengers (who were very wise) – clerks and laymen – and sent them to Calais bearing letters of credence to the King of France.

The bishop of Durham[202] was of their number – so I heard – and Sir Thomas Percy,[203] who was happy to do his master's bidding; also Sir William Heron,[204] who knew what he was doing.

---

[201] Lines 3300–3301. *il avoit fait mourir* ... / *Ses oncles*. *Supra*, l. 1633, note.
[202] Line 3325. *L'evesque de Dureme*. Walter Skirlaw was bishop of Durham, 1388–1406. See *ODNB*, s.v. 'Skirlawe [Skirlaw], Walter (*c*.1330–1406)'.
[203] Line 3327. *de Persi Sire Thommas*. *Supra*, l. 34, note.
[204] Line 3332. *Guillaume Heron*. William Heron, Lord Say, was Steward of the King's household under Henry IV. See Given-Wilson, *Royal Household*, pp. 73, 196.

LA PRINSE ET MORT DU ROY RICHART D'ANGLETERRE 275

  Ses oncles – par son fol oultrage,
  Et qu'il n'estoit prudent ne sage
  Pour le royaume gouverner.
  D'autres choses asez compter   3304
  Vous pourroie que chascun dit,
  Maiz certes je vous[1806] cuide avoir dit
[fo. 72r.] Le vray, comme je puis entendre.
  Et se devoie[1807] l'ame rendre,   3308
  Si[1808] demourroy[1809] je[1810] en ceste colle,
  Car comme gent mauvaise et folle
  Hëent Françoiz mortellement,[1811]
  S'ilz[1812] osoient monstrer comment.   3312

§68 Lines 3313–3405. Henry sends ambassadors to Charles VI: amongst other things he wants a marriage between Queen Isabella and the Prince of Wales.

  Aprés ce que le duc Henry
  Ot achevé et acompli
  De son vouloir la plus grant part
  Et desfait le bon roy Richart,   3316
  Le fist le commun couronner.
  Et puis aprés volt ordonner
  Ses embassadeurs et messages
  Sollempnes, (qui furent moult sages),   3320
  Et les envoia a Callais:
  Gens d'eglise avecques[1813] gens lais,
  Pour venir vers[1814] le roy de France,
  Apportant[1815] lettres de creance.[1816]   3324
  L'evesque de Dureme y fu –
  Ainsi que je l'ay entendu –
  Et de Persi Sire[1817]* Thommas,
  Qui n'estoit travailliés[1818] ne mas[1819]   3328
  De faire le vouloir son maistre;
  Avecque[1820] un, qui sot bien son estre,
  C'on appelle par son droit non
  Monseigneur[1821] Guillaume Heron.   3332

[1806] L *no* vous
[1807] H et se je devoie L et se devoie ABD et se je devoie C et si je devoie
[1808] L *no* si
[1809] L demourray C demoureray D demourroye
[1810] D *no* je
[1811] L mortelment
[1812] AD sil
[1813] LAD aveuc
[1814] L veoir
[1815] LABCD apportans
[1816] A recreance
[1817] *all mss* messire
[1818] LB travaillie
[1819] C las
[1820] H avecque [*small erasure*] ACD avecques
[1821] L messire

These three came across to justify the crime that their new King had committed against the King of France[205] [fo. 72v.] who had showered him with such great honours when he was unhappily banished from England. The said ambassadors promptly sent a herald (who was wise, cunning and circumspect) to Paris to ask for their safe-conduct, for thus were they instructed by their master when they left.

The herald was made to leave Paris swiftly without a reply, a safe-conduct or a summons, for the King would not suffer them to come to negotiate with him. Rather did he send Master Pierre Blanchet[206] and Henart de Kanbenart[207] to them at Calais to find out what they wanted; these two travelled together. There the English ambassadors greeted them – it seems to me – with much reverence and courtesy, saying that there had been a great revolution in their country, and that they had chosen a new King following the decree and good advice of the Commons of England, without anyone finding fault with that.

---

[205] Lines 3336–3339, and *infra*, ll. 3374–3375. Lancaster had been well received in France, when he went there on being banished in 1398. See Given-Wilson, *Henry IV*, p. 119; Saul, *Richard II*, pp. 405–406.

[206] Line 3353. *Pierre Blanchet* was secretary to Charles VI. An editorial note in Froissart, *Oeuvres*, ed. Kervyn de Lettenhove, XVIII, pp. 587–588, contains the instructions given to the bishop of Chartres, Jehan de Hangest, Pierre Blanchet and Gontier Col, when they were sent to speak to the English messengers at Calais.

[207] Lines 3353–3354. *Henart / ... de Kanbenart* was Charles VI's usher of arms. See *Anglo-Norman Letters and Petitions*, ed. Legge, no. 158.

LA PRINSE ET MORT DU ROY RICHART D'ANGLETERRE 277

Ces trois firent lors le passage
Pour venir excuser l'oultrage,
Que leur[1822] roy nouvel avoit fait
Au roy de France, qui de fait[1823]   3336
[fo. 72v.] Ly avoit fait si grant honneur,
Lui estant banis[1824] a douleur
Hors du royaume d'Engleterre.
Aprés envoierent bonne[1825] erre   3340
Les diz messages un herault,
Qui fu sage, soutif[1826] et caut,
A Paris pour[1827] leur saufconduit,
Car ainsi furent introduit   3344
De leur maistre au departir.
Maiz on fist le herault partir
Bien brief de Paris sans reponse
Et sans saufconduit ou semonse,[1828]   3348
Car le roy ne volt pas souffrir
Qu'a ly se[1829] venisent[1830] pour[1831] offrir.
Ains envoia par devers eulx
A Callais pour savoir leurs[1832] veulx   3352
Maistre Pierre Blanchet, Henart
Qu'aucuns[1833] dïent de Kanbenart;[1834]*
Ces deux y alerent ensemble.
La leur firent – comme il me semble –   3356
Reverence et[1835] honneur moult grant
Les messages anglés, disant
Que tresgrande mutasïon
Avoit[1836] eu[1837] en leur regïon,   3360
Et qu'il[1838] avoient fait un roy
Tout nouvel[1839] par[1840] le bon arroy
Et conseil du peuple commun
D'Engleterre, sans ce qu'aucun   3364
D'eulx y eust trouvé que redire.[1841]

[1822] L le
[1823] H de [small erasure] fait
[1824] L bany
[1825] LB bon
[1826] L soubtil AD soubtis
[1827] C par
[1828] AD responce
[1829] L sen B se *changed to* sy
[1830] ACD vinssent
[1831] LC *no* pour
[1832] L les
[1833] H quacuns L que aucuns ABCD quaucuns
[1834] L de cambernart AD de vaubernart B que kaubernart C de karbenart
[1835] C *no* et
[1836] A avoient
[1837] AD eue
[1838] LABD quilz
[1839] L nouvel tout
[1840] BC pour
[1841] L y eust riens trouve que redire [*no* deulx]

Words could not express [fo. 73r.] the great affection that this King felt towards his cousin – the King of France – so tenderly did he love him and would continue to love him throughout his life; for as long as he lived he would be greatly attached to him, as he had received him most splendidly in his country.

'And to nurture the love, well-being, peace and health of the two kingdoms this King would like a marriage to be arranged in France – so it seemed to us – between the Queen and his son, the Prince,[208] and between him and another lady of royal blood who conquers his heart: thus great joy and many advantages could fall on the two kingdoms – certainly no Christian in this world could wish for more – and he would like a lasting peace to be announced throughout the two countries.'

---

[208] Line 3383. *la roÿne et ... son filz,* / *Le prince.* Isabella and Henry of Monmouth.

Du quel roy ne savoient[1842] dire
[fo. 73r.] Le desir ne[1843] la[1844] grant ardeur
D'amour, qu'il avoit sans faveur 3368
Au roy de France – son cousin –
Tant l'amoit de loyal cuer fin
Et aimeroit toute sa vie;
Et que, tant qu'il[1845] seroit en vie 3372
Se tendroit grandement tenu
A ly, car il l'avoit[1846] receu
En son païs moult grandement.
'Et pour connourir[1847]* fermement 3376
'L'amour et[1848] la transquilité,
'Bien, paix, aliance et santé
'Des deux[1849] royaumes tout ensemble
'Desire – selon ce[1850] qu'il nous semble – 3380
'Que mariage se feïst
'En France – comme il nous a dit –
'De la roÿne et de son filz,
'Le prince – soiez ent tous fiz[1851] – 3384
'Et de ly a une autre dame
'Du sanc royal, qui son cuer dame:
'Et par[1852] ainsi pourroit venir
'Es deux royaumes grant plaisir 3388
'Et grant abondance de biens –
'Voire trestous les crestïiens
'De ce monde ne[1853] voulroient[1854] mieulx –
'Et que ferme paix en tous lieux 3392
'Des deux royaumes fust criee.'

[1842] C savoit
[1843] LABC et D de
[1844] B le
[1845] C et tant que il
[1846] B avoit [no le]
[1847] L renourrir
[1848] B de
[1849] B de deux C no deux
[1850] B no ce
[1851] A line 3384 omitted
[1852] C pour
[1853] HLACD en B ne
[1854] LACD vauldroient B vouloient

But when they had delivered their message to the French, these latter replied, before [fo. 73v.] they left the place, saying:[209]

'Messeigneurs, God forbid that we give one word in reply to this matter, for it is too important an affair. We are only instructed to report your request and what you say to the King of France, our master.'

§69 Lines 3406–3494. French ambassadors are sent to Boulogne to hear the English requests and to demand the return of Queen Isabella. She arrives at Calais on 25 July 1401.

Thus without saying another word the French messengers left the English, who once more showed them prodigious honour and reverence. They returned directly to France, to Paris where the King was; he was most anxious to know the English situation, and how they had deposed King Richard and put him to death.

The messengers made their report to the King in full Council, relating accurately the conduct of the English, and how they humbly begged for a safe-conduct. Then the Council very wisely agreed together – it seems to me – to send

---

[209] Line 3396. Monstrelet gives a brief account of the handing back of Isabella. See Monstrelet, *La Chronique*, ed. Douët-d'Arcq, I, pp. 32–36.

Maiz quant[1855] ilz orent bien contee
Leur raison devant les Franchois,
Ilz les[1856] respondirent,* ainchois 3396
[fo. 73v.] Qu'ilz se partissent de la place,
Disant:[1857] 'Seigneurs, ja Dieu ne place
'Que de ceste matiere yci[1858]
'Respondons ne mot ne demi, 3400
'Car c'est une chose trop grant.
'Chargiez ne[1859] sommez plus avant
'Fors seulement de rapporter
'Toute vo[1860]* requeste et parler 3404
'Au roy de France, nostre sire.'

§69 Lines 3406–3494. French ambassadors are sent to Boulogne to hear the English requests and to demand the return of Queen Isabella. She arrives at Calais on 25 July 1401.

Ainsi sans plus[1861] parler ne dire
Se partirent eulx[1862] des Englés,[1863]
Qui de rechief leur firent tres 3408
Grant honneur et grant reverence.
Tout droit retournerent en France
A Paris, ou le roy estoit,
Qui assez grant desir avoit 3412
De savoir des Angloiz le fait,
Et comment[1864] ilz orent desfait
Le roy Richart et mis a mort.
En plain conseil firent rapport 3416
Les messages devant le roy,
Racomptant par tresbel aroy
Des Englés toute la maniere
Et comment[1865] par humble priere 3420
Desiroient un[1866] saufconduit.
Lors le conseil, comme bien duit
Et sage, fu d'accort ensemble
C'on envoieroit – ce me semble – 3424

[1855] B quant *at line end*
[1856] LB ilz leur AD et les
[1857] LB disans
[1858] L cy [*no* y]
[1859] L nen
[1860] HLBCD toute vostre A tout vostre
[1861] B *no* plus
[1862] A ilz
[1863] H engl<u>e</u>s
[1864] B come
[1865] B come
[1866] B *no* un

ambassadors of equal rank to hear their proposition [fo. 74r.] and what the English wanted. They should take pains to enquire about what the English had done; and the English should hand back the Queen with all speed, as they are obliged to do by their pledged word and the seals affixed to the documents drawn up when the marriage was arranged between King Richard and his wife. None of the French should be slow to petition them time and again, otherwise their behaviour will be wicked and disloyal and great harm will ensue in the two countries. They should have only one aim, and hide nothing that is right from the English; they should go directly without delay to Boulogne to hear and know what the English propose.

Thus in February the bishop of Chartres[210] left Paris first along with Monseigneur de Hugueville,[211] stopping nowhere until they came to Boulogne; Master Pierre Blanchet[212] was there, [fo. 74v.] also Master Gontier Col.[213] They had to put up with the rough and the smooth before they could win back the Queen, for

---

[210] Lines 3452–3453. *L'evesque de Chartres.* Jean de Montaigu, bishop of Chartres, 1390–1406, was brother to Jean de Montaigu, first owner of **H**. *Supra*, Introduction, pp. 2–3 nn. 5 and 6.

[211] Line 3453. *Monseigneur de Hugueville.* Jean de Hangest, sire de Hugueville, a member of the king's council. See Given-Wilson, *Henry IV*, pp. 171–173. For a brief biography, see Froissart, *Oeuvres*, ed. Kervyn de Lettenhove, XXI, p. 508. His statement detailing his negotiations in England regarding Isabella's return is printed ibid. XVI, pp. 366–373. See also A. Dubois, *Valère Maxime en français à la fin du Moyen Age* (Turnhout, 2016), p. 81.

[212] Line 3456. *Pierre Blanchet. Supra*, l. 3353, note.

[213] Line 3457. *Gontier Col.* Secretary to Charles VI. He died at the hands of the Burgundians when they took control of Paris in 1418. See R. Bossuat, L. Pichard, and G.R. de Lage (eds), *Dictionnaire des lettres françaises: Le Moyen Age*, new edn (Paris, 1992), s.v. 'Gontier et Pierre Col'. Also Perroy, *La Guerre de Cent Ans*, p. 192.

Messages d'estat tout pareil
A eulx, pour ouÿr leur conseil[1867]
[fo. 74r.] Et[1868] ce qu'ilz[1869] vouldroient requerre.
Et qu'il[1870] mettent paine d'enquerre 3428
De leur fait et de leur convine;[1871]
Et qu'ilz rendent brief la roÿne,
Comme[1872] ilz y sont tous obligiés
Par leur foy et sëaulx fichiés 3432
Aux instrumens qui furent faiz,
Quant le mariage parfaiz
Fu du roy et de sa compaigne.
Et que nesun[1873] d'eulx ne se[1874] faigne 3436
De les en sommer bien souvent,
Ou qu'ilz seroient autrement
Faulx, parjures et desloyaulx,
Et qu'il en pourroit trop de maulx 3440
Avenir es deux regïons.
Ne qu'a autres oppinïons
Nulle quelconque[1875] fors a celle
N'entendent, et c'on ne[1876] leur celle 3444
Riens a dire qui soit de droit;
Et qu'il[1877] s'en voisent trestout droit
A Boulongne sans plus atendre
Pour ouÿr, savoir et entendre 3448
Ce qu'Englés[1878] vouldront[1879] proposer.
Lors partirent sans reposer[1880]
De Paris ou mois de fevrier
L'evesque de Chartres premier[1881] 3452
Et Monseigneur de Hugueville
Sans arrester n'a[1882] champ n'a ville,
Tant qu'a Boulongne sont venu;
Maistre Pierre Blanchet y fu, 3456
[fo. 74v.] Aussi fu Maistre Gontier Col.
Ceulx endurerent dur et mol
Asez, ains qu'ilz peussent ravoir[1883]
La roÿne, car riens de voir 3460

[1867] B pour oyr tout leur conseil [*no* a eulx]
[1868] B de
[1869] C quil
[1870] LACD quilz
[1871] H convi<u>n</u>e
[1872] C et comme
[1873] B neiz un
[1874] C *no* se
[1875] L nulles quelconques
[1876] H ne *superscript* B *no* ne
[1877] LACD quilz
[1878] H que<u>n</u>gles
[1879] BC vouldrent
[1880] C arrester
[1881] H premi<u>er</u>
[1882] L a [*no* ne] B nau
[1883] C avoir

in truth the English would make them no concessions, considering that the negotiations lasted twenty months before they repatriated the young Queen; they were always delaying until she would be twelve years old, so that her deeds and words, and anything they could have had her do, could never be undone. But they were entreated and petitioned so often by the French – showing them that they were very wrong to keep her, considering the agreement that was made on her marriage – that the English ordered her passage [to France].

On Tuesday 25 July around six o'clock in the morning, the Queen of England crossed from Dover to Calais; this was in the year 1401, as I understand. She was in splendid company, for she had with her some of the greatest ladies of England. When they had set foot on shore, [fo. 75r.] Hugueville who had crossed with her did not delay. Rather did he report immediately to the ambassadors at Boulogne what had happened, and how she had crossed over, and that the English intended to hand her back, as they had him understand.

Ne leur tenoient les Englois,
Veu que l'espace de vint mois
Dura la prosecusïon,
Ains que la restitusïon 3464
Feissent de la jeune roÿne;
Atendant[1884] tousjours le termine
Qu'elle eüst douze ans acomplis,
Afin que ses faiz et ses dis 3468
Et ce qu'ilz ly eussent fait faire,
N'eüst on[1885] peu jamaiz[1886] desfaire.
Maiz requis furent si souvent[1887]
Et sommés par françoise gent – 3472
Eulx demonstrant qu'a tresgrant tort
La tenoient,[1888] veü l'accort
Qui en fu fait au[1889] mariage –
Qu'ilz[1890] ordonnerent son passage. 3476
Droit le[1891] mardi .xxvme [1892]
Jour de juillet environ prime
Passa de Douvres a Callais[1893]
La roÿne des Englois, mais 3480
Ce fu en l'an mil quatre cens
Et un – sicomme je l'entens –
Tresgrandement acompaignie,[1894]
Car elle ot en sa compaignie[1895] 3484
Des plus grans dames d'Engleterre.
Quant descendus furent a terre,
[fo. 75r.] Hugueville, qui fu passés
Avecque[1896] elle, ne fu lassés, 3488
Ains escript tantost a Boulongne
Aux embassadeurs la besongne
Et comment[1897] elle estoit passee,
Et qu'ilz avoient tous pensee[1898] 3492
De la restituer et rendre,
Comme ilz ly orent[1899] fait entendre.

[1884] ACD attendans
[1885] D on *superscript*
[1886] C jamais peu
[1887] C *line 3471 omitted*
[1888] ACD retenoient
[1889] B en
[1890] B quil
[1891] A au
[1892] ABD le .xxv.^{e}
[1893] H callais
[1894] L accompaigniee
[1895] L compaigniee C *line 3484 omitted*
[1896] ACD avecques
[1897] B come
[1898] H tous en pensee
[1899] BC ilz lorent

§70 Lines 3495–3509. Queen Isabella moves from Calais to Leulingham.

On the following Sunday, the last day of July, without any more obstruction, the Queen left Calais with the English who could not find any more justifiable cause for delay, so much did the French petition them; they led her straight to Leulingham.[214] Right there she was met by those who were in the picture, that is the honest count of St Pol[215] – as everyone says – and with him the French ambassadors who had moved mountains to get her back.

§71 Lines 3510–3564. The handover of Isabella at Leulingham begins.

Near Leulingham the Queen entered an elegant pavilion that the English had erected in the valley. The high-born ladies of France approached, greatly wishing [fo. 75v.] to meet her. A little later – as it seems to me – they left there and everyone led the Queen to the chapel of Leulingham (which looks like everyone knows who has seen it).[216]

---

[214] Line 3502. *Lolinghehen*. Leulingham, midway between Boulogne and Calais, was used at this time for Anglo-French peace conferences and agreements. See Monstrelet, *La Chronique*, ed. Douët-d'Arcq, I, p. 33 n. 4.

[215] Line 3505. *de Saint Pol le ... conte*. Waleran III of Luxembourg, count of St Pol, 'one of the most powerful of Philip's vassals in Artois', Vaughan, *Philip the Bold*, pp. 89–90.

[216] Lines 3521–3523. *la chappelle / ... (qui est telle / Que chascun scet, qui l'a veüe)*. Creton's energy seems to be flagging here; this is a quite flagrant way of filling out the couplet.

§70 Lines 3495–3509. Queen Isabella moves from Calais to Leulingham.

<blockquote>

Le dimenche aprés[1900] derrenier* jour
De juillet, sans plus de sejour,   3496
Parti de Callais la roÿne
Avec[1901] Englés, qui de termine
Ne porent plus par droit trouver,
Tant les firent Franchois sommer,   3500
Maiz l'amenerent[1902] trestout droit
A Lolinghehen.[1903] La endroit
Alerent ceulx au devant d'elle,
Qui en savoient la nouvelle.   3504
Ce fu de Saint Pol le droit conte[1904] –
Ainsi que chascun le raconte –
Et les embassadeurs de France
Avec[1905] lui, qui grant deligence   3508
Avoient mis pour la ravoir.

</blockquote>

§71 Lines 3510–3564. The handover of Isabella at Leulingham begins.

<blockquote>

Dessoubz Lolinghehen[1906] pour voir
Fu la roÿne descendue[1907]
En une tente, que[1908] tendue   3512
Orent Englois en la valee
Par maniere bien ordonnee.
Vindrent devers elle les dames
De France, qui de cuer et d'ames   3516
[fo. 75v.] La desiroient moult veïr.[1909]
Un pou aprés vouldrent partir
De la – ainsi comme il me semble –
Et enmenerent tous[1910] ensemble   3520
La roÿne a la chappelle
De Lolinghehen[1911] (qui est telle
Que chascun scet, qui l'a veüe).

</blockquote>

[1900] L no apres
[1901] C avecques
[1902] D la demenerent
[1903] L loulinganth
[1904] D droit ~~compte~~ conte
[1905] B avecques
[1906] L loulynganth
[1907] C line 3511 omitted
[1908] BC qui
[1909] A moult a veir B veoir
[1910] AD tout
[1911] L loulynganch

And when she had come they made her enter, in the company of very few people: just the ambassadors of France and England, who had worked hard towards this.

When they were together in the chapel, a knight whom the English hold very dear – Sir Thomas Percy[217] – started speaking and said:

'King Henry of England, my sovereign lord, wishing the fulfilment of his promise, has unconditionally and freely had the Queen of England brought here to hand her back to her father, the King of France; liberated, quit and free of all bonds of marriage and any other debt, [fo. 76r.] due, or commitment.'

Sir Thomas swore on the perdition of his soul that this was so, and furthermore that she was as pure and undefiled as on the day that she was taken in her litter to King Richard. And if there were anyone anywhere – king, duke, earl: Christian or non-believer: of high or low degree – who disputed this, Sir Thomas would straightway find an Englishman of equal rank to support his case; and would reveal the Queen's body[218] to the view of any appropriate judges, to show that she was as he said.

---

[217] Line 3533. *Sire Thommas de Persi. Supra*, l. 34, note.

[218] Line 3564. Percy is offering to have her examined to establish that she is still a virgin, *saine et ... entiere*, l. 3551.

Et quant elle fu[1912] descendue, 3524
Ilz la firent entrer dedens
Avecques asés pou de gens,
Fors les embassadeurs de France
Et d'Engleterre, qui a ce 3528
Faire avoient asez mis.
Quant ilz furent ensemble mis
En la chappelle, un chevallier,
Qui d'Engloiz est tenu moult chier – 3532
C'est Sire Thommas de Persi –
Prinst a parler, disant ainsi:
'Le roy Henry, roy d'Engleterre,
'Mon souverain seigneur en terre, 3536
'Desirant l'acomplissement
'De sa[1913] promesse, ligement[1914]
'Et de voulenté tresaffine,
'A cy Madame la roÿne 3540
'D'Engleterre fait amener
'Pour la rendre et restituer
'A son pere – le roy de Franche[1915]* –
'Bien deliee, quitte et franche 3544
'De tous lïens de mariage
'Et de trestout autre servage,
[fo. 76r.] 'Debte ou obligacïon.'
Et que sur la dampnacïon 3548
De son ame ainsi le prenoit,
Et oultre plus quë elle[1916] estoit
Aussi saine et aussi entiere
Qu'au[1917] jour que dedens sa litiere 3552
Fu amenee au roy[1918] Richart.
Et s'il estoit nul quelque part –
Fut* roy, duc, conte: crestïen
Ou d'autre estat: grant ou moien – 3556
Qui voulsist a ce contredire,
Il trouveroit sans plus riens dire,
Ne sans[1919] querir plus long[1920] conseil,
Un homme d'estat[1921] tout pareil 3560
En Engleterre, soustenant
Ceste querelle; et par devant
Tout bon juge exposeroit
Son corps,* que tout ainsi estoit. 3564

[1912] AD la fust
[1913] LB la
[1914] A lyement
[1915] LABD france
[1916] H que elle C quelle
[1917] C qua
[1918] L no roy
[1919] B no sans
[1920] AC loing
[1921] B ung [mark of omission] destat [homme in left margin]

§72 Lines 3565–3601. The handover is completed and Isabella is back on French soil.

When he had had his say, the count of St Pol very smartly told him that – Jesus Christ be praised – they all firmly believed him without harbouring any doubts.

Then Sir Thomas Percy, weeping bitterly,[219] took the young Queen by the arms and handed her to the ambassadors there. And also they were given [fo. 76v.] certain letters of quittance which the French had promised; you should know that before the two sides left there, they shed most piteous tears. But when it came for her to leave the chapel, the Queen – whose heart shines with goodness – led out all the English ladies and gentlemen who were expressing their great sorrow in the French pavilions. They agreed to dine together; and so they did, as it seems to me. After the dinner the Queen called for a great quantity of very fine jewels and had them given to the noble English ladies and gentlemen who were weeping in great grief.

---

[219] Line 3573. *en plourant*. This could refer either to Percy or to Isabella. *Supra*, ll. 349–350, note. At first glance Isabella is the more likely candidate, but the whole English party is described as weeping, *infra*, ll. 3579–3581, 3586–3587, 3595–3597.

§72 Lines 3565–3601. The handover is completed and Isabella is back on French soil.

 Et quant il ot[1922] dit son vouloir,
Tressagement – sachiez[1923] de voir –
Le conte de Saint Pol lui dist
Que loué en fut Jhesucrist,   3568
Et qu'ainsi[1924] le creoient[1925] eulx
Fermement sans estre doubteulx.
Lors Sire Thommas de Persi
La jeune roÿne saisi   3572
Par les bras en plourant moult fort
Et la livra[1926] par bon accort
Aux[1927] messages qui furent la.
Et aussi on leur delivra   3576
[fo. 76v.] Certaines lettres de quittance,
Qu'avoient promis ceulx de France;
Et sachiez que les deux parties,
Ains que de la fussent[1928] parties,   3580
Plourerent moult piteusement.
Maiz quant ce vint[1929] au partement
De la chappelle, la roÿne –
Qui son cuer de[1930] bien enlumine –   3584
En admena tous les Englés
Et les dames, qui firent[1931] tres
Grant douleur[1932]* aux franchoises tentes.
Et si estoient leur[1933] ententes   3588
De disner la trestous ensemble;
Si firent ilz,[1934] comme[1935] il me semble.
Maiz quant ce vint aprés disner,
La roÿne fist ordonner   3592
De tresbeaux joiaux grant foison,
Et les fist presenter par don
Aux grans dames et aux seigneurs
D'Engleterre, qui de douleurs   3596
Et de dueil plouroient[1936] moult fort.

[1922] C eust
[1923] H sachie [z *squeezed in later*]
[1924] C quausi
[1925] LBC croyent
[1926] B laissa
[1927] B au
[1928] H fus*sent*
[1929] B vient
[1930] A en
[1931] LB furent *changed to* firent [*dot beneath second minim of* u]
[1932] *all mss* grant dueil
[1933] LACD leurs
[1934] C il
[1935] D si comme
[1936] C plourerent

But the Queen comforted them and bade them farewell; then their lamentations broke out again when she had to take her leave.

§73 Lines 3602–3712. Isabella returns to Paris. Creton finishes by cursing the English; he wrote the *Prinse et mort* so that the truth of Richard's capture might be known.

The English and the French then parted, but I know it to be true that before the Queen of England was one league further on, [fo. 77r.] she came across my lord of Burgundy,[220] who had come from Boulogne to lay a secret ambush. The count of Nevers,[221] his elder son was there – you can all be sure of that – Monseigneur Antoine[222] was there too; there was also another great lord, the duke of Bourbon.[223]

They were accompanied by 500 lancers on foot, drawn up armed in the fields, so that if the English had changed their plans, or if they had thought to take the Queen away again – because of

---

[220] Line 3607. *Monseigneur ... de Bourgongne*. Philip the Bold.
[221] Lines 3611. *De Nevers le conte*. Burgundy's elder son, the future John the Fearless.
[222] Line 3613. *Anthoine Monseigneur*, his younger son. For Burgundy's family, see Vaughan, *Philip the Bold*, p. 82.
[223] Line 3616. *le duc de Bourbon*. Louis II of Bourbon, brother-in-law to the late Charles V, who had married one of Louis' sisters, Jeanne de Bourbon. Louis was uncle to Charles VI. See also Monfrin, 'Humanisme et traductions', p. 177.

Maiz la roÿne reconfort
Leur donna et prinst congié d'eulx;
Et lors renouvela leurs deulx,[1937]   3600
Quant d'avecque[1938] eulx se dust[1939] partir.

§73 Lines 3602–3712. Isabella returns to Paris. Creton finishes by cursing the English; he wrote the *Prinse et mort* so that the truth of Richard's capture might be known.

Ainsi se voldrent departir
A celle heure Angloiz et Franchois,
Maiz je sçay bien[1940] de vray, ainchois[1941]   3604
Que la roÿne d'Engleterre
Fust loings une lieue de terre,
[fo. 77r.] Trouva Monseigneur de Bourgongne
Qui estoit venu de Boulongne[1942]   3608
En enbuche secretement.
Avec ly estoient[1943] present
De Nevers le conte, son filz
Aisné – de ce soiez tous[1944] fiz –   3612
Si fu Anthoine Monseigneur;
Encor y ot un grant seigneur,
C'on appelle[1945] par[1946] son droit non
Monseigneur le duc de Bourbon.   3616
Ceulx estoient acompaignié
De[1947] .v.ᶜ lances tout[1948] a pié
Rengiés sur les champs et armés,
Afin que, se[1949] la[1950] voulentés   3620
Des Engloiz fust* mal[1951] retournee,
Ou qu'ilz[1952] eüssent eu[1953] pensee
De la roÿne remener –
Pour aucun estrif[1954] ou parler   3624

[1937] B leurs ~~pleurs~~ deulx
[1938] HACD davecques L daveuc B quant ~~ave~~ davecques
[1939] H dult L dut ABCD dust
[1940] AD *no* bien
[1941] A que aincois
[1942] B qui estoit [*mark of omission*] de boulongne [venu *in left margin*]
[1943] A avecques luy estoit B avec luy estoit
[1944] HABCD aisne soiez ent tous fiz [D soies *superscript*] L aisne de ce soyes tout fiz
[1945] A appelloit
[1946] C pour
[1947] D a
[1948] AB tous
[1949] C si
[1950] *all mss* les
[1951] C fust en mal
[1952] BC quil
[1953] LACD eussent en B eussent [eu *superscript*] en
[1954] H estrif C rescript

some dispute between the two sides – everyone would have done his duty to rescue her: and they would have charged the English through hills, plains and valleys until, despite them, the French would have taken the Queen forcibly back to her father, the King of France.

But I want you to see that they did not need to do this, for the English intended to restore [fo. 77v.] her out of England into her own country, with all the jewels she had in her possession when she left France after her marriage. She journeyed through France to Paris, where there were many tears shed and much joy on her arrival.

Now let us pray to God – who meekly let his naked body hang on the Cross to redeem sinners out of the hands of their false enemies in Hell – that He may take speedy revenge on the great evils, ingratitude, outrage and injustice committed by the foul English against their King and Queen; but let this be soon, for I swear in truth to you that I have a great desire to see it done, on account of the evil I have seen amongst them. If everyone knew what they want

Qu'ilz eussent peu entre[1955] eulx avoir –
Que chascun de ceulx[1956] leur devoir
Eüssent fait de la rescoure:
Et qu'ilz eüssent laisié coure 3628
Sur Engloiz a fort leurs chevaulx
Parmi montaignes, plains et vaux,
Tant que par force et maugré eulx
L'eüssent ramenee entr'eulx 3632
Au roy de France, son beau pere.*
Maiz je vueil bien[1957] qu'il vous apere
Qu'ilz n'orent mestier de ce faire,
Car les Engloiz voldrent parfaire 3636
[fo. 77v.] D'elle la restitucïon
D'Engleterre en[1958] sa regïon
Et de tous ses joyaulx aussi
Qu'elle avoit, quant elle parti 3640
De France aprés son mariage.
Et depuis fist elle passage
Parmi France jusqu'a[1959] Paris,
Ou[1960] maintes larmes et maint[1961] ris 3644
Furent geteez[1962]* pour sa venue.
Or prions Dieu – qui sa char nue
Leissa humblement en croix[1963] pendre
Pour pecheurs rachetter et rendre 3648
Hors des mains des faulx ennemis
D'enfer, qui ne sont noz amis –
Qu'il vueille brief prendre vengance[1964]
Des grans maulx et desconnoissance, 3652
De l'oultrage et injuste fait,
Que les mauvaiz Engloiz ont fait
A leur roy et a leur roÿne;
Maiz que ce soit en brief termine, 3656
Car je vous jure a dire voir
Que je le[1965] desire moult voir
Pour le mal que j'ay veu entre eulx.
Et se chascun savoit leur[1966] veulx 3660

[1955] B eussent ~~seu~~ [peu superscript] entre
[1956] H chascun de ceulx B chascun deulx
[1957] BD no bien
[1958] L en superscript
[1959] B jusques a
[1960] C print [sic]
[1961] LABD mains
[1962] HLCD fu jettee A furent geteez B fu jecte
[1963] B en croix humblement
[1964] B vueille [mark of omission] prendre vengance [brief at line end]
[1965] C no le
[1966] LACD leurs

and how they hate the French, I think that within three months one would see many ships filled with provisions and supplies carrying battle to them, [fo. 78r.] for these are very wicked people, slow to do good; anyone can clearly see that.

If I have spoken too much about them in any way that causes offence, I humbly beg without bitterness to be pardoned. I swear by God and on my soul that to the best of my ability I have not laid at their door any wrongs that they have not committed, considering that I saw their actions for seven[224] whole months and rode with them in diverse countries and places, in Ireland and England. And the good earl of Salisbury earnestly asked and begged me, when he was captured with King Richard, to spread abroad their crimes and disloyal treachery if I were able to return to France.

I gave him my faithful promise of my own free will, and for this reason I have taken pains to honour the vow I made him in the great distress and danger in which I left him; and also because I know

---

[224] Line 3678. *sept mois*. For an explanation for this error, *supra*, l. 3288, note.

Et comment[1967] ilz hëent Franchoiz,
Je cuide fermement ainchoiz[1968]
Que trois mois fussent acomply,
C'on verroit maint vaissel[1969] empli[1970]   3664
De garnison et de vitaille
Pour eulx aler faire bataille,
[fo. 78r.] Car ce sont tresmauvaises gens
Et de bien faire negligens;   3668
Chascun le puet veoir[1971] clerement.
Et se parlé trop largement
Ay d'eulx, en aucune maniere
Qui desplaise, d'umble[1972] priere   3672
Requier, et de cuer sans amer,
C'on le me vueille pardonner.
Car je prens sur[1973] Dieu et sur[1974] m'ame
Qu'a mon povoir, mal ne diffame   3676
Je n'ay dit d'eulx, qu'ilz n'aient fait,
Veu que sept mois entiers[1975] leur fait
Vy, et chevauchay[1976] avecque[1977] eulx
Par plusieurs contrees et lieux,   3680
En Yrlande[1978] et en[1979] Engleterre.
Et si me voult moult fort requerre
Et prier de bon cuer aussi
Le bon[1980] conte de Salsebery,   3684
Quant il fu pris avec le roy
Richart, que de tout le desroy
Et desloyale traïson
Voulsisse faire mensïon,   3688
Se retourner povoie en Franche.
Et certes de voulenté franche
Et de cuer loyal ly[1981] promis,
Et pour ceste cause j'ay mis   3692
Paine d'acomplir la promesse,
Que ly fis en la grant tristesse
Et peril, ou je le laissay;
Et aussi pour ce que je sçay   3696

[1967] LB comme
[1968] A quaincois
[1969] H vaissel L mains vaisseaulx
[1970] L emplis
[1971] H ve<u>o</u>ir
[1972] LBC durable
[1973] L sus
[1974] L sus
[1975] C entiers *superscript*
[1976] L chevauchie
[1977] ABD avecques
[1978] H yr<u>lande</u>
[1979] C *no* en
[1980] L *no* bon
[1981] C cy

[fo. 78v.] for sure that no one could have known the truth about the King's capture, and how he was falsely lured from his fine, strong Welsh castles through concord and negotiation with the earl of Northumberland, as I said before. And so I sincerely beg all who read to the end of this account which I wrote about the English and what they did, to pardon me if I made mistakes in versification, in rhyme or in my prose, for I am not skilled in them.

                Amen.

[fo. 78v.] De certain c'on[1982] n'eust[1983] peu savoir
De la prise du roy le voir,
Et[1984] comment[1985] il fu faulsement[1986]
Par traittié et par[1987] parlement 3700
Atraiz[1988] hors de ses[1989] forts[1990] chastiaulx,
Qui sont en Galles bons et biaulx,
Du conte de Northomberlant,
Comme j'ay dit ycy devant. 3704
Si prie a tous ceulx[1991] de cuer fin,
Qui verront jusques a la fin
Ce traittié, que j'ay voulu faire
Des Engloiz et de leur affaire, 3708
Que se j'ay mespris en rimer,
En prose ou en leonimer,
C'on m'en[1992] tiengne pour excusé,
Car je n'en sui pas bien rusé. 3712

Amen.[1993] 3714

[1982] B com
[1983] C con eust [no ne]
[1984] ACD ne
[1985] B come
[1986] B faulcessement
[1987] C no par
[1988] L attrait
[1989] C no ses
[1990] H forts *superscript*
LB *no* forts
[1991] A dieu que
[1992] AD me [no en]
[1993] L explicit A amen deo gracias B explicit lystoire du roy richart dengleterre composee par [blank] creton C deo gracias D deo gracias cy fenist le roy richart deo gracias

[EPISTLES AND *BALLADES*]

[The epistles and *ballades* are found only in B, fos 32v.–36r. Its copy of the *Prinse et mort* finishes with: *Explicit l'ystoire du roy Richart d'Engleterre composee par* [blank] *Creton*. This MS has been compiled in a careless and hasty manner with many crossings out and expunctions, false starts and obvious scribal errors. All rejected readings can be found at the foot of each page in the French text and referenced by a superscript.]

[fo. 32v.] Epistle [I, to King Richard] written by the said Creton

As faithful love demands, I Creton – your devoted servant – send this letter to you Richard of England, most noble Christian Prince. And you should know that, as I write, the anger in my heart makes tears flow down my face when I think of your unhappy life. And yet my spirits are greatly comforted and I have high hopes for your well-being, because it is said over here that you are free and in good health; I pray to Our Lord that this may be so.

Alas! Most mighty Sire, how has your solitary self been able to bear such grievous sadness and live? Certainly everyone who talks about this or hears it talked about is greatly astonished, and most men cannot believe it. But through this it can be shown that Our Lord God, who is a righteous judge, has held you in His holy safe-keeping while you were in your enemies' hands, and visited you with capricious and bitter misfortunes, in order perhaps to test the strength and firmness of your strong Christian faith; and – recognizing God's power and wishing to attain everlasting glory – you have borne them with true patience, giving Him thanks and praise for everything that it pleases Him to have done. Thus it appears that you are God's friend, or otherwise your life would have been over a long time since; perhaps these things were predestined before your birth.

[EPISTLES AND *BALLADES*]

[The epistles and *ballades* are found only in B, fos 32v.–36r. Its copy of the *Prinse et mort* finishes with: *Explicit l'ystoire du roy Richart d'Engleterre composee par* [blank] *Creton*. This MS has been compiled in a careless and hasty manner with many crossings out and expunctions, false starts and obvious scribal errors. All rejected readings can be found at the foot of each page in the French text and referenced by a superscript.]

[fo. 32v.] Epistre faicte par ledit Creton*

Ainsy come* vraye amour requiert, a tresnoble Prince et vray catholique, Richart d'Engleterre, je[1994] Creton – ton lige serviteur – te envoie ceste epistre. Et saches que en l'escripsant, l'yre de mon cuer espandoit mes larmes par mes joes, pensant a ta douloureuse vie. Et toutesfoiz mon esperit est moult reconforté, et ay vertueuse esperance pour ta santé,[1995] et pour ce que on dit par deça que tu es sains et alegiés, desquelles choses je pry Nostreseigneur que ainsi soit.

Helas! Tresredoubté Sire, et coment a peu ton seul corps soustenir ne porter tant de doulereuse tristresse sans mort? Certes toutes les creatures, qui en parlent ou oent parler, s'en esbaÿssent moult, et la plus grant partie[1996] des homes ne le peut croire. Maiz par ce leur peut apparoir que Nostresire Dieux, qui est vray juge, toy estant es mains[1997] de tes ennemis, t'a tenu en sa saincte garde, en toy demonstrant perverses et ameres fortunes, et par avanture pour esprouver la constance et l'estableté de ta ferme foy[1998] catholique; et toy – congnoissant la puissance divine [et][1999] desirant parvenir a la gloire qui est sans fin – les as portees en vraye pacience, en ly rendant graces et loenges de tout ce qu'i* ly plaist estre fait. Et par ainsi appert que tu es amy de Dieu, ou autrement ta vie fust pieça finee; et peut-estre que ces choses te sont predestinees devant ta nativité.

[1994] p̄ je
[1995] par ta sanite
[1996] parties
[1997] es mains [*in left margin*]
[1998] loy
[1999] no et

Now hold fast to hope in Our Lord more than ever before, for well do I know that if you are alive – despite perfidious Lancaster and all his men – you will be restored to great honour and authority in your kingdom. Your body is more suited to Mars than to Jupiter or Venus, and God has formed you for this; your actions are fierce enough for war and men bear witness to this.

Ah! Most mighty and powerful Prince, when I remember that, while you were conquering lands in Ireland devoid of Christians and full of wild places, the perfidious scoundrel – Lancaster – landed in your kingdom and turned the hearts of your subjects against you with his falsehoods, my whole mind is moved to madness. Cursed be the hour when he crossed the sea to England, that Neptune[225] – the god of the winds – did not play havoc with his sails on the high seas, in order that his ship might have been destroyed and that the days of his wicked and shameful life ended at that time: that his flesh might have been eaten by birds or fish, his furious spirit driven through the heavens, and his bones driven down into the sand of the seashore by the pounding of the waves; certainly they merited such a grave and none other.

Ah! most mighty Prince [fo. 33r.], the warm love which you showed towards the most false earl of Rutland[226] has cost you dear, for by him alone and his dishonest deception was your return from Ireland to England delayed by sixteen to eighteen days, after you had heard news of your enemies. Alas! And why did you believe him more than the members of your Council, who ardently desired your swift return? Certainly I am much amazed that the sea gods favoured you so, sending you winds to reach the port of Milford Haven;[227] it would have been better for you to have landed elsewhere, but none can resist what Our Creator has preordained.

---

[225] Page 303, line 13. *Neptunus – le dieu des vens*. Neptune was god of the sea. Professor Strohm has misunderstood Creton here: 'rewriting history via a remarkable imaginative flight', Strohm, 'The Trouble with Richard', p. 88. Creton did not suppose Henry shipwrecked, he wished that he had been. The verbs are subjunctives, telling what should have happened, not what did.

[226] Page 303, lines 22–25. *conte de Rotelant ... son faulx enginement*. For Rutland's role in delaying the return from Ireland, *supra*, ll. 527–557.

[227] Page 303, line 28. *Milleforde*. *Supra*, ll. 805–809.

Or ayes doncques ferme esperance en Nostreseigneur plus que oncques maiz, car je sçay bien que, se tu es vif – maugré le traïstre de Lencastre et toutes ses batailles – tu seras restabli a grant honneur et a grant puissance en ton royaulme, car ton corps et ta personne est plus convenable a Mars que a Jupiter ne a Venus, et Dieu t'a formé ad ce; et sont tes faiz dignes de batailles, et de ce te portent les homes tesmoignage.

Ha! Tresredoubté et puissant[2000] Prince, quant il me souvient que, toy conquerant terres deshabitees de crestiens et plaines de desers en Hybernie, et come le lierre [et][2001] traïstre de Lencastre entra en ton royaulme et soubvertist les cuers de tes soubgez par son faulx art contre toy, tout mon sens s'esmeut a forsenerie. Et maudite soit l'eure quant il passa en Albion, que Neptunus – le dieu des vens – ne fist ses batailles enmi ses voiles ou hault pelage[2002] de la mer, affin que* sa nef fust rompue, et que a celle heure les jours de sa malvaise et honteuse vie fussent finés: et que sa chair fust devouree, viande a oyseaux ou aux poissons, et son esperit folié[2003] par diverses regions de l'air, et ses os sustraiz en la rive de la mer dedens le sablon par le deboutement des eaues; certes de telle sepulture* estoient ilz dignes et non d'autre.

Ha! Tresredoubté Prince, [fo. 33r.] l'ardant affection d'amour que tu avoies au tresfaulx conte de Rotelant t'a esté moult chier vendue, car par luy seul fut ton passage retardé de .xvi. a .xviii. jours d'Ybernie en Angleterre, toy avoir oÿ* nouvelles de tes ennemis, par son faulx engineement. Helas! Et pour quoy le crus tu plus que ceulx de ton conseil, qui desiroient moult ta briefve retournee? Et certes je me esmerveille moult come les dieux de la mer te furent ay favourables, qui te mandoient vent pour arriver au port de Milleforde; mielx eust esté pour toy d'estre arrivé a port[2004] d'autre region, maiz ce qui est predestiné du Createur[2005] ne peut nul contrester.

[2000] et puissant <u>puissant</u> prince
[2001] no et
[2002] ses batailles ou ses voiles non mie en ou hault pelage
[2003] foliable
[2004] a u port
[2005] du r createur

Furthermore, most mighty Prince, when I remember the earl of Northumberland[228] I curse him, for he came to you at Conway and swore on the Host that your enemy – Henry Lancaster – only wanted his own estates and that he felt remorse for setting foot in your kingdom. Thus I am greatly astonished that the land of his fathers can permit him [Northumberland] to live, for all his promises were empty and steeped in treason; by reason of them he took you to Flint accompanied by a great number of his men-at-arms whom he had left treacherously hidden behind boulders between Conway and Rhuddlan. In this castle of Flint, dear Sire, you spent a most sorrowful night and understandably so, for you could see that you were surrounded on all sides by your enemies, who craved your death more than any other thing. And at that time I myself firmly believed that the end of my days had come, and my heart was filled with great sorrow, as much for you as for me.

The next day the scoundrel – Lancaster[229] – led you in humiliation to London and handed you over to the citizens, who wickedly condemned you to imprisonment for life, from which Our Lord God has delivered you. Now you should thank Him steadfastly and foster a righteous hope that you can have revenge on your enemies; and that the slaughter is so great that their blood flows in rivers throughout your kingdom, so that the ends of their cruel lives may be an example to all other traitors for all time to come.

And you should know that I have documented – in pictures and words[230] – throughout the kingdom of France all the evil and hateful acts of treason that they have committed against you, in order that their lives might be filled with shame and condemnation. And certainly, most mighty Seigneur, I know not how it is that your person appears so often to my inner eye, for day and night all my thoughts and suppositions concern you alone. And had it been the Creator's will that I – sorrowful and sad – should have seen you again before I died, my heart would be eased. But although I cannot see you with the eyes in my head, yet you are always presented to my inner eye, and it sometimes appears to me that I see and speak to you. Thus do illusory joys delight me when I cannot experience real gratification, and for this reason my mindful heart offers up vows and prayers every day to Our Creator, that I may soon see you with all the joy that I desire.

---

[228] Page 305, lines 1–9. *conte de Northomberlant ... entre Cornüay et Rothelant. Supra*, ll. 1765–1792, 1839–1925.

[229] Page 305, lines 15–16. *le lierre de Lencastre ... te livra au turbe*. Creton is omitting their return to Chester and the three days spent there. *Supra*, p. 203, l. 3–p. 205, l. 11. *Turbe* = 'citizens'; these were the liverymen of London.

[230] Page 305, line 24. *j'ay manifestees par figures [et] par diz*. Creton has written an illustrated account of the usurpation.

Encore, tresredoubté Prince, quant il me souvient du conte de Northomberlant, je maudiz sa vie, car[2006] il te vint jurer a Cornüay sur le corps Nostreseigneur que ton ennemy – Henry de Lencastre – ne vouloit que sa terre, et qu'il se repentoit de tant qu'il estoit entré en ton royaulme, dont[2007] je suy moult esbahy come la terre paternelle [le][2008] peut soustenir en vie, car toutes ses convenances estoient faulces et plaines de traÿsons; et par ycelles t'enmena a Flint avec grant quantité de ses gens d'armes, qu'il avoit laissiés traïteusement tapis de roches[2009] entre Cornüay et Rothelant. Ouquel chastel de Flint, chier Sires, la nuyt te fu moult douleureuse et a bon droit, car tu te[2010] vëoies environné de tes ennemis de toutes pars, lesquiex desiroient ta mort plus que nulle autre chose. Et moy mesme cuiday a celle heure fermement que la fin de mes jours fust venue, et avoie grant douleur au cuer, tant pour toy come pour moy.

Et le lendemain le lierre de Lencastre te enmena honteusement a Londres et te livra au turbe, lesquiex par[2011] leur faulx conseil te condampnerent en chartre perpetuelle, dont Nostreseigneur Dieu t'a delivré. Or penses donc de luy rendre graces de ferme entencion, et ayes vertueuse esperance de prendre vengeance de tes ennemis; et que ce soit par sy grant occision, que de leur sang courent fleuves par ton royaulme, sy que la fin de leur doleureux jours soit exemple a tous autres traïstres a tous temps a venir.

Et saiches que tous les maulx et horribles traÿsons, qu'ilz t'ont faictes, j'ay manifestees par figures [et][2012] par diz* ou royaulme de France, affin que leur vie soit honteuse et plaine de reproche. Et certes, tresredoubté Seigneur, je ne sçay come la representacion de ton ymage me vient sy souvent devant les yeux de mon cuer, car de jour et de nuyt toutes mes pensees et ymaginacions* ne sont autres sy non penser a toy. Et se la voulenté du Createur estoit telle, que moy – doleureux et triste – eusse veu ta figure devant ma mort, tout mon esperit en seroit reconforté. Maiz combien que je ne la puisse veoir des yeulx de mon chief, sy est elle tousdiz presentee devant les yeulx de ma pensee, et m'est aucunesfoiz advis que je te voy et que je parle a toy. Ainsi me delictent les faulces joyes, quant les vraies je ne puis avoir, et pour ce je faiz sacrefice de voeux,[2013]* d'oroisons et de prieres tous les jours de cuer ententif a nostre Createur, que bien brief je te puisse veoir, a telle joye come je le desire.

[2006] cas
[2007] donc
[2008] *no* le
[2009] ~~tampis~~ tapis de robes
[2010] [te *superscript*]
[2011] pour
[2012] *no* et
[2013] feu

Most noble and true Christian Prince, remember your noble and loyal wife, who spends day and night weeping as she waits for you, wishing to hear reliable news of your well-being. Send your instructions over here, so that we can clearly see that you are free and in good health, for all men, great and small, rejoice that you are alive. And do not feel sorrow or shame that revenge for you has not been taken a long time ago, for you well know the adversities and tribulations of this kingdom and especially of your father-in-law Charles, King of France; you can be sure that nothing else has delayed it. And if it is your pleasure to come over here, you will find the greater part of the chivalry of France ready to live and die with you.

And also you will find your noble wife, whom your mother-in-law has been keeping most carefully for you, since she was handed back[231] by your enemy, the scoundrel, Lancaster; he dragged out the negotiations for twenty-two months without wanting to give her back, so that she would have been twelve years old, and anything he would have had her do or say would have been unalterable. For his wicked intention was to betroth her to his eldest son, whom you knighted with great honour and joy in Ireland.[232] But it can be shown that she was entreated and petitioned for diligently by the Council of France, so that she was handed back before she attained her majority. And you should know that today she is as chaste and undefiled[233] as she was when you parted from her at Windsor to go on your Irish expedition; she herself bears witness to this. Thus, most mighty Prince, you must greatly wish to see her, for it is a very precious thing to cull the first flower from the tender body of such a noble virgin as your wife.

Now come over here, dear Sire, set sail and Hippotes,[234] the gentle wind, will waft you to safe port. And I am sure that all the gods of the winds and the sea will aid your passage and Stella Maris – the star of the sea – [fo. 33v.] will point you to safe harbour, for your cause appears just to Our Lord, considering that He has delivered you from such grave danger as you have been in for a very long time.

---

[231] Page 307, lines 14–15. *depuis la restitucion faicte de ton ennemy. Supra*, ll. 3318–3601.
[232] Page 307, lines 19–20. *son filz aisné, lequel tu feis chevalier ... en Yrlande. Supra*, ll. 138–144.
[233] Page 307, lines 22–25. *Et sachies ... tesmoignage. Supra*, ll. 3550–3564.
[234] Page 307, line 30. *Ypothades* = Hippotes, father of Aeolus, ruler of the winds.

O, tresnoble Prince et vray catholique, ayes remembrance de ta noble et loyal compaigne, qui espant ses larmes jour et nuyt en toy actendant, desirant oÿr vraies nouvelles de ta santé. Fay tes mandemens par deça, affin qu'il appere clerement que tu es sains et alegiés, car tous homes nobles et nonnobles se resjoïssent de ta vie. Et n'ayes doleur ne vergoigne au cuer, se ta vengeance n'a esté faicte des pieça, car tu peus congnoistre et savoir clerement les adversités, douleurs et tribulacions de cest royaulme et en especial de ton beau pere, Charles, roy de France; et soies ferme et certain que nulle autre chose ne l'a retardee. Et s'il te plaist venir par deça, tu[2014] trouveras la plus grant partie de la chevalerie preste pour vivre et mourir[2015] avec toy.

Et sy trouveras ta noble compaigne, que ta belle mere t'a moult precieusement gardee depuis la restitucion faicte de ton ennemy – le lierre de Lencastre – lequel delaia la[2016] prosecucion par l'espace de .xxii. moiz sans la vouloir rendre, affin telle que elle eust .xii. ans acomplis, et que ce qu'il [ly]* eust[2017] fait faire ou dire eust esté ferme et estable. Car sa faulce entencion estoit telle de la donner a son filz aisné, lequel tu feis chevalier a grant honneur et a grant joye en Yrlande. Maiz par ce peut apparoir que diligeaument a esté requise et sommee par le conseil de France, et tant que elle a esté rendue, ainz que le jour de son aage fust acomplis. Et sachies que aussi chaste et aussi entiere que elle estoit, quant tu[2018] partis d'elle a Windesore pour aler en ton voyage d'Yrlande, elle est au jour d'uy, et de ce porte elle mesmez tesmoignage. Et pour ce, tresredoubté Prince, tu doiz avoir tresgrant desir de la veoir, car moult precieuse chose est de cuillir la premiere[2019] fleur du tendre corps de sy noble pucelle come de ta compaigne.

Or viens doncques par deça, chiers Sires, et met tes voiles en mer, et Ypothades, le[2020] doulx vent, te fera arriver a bon port. Et suy certain que tous les dieux des vens et de la mer te feront ton passage, et te fera l'estoile [fo. 33v.] d'eaue demonstrerresse de vray port, car ta cause appert juste a Nostreseigneur, veu qu'il t'a delivré de sy grant peril, ouquel tu as esté moult longuement.

[2014] deca te tu
[2015] mouru
[2016] delaie sa
[2017] no ly
[2018] quant p tu
[2019] premere
[2020] ile

Ah! Most mighty Prince, how many noble ladies and knights will flock to meet you, weeping as much for joy at your well-being as for the bitter misfortunes that you have suffered. Certainly you will see all men praise Our Creator and enthusiastically lay hands on their weapons to go with you to fight your enemies. And if you cannot come here, because someone impedes your passage, at least, Sire, be pleased to tell us your heart's intent, and you will find that most of the nobles of the royal blood of France are your true friends and will not fail you, even unto death. And certainly if you do not arrive here soon, I shall go to you, wherever you are, and shall bring to you – in writing and pictures – a great portion of your bitter misfortunes and calamities as I saw them happen, I being with you in Ireland and in England.

Now at the end of my epistle I beg you, most mighty and true Christian Seigneur, that you do not despise it and that my shortcomings do not cause you displeasure. Read it with care and perhaps you will find in it something to please you in some way. And I promise you – in the name of God who is omnipotent over all beings – that the intense love that I bear you makes me write it, wishing with all my heart for the fulfilment of all your good pleasures and desires. Certainly if the sea gods favour me, I will swiftly follow, and soon set off after it.

Ballade [I] by the said Creton

Lords of the royal blood of France, lay hands on your weapons with all speed if you have reliable news about the King who has undergone so much suffering at the hands of the perfidious English; they have robbed him of his authority and then condemned him to death. But God, who is our righteous judge in Heaven above, has saved his life. Everyone – young and old – says so everywhere; it is noble King Richard of England.

Ha! Tresredoubté Prince, quantes nobles dames et chevaliers yront a l'encontre de toy, espandant leurs larmes, tant pour la joye de ta santé come pour les ameres fortunes et douleurs que tu as souffertes. Certes tu verras tous les homes loer nostre Createur et mettre les mains aux armes ententivement pour aler avecques toy contre tes ennemis. Et se tu ne peus venir par deça, et que aucun empesche ton passage, au moins, Sire, qu'il te plaise mander l'entencion de ton courage, et tu trouveras la plus grant partie des nobles du sang de France tes vrais amis, et qui ne te fauldront jusques a la mort. Et certes se tu ne viens bien brief par deça, je yray[2021]* a toy en quelque lieu que tu soyes, et te porteray – par escript et par figures – une grant partie des ameres fortunes et doleurs, come je les vy avenir,[2022] moy estant avecques toy en Ybernie et en Angleterre.

Or te prie je, mon tresredoubté Seigneur et vray catholique, en la fin de mon epistre, que tu ne la vueilles prendre en desdaing, et que la faulte de mon povre[2023] corps ne te desplaise point. Et la parlis ententivement, et par avanture que tu y trouveras chose qui te pourra aucunement plaire. Et sy te promet – par Dieu qui est puissant sur toutes creatures – que l'ardant desir d'amour que j'ay a toy le me fait faire, desirant de tout[2024] mon cuer l'acomplissement de tes bons plaisirs et desirs.[2025] Et certes se les dieux de la mer me sont favourables, je la suyvray tost et yray briefment aprez.

Balade [I] par ledit Creton

O vous Seigneurs du sang royal de France,
Mettés la main aux armes vistement,
Se vous avez certaine congnoissance
Du roy, qui tant a souffert de tourment
Par faulx Anglois, qui traïteusement
Luy ont tollu la dominacïon
Et puis de mort fait condampnacïon.
Maiz Dieu, qui est le vray juge es sains cieulx,
Luy a sauvé la vie. Main et tart
Chascun le dit partout, jennes et vieulx;
C'est d'Albïon le noble roy Richart.

[2021] yroy
[2022] vy a̶-e̶ avenir
[2023] poivre
[2024] tou
[2025] desiirs

And if it is so, for greater increase of honour you should swiftly have your men armed, for all his hope was in you; I know this to be true. Often in Wales did I hear him weep bitterly and praise[235] King Charles of France, and all of you, while the perfidious English hounded him most cruelly. Alas and alack! Help him to improve his lot; it is noble King Richard of England.

He is of your blood and allied to you; everyone knows it plainly. Thus you have no excuse to refuse him aid. Do not await a call to arms, as for lesser cause was the palace of Ilium set ablaze and Priam[236] and four of his sons killed. Make haste then to send help over there and you will be praised in all quarters; it is noble King Richard of England.

Princes, do not take it amiss that he does not tell you of his affairs; you should not be surprised. Cross the sea and help the stricken leopard[237] to rise again; it is noble King Richard of England.

[Epistle II, to Philip the Bold, duke of Burgundy]

[The passages in italic type represent borrowings from Valerius Maximus, as translated by Simon de Hesdin.]

[fo. 34r.] *The fragility and mutability*[238] of public affairs rightly demand a leader who is wise, prudent and endowed with good governance.

---

[235] Page 311, line 6. *renon*. The usual meaning is 'fame', *infra*, p. 311, l. 21. However, Froissart, *Chroniques de France et d'Angleterre, livre quatrième*, p. 123, l. 5, and p. 436, l. 7, has *renommer* = *célébrer* = 'to praise'. 'Praise' fits *renon* here.

[236] Page 311, lines 18–19. *Fu mis en feu le palais d'Ylion / Et Priant mort et quatre de ses fieulx*. This is perhaps taken from Valerius Maximus, [*Les*] *Grejois ... mirent siege devant Troyes ... ouquel ... furent tués les enffans Priamus, c'est assavoir Hector, Troylus, Deyphebus, Paris ... Et finablement sa citié prise et mise en feu et lui meismes fu mis à mort*: 'La Traduction de Valère Maxime par Nicolas de Gonesse', ed. Charras, Book 7, p. 378, ll. 16–21. *Priant* is what Creton wrote. The scribe of **B** mistook *priant* for a verb – present participle < *prier* which makes no sense; he changed it to *prirent* – 6th person past historic < *prendre* – which equally makes no sense. *Priant* is a proper name = 'Priam', king of Troy. This is the form used by Deschamps. *Oeuvres complètes*, ed. de Queux and Raynaud, VIII, no. 1457, pp. 149–150, l. 3.

Filz does not rhyme with *lieux*; the Northern form *fieulx* is found in Christine de Pizan, *Oeuvres poétiques*, ed. M. Roy, 3 vols (Paris, 1886–1896), I, s.v. Autres Balades, no. 37, pp. 250–251, l. 30. See also Pope, *From Latin to Modern French*, §391 (4), p. 155.

[237] Page 311, line 26. *le liepart*. For the leopard as the King of England, *supra*, ll. 133–134, note.

[238] Page 311, line 32. *La fragilité avecques l'inconstance*. Probably from Valerius Maximus, *Facta et dicta memorabilia*, ed. Enriello and others, I, p. 1. See also, *infra*, p. 313, ll. 7–8.

Et s'il est vray, pour avoir acroissance
De grant honneur faictes hastivement
Voz gens armer, car toute s'esperance*
Estoit en vous; je le sçay vraiement.
Par maintesfoiz plourant piteusement
Luy oÿ faire en Gales maint renon
Du roy françois, qui Charles a a non,
Et de vous tous, quant faulx Anglois crueulx
Le chassoient plains de [tres]crueulx[2026]* art.
C'est grant pitié! Aidiés luy* pour le mieulx;[2027]
C'est d'Albïon le noble roy Richart.

C'est vostre sang de ligne et d'aliance;
Chascun le scet et congnoist clerement.
Vous ne povés donc trouver excusance,
Que ne soiés tenus tresgrandement
De luy aidier. N'atendés mandement
Nul quelconque, car pour moins d'achoison
Fu mis en feu le palais d'Ylion,
Et Priant[2028] mort et quatre de ses fieulx.[2029]*
Hastés vous donc d'envoier celle part,
Sy en aurés bon renon en tous lieux;
C'est d'Albïon le noble roy Richart.

Princes, n'ayés en indignacïon,
S'il ne vous fait de son fait mencïon;
Vous n'en devez pas estre merveilleux.
Passez la mer et aydiés le liepart
A relever, qui est moult[2030] douleureux;
C'est d'Albïon le noble roy Richart.[2031]

[Epistle II, to Philip the Bold, duke of Burgundy]

[The passages in italic type represent borrowings from Valerius Maximus, as translated by Simon de Hesdin.]

[fo. 34r.] *La fragilité avecques l'inconstance*[2032] de la chose publique doit ou doivent* desirer par droit cours de Nature chief sapient, prudent et plain de bon gouvernement.

[2026] *no* tres
[2027] mielx
[2028] prirent
[2029] filz
[2030] relever qui est qui est moult
[2031] le roy noble roy richart
[2032] fragilite avecques avecques linconstance

And because the head of this kingdom[239] has suffered or is suffering still from a strange and possibly unidentifiable injury – perhaps by the will of Our Creator, who was or still is angry at the multitude of sins committed by him or by others in his kingdom, punishment for which is sent him by His Celestial Majesty – or because of the sins of our fathers, of which *the Holy Scriptures say: 'Our fathers have sinned, but we will carry the blame'*[240] – or perhaps because of various wicked and hateful actions carried out by Fate:

Yet for the common good, most mighty Christian Prince, Philip – son of a King of France[241] and duke of Burgundy – you should consider the kingdom's poor and miserable people, responsibility for whom you received at one time through the consent and command of your brother Charles, formerly King of France, which responsibility, most mighty Seigneur, you have exercised most wisely and beneficially to this day.

And in carrying out the work which you have begun – which needs help more than ever – I can compare you very well to the beginning, not the end, of the rule of the Roman emperor, Tiberius Caesar. In accomplishing the good works which you have begun, you are his only successor on earth, *for Suetonius*[242] *says in his book The Twelve Caesars that he was so overflowing in humility, chastity, good sense, wisdom and all other virtues, that he surpassed all other men; and at the same time he had such a great and special knowledge of the ceremonies due to the gods that it was most marvellous.*

And from the beginning of his reign until almost the end, he would not tolerate being called emperor or father of the country, and could scarcely suffer anyone to kneel before him, and sharply reprimanded anyone who did. And especially did he mortally hate those who flattered him, which is very like how some great lords behave today, which is a matter of regret; and perhaps some lose their self-awareness. He never had harm done to anyone for what was said of him – be it good or bad – but said that in a free city all tongues should be free. He spoke so well to everyone and so honoured all those who spoke to him, that in doing so he almost overstepped the bounds of humanity.

---

[239] Page 313, line 1. *en ce royaulme le chief principal*. Charles VI of France, who suffered from recurring bouts of insanity.

[240] Page 313, lines 7–8. *l'Escripture Saincte dit: 'Noz peres ont pechié, maiz nous emporterons le mal'*. This is the first indisputably identified borrowing from Simon de Hesdin's translation of Valerius Maximus: *si comme dist la Sainte Escripture* … «*Nos peres pecherent et ne sont plus, et nous portons leurs iniquités*», Valère Maxime, *Facta et dicta memorabilia*, ed. Enriello and others, I, p. 70. Also, A. Vitale-Brovarone, 'Notes sur la traduction de Valère Maxime par Simon de Hesdin', in M.C. Timelli and C. Galderisi, *Pour acquérir honneur et pris: Mélanges de Moyen Français offerts à Giuseppe Di Stefano* (Montreal, 2004), pp. 183–191; and *supra*, Introduction, pp. 34–35.

[241] Page 313, line 11. *Philippe – filz de roy de France*. Philip was the fourth son of King John the Good, and brother of Charles V, *infra*, p. 313, 14.

[242] Page 313, lines 22–37. *car Suetonius dit ou livre Des .xii. Cesarres … a pou que … il ne passoit les mectes de humanité*. This passage comes from Valerius Maximus: *Suetonius ou livre des .XII. Cesaires dist … que a pou que … ne passoit les mettes de humanité*, Valère Maxime, *Facta et dicta memorabilia*, ed. Enriello and others, I, p. 9.

Et pour ce que en ce royaulme le chief principal se peut estre dolu ou deult encore de bleceure merveilleuse et par avanture incongneue – et peut-estre par la voulenté du Createur, lequel peut avoir esté ou est indigné aucunement par la moultiplicité d'aucuns pechiés commis par luy ou par autres de son royaulme, dont pugnicion luy est transmise de la majesté celestiele – ou par le pechié de noz peres, desquiex *l'Escripture Saincte dit: 'Noz peres ont pechié, maiz nous emporterons le mal'* – ou par avanture [par] aucunes malvaises oevres et detestables[2033] faictes par [le][2034] sort ou autrement:

Toutesvoiz loist il pour le bien publique, tresredoubté Prince et vray catholique, Philippe – filz[2035] de roy de France, duc de Bourgoigne – que tu ayes regard a son povre et miserable peuple, duquel tu as une foyz receu la charge et garde par le consentement et commandement de ton beau frere Charles, jadix roy de France, auquel gouvernement, mon tresredoubté Seigneur, tu as esté moult prudent et favorable jusques au jour d'uy.

Et en poursuyvant l'euvre que tu as commencee – laquelle a greigneur mestier d'aide que oncques mayz[2036] – je te puis assez comparer au commencement de la seignourie de Tybere Cesar – empereur des Rommains – non pas a la fin de son empire. Maiz en acomplissant les oeuvres[2037] vertueuses que tu as commencees, tu peus estre son seul successeur en terre, *car Suetonius dit ou livre Des .xii. Cesarres*[2038] *qu'il fut sy habondant en humilité, en chasteté, en sens, en prudence et en toutes autres operations vertueuses, qu'il en passa tous les autres; et avecques ce il fu de sy grant congnoissance et especial cultivement des*[2039] *cerimonies aux dieux, que ce fu grant merveille.*

Et tant que du commancement[2040]* *de son empire et prez jusques a la fin, il ne voult souffrir non d'empereur ne surnon de pere du païs,*[2041] *ne a paine vouloit il souffrir que on se agenoillast devant luy, et reprovoit aigrement ceulx qui*[2042] *le faisoient. Et especialment ceulx qui le blandissoient ou flatoient heoit il mortelment, laquelle chose est au jour d'uy moult prouchaine, collateral et familliant d'aucuns grans seigneurs, dont est pitié et domage; et par avanture peut-estre que aucuns en perdent la congnoissance d'eulx mesmes. Il ne faisoit fere mal a nul pour chose que on dist de luy – feust bien ou mal – maiz [disoit]*[2043] *que en franche cité toutes langues devoient estre franches. Il parloit sy bel a chascun et honnouroit aussi tous ceulx qui parloient a luy, que a pou que en ce faisant il ne passoit les mectes de humanité.*

[2033] par avanture s [*no* par] aucunes malvaise oevres et destables
[2034] *no* le
[2035] philippe ro filz
[2036] oncques ma mayz
[2037] oeivres
[2038] cesarrens
[2039] de
[2040] commandement
[2041] de paix
[2042] ceulx [*one letter scored out*] qui
[2043] *no* disoit

And then when the Romans saw the very special way he governed and that he had such keen regard for public affairs, *there were some men burning with avarice who advised*[243] *him to increase the country's dues and taxes. He replied to them most severely that they showed no love for the common good, and that a good shepherd did not swallow or devour his sheep but sheared it closely*; and he did so many good things that he demonstrated in his own person how everyone ought to behave and live.

Considering the great virtues in Tiberius Caesar from the beginning of his rule almost to the end, I have been able to compare you to him, since you have been recently following in his excellent footsteps, in as much as you have become shepherd to the poor sheep – as he was – and have not been willing for them to be devoured, but have most energetically laid hands on your victorious weapons to protect them. For this, most mighty Christian Seigneur, your wisdom will be exalted and spread amongst all Christians today and for all time to come.

And you should know that by working in this way you gain a second life, which is called everlasting glory: for glory – that is to say good repute – gives all good men a second life after their deaths, and the repute which lives on following their good works makes it seem as if they were still alive. Also glory stops those who are praiseworthy from dying. Therefore, most mighty Seigneur, be pleased to continue the good work which you have begun, for your feats of arms are not violent or oppressive, but are gentle and shining like Jupiter's star to serve the common good. And you can see this clearly, for out of all other Christian princes you are courted by several places and nations, especially by the Bretons,[244] who want to hand over to you alone all their government and safe-keeping; this is most honourable, considering their nobility and strength and that of their country.

And because your strength and power, after those of the head of this kingdom are greater than other men's – as I can see – may it please you to apply yourself to two things which will make your good name live for ever: that you consider the most merciless and unhappy strife within our Holy Mother Church,[245] in order that she may be united and

---

[243] Page 315, lines 2–6. *il y ot d'aucuns ... qui a luy conseillerent ... de la tondre justement*. This comes from Valère Maxime, *Facta et dicta memorabilia*, ed. Enriello and others, I, p. 9. *ce n'estoit pas fait de bon pastre ... de vouloir transgloutir ... sa beste, maiz de la tondre justement*. Hesdin has made a mistake in translation here, and Creton follows him. He contrasts the good shepherd who shears (*tondre*, p. 315, l. 6) his sheep with the bad who devours (*transgloutir*, p. 315, l. 6) it. Hesdin has translated *degluttire* 'to devour' instead of *deglubere* 'to flay'. Creton uses *escorchier* 'to flay', *supra*, l. 2001.

[244] Page 315, lines 29–31. *tu es desiré ... mesmement des Bretons*. In October 1402, Philip the Bold became regent of Brittany and guardian of the young duke John V. This prevented Brittany from falling under English influence, as Joan of Navarre, widow of duke John IV had married Henry IV. See Vaughan, *Philip the Bold*, pp. 52–53.

[245] Page 315, lines 37–38. *la trescrueuse ... discorde de nostre mere Saincte Eglise*. The papal Schism: ibid. pp. 45–47.

Et lors, quant les Rommains virent son tresespecial gouvernement et qu'il avoit sy aspre[2044] regart a la chose publique, *il y ot d'aucuns ardans en convoitise, qui a luy conseillerent qu'il creust les threuz et redevances du païs, de quoy il respondi a eulx*[2045] *moult crueusement qu'ilz n'amoient pas le bien publique, et que ce n'estoit pas fait de bon pastre ou pastour de vouloir transgloutir ou mengier sa beste, maiz de la tondre justement;* et tant fist de biens, qu'il monstra en luy par exemples come chascun se devoit gouverner et vivre.

Et pour l'influence des grans biens habondans en ycellui Tybere Cesarre du commancement[2046] de son empire et pres jusques a la fin, je te puis bien avoir comparé a luy, car encores depuis nagueres tu as moult habondaument enssuy les vertus de sa succession, de tant que tu as voulu devenir pastour des povres bestes – come il fut – et n'as pas voulu souffrir leur transgloutissement, maiz as tresviguereusement mis la main aux armes vainquerresses pour les garder. Pour laquelle chose, mon tresredoubté Seigneur et vray catholique, la prudence de toy sera essaucee et divulguee entre tous les crestiens de cest monde et entre les aages a venir.

Et sachies que en faisant telles oevres tu peus acquerir une vie seconde, qui est appellee gloire perdurable: car la gloire – qui vault autant a dire come bone renommee – donne a tous preudommes une vie seconde aprés la mort, et la renommee, qui remaint de leurs bones oevres, fait sembler qu'ilz soient encores vifs. Encore deffent la gloire que ceulx ne soient mors qui sont dignes de loenges. Et pour ce, mon tresredoubté Seigneur, vueillies soustenir vertueusement la[2047] oevre* que [tu][2048] as commencee, car tes armes ne sont pas armez forcenees ne persecutoires, maiz sont doulces et reluisans come l'estoille de Jupiter pour le bien publique. Et tu le peus appercevoir clerement, car entre tous les autres princes des crestiens tu es desiré en plusieurs lieux et plusieurs nacions mesmement des Bretons, lesquiex singulierement[2049] et seulement a toy veulent baillier toute leur seignourie et garde et gouvernement; laquelle chose est moult honnourable, veu la noblesse et force d'iceulx et de leur païs.

Et pour ce que ta force et puissance, aprez[2050] celle du chief de ce royaume surmonte les autres – come je puis appercevoir – qu'il te plaise mettre ententive a deux choses, lesquelles feront vivre ta renommee perdurablement: c'est que tu ayes regard a la trescrueuse et miserable discorde de nostre mere Saincte Eglise, affin que par toy elle puisse estre unie et mise en paix et en repos. Car [fo. 34v.] certes

---

[2044] sy ~~apre~~ aspre
[2045] ceulx
[2046] comman ~~dement~~
[cement *superscript*]

[2047] le
[2048] *no* tu
[2049] singlierement

[2050] ta force et puissance est force aprez

pacified by you. For [fo. 34v.] certainly I truly believe that all the trials and tribulations which are happening in this country or have been happening for a long time past, only come about through our sins and through our disregard for or disobedience towards Our Creator.

Valerius Maximus shows many fine examples of this when he deals with the Romans, saying: *'It is no surprise*[246] *that the benevolence or goodwill of the gods have been constant in protecting and enlarging the Roman empire, which has had the petty misdeeds against their honour or service examined with such scrupulous care, for no one should think that our city was ever backward with regard to the most conscientious observance of the ceremonies due to the gods.'* And he proves this with a multitude of examples, one of which I want to relate to you and which we ought to remember.

'In Rome two consuls were appointed, one of whom was named Scipio Nasica and the other Gaius Figulus. They were sent to wage war, one in Corsica and the other in Gaul; they subjected these lands to Roman rule. But notwithstanding their excellent feats of arms, they were recalled to Rome and stripped of their estates and situations simply *because Tiberius Graccus*[247] *had written to tell the College of Augurs in Rome that they had held meetings in the temple or tabernacle of the gods, to hear matters*[248] *of little and trivial significance, the noise from which might perhaps have disturbed the sacrifices to the gods.'*

We ought to mark well this example[249] *and treat our holy places and churches with great reverence, for as St Isidore says in the fifteenth book of his Etymologies:* 'If pagans could bestow such great honour on the temples or tabernacles not of their gods but of their idols, Christians ought to be most ashamed to show so little reverence to God Himself who is Our Creator.' Livy and Valerius Maximus relate many other marvellous things concerning this subject; through them they seemed to mean that *the great benevolence*[250] *and goodwill of the gods favoured and helped the Romans.*

---

[246] Page 317, lines 6–10. *Ce n'est pas merveille ... des cerimonies aux dieux*. This comes from *nulz ne se doit mervillier ... des cerimonies aus diex*, Valère Maxime, *Facta et dicta memorabilia*, ed. Enriello and others, I, p. 31.

[247] Page 317, lines 18–20. *Tyberius Graccus avoit escript ... tabernacle aux dieux*. Comes from *Tyberius Graccus ... envoia lectres ... le tabernacle des diex*, ibid. I, p. 26.

[248] Page 317, lines 20–22. *pour oÿr questions de petites choses et inutiles, desquelles la noÿse par avanture povoit avoir empeschié le sacrefice des dieux*. Comes from *il avoit oïes ou temple questions de petites choses et inutiles, desquelles la noïse par avanture avoit empeeschié le service des diex*, ibid. I, pp. 28–29.

[249] Page 317, lines 23–27. *Ceste exemple devroit on bien noter ... qui est nostre Createur*. This comes from *En cest exemple puet on noter ... au vray Dieu du ciel*, ibid. I, p. 26. *Ysidore*, p. 317, l. 24. St Isidore of Seville (560–636), author of the *Etymologiae*. See Bossuat and others (eds), *Dictionnaire des lettres françaises: Le Moyen Age*, s.v. 'Isidore de Séville'.

[250] Page 317, lines 30–31. *la grant indulgence et bone voulenté des dieux les Rommains ont esté favourables et aydans*. Comes from *l'indulgence ou bonne voulenté des diex a esté ferme et constans de garder et augmenter le empire*, Valère Maxime, *Facta et dicta memorabilia*, ed. Enriello and others, I, p. 31. **B**'s reading has *dieux* and *Rommains* transposed, *supra*, p. 317, l. 30.

je croy veritablement que toutes les tribulacions et maulx, qui aviennent ou sont avenus en ce royaume depuis longtemps a, ne viennent sy non des pechiés commis par nous et par la descongnoissance ou desobeïssance que nous avons de nostre Createur.

Moult de beaux exemples en monstre Valerius, ou il traicte des faiz des Rommains, en disant ainsi: *'Ce n'est pas merveille, se indulgence ou bone voulenté des*[2051] *dieux a esté ferme et constant de garder et acroistre l'empire de Romme, lequel a voulu par sy scrupuleuse cure estre examinez les petis mesfaiz encontre leur honneur ou service, car on ne doit pas cuidier que nostre cité eust oncques les yeulx arriere du tresespecial cultivement des cerimonies aux dieux.'* Et il le monstre[2052] bien par moult d'exemples, entre lesquiex je t'en vueil raconter[2053] un, duquel nous devrions bien avoir la souvenance.

'Il fu ordonné a Romme deux consules, dont l'un fu appellé Scipio Nasica et l'autre Gayus Figulus,[2054] lesquiex furent envoiés pour fere guerre, l'un en Corsique et l'autre en Gale, lesquelles terres ilz soubzmistrent a la seignourie de Romme. Maiz nonobstant leurs armes vertueuses furent ilz remandez a Romme et furent privez de leurs estas ou offices, pour ce seulement que *Tyberius Graccus avoit escript au college des augures a Romme qu'ilz avoient*[2055] *fait assemblees de gens dedens le temple ou tabernacle aux dieux pour oÿr questions de petites choses et inutiles, desquelles la noyse par avanture povoit avoir empeschié le sacrefice des dieux.'*

Ceste[2056] exemple devroit on bien noter, et avoir les sains lieux et eglises en grant reverence, car sycome dit Ysidore ou .xve livre d'Ethimologies: *'Se les paiens faisoient aussi grant honneur aux tabernacles ou temples non pas de leurs dieux maiz de leurs ydoles, bien devroient les crestiens grant vergoigne avoir de fere si pou de reverence au vray Dieu, qui est nostre*[2057] *Createur.'* Moult d'autres grans misteres en raconte Titus Livius et Valerius Maximus touchans ceste matiere, par lesquiex[2058] il semble qu'ilz veulent dire que *la grant indulgence et bone voulenté des dieux les Rommains*[2059] *ont esté favourables et aydans.*

[2051] de
[2052] ilz le monstrent
[2053] vueil monstrer raconter
[2054] siculus
[2055] quil avoit
[2056] e ceste
[2057] nostre *superscript*
[2058] lesquuex
[2059] bone voulente des rommains les dieux

Next, most mighty Seigneur, you should see that revenge is taken or punishment meted out for the spilling – so sinfully and so treacherously – of the royal blood of that good Christian, King Richard; certainly it is most pitiful and distressing to hear of the end of his days which have been cut short before his lifespan was reached, on account of the true and loyal love which he had for this country. Alas! If you knew what sad laments and piteous regrets he voiced to all the royal princes of France – and especially to you and to the Count of St Pol[251] – when he was a fugitive in Wales, in fear of those traitors, his enemies, who pursued him on all sides in order to put him to death, certainly you would gather large companies of men and cross to their island, for the long duration of peace makes good men become gross and lazy.

And therefore, Sire, do not agree to any further truce, but let revenge be taken, proportionate to the crime. And truly I think that there would be no more honourable conquest made or talked about than this, since the time that the Gauls destroyed the sovereign empire of Rome *after they had crossed*[252] *the frozen, wild and impassable Alps, which no man had crossed before except Hercules*. And fear not their furious strength, for Our Lord God who is a righteous judge, knowing their wickedness, would not allow them to be victorious in battle – as we can clearly see – for since their rebellion[253] they have known only failure and defeat. Therefore, Sire, should it please you to set sail when you can, and unfurl in the wind those banners sent to your lineage by divine omnipotence, you will see the greater part of the nobility laying hands on their weapons to go along with you, seeking revenge for the royal blood shed in England.

Now I beg you, most mighty Christian Seigneur, at the end of my epistle, if I have misspoken in any way, please excuse me and bear with my ignorance, for I am only a lay person with little learning, and my knowledge is scant. But the faithful love I bear you made me write it, wishing with all my heart to serve you. May the God who broadcasts His riches and bestows His abundance on wise men grant you victory.

Amen.

---

[251] Page 319, line 9. *Monseigneur de Saint Pol.* For Waleran of Luxembourg, *supra*, l. 3505, note. In the *Prinse et mort* we read only that Richard invoked Charles VI and Isabella.

[252] Page 319, lines 17–19. *qu'ilz orent passees les Alpes tresfroides, rudes et incertables, que oncques home par avant n'avoit passees que Hercules seulement.* Comes from *qui premierement passerent les Alpes tres froides, rudes et intraitables, c'est a dire les mons qui n'avoient esté passé par devant, fors de Hercules*, Valère Maxime, *Facta et dicta memorabilia*, ed. Enriello and others, I, pp. 34–35. Creton's *incertables* should be Hesdin's *intraitables*.

[253] Page 319, lines 23–25. *depuis ... leur rebellion ilz n'ont eu ... que fortunes et desconfitures*. The deposition of King Richard in 1399 was followed in 1401 by the uprising of Owen Glendower in Wales, and trouble on the border with Scotland. See Given-Wilson, *Henry IV*, pp. 190–215.

Aprés, mon tresredoubté Seigneur, vueillies que vengeance ou[2060] pugnacion soit faicte du noble sang du bon catholique le roy Richart, lequel a esté espandu tant villainnement, tant traïcteusement, que certes c'est moult misericordieuse et piteuse chose a oÿr la fin[2061] de ces* jours lesquiex, par la vraye et loyale[2062] amour qu'il avoit par deça, ont esté finiz, ainz que son aage deust estre acompli. Helas! Se tu savoies bien les tristes complaintes et les piteux regrés qu'il faisoit a tous les seigneurs du sang de France – et especialment a toy et a Monseigneur de Saint Pol – quant il estoit fuitif en Gales pour la crainte des traïctres ses ennemis, qui le chassoient de toutes pars pour le mettre a mort, certes tu feroies assembler tumultes de batailles pour passer en leur ysle, car la longue demeure de paix fait les bons homes a rudir* et devenir paresceux.

Et pour ce, Sires, ne soies consentans de leur plus donner treves, maiz que vengeance en soit prise, telle come il appertient au mesfait. Et vrayement je cuide que – depuis le temps que les Gaulx destruisirent[2063] le souverain empire de Romme et *qu'ilz orent passees[2064] les Alpes tresfroides, rudes et incertables,* que oncques home par avant n'avoit passees que Hercules seulement* – ne fu plus honnourable conqueste faicte come ceste, ne dont il fut plus parlé. Et ne doubte point leur force forcenee, car Nostreseigneur Dieux, qui est vray juge, congnoissant leurs maulx, ne les pourroit souffrir ne soustenir en armes victorieuses – come on le peut clerement appercevoir – car depuis le temps de leur rebellion ilz n'ont eu gaires que fortunes et[2065] desconfitures. Et pour ce, Sires, s'il te plaist metre tes voiles en mer maiz que temps convenant soit venu, et tes enseingnes au vent – lesquelles furent envoiees a ton sang par la puissance divine – tu verras la plus grant partie des nobles homes mettre la main aux armez ententivement pour aler avecques toy, desirans la vengeance du noble sang espandu en Albion.

Or te prie je, mon tresredoubté Seigneur et vray catholique, a la fin[2066] de mon epistre que, se j'ay aucunement mespris en parler, qu'il te plaise le moy pardonner et supporter l'ignorance de moy, qui ne suys que home lay et pou sachant; et est mon entendement de pou de congnoissance. Maiz la vraie amour que j'ay a toy le m'a fait faire, desirant de tout mon cuer ton service. Ycellui Dieu, qui ses richesses eslargist et donne habondament a la vie des saiges, te vueille octroier vie victorieuse.

         Amen.

[2060] vengeance ~~soit faicte~~ ou
[2061] la ~~v~~ fin
[2062] loyal
[2063] destruisierent
[2064] passes
[2065] de
[2066] affin

Ballade [II] by Creton

Come, come from the Empire and from France, come and see an excellent company, come and see an alliance renewed. Come and see noble knights, come and see how they both act as one, come and see Caution coupled with Youth.[254] Come and see the scourge of sloth who labours diligently night and day for the common good. Come and see triumphant love, come to him bearing branches of laurel.

Do this to strengthen the old custom,[255] established long ago by the Romans; [fo. 35r.] it is the true symbol of victory, awarded for loyalty – as formerly the Romans used to award it for wisdom or valour – for it was the supreme earthly prize, given for worthy deeds and honour. If you follow the Romans, everyone will hold you dear, and if a prince's work leads to victory, come to him bearing branches of laurel.

The man who brings safety where there was danger saves the lives of many valiant men. And perhaps France[256] would shortly have been enslaved by the jealous English,[257] since previously they showed that they had the ability to do so. Thus it seems to me that the man who extinguishes such a misfortune should have many triumphs.[258] Come and see him to thank him, everyone in turn should come and see him, come to him bearing branches of laurel.

---

[254] Page 321, line 7. *Prudence avec Jennesse*. 'Caution' is certainly Philip the Bold. 'Youth' has been suggested as the young duke of Brittany (*supra*, p. 315, ll. 29–31); see Creton, 'Trois ballades politiques inédites', ed. Roccati, pp. 1102–1103; but Louis d'Orléans (1372–1407), younger brother of Charles VI, may be a securer identification. Creton is celebrating the outbreak of peace at the beginning of 1402. *Supra*, Introduction, p. 22.

[255] Page 321, lines 13–14. *l'anciennë ordonnance / ... des Rommains*. Creton is referring to the Roman custom of awarding a crown of laurel to a victorious commander. See *Oxford Classical Dictionary*, s.v. 'Crowns and Wreaths, Roman'.

[256] Page 321, line 26. *la province – France* – does not refer to Brittany, a province of France, but to France herself. See *infra*, p. 327, l. 28, *leur province* = England. Creton also uses *region* = *pays* to refer to France. *Supra*, l. 3638, *D'Engleterre en sa region* = 'out of England into her own country'.

[257] Page 321, line 28. *Albïons* = Englishmen. This form is also found in Deschamps, *Oeuvres complètes*, ed. de Queux and Raynaud, I, no. 153, p. 281, l. 22; III, no. 362, p. 100, l. 21.

[258] Page 321, line 30. *triumphes*. A triumph, a celebratory procession, was awarded by the Romans to a successful general. See *Oxford Classical Dictionary*, s.v. 'Triumph'.

Balade [II] par Creton

Venez, venez de l'Empire et de France,
Venez vëoir tresbelle compaignie,
Venez vëoir renouvel d'aliance.
Venez vëoir gente chevalerie,
Venez vëoir comë elle est unie,
Venez vëoir Prudence avec Jennesse.
Venez vëoir l'ennemy de paresce,
Qui pour le bien publique nuyt et jour
Diligeaument ne fait que travaillier.
Venez vëoir victorïeuse amour,
Venez vers luy portant raim de lorier.

Pour augmenter l'ancïenne ordonnance,
Qui des Rommains fu pieça establie;
[fo. 35r.] Et pour monstrer vraie signifiance
De victoire par[2067] loyaulté gaingnie[2068] –
Come jadiz la rommaine lignie
Souloit faire par senz ou par prouesce –
Faictes ainsi, car ce fu la maistresse
Des biens mondains, de vaillance et de honnour.[2069]*
D'ensuyvre les chascun vous aura chier,
Et se prince conqueste par labour
Venez vers luy portant raim de lorier.

Car qui fait seur ce qui est en balance,
De maint vaillant home gaigne la vie.
Et peut-estre que la province – France –
En eust esté en brief temps asservie
Par Albïons, qui sont tous plains d'envie,
Veu que pieça en ont monstré l'adresse.
Sy doit avoir triumphes a largesse,
Ce m'est advis, qui estaint tel dolour.[2070]
Venez le veoir pour le remercier,
Venez le veoir un chascun a son tour,
Venez vers luy portant raim de lorier.[2071]*

[2067] pour
[2068] gaingnee
[2069] honneur
[2070] doleur
[2071] venez le veoir portant rains de lorier

Another *ballade* [III] by the said Creton

All[259] the lands of Asia and Europe, Africa also and India were formerly conquered by the ancient Romans' mighty feats of arms, so strong were their noble levies, until Sulla and Marius[260] were elected to rule as consuls. Then began the cruel jealousy from which many Romans died. The strength of Rome was almost destroyed by their quarreling and hostility; reflect on this, noble blood of France.

Sulla, who was full of self-will, planned to go and conquer the lands of noble King Mithridates.[261] But before he had led his army from the Campania,[262] Marius said that he would lead the armies himself and that he was consul; he had been consul for six years or more. Then Sulla appeared, full of rage, and put all those of Marius' party to death. Marius took revenge when he returned from his flight to Ostia;[263] reflect on this, noble blood of France.

A long time afterwards Caesar[264] – the first emperor – won many noble victories, and you can be sure that in under three years he subjugated fourteen kings with his fierce fighting. Pompey feared his receiving a triumph from those he had defeated, and ordered him not to enter Rome. Julius Caesar said to his men, who knew how to fight to the death: 'Those who have enslaved Rome will die'; reflect on this, noble blood of France.

---

[259] Page 323, line 1. *Autre balade*. With five stanzas and an *envoi*, this is a *chant royal*. See L.A. Finlay [formerly Stewart], 'The *Chant Royal*: A study of the evolution of a genre', *Romania*, 96 (1975), pp. 481–496; also L.E. Kastner, *History of French Versification* (Oxford, 1903), pp. 268–271.

[260] Page 323, line 7. *Scilla, Marius*. Creton had read Valerius Maximus' account of the enmity between Sulla and Marius: *Silla et Marius si orent grant guerre ensamble, par laquelle la vertu et poissance de Rome fu aussi comme toute perie et perdue*, Valère Maxime, *Facta et dicta memorabilia*, ed. Enriello and others, I, p. 114.

[261] Page 323, line 16. [*le*] *roy Mitridates*. See *Oxford Classical Dictionary*, s.v. 'Mithridates II, king of Parthia, 125/121–91 BCE', also s.v. 'Parthia, Parthian empire'.

[262] Page 323, line 17. *Campaigne* is the correct reading. See *Quant Silla sot ceste chose ... il revint de Champaigne vers Rome*, Valère Maxime, *Facta et dicta memorabilia*, ed. Enriello and others, I, p. 114. **B**'s *compaignie* also makes the line hypermetric. The Campania = the region of west central Italy. See *Oxford Classical Dictionary*, s.v. 'Campania'.

[263] Page 323, line 24. *Ostie*. Ostia was a harbour-town at the mouth of the Tiber. See *Oxford Classical Dictionary*, s.v. 'Ostia'. Ostia's importance to Rome is well illustrated by the fighting between Marians and Sullans. When Marius returned from Africa, he captured Ostia before advancing on Rome; he knew that by controlling Ostia and the Tiber he could starve Rome.

[264] Page 323, lines 26–27. *Cesar – le primerains / Emperiere*. Caesar's great-nephew Augustus was the first emperor. The rivalry between Caesar and Pompey is treated in Valère Maxime, *Facta et dicta memorabilia*, ed. Enriello and others, I, pp. 124–127, and 265–268.

Autre balade [III] par ledit Creton

Par les grans faiz des ancïens Rommains
Furent jadiz les terres soubjuguees
De toute Aise et d'Orreup[2072] pour [le][2073] mains,
D'Auffrique aussi avecques les Indees;
Tant furent fors leurs nobles assemblees,
Jusques au temps que Scilla, Marius
Pour gouverner furent consule esleus.
Lors commença la doleureuse envie,
Dont mains[2074] Rommains depuis perdirent vie.
Par le discorde[2075]* d'eulx et malveillance
Fut la force rommaine prez perie;
Advisés y, le noble sang de France.

Scilla, qui fu de sa voulenté plains,
Tenoit aler conquerre les contrees
Du noble roy Mitridates. Mes ainz
Que de Campaigne[2076] eust ses gens amenees
Dit Marius qu'il feroit les armees
Luy mesme, et que consule il fust tenus;[2077]
Sy avoit il esté six ans ou plus.
Lors vint Scilla plain de forcenerie
Et mist a mort tous ceulx de la partie
De Marius, qui puis en prist vengeance,
Quant il revinst de sa fuyte d'Ostie;
Advisés y, le noble sang[2078]* de France.

Grans temps aprez Cesar – le primerains
Emperiere – maintes nobles journees
Ot[2079]* de victoire, et sy soiés certains
Qu'a luy soubzmist en moins de troiz annees
.xiiii. roys par ses fieres meslees.
Pompee ot paour qu'il ne fust lors reçus
A triumphe, par ceulx qu'il ot vaincus,
Sy luy manda que a Romme n'entrast mie.
Jules Cesar dist a sa compaignie,
Qui furent duys d'armes faire a oultrance:
'Ceulx seront mors, qui ont[2080] Romme asservie;'
Advisez y, le noble sang de France.

[2072] dorreut
[2073] no le
[2074] maint
[2075] discord
[2076] compaignie
[2077] tenu
[2078] roy
[2079] et
[2080] qui ~~mo~~ ont

Then was Caesar feared so much by Pompey that he fled, having called up his men. Then were father and cousin fighting against one another with bloodied weapons. Caesar's men were slaughtered, but then Pompey was defeated and his people killed; not one of them survived. He fled to Ptolemy[265] by sea, [fo. 35v.] and did not survive there long; Ptolemy had him executed without warning. After this Rome lost her ascendancy; reflect on this, noble blood of France.

Now Lucan,[266] an upright and worthy man, said that these misfortunes were brought about because the one did not want another to rule over him, considering the honours he had won. 'The other, full of pride, would bear no equal, thus the whole empire was lost,' said Valerius. At one time Caesar and Pompey held sway over all the world. Alas! Had there been enduring peace between them,[267] no city would have been hostile to them; reflect on this, noble blood of France.

Princes, be clothed in harmony – that is a garment of great virtue – behave so that it is not torn by you. No one will take sides against you, for you have a huge amount of righteous power. Rome was despoiled by strife; reflect on this, noble blood of France.

---

[265] Page 325, lines 8–10. *A Tholomee s'en fouÿ par navye / ... Trenchier luy fist le chief*. See Valerius Maximus, *Photin osta a Pompee la teste et la presenta au roy Ptholomee ... Qui veult savoir plus a plain de ceste matere si voie Lucan ...*, Valère Maxime, *Facta et dicta memorabilia*, ed. Enriello and others, I, p. 266. Photinus (d. AD 376), bishop of Sirmium (in Serbia), denied the incarnation of Christ, and was therefore considered a heretic. See *The Catholic Encyclopedia*, ed. C.G. Herbermann and others, 18 vols [in 19] (New York, 1907–1950); https://www.catholic.org/encyclopedia/, XII, s.v. 'Photinus'.

[266] Page 325, line 13. *Lucan*. Roman poet, whose *Pharsalia* deals with the civil war between Julius Caesar and Pompey. See *Oxford Classical Dictionary*, s.v. 'Annaeus Lucanus, Marcus, the poet Lucan (39–65 CE)'.

[267] Page 325, lines 21–23. *Se paix unye / Eûst esté entre eulx ... / Nulles cités ne leur fut enemie*. Comes from Valère Maxime, *Facta et dicta memorabilia*, ed. Enriello and others, I, p. 126.

Lors fu Cesar de Pompee sy crains
Qu'il s'en fouy, tant qu'ot ses gens mandees.
La fu le pere et le cousin germains,
L'un contre l'autre en armes sanglantees.
Les gens Cesar y furent decoupees,
Maiz depuis [fu][2081] vaincus Pompeius
Et ses gens mors, qu'il n'en demoura nulz.
A Tholomee s'en fouÿ par navye,
[fo. 35v.] Ou il ne fu pas longuement en vie;
Trenchier luy fist le chief sans deffiance.
Depuis perdy Romme sa seignourie;
Advisez y, le noble sang de France.

Or dist Lucan, qui fu preudoms et sains,
Que ses[2082] douleurs sy furent engendrees
Pour ce que l'un ne voult nulz souverains,
Veu les honneurs qu'il avoit conquestees.
'L'autre, qui fu plain de fieres pensees,
'Ne voult avoir pareil, dont tous perdus
'Fut tout l'empire,' ce dit Valerius.
Sy tindrent eulx un jour la monarchie
De tout le monde. Helas! Se paix unye
Eüst esté entre eulx sans variance,
Nulles cités* ne leur fut[2083]* enemie;
Advisez y, le noble [sang de France.][2084]*

Princes, soyés de concorde vestus –
C'est un habit qui est de grant vertus –
Faictes que ne soit de vous departie.
Nul ne fera encontre vous partie,
Car trop avés vertueuse puissance.
Romme sy fu par discorde ravie;
Advisez y, le noble sang de France.

[2081] *no* fu
[2082] se
[2083] fut *superscript*
[2084] *no* sang de france

Another *ballade* [IV] by the said Creton.

Lay hands on your weapons with all speed to win honour and renown, to improve your standing amongst noble men, to be like Judas Maccabaeus,[268] to emulate the valiant deeds of Alexander, who was bold and brave. If you have any thought of defeating a king,[269] muster troops against this summer season, then throw down a challenge to Henry who has falsely accused you of treachery, in the letters sent to France.

Do not lead your army into Italy[270] – that is a country full of dangerous people – even if you had conquered them, that would not win you any security. Do not hate the Germans, but be ready, willing and able to attack those most wicked people[271] who have long been hostile to the royal blood from which you sprang and to which you belong today. Do not look elsewhere; you can see the truth of this, in the letters sent to France.

Do not wait until they have crossed the sea, for advantage very often lies with the aggressor. But let their land be pillaged by you, riding hard and setting fire[272] like they did here in many districts, until fire appears in more than a hundred places. Repay them what they did to us in their great perfidy. You will be obeyed and feared for evermore if you exact revenge, you whom they have greatly insulted, in the letters sent to France.

---

[268] Page 327, lines 4–6. *Judas Machabee / ... Alixandre*. These were two of the Nine Worthies, a group of historic and legendary figures popular in the Middle Ages, embodying the virtues of a perfect knight. There were three pagans (including Alexander the Great), three Jews (including Judas Maccabeus), and three Christians (including Charlemagne. *Supra*, l. 1492, note). See J. Huizinga, *The Autumn of the Middle Ages*, trans. R.J. Payton and U. Mammitzach (Chicago, 1996). pp. 76–77.

[269] Page 327, lines 8–9. *Se vous avés pensee ... / De conquerir royale majesté*. This *ballade* is addressed to Louis d'Orléans, and refers to an exchange of letters between him and Henry IV in 1402–1403. *Supra*, Introduction, p. 28.

[270] Page 327, lines 14–18. *En Ytalie ne conduisiés armée / ... D'Alemaigne ne soiés envïeux*. Louis d'Orléans was known to have ambitions in Italy and Germany. See Palmer, *England, France and Christendom*, pp. 222–223.

[271] Page 327, line 20. *la tresmalvaise gent* = the English.

[272] Page 327, line 29. *En chevauchant de force et boutant feux*. During the fourteenth century, English tactics in the war against France generally involved a *chevauchée*: the army rode on a broad front, plundering and burning as they went. See Palmer, *England, France and Christendom*, pp. 5–6. Creton advocates turning these tactics against the English.

Autre balade [IV] par ledit Creton

Pour acquerir honneur et renommee,
Pour mielx valoir entre les gracïeux,
Pour ressembler a Judas Machabee,
Pour enssuïr les faiz chevalereux
D'Alixandre, qui fu hardyz et preux,
Mettés la main aux armes vistement.
Se vous avés pensee aucunement
De conquerir royale[2085] majesté,
Assemblés gens contre cest temps d'esté,
Et puis mandés a Henry deffiance,
Qui vous met sus sans cause faulseté
Par [les][2086] lettres envoiees en France.*

En Ytalie[2087] ne conduisiés armee –
C'est un païs plain de gens perilleux –
Se vous aviez la terre conquestee,
Sy n'auriés vous asseurance par eulx.
D'Alemaigne ne soiés envïeux,
Maiz soiés prest, hastif et diligent
De courre sus la tresmalvaise gent,
Qui sy longtemps ennemis[2088] ont esté
Du sang royal, dont pieça fustes né,
Et sont encores. N'ayés autre esperance;
Vous en povés savoir la verité
Par [les][2089] lectres envoiees en France.

N'attendés pas qu'ayent la mer passee,
Car assaillans sont bien souvent eureux.
Maiz par vous soit leur province fustee
En chevauchant de force et boutant feux,
Come ilz ont fait par deça en mains[2090] lieux,
Tant qu'il y pert en places plus de cent.
Rendés leur donc leurs biens pareillement
Qu'ilz nous ont fait par grant desloyauté.
Vous en serez servi, craint et doubté
A tousjours maiz, se prise en est vengeance
De vous, a qui ilz ont moult offensé
Par [les][2091] lettres envoiees en France.

[2085] royal
[2086] no les
[2087] ytale
[2088] ennemie
[2089] no les
[2090] maint
[2091] no les

[fo. 36r.] Prince, go to war with Perfidy, who ought to make you want to punish boldly, in faith and in hope, those who show you no love, in the letters sent to France.

[fo. 36r.] Prince, querele avec[2092] Desloyauté,
Qui vous doit bien donner la voulenté
De hardement, de foy et d'esperance
De pugnir ceulx, dont vous n'estes amé,
Par les lectres envoiees en France.

[2092] avecques

ILLUSTRATIONS

Reproductions of the pages containing all
sixteen miniatures (Figures I–XVI)

ILLUSTRATIONS 331

Figure I. Creton makes obeisance to Jean de Montaigu, the first owner of **H** (BL MS Harley 1319 fo. 2r.) © The British Library Board.

Figure II. King Richard knights Henry of Monmouth (BL MS Harley 1319 fo. 5r.) © The British Library Board.

Figure III. Three ships arrive from Dublin (BL MS Harley 1319 fo. 7v.) © The British Library Board.

Figure IV. McMurrough gallops downhill out of the woods (BL MS Harley 1319 fo. 9r.) © The British Library Board.

ILLUSTRATIONS 335

Figure V. The Archbishop of Canterbury, holding the papal bull, preaches from the pulpit (BL MS Harley 1319 fo. 12r.) © The British Library Board.

Figure VI. Salisbury's ships arrive at Conway (BL MS Harley 1319 fo. 14v.) © The British Library Board.

Figure VII. King Richard's fleet leaves for Wales, one of the ships bearing his sunburst badge on her sail (BL MS Harley 1319 fo. 18r.) © The British Library Board.

Figure VIII. King Richard, in black cowl, meets Salisbury and other companions at Conway (BL MS Harley 1319 fo. 19v.) © The British Library Board.

Figure IX. Exeter and Surrey ride out on their embassy to Lancaster (BL MS Harley 1319 fo. 25r.) © The British Library Board.

Figure X. Exeter and Surrey make obeisance to Lancaster at Chester (BL MS Harley 1319 fo. 30v.) © The British Library Board.

ILLUSTRATIONS 341

Figure XI. Northumberland makes obeisance to King Richard at Conway (BL MS Harley 1319 fo. 37v.) © The British Library Board.

Figure XII. Northumberland kneels before the Host (BL MS Harley 1319 fo. 41v.) © The British Library Board.

Figure XIII. King Richard is ambushed by Northumberland (BL MS Harley 1319 fo. 44r.) © The British Library Board.

Figure XIV. Lancaster makes obeisance to King Richard at Flint (BL MS Harley 1319 fo. 50r.) © The British Library Board.

Figure XV. Lancaster hands King Richard over to the liverymen of London (BL MS Harley 1319 fo. 53v.) © The British Library Board.

Figure XVI. The Deposition Parliament. The empty throne, with Lords Spiritual on the left and Lords Temporal on the right (BL MS Harley 1319 fo. 57r.) © The British Library Board.

NOTES ON TRANSLATION

The bold numbers refer to the appropriate line in the French text where the presence of the note is indicated by an asterisk.

3. *De verdure, et.* The first example of lyric caesura, also in ll. 105, 181, 249 and so forth, and less common here than epic caesura. The final *e* of *verdure* is not elided into the following initial vowel, as it would normally be, and counts as a syllable.

8. *Joyeux et gay.* In MidF it was common to use pairs of words meaning the same, or almost the same. See also *infra* l. 10, *dueil et esmay*; l. 38, *les despiz et deulx*; l. 43, *a repoz në a paix.* See *Chrestomathie*, ed. Rickard, no. 1, p. 40, l. 1, note. In the prose section and epistles Creton occasionally launches into triplets. *Infra*, p. 195, l. 11; p. 201, ll. 8–9; p. 307, ll. 7–8.

13. *je vous pri.* 1st person present indicative of *-er* verbs are more common with an analogical *e* than without, e.g. ll. 719, 1141, *prie*; ll. 912, 1346, *crie*; l. 3658, *desire*. But cf. also ll. 313, 611, *affi*; l. 712, *pri*; ll. 1657, 2089, *lo*.

24, 26. *certains…plains.* The OF form of the masculine singular noun and adjective, with *-s*, occurs alongside the ModF form, e.g. l. 346, *grans homs*; l. 1055, *li sires de Persi*; l. 1071 *li homs*.

38, 39. These are the first examples of epic caesura: at the break in the line the final unstressed *e* of *salee* and *Ymbernie* is not counted, even preceding a consonant. See also ll. 46, 78, 102, and following. Epic is more common than lyric caesura in the *Prinse et mort*.

41. *Grant quantité.* The ModF form *grande* occurs only twice, ll. 3246, 3359. The usual form of the feminine adjective is *grant*. On the other hand, the usual form of the adverb is ModF *grandement*, e.g. ll. 427, 1579, 3373. OF *granment* is only found twice, ll. 151, 245.

63. *guinder* = 'to hoist up'. Creton must have written *guinder* – **AD**'s reading – not *wuidier* = 'to unload'; the horses were being loaded on to ships for passage to Ireland.

70–71. *tour* / ... *tour*. The first *tour* (noun masculine) = 'skill', the second (noun feminine) = 'tower', an acceptable rhyme in MidF. Less acceptable was to have a word rhyming with itself, e.g. ll. 81, 83, *gent* / ... *gent*. Some other examples are at ll. 164–165; 832, 835; 1377–1378.

73–75. *gens vi laide et orde,* / *L'un desciré* ... / *L'un ot un trou*. Creton treats cavalierly the collective noun *gent* (noun feminine singular) and *gens* (noun masculine plural), both meaning 'people', 'army', or 'retinue'. *Gent* is feminine, e.g. ll. 222, 573, except for l. 1031, *gent desrouté*. Adjectives preceding *gens* are feminine, ll. 473, 949; following are masculine, ll. 721, 847. However, at p. 323, l. 17, and p. 325, l. 2 the past participles agree with *gens* feminine; at p. 325, ll. 5, 7, the past participle agrees with *gens* feminine, then masculine in the same sentence. See also ll. 737–740, *ceste gent s'esmaie* / *De peur qu'ilz ont* ... / *Il me lairont; ce ne sont que gens laie* / *Et non saichans*. The question of number is equally confused; l. 2139, *gens* has a singular verb, and in ll. 737–738, and 2544–2547, *gent* first has a singular verb then a plural one. Creton is driven by demands of rhyme and especially metre.

Ot ... *avoit*. In MidF the past historic tense is frequently used where ModF would use the imperfect, *infra* ll. 801, 2693. A mixture of the two is not uncommon, as here and at ll. 271–275; p. 187, l. 20, and ll. 2693–2694.

107–108. *son* ... / *avec*. See the variant readings in these lines. Words and letters in **H** with an underlining have been written over an erasure. It is certain that in l. 107, **H** originally had **LB**'s reading *le*, and in l. 108, **LB**'s *et*.

117–119. *hardi* / ... *apers* ... / ... *esbahi*. Creton is inconsistent in the form of the masculine plural adjective, as he is in the singular, *supra* ll. 24–26; *hardi* and *esbahi*, rhyming with *lui* and *vy*, are the OF forms; *apers* is the ModF form. Further examples are ll. 206, 685, 1301, and 2125.

151. *granment*. For the OF form of *grandement*, *supra*, l. 41, endnote (hereafter 'note').

155. For *desir* meaning 'regret' see E. Huguet, *Dictionnaire de la langue française du XVIe siècle*, 7 vols (Paris, 1925–1967), s.v. '*desir*'.

NOTES ON TRANSLATION 349

175. *homs* = *homme*; a relic of OF nominative case, singular, but the *s* is analogical. *Homs* < *homo*, *infra*, ll. 346, 348, 2027.

177. *tant sont boiz pereilleux*. All MSS have *les boiz*, which gives one syllable too many. Creton omits the definite article, *infra*, l. 202, *Que cerf ne fait*; also l. 2699, *Ly metoient croix sur la teste*.

190. *esragoient*. *g* before *a/o* is sometimes used to represent a soft *g*. Other examples are l. 389, *desloga*; l. 1214, *changable*; l. 3239, *manga*.

213. *Col* = ModF *cou*. Nouns which owe their ModF forms to a back-formation from their plural, appear here in their OF form. Some other examples are, l. 344, *ruissel*; l. 982, *mantel*; l. 1834, *vaissel*; l. 2071, *morsel*.

222. *desoremaiz* counts as only three syllables, also at ll. 1498, 1634, 1842. It counted as four at l. 143. Interconsonantal *e* is weak by MidF but this is often not reflected in the spelling, e.g. l. 483, *aideront*; l. 591, *parlera*; l. 921, *souverain*; ll. 2042, 2181, *serement*; ll. 3263, 3495, *derrenier*, are all of two syllables. *Salsebery*, ll. 546, 1182 is of three syllables; l. 2156 of two syllables only. See *Chrestomathie*, ed. Rickard, p. 19.

243. *nulle riens*. There are some other examples of OF feminine nouns with a flexional *s* in the singular, *infra* l. 1538, *saisons*; l. 2323, *raisons*; l. 3620, *voulentes*; p. 185, l. 17, *cités*.

254–255. **H** has a minor correction in both of these lines; l. 254 originally read *Maquemoire*, the *i* has been erased but is just visible. In l. 255 the *z* of *painez* has been squeezed in later. *Z* is often used for *s*, a final *ez* does not necessarily indicate that the *e* is stressed, e.g. l. 346, *a merveillez*; l. 405, *nous y fusmez*; l. 729, *maintez foiz*.

281. **H**'s original reading lacks one syllable, *si* has been added from AD's reading. The same emendation has been made at l. 419.

290. *Ses amis*. *Ses* is the first of only two examples of the OF masculine singular possessive adjective, *infra* l. 3064, *ses corps*. There is one example of the OF masculine plural possessive adjective, l. 709, *my compaignon*.

294. **H**'s line as it stands has one syllable too many. **ABCD**'s *soit*, singular, has been preferred to *soient*, plural; only one *seigneur* – the earl of Gloucester – went to parley with McMurrough. In the preceding line, **H** originally read *moins*; an *a* has been written over the *o*.

302. *qu'i* = *ce qu'il*, *l* in pre-consonantal position – *qu'i seroit* – was silent by now, so that *qui* and *qu'il* became homophonous and were often confused. Cf. *infra* ll. 373, 382, 1211, *qu'i* = *qu'il*; l. 794, *quil* = *qui*; l. 2757, *qu'i* = *qu'ilz*.

309. *Present le roi* = (literally) 'the king being present', a construction based on the Latin ablative absolute. See *Chrestomathie*, ed. Rickard, p. 13. Other examples are l. 1911, *ce fait*; p. 189, ll. 17–18, *la messe oïe*; ll. 2662–2663, *presens / Tous ceulx*.

335. *N'autre.* **H** originally read Autre, as in **B**; the *N* is written over an erasure, and the *a* is written in the space between the initial letter and the rest of the line.

339–340. *Sa semblance... / Veez pourtraite*. Around 1400 *semblance* = 'portrait'. *Portraire* = to delineate any subject, not necessarily a likeness. See Musée du Louvre, *Paris 1400: Les Arts sous Charles VI*, ed. E. Taburet-Delahaye (Paris, 2004), p. 28.

340. *Vëez* counts as two syllables here, only one at l. 1133.

343. As they stand, **HABCD** lack one syllable. **L**'s reading – *et deulx deux* – has been preferred.

349–350. *Lui et le conte parlerent... / En racontant*. In MidF the present participle, *racontant*, does not always refer to the subject of the main clause, *Lui et le conte*. Here it refers only to *le conte*: Gloucester is enumerating McMurrough's crimes against Richard. *Infra*, ll. 2117–2118, 2165; p. 189, l. 4; l. 3573.

363. *moult lui estoit tart* = 'he was very impatient'. Di Stefano, *Dictionnaire des locutions*, s.v. '*tard*': *il m'est tart que*: *indique surtout l'impatience de, l'empressement à*.

373. Et qu'i cuidra avoir bon, si l'envie. Ibid. s.v. '*bon*': *avoir de bon sur qqn* = *l'emporter* = 'to get the upper hand of', and *avoir du bon* = *avoir le dessus* = 'to have the upper hand'.

390. *une meure* = 'a blackberry', something of little value. *OED*, s.v. 'fig, 4. a.', 'As a type of anything small, valueless, or contemptible'.

406. *Aises du corps comme poisson en Saine* = 'as happy as fish in water'. See Di Stefano, *Dictionnaire des locutions*, s.v. '*poisson*'.

419. HBC's hypometric line has been amended following **AD**. Cf. *supra*, l. 281, note. D was originally short of one syllable also, *si* having been added later. At ll. 1094 and 2673, **A** has a regular line and D's correction makes it the same. **L** has a regular line, but its reading is further from that of the other MSS.

432. *se m'ait Dieux* (also l. 999). The OF 3rd person present subjunctive of *-er* verbs, i.e. the form without final *e*, survives in a few stereotyped expressions. Other examples are ll. 1515, 1674 *doint* (< *donner*); ll. 792, 1444, *gart* (< *garder*). See *Chrestomathie*, ed. Rickard, no. 13, p. 95, l. 87 and note.

443. *rebous* was originally written *rebours*, the scribe later crossing out the *r* to make a better rhyme for the eye with *nous: tous: doulx*. These rhymes – also ll. 1384–1387, *m'ame: larme: ferme: diffame* – illustrate the weakness of a pre-consonantal *r* at this time.

463. *Quant au roy pleut, qui.* Although *que* was commonly used as a subject form in MidF – see **D**'s reading at l. 239 and **B**'s at l. 326 – the single example in **H**, unsupported by the other MSS has been amended.

483. *lui aideront. Aideront* counts as two syllables, *supra*, l. 222, note. *Aidier* can still be intransitive (as in OF) as used here, also l. 489; p. 311, ll. 10, 16. The ModF transitive usage co-exists, *supra* l. 1550, p. 311, l. 26.

487. *envoiee.* Considering that *donnee* agrees with the preceding direct object – *que*, l. 486, whose antecedent is *la bulle sëellee*, l. 485 – **LB**'s reading has been preferred to **HACD**'s.

493. *Lors veïssiez.* An OF figure of speech that was still being used right up into the fifteenth century. See N. Andrieux-Reix, '*Lors veïssiez*, histoire d'une marque de diction', *Linx*, 32 (1995), pp. 133–145. Creton is referring beyond the text to the action he is describing; he is inviting the listener or reader to step into the scene and witness it for himself.

520. *Biau* for *beau*. The first of a sprinkling of Northern forms, probably scribal in origin. *Infra* ll. 1765–1767, *mangonniaulx: monchiaulx: nouviaulx*; and ll. 3701–3702, *chastiaulx: biaulx*. See also *le* for *la*, p. 193, l. 31 and note, *je prendray la mort en pasience, comme tu le prins*; and forms in *ch*, *infra* ll. 2555, 2617, *commencha*; l. 3043, *aperchevoir*; l. 3207, *chieulx*. See Pope, *From Latin to Modern French*, § 1320 Northern

Region; *Phonology*: §§ i, viii, pp. 486–488. These spellings are not in the other MSS, except for **C**, which only has them where **H** does. This suggests that they were in the exemplars which **H** and **C** copied; the other MSS 'corrected' them out. *Infra* ll. 1142, 1977, *no* for *nostre*, is a Northern form, ibid. *Morphology*, § xxv (b), p. 490, but this comes from Creton, as it affects the syllable count.

543. All MSS have one syllable too many. The removal of the conjunction *et* is a suggested correction. *S'est li fons* = (*aus*)*si est li fons*.

Li fons. There are four other examples of the OF masculine nominative singular definite article, ll. 850, 1055, 1071, and 2027 In the last two cases *li homs* avoids elision, thus giving the correct number of syllables.

572–573. *emprinse* / ... *prinse*. The rhymes at ll. 574–575, *guise* / ... *mise* show that the *n* is not sounded. The rhymes at ll. 1576–1579 show this also. This pronunciation is not peculiar to Creton. In the mid 14th-century *Les Voeux du héron* written in monorhymed *laisses*, *prins(s)*, ll. 28, 52, 71, 121, rhymes with *païs*, *avis*, *paradis* and other rhymes in -*i* in the *laisse*, ll. 27–144; also ll. 205–220. See *Vows of the Heron*, ed. Grigsby and Lacy.

591. *parlera* counts as two syllables. *Infra* l. 2001, *feray*, counts only as one syllable, but ll. 578, 590 and elsewhere counts as two. See above l. 222 and note.

626. *merveilles*. The form with *s* is well attested. *Infra*, ll. 951, 1425, 2640. See also Huguet, *Dictionnaire*, s.v. '*merveille*', and Tobler and Lommatzsch, *Altfranzösisches Wörterbuch*, s.v. '*merveille*'.

638. *qui ne les haioit mie*. An example of litotes. See *OED*, s.v. litotes. Ironical understatement ... in which an affirmation is expressed [King Richard loved the Welsh and men of Cheshire] by the negative of the contrary [he did not hate them].

640–641. *Cuidant* ... / *Qu'arrivé feust le roy*. Verbs of thinking, used affirmatively, are followed by the subjunctive, *infra*, l. 693, *nous pensons ... que le roy soit mort*; or the indicative, l. 734, *je croy ... que vous estes traÿs*; p. 191, l. 20, *je croy ... qu'il lui osta*.

709. *my compaignon*. An isolated example of the OF masculine plural possessive adjective. Cf. *supra*, l. 290 and note.

737–740. *ceste gent s'esmaie / De peur qu'ilz ont ... / gens laie / Et non saichans.* Supra, ll. 73–75, note. Also, l. 739, *il me lairont*. There are a few instances of OF *il* masculine plural pronoun, *infra*, l. 1571; p. 201, l. 8; l. 3018, but *ilz* is the usual form.

764. All MSS lack one syllable. There is *enjambement* between this line and the next. Creton may have regarded ll. 764–765 as one 14-syllable line, in which case the final, unstressed, *e* of *deffendre* would count as a syllable.

794. *quil* is a spelling variant of *qui*. Cf. *supra*, l. 302, note.

864. *voise*. OF 3rd person present subjunctive < *aler*.

891. *quant il vit sa queue luire* (literally) = 'when he saw his tail shining'. There was a bizarre belief in France in the Middle Ages that Englishmen had tails: see P. Rickard, '*Anglois coué* and *l'Anglois qui couve*', *French Studies*, 7 (1953), pp. 48–55; but this seems not to be pertinent here. See *DMF*, s.v. '*luire*', I.C.: *Voir sa queue luire* = *voir le moment favorable*. I thank Professor Roccati for this reference.

896–899. *haultaine: plaine: quinzaine: aime*. The first three rhymes are good, there is assonance only with the fourth. This occurs occasionally elsewhere, e.g. ll. 1240–1243, 2144–2147.

918. *qu'on* = *ce qu'on*.

921. *souverain* counts as two syllables, *supra*, l. 222, note.

950. *arme* = *âme*, 'soul'. In negative construction = 'no one'. Cf. *infra*, l. 1550. See *Chrestomathie*, ed. Rickard, p. 372.

967. *fouyus*. Creton appears to have coined this past participle < *fouir* to fit the rhyme.

993. *de la se departirent*. It is obvious from what follows that the verb does not refer only to Rutland and Percy, *infra*, l. 1277, note.

1047. *estourdiz* has no pejorative meaning here, = 'daring'.

1084. *son beau frere* = 'brother', also at ll. 1135, 1746. The usual meaning of *beau frere* is 'brother-in-law', ll. 1463, 1466, 1526. Similarly *beau pere* usually means 'father-in-law', ll. 1356, 2241, but can mean 'father', l. 3633.

1085. *Die* (subjunctive) has been changed from *dit* (present indicative); the *e* is written over the *t*.

1097. The break comes after the seventh syllable. There is lyric caesura in this line, as in l. 1094.

1133. *veez* counts as only one syllable, as in ll. 1541, 1939.

1142. *no vie*. Creton uses the Northern form of the feminine singular possessive adjective, instead of *nostre*, evidently because it is a monosyllable. This happens once more, at l. 1977. *Supra*, l. 520, note.

1207. *Lui estre ... demené*. In ModF, *étant*, a present participle, would be expected rather than an infinitive. But cf. *infra*, p. 191, l. 12, *les avoir veuz*; p. 303, l. 24, *toy avoir oü*.

1230. *chascun*. **H** originally read *chaccun*, an *s* being written over the first of the double *c*s.

1241. *trestout*. **H** reads *tout*, the initial *t* being a large majuscule written over an erasure. It seems likely that **H** originally read *trestout* (**LC**'s reading), and that has been preferred, otherwise the line lacks a syllable. Something similar occurs at l. 1479.

1277. *S'en alerent*. The verb does not refer only to Rutland and Percy, *supra*, l. 993, note.

1287. *venoit ... / Meschief et paine*. The verb is agreeing with the nearer of two related subjects. Cf. p. 191, ll. 16–18, *En ceste ... compaignie estoit l'arcevesque de Cantorbie, Messire Thomas de Persi et le conte de Rotelant*; p. 303, ll. 4–5, *ton corps et ta personne est plus convenable a Mars*. The ModF construction is also found, p. 197, ll. 6–7, *l'archevesque de Cantorbie et le conte de Northomberlant alerent querre le duc de Lancastre*.

1304–1306. *juge ... / juge*. The first *juge* = 'judge'; the second = 'judgment', an acceptable rhyme in MidF. Cf. *supra*, ll. 70–71, note.

1312–1314. *loy ... / loy*. The same word rhyming with itself would have been frowned upon; also ll. 1377–1378, *estuet ... / estuet*.

1355. *j'espoir*. *Espoir*, first person present indicative < *esperer*, is one of a handful of relics of OF vocalic alternation. See also l. 1408, *muir* < *morir*; and l. 1947, *ains* < *amer*. See *Chrestomathie*, ed Rickard, no. 13, p. 95, l. 82 and note.

1384. *m'ame* is the first of a handful of OF elided forms of a possessive adjective before a feminine noun beginning with a vowel. Some others are l. 1404, m'amie; l. 1415, *m'esperance*; l. 2294, *s'image*; p. 311, l. 3, *s'esperance*. Generally the ModF forms are used, supra l. 786, *son ame*; l. 515, *son emprise*; infra, p. 305, l. 27 *ton ymage*. See *Chrestomathie*, ed. Rickard, no. 1, p. 41, l. 32 and note.

1389. *Encore*. **HBC**'s *encores*, makes the line hypermetric; **AD**'s *encore* has been preferred to **L**'s *encor*, as that is the usual spelling here. There is a similar situation with *avecque(s)* at ll. 3009, 3601.

1462. *d'Excestre*. **H**'s original reading was *decestre*, the *x* added superscript; also *infra*, l. 1502.

1466. *Ilz sont ... y ne sont pas. Ilz*, also spelled *y*, is used here twice rather than the ModF *elles*, because it is a monosyllable. See *Chrestomathie*, ed. Rickard, no. 17, p. 112, l. 116 and note; also no. 23, p. 140, l. 100 and note.

1469. Va comptant = *compta. Infra*, l. 1759, *a la pensant* = *pensa*.

1469–1501. *Et lors lui va comptant ... / ... ce que fait lui a.* This very long sentence has been broken at ll. 1484 and 1496 for the sake of clarity. The principal verb *va comptant* governs *tout ce que*, l. 1470, and eight noun clauses introduced by *que*, ll. 1473, 1475; *comment*, l. 1478; *que*, ll. 1480, 1482, 1485, 1497, and 1499.

1475. *Et*. **H** originally seems to have read *Si*. The scribe had changed *S* majuscule into an *E*; the *E* is written in darker ink over an *S*, and the *t* is written over an erasure.

1479. *tresgrant*. **H** reads *grant* preceded by an erasure. The descender of the *g* has been looped up to the left to form a *T* majuscule, which is an abbreviation of *tres*. **C**'s reading is *tresgrant*, which gives the correct number of syllables. See also *supra*, l. 1241, note.

1515. *doint*. 3rd person present subjunctive < *donner*; also at l. 1674. *Supra*, l. 432, note.

1541. *veez* counts as one syllable only.

1568. *cependent.* = *cependant*. There is hesitation in the MidF period between *a/e* befora a nasal consonant. *Infra*, also l. 1878, *atendant* = *atendent*; l. 1969, valissent = valissant. See *Chrestomathie*, ed. Rickard, no. 5, p. 59, l. 27; and no. 6, p. 64, ll. 104, 106, note.

1577. *prins*. For the pronunciation, *supra*, ll. 572–573, note.

1603. *artillerie* counts as four syllables only. *Supra*, l. 222, note.

1639. *monne* = 'nun'. **LABD** have *moine* = 'monk', which makes better sense but does not rhyme.

1661. *qu'avec*. **HB**'s reading, *avecques*, makes the line one syllable too long. **AD**'s reading makes the syllable count correct, and also makes the construction of the sentence clearer.

1705. *fu* is the imperfect subjunctive, as is *fut*. Cf. *infra*, ll. 3555, 3568. The usual form is *feust*, *supra*, ll. 641, 1018, or *fust*, *infra*, l. 2417, 3065.

1745. *feïstes*. **HB**'s *fistes* gives a line of only nine syllables. **LACD**'s *feïstes* has been preferred.

1752. *Ne quë en dire*. **H**'s reading, *Ne qu'en dire*, lacks one syllable.

1759. *ala pensant* = *pensa*. *Supra*, l. 1469, note.

1765–1767. *mangonniaulx*: *monchiaulx*: *nouviaulx*. *Supra*, l. 520, note.

1766. *roide*. *OED*, s.v. 'stiff, 6.', 'Tight, closely packed. Now *hyperbolically* in colloquial use: Densely crowded (*with*). Also *figurative*'. 'Densely crowded with' is clearly the meaning of *roide* here.

1777–1778. *On les devroit tenir… / Et que croniques nouviaulx en feussent faiz*. The ModF hypothetical construction (conditional) is followed by the OF (imperfect subjunctive).

1784. *Moy le sisisme*. All MSS read *Moy sixiesme*. The other rhymes of the quatrain are *prime*, *rime*, *lime*, and at l. 3477 .xxv.[me] rhymes with *prime*; thus the form *sisisme* would be expected here. See Pope, *From Latin to Modern French*, § 825, pp. 318–319. Also, the line is hypometric; thus *Moy le sisisme* is suggested as Creton's original reading.

1809. *Northomberlant* counts here, and at l. 2008, as three syllables. *Supra*, l. 222, note.

1838. *esvesque ... autresi. Esvesque* is attested in Huguet, *Dictionnaire*, s.v. '*evesque*'. It is attributed to the rarity of initial *e* + consonant other than *s*; see *Chrestomathie*, no. 53, p. 274, l. 106, note. **H** originally had **LBC**'s *aussi*; a *t* and a contraction mark have been written in very dark ink over the first *s*. The same change has been made by the scribe at l. 2266 and editorially at l. 1870. *Autresi* would have been what Creton wrote to give the correct syllable count.

1878. 1878 *atendant* = *atendent*. *Supra*, l. 1568, note.

1911. *Ce fait* = (literally) 'this having been done'; *supra*, l. 309, note.

1933. *Lors veïssiez*. *Supra*, l. 493, note.

1939. *veez* counts as one syllable, as in ll. 1133, 1541.

1947. *ains* < *amer*. *Supra*, l. 1355, note.

1977. *no gent*. *Supra*, l. 520, note.

2001. *feray* counts as only one syllable. *Supra*, l. 222, note.

2008. *Northomberlant* counts as three syllables. *Supra*, l. 222, note.

2028–2031. *mure* is the form required by the rhyme. See Huguet, *Dictionnaire*, s.v. '*morir*'. However, *supra*, ll. 888–891, *conduire*: *muyre*: *duire*: *luire*; *infra*, ll. 2236–2239, *destruire*: *muire*: *conduire*: *fuire*.

2042. *serement* counts as two syllables here and at l. 2181, but three syllables at ll. 2046 and 2055. *Supra*, l. 222, note.

2099. *Du pas garder* = *de garder le pas*. *Infra*, l. 3002, *Du duc Henry faire mourir* = *de faire mourir le duc Henry*. See *Chrestomathie*, ed. Rickard, no. 39, p. 213, l. 151.

2111. *qu'a*. **H** originally read *que*, an *a* being written over the *e* in very dark ink.

2133. *Jusqu'a*. **H**'s original reading was *jusque*; *a* has been written over the *e*.

2139. *Des gens* (two syllables) gives the correct syllable count, *de la gent* (three syllables) does not. Creton is using *gens* (plural) as if it were *gent* (singular), *supra*, ll. 73–75, note.

2144–2147. *paine: enmaine: aime: souveraine.* There is assonance only between *aime* and the other rhyme-words. *Supra*, ll. 896–899, 1240–1243.

2165. *Ainsi parlant, nous convint aprochier. Supra*, ll. 349–350, note.

2187. *deshonnour* is the form required by the rhyme. The same applies at *infra*, *honnour*, p. 321, l. 20, and *dolour*, p. 321, l. 31. Cf. *supra, honnour*, l. 1533; *doulour*, l. 870.

2249. *Sceü le fait. Supra*, l. 309, note.

2266. *autresi.* For the alteration in **H**, *supra*, l. 1838, note.

2270. *Trestoute nuit* = 'overnight'. By MidF, *toute la nuit* and *toute nuit* could both refer to one night in particular or to an unspecified night. See *Chrestomathie*, ed. Rickard, no. 42, p. 227, l. 205, note.

page 187, line 15. *catholique* = 'Christian'. For this interpretation, see *Le Grand Robert*, s.v. *catholique*, II, 1°.

page 193, line 31. *je prendray la mort ... comme tu le prins.* There are another two instances of the Northern *le* for *la*, 3rd person pronoun feminine, direct object, p. 199, l. 8, and l. 2801. See *Chrestomathie*, ed. Rickard, no. 27, p. 155, l. 38 and note; no. 39, p. 210, l. 23 and note. Also *supra*, l. 520, note.

page 195, line 11. *bons, vrais et loyaulx* is a triplet. *Supra*, l. 8, note.

page 197, line 12. *et lui dist* is the reading of all MSS; the syntax is rather confused. I suggest that *et* is a corrupt reading.

page 199, line 17. *le mes* = *les me*, a Northern form.

page 199, line 25. *Albie* = *Albion* = 'England'. This is found also in Deschamps, *Oeuvres complètes*, ed. de Queux and Raynaud, I, no. 26, p. 106, l. 4; II, no. 285, p. 139, l. 12.

page 201, line 8. *il sont. Supra*, ll. 737–740, note.

page 211, line 6. *tourna*. It appears that **H** originally read *tournoya*, **ACD**'s lesson; the *a* has been written over the second *o* and an erasure follows.

page 213, lines 1–4. *Ainsi partismes ... d'estre en France*. These lines are only in **AD**. The reason behind the omission is unclear.

2296–2334. The imprecatory *ballade* (lines 2296–2334) has three stanzas on identical rhyme-schemes plus an *envoi* (the *envoi* sends – *envoyer* = 'to send' – the *ballade* to its addressees). See S.V. Spilsbury, 'The Imprecatory *Ballade*: A fifteenth-century poetic genre', *French Studies*, 23 (1979), pp. 385–396. Creton's language is restrained compared to that of Deschamps and François Villon.

2300. The missing line in **C** – as given in **D** – has been written in the right-hand margin by a modern hand.

2331. *deveroient* counts as three syllables, *supra*, l. 222, note; the break in the line comes after the sixth syllable. This has the effect of stressing *toy*, the object of Creton's execration.

2358. *visce*. Creton has made up a verb modelled on the noun *vice*. The scribes were thrown into confusion by it, as witness the variant spellings.

2437. desfaire (= 'to depose' or 'to kill') is written over an erasure. **LABCD** read *faire mourir*, certainly **H**'s original reading. **H**'s revised reading introduces an element of uncertainty: was Richard murdered or merely deposed? **H**'s original reading was unambiguous.

2442. *dis*. **H**'s original reading was *diz*. An *s* was written over the *z*, making a more satisfying rhyme for the eye.

2447–2478. *hors de la ville / De Londres – ce ne fu pas guille*. There is no *de* in **HLBCD**, l. 2447, which makes the line short by one syllable. A's *hors de la ville* gives a regular line. In l. 2448, all MSS originally read *ce n'est pas guille*, and the line again lacks a syllable. On the analogy of l. 3250 – where the scribe of **H** has changed *nest* > *ne fu* – *ne fu* has been judged to be what Creton originally wrote.

2501. All MSS read *Norvic* and the line is hypometric. *Norvic* has been amended to *Norevic*, on the analogy of *Panebroc*, l. 2510, to make eight syllables. Similarly *Werwic*, l. 2937, has been amended to *Werewic*.

2513. In **BC**, l. 2515 originally followed on l. 2513. The mistake was realized and l. 2515 scored out. l. 2514 follows, then l. 2515 in its correct place.

2525. *Toute jour* arose from a wish to avoid confusing *tot jor* (= *toute la journée* = 'all day long') with *toz jorz* (= *toujours* = 'always'), perhaps on the analogy of *toute nuit*. See P. Rickard, 'Toute jour, tout le jour, et toute la journée', *Romania*, 85 (1964), pp. 145–180.

2536. *Fïlz dë Isaac.* **HLB**'s *f. disant* is an obviously corrupt reading.

2541. *la couronne* means, by extension, 'kingdom', also *infra*, l. 2563. Tobler and Lommatzsch, *Altfranzösisches Wörterbuch*, s.v. '*couronne*', has the meaning 'royal domain'. 'Kingdom' is also the meaning of *royauté*, *infra*, l. 2790, but *infra*, l. 2681 it means 'crown'.

2573. Without *si*, all MSS lack one syllable. The correction has been made following **AD**'s reading at ll. 281, 419. In **C**, ll. 2572–2573 have been omitted.

2617. *Il commencha imterroger.* The construction *commencer* + infinitive (no *a*) was still current in the sixteenth century; see Huguet, *Dictionnaire*, s.v. '*commencer*'. For other forms in *ch* and other Northern forms, *supra*, l. 520, note.

2648. *interrogasïon* counts as six syllables, but *interrogasion*, l. 2658, counts as five.

2656. *yert.* A solitary example of the OF 3rd person imperfect < *estre*. Creton regularly uses *estoit*, *supra* l. 2655; *infra*, ll. 2664, 2670; which has two syllables.

2660. *A tousjours leur sera lait vice.* A cliché, repeated *infra*, l. 2840.

2662. *presens / Tous ceulx.* *Supra*, l. 309, note.

2673. *deulx en disant ainsi.* **HBC**'s reading lacks two syllables. **AD**'s *ambedeulx* has been preferred to **L**'s *humblement*, which was probably a mis-hearing of *ambedeulx*. *Infra*, ll. 2692–2693, where *humblement* does not figure.

2681. *la royauté* = 'the crown'. *Supra*, l. 2541, note.

2688. *Ce ly mist la pusse en l'oreille* = (literally) 'this put a flea in his ear'. *DMF*, s.v. '*puce*': m*ettre la puce en l'oreille a qqn* = *Inspirer des inquiétudes à quelqu'un*. But Lancaster would not have been worried by the peers' response, it must mean that the loud acclamation roused, stirred him.

2693–2694. *Furent … / … estoient.* For the juxtaposition of tenses, *supra*, l. 75 and note.

2702. *Baisa.* A singular verb has been used instead of the grammatically correct plural – *baiserent* – for the sake of metre and rhyme.

2725–2726. *Le roy baisa parmi la bouche / Le connestable.* ModF word order – subject, verb, object – was not yet fixed in MidF. See *Chrestomathie*, ed. Rickard, pp. 27–28. In these two lines *le roy* is the object, *le connestable* the subject; it is the Constable who has the active role. This is not a common feature of Creton's language, but see p. 197, ll. 11–12, l. 2812; he uses it here for the sake of the metre in order to have eight syllables in either line.

2788. *de cuer fin.* H's isolated *le cuer* has been amended following the other MSS here, and following all six MSS at ll. 1166–1167 and 2514.

2790. *royaulté* = 'kingdom'. *Supra*, l. 2541, note.

2810. B's reading, the only regular one, has been preferred.

2826–2827. *moult tart / Leur estoit de si long sejour. Supra*, l. 363, note.

2830. *l'elexsion.* This word seems to have caused confusion among the scribes, whereas at l. 2647 it was copied without question.

2833. *com.* L's reading has been preferred to *comme*, otherwise the line is hypermetric; l. 3267 is a similar case.

2836. *compter.* **H**'s reading was originally *conter*; the scribe subsequently wrote a contraction mark over the *o* and a *p* over the *n*.

2900. *feste* = ModF *faîte* = 'highest point'.

2937. For all MSS, *werwic* > *werewic*, *supra*, l. 2501 and note, *norvic* > *norevic*.

2963–2964. *oultrance* / ... *qui a ce*. This is a doubtful rhyme, also infra, ll. 3013–3014, *aliance* / ... *qui a ce*; ll. 3527–3528, *France* / ... *qui a ce*.

3002. *Du duc Henry. Supra*, l. 2099, note.

3009. HACD are hypermetric. *Avecque* has replaced *avecques*, on the analogy of ll. 3330, 3488, and 3679. The same correction has been made, *infra*, l. 3601.

3018. il *avoient. Supra*, ll. 737–740, note.

3030. *Salsebery* = three syllables, also at ll. 3058, 3189. *Supra*, l. 222, note.

3064. *ses corps* = son *corps*, singular. *Supra*, l. 290, note.

3083. *pere* = third person present subjunctive < *paroir*, 'to appear'. See Pope, *From Latin to Modern French*, § 1060, pp. 398–399.

3197. HL's *puet* is either a historic present tense (see *Chrestomathie*, ed. Rickard, no. 26, p. 153, l. 138, note), or an orthographic variant of *peust*, imperfect subjunctive, *supra*, ll. 565, 1801. The usual form of the past historic here is *pot*, *supra*, ll. 98, 177, 409.

3250. *ne fu*. The scribe has changed *nest* into *ne fu*. The *f* is formed from the long-tailed *s* with a cross-stroke, the *u* is written over an erasure.

3263. *Supra*, l. 222, note

3277. *Le resembloit*. In MidF *resembler* was in course of transition from a transitive (OF) to an intransitive (ModF) verb. For ModF usage, *supra* ll. 3148–3149; *infra*, p. 327, l. 13. See *Chrestomathie*, ed. Rickard, no. 40, p. 217, l. 118, note.

3298. *la rachine de l'envie*. The sense requires *de* instead of *et*.

3327. All MSS are hypermetric. *Messire* has been altered to *Sire* on the analogy of ll. 3533, 3571.

3353–3354. *Maistre Pierre Blanchet, Henart* / ... *de Kanbenart*. This is not the only time that Creton omits the conjunction [*et*] between two names. See p. 323, l. 7, *Scilla, Marius*.

3376. *connourir*. A further word not found elsewhere. The scribe of **L** found it unfamiliar and substituted *renourrir*.

3396. *Ilz les respondirent*. A rare example of the transitive (OF) use of *respondre*. See A. Tobler and E. Lommatzsch, *Altfranzösisches Wörterbuch*, 12 vols (Berlin, Wiesbaden, Stuttgart, 1925–2018), s.v. 'respondre', and Huguet, *Dictionnaire*, s.v. 'respondre'.

3404. *vo requeste*. All MSS have *vostre requeste*, and the line is hypermetric. The Northern *vo* is substituted on the analogy of l. 1142, *no vie*; l. 1977, *no gent*. See Pope, *From Latin to Modern French*, § 1320, p. 1490, Morphology, §xxv (b); and *Chrestomathie*, ed. Rickard, no. 4, p. 57, l. 9. Another example from Deschamps is: Deschamps, *Oeuvres complètes*, ed. de Queux and Raynaud, V, no. 893, pp. 79–80, refrain: *Lors dis: «Oïl, je voy vo queue»*.

3495. *derrenier*. Of two syllables only. *Supra*, l. 222, note.

3543. *Franche*. **H**'s reading was originally *France*; the scribe then wrote an *h* over the original *e* and added an *e*. The same alteration has been made *infra*, l. 3689.

3555. *Fut* is the imperfect subjunctive, also l. 3568. *Supra*, l. 1705, note.

3564. *Son corps*. In MidF the possessive adjective did not necessarily refer to the nearest antecedent. Here, *Son* clearly refers to *la roüne*, l. 3540.

3587. *Grant douleur*. All MSS read *grant dueil* which makes the line hypometric. *Douleur* is suggested as what Creton originally wrote, on the analogy of ll. 3596–3597.

3620–3621. *la voulentés / ... fust*. All MSS have *les voulentés*, amended to singular because of the singular verb. For OF feminine singular nouns with a flexional *s*, *supra*, l. 243, note.

3633. *Son beau pere* = her father. *Supra*, l. 1084, note.

3645. *Furent geteez*. **A**'s reading alone is grammatically correct. In MidF a verb could agree with the nearer of two or more co-ordinated subjects, *supra*, p. 191, ll. 17–18; *infra*, p. 303, ll. 4–5. See *Chrestomathie*, ed. Rickard, p. 31. Here Creton has it agreeing with the further, *maintes larmes* (l. 3644). For the ModF usage, *supra*, p. 197, ll. 5–7.

page 301, line 10–page 329, line 5.

*Due to the indifferent quality of **B**, endnotes have been written for only a selected number of the many scribal errors and amendments.*

page 301, line 11. *come.* B reads *coe* [with a mark of contraction above]. This has been extended with only one *m*, considering *infra*, p. 301, l. 24, *e* [contraction] *nemis*; p. 303, l. 5, *p* [contraction] *so* [contraction] *ne*; p. 317, l. 8, *Ro* [contraction] *me*; and so forth. Had the scribe meant *comme*, he would have written *co* [contraction] *me*. Similar cases are *bone renommee*, p. 315, l. 21; *les bons homes*, p. 315, l. 13.

page 301, line 12. For *catholique* = 'Christian', *supra*, p. 187, l. 15, note.

page 301, line 28. *tout ce qu'i* = *tout ce qu'il*. Supra, l. 302, note.

page 303, lines 15–18. *affin que* governs five clauses, the verbs of which are 1. *fust rompue*, 2. *fussent finés*, 3. *fust devouree*, 4. [*fust*] *folié*, and 5. [*fussent*] *sustraiz*. It was quite normal for the auxiliary verb to be merely understood in 4 and 5. In 4, **B**'s *foliable* is corrupt, a past participle *folié* is required.

page 303, line 19. *telle sepulture.* **B**'s reading was *telles sepultures*. The *s* of *telles* has almost been erased, and there are two dots beneath the final *s* of *sepultures*.

page 303, line 24. *toy avoir oÿ.* Supra, l. 1207, note.

page 305, line 24. *par figures* [*et*] *par diz.* The *et* is needed to complete the sense, on the analogy of p. 309, l. 11, *par escript et par figures*.

page 305, line 28. *pensees et ymaginacions.* This is a doublet, two words meaning the same, or almost the same. Professor Strohm has been led astray by Dillon's careless transcription: the ampersand between the two nouns has been omitted. Creton, 'Remarks on the Manner of the Death of King Richard', ed. Dillon, p. 88; Strohm, 'The Trouble with Richard', pp. 96–97.

page 305, line 35. *sacrefice de voeux.* **B**'s reading, *de feu*, is obviously corrupt. *De voeux, d'oroisons et de prieres* is a triplet.

page 307, line 17. *ly* has been added to complete the sense. *Supra*, l. 3469, *Et ce qu'ilz ly eussent fait faire*.

page 309, line 10. *je yray*. Creton would not have used the conditional tense – *yroy* – here, but the future tense. *Infra*, p. 309, l. 11, *te porteray*; p. 309, l. 22, *je la suyvray ... et yray*.

page 311, line 3. *s'esperance*. *Supra*, l. 1384, note.

page 311, line 9. The line as it stands lacks one syllable. Substituting *trescrueulx* for **B**'s *crueulx* gives ten syllables. *Infra*, p. 315, l. 37, *trescrueuse*.

page 311, line 10. *Aidiés luy*, also *infra*, p. 311, l. 16, *luy aidier*. For the intransitive use of *aidier*, *supra*, l. 483, note.

page 311, lines 18–19. *Fu ... / ... Priant mort et quatre de ses fieulx*. **B** reads *prirent mort*: the scribe mistook Creton's *priant* for a verb – present participle < *prier* – which makes no sense, and changed it to *prirent* – 6th person past historic < *prendre* – which makes hardly any more sense. But *priant* = 'Priam', king of Troy: this is the form used by Deschamps, *Oeuvres complètes*, ed. de Queux and Reynaud, VIII, no. 1457, pp. 149–150, l. 3.

Fu ... mort. In MidF *mourir* was still used transitively = 'to kill', as well as ModF intransitively = 'to die', *supra*, p. 307, l. 12.

Fieulx. **B**'s reading: *filz* – does not rhyme with *lieux*. *Fieulx* is found in Christine de Pizan, *Oeuvres poétiques*, ed. M. Roy, I, s.v. *Autres Balades*, no. 37, pp. 250–251, l. 30. See also Pope, *From Latin to Modern French*, §391 (4), p. 155

page 311, line 33–page 313, line 4. *doit ou doivent ... se peut estre dolu ou deult encore ... peut avoir esté ou est*. Creton adopts a more pedantic and legalistic style in this epistle, in order that his borrowings from Valerius Maximus do not stand out.

page 313, line 27. B originally read *commandement*. It has been corrected editorially to *commencement*: *supra*, p. 313, l. 19. The scribe made the same mistake, p. 315, l. 10, but corrected it himself.

page 315, line 26. *la oevre*. *Oevre* is feminine, considering *commencee* in the following line.

page 319, line 5. *ces = ses.*

page 319, line 13. *rudir.* Another of Creton's made-up words = 'to become gross'.

page 319, line 18. *incertables.* This is an error for Hesdin's *intraitables* = '*impassable*'.

page 321, line 20. *honnour* is the form required by the rhyme. *Supra*, l. 1533, *honnour*; p. 319, l. 19, *honnourable.* Similarly, *infra*, p. 321, l. 31, *dolour* would have been what Creton wrote. *Supra*, ll. 387, 769, 870.

page 321, line 34. *Venez vers luy portant raim de lorier.* Creton is more likely to have repeated the same refrain as in the preceding stanzas; this is what he did in the preceding *ballades.* **B**'s – *venez le veoir* – was probably a scribal error, the result of contamination from the preceding lines.

page 323, line 11. *discorde.* **B**'s *discord* has been amended – the line lacks one syllable, *infra*, p. 325, l. 30.

page 323, line 25. *sang de France.* **B**'s *roy de France* is an obvious scribal error.

page 323, line 28. *Ot.* **B**'s first *et* has been changed. Creton would have had a verb here.

page 323, line 23. *nulles cités*, (also *grant vertus*, p. 325, l. 26). *Supra*, l. 243, note. *Fut* is a subjunctive.

page 325, line 24. *sang de France.* The missing portion of the line is supplied from the other refrains.

page 327, line 13. The three refrains are lacking one syllable; the reading in the *envoi* has been preferred, p. 329, l. 5.

BIBLIOGRAPHY

Primary Printed Sources

Anglo-Norman Letters and Petitions, ed. M.D. Legge (Oxford, 1941).
Carew, George, earl of Totnes (trans.), 'The Story of King Richard the Second, His Last being in Ireland, Written by a French Gentleman, who Accompanied the King in that Voyage to His Leaving Ireland in 1399', in *Hibernica, or, Some Antient Pieces Relating to Ireland*, Part I, ed. W. Harris (Dublin, 1757; originally published 1747), pp. 23–28.
Chandos Herald, *La Vie du Prince Noir*, ed. D.B. Tyson (Tübingen, 1975).
Chartier, Alain, *The Poetical Works of Alain Chartier*, ed. J.C. Laidlaw (Cambridge, 1974).
Christine de Pizan, *Ditié de Jehanne d'Arc*, ed. A.J. Kennedy and K. Varty (Oxford, 1977).
Christine de Pizan, *Le Livre de l'advision Cristine*, ed. C. Reno and L. Dulac (Paris, 2001).
Christine de Pizan, *Le Livre des fais et bonnes meurs du sage roy Charles V*, ed. S. Solente, 2 vols (Paris, 1936–1941).
Christine de Pizan, *Le Livre du corps de policie*, ed. A.J. Kennedy (Paris, 1998).
Christine de Pizan, *Oeuvres poétiques*, ed. M. Roy, 3 vols (Paris, 1886–1896).
Christine de Pizan, *The Love Debate Poems of Christine de Pizan: Le Livre du Debat de deux amans, Le Livre des Trois jugemens, Le Livre du Dit de Poissy*, ed. B.K. Altmann (Gainesville, FL, 1998).
Chronicles of the Revolution 1397–1400: The Reign of Richard II, ed. C. Given-Wilson (Manchester, 1993).
Chronicque de la traïson et mort de Richart Deux roy dengleterre, ed. B. Williams, English Historical Society (London, 1846).
Chrestomathie de la langue française au XVe siècle, ed. P. Rickard (Cambridge, 1976).
Creton, Jehan, 'Translation of a French Metrical History of the Deposition of King Richard the Second ... with a Copy of the Original', ed. J. Webb, *Archaeologia*, 20 (1824), pp. 1–423.
Creton, Jehan, 'Histoire de Richard II', ed. J.A. Buchon, in *Collection des Chroniques*, XXIV (Paris, 1826), pp. 321–466.
Creton, Jehan, 'Remarks on the Manner of the Death of King Richard the Second', ed. P.W. Dillon, *Archaeologia*, 28 (1840), pp. 75–95.
Creton, Jehan, 'Trois ballades politiques inédites de Jean Creton (début du XVe siècle)', ed. G.M. Roccati, in *Lingua, cultura e testo: Miscellanea di studi francesi in onore di Sergio Cigala*, ed. E. Galazzi and G. Bernardelli, 3 vols (Milan, 2003), II, pt. 2, pp. 1099–1110.

Deschamps, Eustache, *Oeuvres complètes d'Eustache Deschamps*, ed. Marquis de Queux de Saint Hilaire and G. Raynaud, 11 vols (Paris, 1878–1903).
Froissart, Jean, *Oeuvres de Froissart*, ed. J. Kervyn de Lettenhove, 25 vols (Brussels, 1866–1877).
Froissart, Jean, *Chroniques ... premier livre*, ed. G.T. Diller (Geneva, 1972).
Froissart, Jean, *Chroniques de France et d'Angleterre, livre quatrième*, ed. A. Varvaro (Brussels, 2015).
Froissart, Jean, *Oeuvres de Froissart: Poésies*, ed. A. Scheler, 3 vols (Brussels, 1870–1872).
Historia Vitae et Regni Ricardi Secundi, ed. G.B. Stow (Philadelphia, PA, 1977).
Holinshed, Raphael, *Chronicles of England, Scotland and Ireland*, 6 vols (London, 1807–1808).
Lorris, Guillaume de, and Meun, Jean de, *Le Roman de la Rose*, ed. F. Lecoy, 3 vols (Paris, 1965–1970).
Machaut, Guillaume de, *Le Jugement du roy de Behaigne and Remede de Fortune*, ed. J.I. Wimsatt and W.W. Kibler (Athens, GA, 1988).
Monstrelet, Enguerran de, *La Chronique d'Enguerran de Monstrelet*, ed. L. Douët-d'Arcq, 6 vols (Paris, 1857–1862).
Stow, John, *The Chronicles of England from Brute* (London, 1580; Text Creation Partnership), www.name.umdl.umich.edu/A13043.0001.001.
Stratford, J. (ed.), *Richard II and the English Royal Treasure: [An Inventory of Richard's Treasure in 1399]* (Woodbridge, Suffolk, 2012).
Usk, Adam, *The Chronicle of Adam Usk 1377–1421*, ed. C. Given-Wilson (Oxford, 1997).
Valerius Maximus [Valère Maxime], *Facta et dicta memorabilia*, trans. Simon de Hesdin, Books I–III, ed. M.C. Enriello, C. Di Nunzio, and A. Vitale-Brovarone, www.pluteus.it.
Valerius Maximus, 'La Traduction de Valère-Maxime par Nicolas de Gonesse', ed. C. Charras, PhD thesis, McGill University, Montreal, 1982.
The Vows of the Heron (Les Voeux du héron): A Middle French Vowing Poem, ed. J.L. Grigsby and N.J. Lacy, trans. N.J. Lacy (New York, 1992).
Walsingham, Thomas, *Annales Ricardi Secundi et Henrici Quarti*, in J. de Trokelowe et Anon., *Chronica et Annales*, ed. H.T. Riley, Rolls Series (London, 1866).
Wanley, Humphrey, *The Diary of Humphrey Wanley 1715–1726*, ed. C.E. and R.C. Wright, 2 vols (London, 1966).

Dictionaries and Finding Aids

Barrois, J. *Bibliothèque protypographique, ou, Librairies des fils du roy Jean: Charles V, Jean de Berri, Philippe de Bourgogne et les siens* (Paris, 1830).
Bossuat, R., Pichard, L., and Lage, G.R. de (eds), *Dictionnaire des lettres françaises: Le Moyen Age*, new edn (Paris, 1992).
Brewer, J.S., and Bullen, W. (eds), *Calendar of the Carew Manuscripts: Preserved in the Archiepiscopal Library at Lambeth*, 6 vols (London, 1867–1873).
British Library, *Catalogue of Illuminated Manuscripts*, www.bl.uk/catalogues/illuminatedmanuscripts.
Briquet, C.M., *Les Filigranes*, 4 vols (Geneva, 1907).

BIBLIOGRAPHY

The Catholic Encyclopedia, ed. C.G. Herbermann and others, 18 vols [in 19] (New York, 1907–1950); https://www.catholic.org/encyclopedia/.
Catholic Hierarchy, *The Hierarchy of the Catholic Church, Current and Historical Information about Its Bishops and Dioceses*, www.catholic-hierarchy.org.
Cockayne, G.E.C. (ed.), *The Complete Peerage*, 12 vols (London, 1910–1959).
Delisle, L.V., *Le Cabinet des manuscrits de la Bibliothèque nationale*, 4 vols (Paris, 1868–1881).
Delisle, L.V., *Recherches sur la librairie de Charles V*, 2 vols (Paris, 1907).
Di Stefano, G., *Dictionnaire des locutions en moyen français* (Montreal, 1991).
Dictionnaire du Moyen Français (1330–1500), www.atilf.fr/dmf.
Godefroy, F., *Dictionnaire de l'ancienne langue française*, 10 vols (Paris, 1881–1902).
Gossen, C.T., *Grammaire de l'ancien picard* (Paris, 1970).
Le Grand Robert, www.lerobert.com.
Huguet, E. *Dictionnaire de la langue française du XVIe siècle*, 7 vols (Paris, 1925–1967).
Hunt, R.W., Madan, F., Craster, H.H.E., Denholm-Young, N., and Record, P.D., *A Summary Catalogue of Western Manuscripts in the Bodleian Library at Oxford*, 7 vols [in 8], (Oxford, 1895–1953).
James, M.R., *A Descriptive Catalogue of the Manuscripts in the Library of Lambeth Palace*, 5 pts, continuously paginated (Cambridge, 1930–1932).
Lewis, C.T., and Short, C., *A Latin Dictionary* (Oxford, 1879).
Littré, P.E., *Dictionnaire de la langue française*, 4 vols (Paris, 1969–1971).
Omont, H., *Bibliothèque Nationale: Catalogue général des manuscrits français: ancien supplément français*, 3 vols (Paris, 1895–1896).
Omont, H., *Bibliothèque Nationale: Catalogue général des manuscrits français: nouvelles acquisitions françaises*, 4 vols (Paris, 1899–1918).
The Oxford Classical Dictionary, 4th edn (Oxford, 2012); https://oxfordre.com/classics.
Oxford Dictionary of National Biography, www.oxforddnb.com.
Oxford English Dictionary, www.oed.com.
Peignot, G., *Catalogue d'une partie des livres composant la bibliothèque des ducs de Bourgogne au XVe siècle*, 2nd edn (Dijon, 1841; originally published Paris, 1830).
Pope, M.K., *From Latin to Modern French with Especial Consideration of Anglo-Norman, Phonology and Morphology*, rev. edn (Manchester, 1952; originally published 1934).
Roberts, J., and Watson, A.G., *John Dee's Library Catalogue* (London, 1990).
Samaran, C., and Marichal, R., *Catalogue des manuscrits en écriture latine, portant des indications de date, de lieu ou de copiste*, 7 vols (Paris, 1959–1984).
Taschereau, J.A., Michalant, H., and Delisle, L. *Bibliothèque nationale, Département des manuscrits: Catalogue des manuscrits français, Ancien fonds*, 5 vols (Paris, 1868–1902).
Tobler, A., and Lommatzsch, E., *Altfranzösisches Wörterbuch*, 12 vols (Berlin, Wiesbaden, Stuttgart, 1925–2018).
[Wanley, H.], *A Catalogue of the Harleian Collection of Manuscripts*, 2 vols (London, 1759).
Watson, A.G. *Catalogue of Dated and Datable Manuscripts c.700–1600 in the Department of Manuscripts, the British Library*, 2 vols (London, 1979).
Wright, C.E. *Fontes Harleiani: A Study of the Sources of the Harleian Collection of Manuscripts Preserved in the Department of Manuscripts in the British Museum* (London, 1972).

Secondary Sources

Ainsworth, P. 'Style direct et peinture des personnages chez Froissart', *Romania*, 93 (1972), pp. 498–522.
Andrieux-Reix, N., '*Lors veïssiez*: Histoire d'une marque de diction', *Linx*, 32 (1995), pp. 133–145.
Armitage-Smith, S. *John of Gaunt: King of Castile and Leon, Duke of Aquitaine and Lancaster, Earl of Derby, Lincoln and Leicester, Seneschal of England* (Westminster, 1904).
Barron, C.M. *London in the Later Middle Ages: Government and People 1200–1500* (Oxford, 2004).
Bennett, M., *Richard II and the Revolution of 1399* (Stroud, Gloucestershire, 1999).
Biggs, D., *Three Armies in Britain: The Irish Campaign of Richard II and the Usurpation of Henry IV 1397–1399* (Leiden, 2006).
Bratu, C., '«Or vous dirai»: La Vocalité des récits historiques français du Moyen Age (XIIe–XVe siècles)', *Neophilologus*, 96 (2012), pp. 333–347.
Clarke, M.V., *Fourteenth-Century Studies* (Oxford, 1937).
Cockshaw, P., 'Mentions d'auteurs, de copistes, d'enlumineurs et de libraires dans les comptes généraux de l'état bourguignon (1384–1419)', *Scriptorium*, 23 (1969), pp. 122–144.
Colvin, H.M. (ed.), *The History of the King's Works*, 6 vols (London, 1963–1673).
Cropp, G.M., and Hanham, A., 'Richard II from donkey to royal martyr: Perceptions of Eustache Deschamps and contemporary French writers', *Parergon*, 24 (2007), pp. 101–136.
Davies, R.R., 'Richard II and the principality of Chester 1397–9', in F.R.H. du Boulay and C.M. Barron (eds), *The Reign of Richard II: Essays in Honour of May McKisack* (London, 1971), pp. 256–279.
De Winter, P.M. *La Bibliothèque de Philippe le Hardi, duc de Bourgogne (1364–1404)* (Paris, 1985).
Dodd, G., 'The road to Richard II's downfall: A visual journey', in Dodd, G. (ed.), *The Reign of Richard II* (Stroud, Gloucestershire, 2000), pp. 111–118.
Dorling, E.E., *Leopards of England and Other Papers on Heraldry* (London, 1912).
Doutrepont, G., *La Littérature française à la cour des ducs de Bourgogne* (Paris, 1909).
Dubois, A., *Valère Maxime en français à la fin du Moyen Age* (Turnhout, 2016).
Duls, L.D., *Richard II in the Early Chronicles* (The Hague, 1973).
Ferrier, J.M., 'The theme of Fortune in the writings of Alain Chartier', in F. Whitehead, A.H. Diverres, and F.E. Sutcliffe (eds), *Medieval Miscellany Presented to Eugène Vinaver* (Manchester, 1965), pp. 124–135.
Finlay [formerly Stewart], L.A., 'The *Chant Royal*: A study of the evolution of a genre', *Romania*, 96 (1975), pp. 481–496.
Fletcher, D., 'The Lancastrian Collar of Esses: Its origins and transformations down the centuries', in J.L. Gillespie (ed.), *The Age of Richard II* (Stroud, Gloucestershire, 1997), pp. 191–204.
Foulet, A., and Speer, M.B., *On Editing Old French Texts* (Lawrence, KS, 1979).
Given-Wilson, C., *Henry IV* (New Haven, CT, 2016).
Given-Wilson, C., *The Royal Household and the King's Affinity: Service, Politics and Finance in England 1360–1413* (New Haven, CT, 1986).
Gordon, D., Monnas, L., and Elam, C. (eds), *The Regal Image of Richard II and the Wilton Diptych* (London, 1997).

Gransden, A., *Historical Writing in England*, 2 vols (London, 1974–1982).
Hedeman, A.D., 'Advising France through the example of England: Visual narrative in the *Livre de la prinse et mort du roy Richart* (Harl. MS. 1319)', *Electronic British Library Journal* (2011), Article 7, 22 pp., www.bl.uk/eblj/2011articles/article7.html.
Hughes, M.J., 'The Library of Philip the Bold and Margaret of Flanders', *Journal of Medieval History*, 4 (1978), pp. 145–188.
Huizinga, J. *The Autumn of the Middle Ages*, trans. R.J. Payton and U. Mammitzach (Chicago, 1996).
Johnston, D.B., 'Richard II's departure from Ireland, July 1399', *English Historical Review*, 98 (1983), pp. 785–805.
Jones, E.J., 'An examination of the authorship of the deposition and death of Richard II attributed to Creton', *Speculum*, 15 (1940), pp. 460–477.
Kastner, L.E., *A History of French Versification* (Oxford, 1903).
Kastner, L.E., 'A neglected French poetic form', *Zeitschrift für französische Sprache und Literatur*, 28 (1905), pp. 288–297.
Kervyn de Lettenhove, J., 'Les Chroniques inédites de Gilles le Bel', *Bulletins de l'Académie royale des sciences, des lettres et des beaux-arts de Belgique*, 2nd ser., 2 (Brussels, 1857), pp. 430–460.
Lechat, D. 'L'Utilisation par Christine de Pizan de la traduction de Valère Maxime par Simon de Hesdin et Nicolas de Gonesse dans *Le Livre du chemin de long estude*', in E. Hicks (ed.), *Au champ des escriptures, IIIe Colloque international sur Christine de Pizan* (Paris, 2000), pp. 175–196.
Leclerc, V., *Histoire littéraire de la France au quatorzième siècle*, 2 vols (Paris, 1865).
Lecuppre, G., *L'Imposture politique au Moyen Age: La Seconde Vie des rois* (Paris, 2005).
Lehoux, F. *Jean de France, duc de Berri: Sa vie, son action politique (1340–1416)*, 4 vols (Paris, 1966–1968).
Louvre, Musée du, *Paris 1400: Les Arts sous Charles VI*, ed. E. Taburet-Delahaye (Paris, 2004).
McGettigan, D., *Richard II and the Irish Kings* (Dublin, 2016).
McKisack, M., *The Fourteenth Century 1307–1399* (Oxford, 1959).
McKisack, M., 'London and the succession to the Crown during the Middle Ages', in R.W. Hunt, W.A. Pantin, and R.W. Southern (eds), *Studies in Medieval History Presented to F.M. Powicke* (Oxford, 1948), pp. 76–89.
Mathew, G., *The Court of Richard II* (London, 1968).
Meiss, M., 'The Bookkeeping of Robinet d'Estampes and the chronology of Jean de Berry's manuscripts', *Art Bulletin*, 53 (1971), pp. 225–235.
Meiss, M., *French Painting in the Time of Jean de Berry: The Late Fourteenth Century and the Patronage of the Duke*, 2 vols (London, 1967).
Merlet, L. 'Biographie de Jean de Montagu [*sic*], grant maître de France (1350–1409)', *Bibliothèque de l'école des chartes*, 13 (1852), pp. 248–284.
Messham, J.E., 'Henry Coneway, Knight: Constable of the Castle of Rhuddlan, 1390–1407', *Flintshire Historical Society Journal*, 25 (1999), pp. 11–55.
Mirot, L., 'Isabelle de France, reine d'Angleterre (1389–1409)', *Revue d'histoire diplomatique*, 18 (1904), pp. 545–573; 19 (1905), pp. 60–95, 161–191, 481–508, and 510–522. The articles were later issued in book form (Paris, 1905).
Monfrin, J., 'Humanisme et traductions au Moyen Age', *Journal des Savants* (1963), pp. 161–190

Morrison, E., and Hedeman, A.D., *Imagining the Past in France: History in Manuscript Painting* (Los Angeles, CA, 2010).
Muscatine, C., *Chaucer and the French Tradition* (Berkeley, CA, 1957).
Palmer, J.J.N., 'The authorship, date and historical value of the French Chronicles on the Lancastrian Revolution', *Bulletin of the John Rylands Library*, 61:1 (1978), pp. 145–181, and 61:2 (1979), pp. 398–421.
Palmer, J.J.N., *England, France and Christendom 1377–1399* (London, 1972).
Perroy, E., *La Guerre de Cent Ans* (Paris, 1945).
Pocquet du Haut-Jussé, B.A., *La France gouvernée par Jean sans Peur: Les Dépenses du receveur général du royaume* (Paris, 1949).
Ramsay, J.H., *The Genesis of Lancaster, or, The Three Reigns of Edward II, Edward III, and Richard II, 1307–1399*, 2 vols (Oxford, 1913).
Rey, M., *Le Domaine du roi et les finances extraordinaires sous Charles VI 1388–1413* (Paris, 1965).
Rey, M., *Les Finances royales sous Charles VI: Les Causes de déficit 1388–1413* (Paris, 1965).
Richardson, H.G., 'Richard II's last parliament', *English Historical Review*, 52 (1937), pp. 39–47.
Rickard, P., '*Anglois coué* and *l'Anglois qui couve*', *French Studies*, 7 (1953), pp. 48–55.
Rickard, P., *Britain in Medieval French Literature 1100–1500* (Cambridge, 1956).
Rickard, P., 'Toute jour, tout le jour, et toute la journée', *Romania*, 85 (1964), pp. 145–180.
Saul, N., *Richard II* (New Haven, CT, 1997).
Sayles, G.O., 'Richard II in 1381 and 1399', *English Historical Review*, 94 (1979), pp. 820–829.
Sherborne, J., *War, Politics and Culture in Fourteenth-Century England* (London, 1994).
Short, I., 'On bilingualism in Anglo-Norman England', *Romance Philology*, 33 (1980), pp. 467–479.
Speer, M.B., 'Editing Old French texts in the eighties: Theory and practice', *Romance Philology*, 45 (1991), pp. 7–43.
Spilsbury, S.V., 'The imprecatory *Ballade*: A fifteenth-century poetic genre', *French Studies*, 23 (1979), pp. 385–396.
Steel, A., *Richard II* (Cambridge, 1941).
Strohm, P., 'The trouble with Richard: The reburial of Richard II and Lancastrian symbolic strategy', *Speculum*, 71 (1996), pp. 87–111.
Strohm, P., *England's Empty Throne: Usurpation and the Language of Legitimation 1399–1422* (New Haven, CT, 1998).
Taylor, C., ' "Weep thou for me in France": French views of the deposition of Richard II', in W.M. Ormrod (ed.), *Fourteenth Century England*, III (Woodbridge, Suffolk, 2004), pp. 207–222.
Taylor, H., *Historic Notices, with Topographical and Other Gleanings Descriptive of the Borough and County-town of Flint* (London, 1883).
Thompson, E.M., 'A contemporary account of the fall of Richard II', *Burlington Magazine*, 5 (1904), pp. 160–172, 267–277.
Tuck, A., *Richard II and the English Nobility* (London, 1973).
Tyson, D.B., 'Jean le Bel: Portrait of a chronicler', *Journal of Medieval History*, 12 (1986), pp. 315–332.
Unwin, G., *The Gilds and Companies of London*, 4th edn (London, 1963; originally published 1908).

Ure, P., 'Shakespeare's play and the French sources of Holinshed's and Stow's account of Richard II', *Notes and Queries*, 53 (1953), pp. 426–429.

Vale, M., 'An Anglo-Burgundian nobleman and art patron: Louis de Bruges, Lord of la Gruthuyse and Earl of Winchester', in C. Barron and N. Saul (eds), *England and the Low Countries in the Late Middle Ages* (Stroud, Gloucestershire, 1995), pp. 115–131.

Varvaro, A., 'Jean Froissart, la déposition et la mort de Richard II: Construction du récit historique', *Romania*, 124 (2006), pp. 112–161.

Vaughan, R., *Philip the Bold: The Formation of the Burgundian State* (London, 1962).

Vaughan, R., *Valois Burgundy* (London, 1975).

Victoria History of the Counties of England: Middlesex, 13 vols (London, 1911–2009), www.british-history.ac.uk/vch/middx.

Vinaver, E., 'Principles of textual emendation', in *Studies in French Language and Mediæval Literature Presented to Professor Mildred K. Pope* (Manchester, 1939), pp. 351–369.

Vitale-Brovarone, A., 'Notes sur la traduction de Valère Maxime par Simon de Hesdin', in M.C. Timelli and C. Galderisi, *Pour acquérir honneur et pris: Mélanges de Moyen Français offerts à Giuseppe Di Stefano* (Montreal, 2004), pp. 183–191.

Walker, S., *The Lancastrian Affinity 1361–1399* (Oxford, 1990).

Walker, S., *Political Culture in Later Medieval England: Essays* (Manchester, 2006).

Wallon, H. *Richard II, épisode de la rivalté de la France et de l'Angleterre*, 2 vols (Paris, 1864).

Whittingham, S., 'The chronology of the portraits of Richard II', *Burlington Magazine*, 113 (1971), pp. 12–21.

Wylie, J.H., *History of England under Henry the Fourth*, 4 vols (London, 1884–1898).

INDEX OF NAMES

All entries for the verse sections are for line numbers; page and line numbers are given for the prose sections. Initial Y has been treated as I.

Aise, Asia p. 323, l. 4
Albie, England p. 199, l. 25
Albïon: England 14; p. 303, l. 13; p. 309, l. 34; p. 311, ll. 11, 22, 28; p. 319, l. 30; Englishman p. 321, l. 28
Alemaigne, Germany p. 327, l. 18
Alemans, Germans 2330
Alixandre, Alexander the Great, king of Macedon, one of the Nine Worthies who personify the ideals of medieval chivalry p. 209, l. 12; p. 327, l. 6
Alpes, les, the Alps p. 319, l. 18
Anthoine, Monseigneur, Anthony, younger son of Philip the Bold, duke of Burgundy 3613
Arondel, Arundel, conte de, Richard Fitzalan, 4th earl of Arundel, *see* Arundel, Thomas, 5th earl and Richard Fitzalan's son
Arundel, Thomas, 5th earl of p. 203, l. 14; 2499, 2941
Auffrique, Africa p. 323, l. 5
Aumarle, duc de, *see* Rotelant, conte de

Beaumarey, Beaumaris, Anglesey, island off the coast of north Wales 1321; map p. ii
Bede, the Venerable Bede, English Benedictine monk p. 199, l. 20
Blanchet, Maistre Pierre, secretary to Charles VI of France 3353, 3456
Boulongne, Boulogne, south of Calais 3447, 3455, 3469, 3608
Bourbon, Monseigneur le duc de, Louis II, duke of Bourbon, brother-in-law to the late Charles V of France 3616
Bourgongne, Monseigneur de, Philip the Bold, duke of Burgundy 3607; p. 313, l. 12
Bretons, Celtic inhabitants of Brittany 2330; p. 315, l. 31

Buckingham, Humphrey Plantagenet, earl of, son of Thomas of Woodstock, duke of Gloucester p. 203, ll. 13–14

Callais, Calais, held by the English at this time p. 213, l. 3; 3321, 3352, 3479, 3497
Campaigne, the Campania, region around Naples p. 184, l. 17
Cantorbie, arcevesque de, Thomas Arundel, Archbishop of Canterbury 471, 1617; p. 191, l. 17; p. 197, l. 6; p. 203, l. 19; 2530, 2895
Cesar, Jules, Julius Caesar, Roman general and statesman, one of the Nine Worthies p. 323, ll. 26, 34; p. 325, ll. 1, 5
Cessiers, the Cheshire archers 882
Cestre, Chester, north-west England, near the Welsh border 634, 1082, 1446, 1558, 1613, 1670, 1747, 1867, 2207, 2271, 2278; p. 94, l. 4; p. 188, l. 4; p. 193, l. 12; p. 199, l. 20; p. 203, ll. 4, 9; p. 205, ll. 4, 10; map p. ii
Charles V, roy de France, king of France p. 313, l. 14
Charles VI, roy de France, king of France 2241, 3295, 3323, 3336, 3369, 3405, 3543, 3633; p. 307, l. 9; p. 311, l. 7
Chartres, evesque de, Jean de Montaigu, bishop of Chartres 3452
Chipstrate, la, Cheapside, the principal street in medieval London p. 211, l. 8
Clocestre, conte de, Thomas Despenser, earl of Gloucester 305, 831
Clocestre, duc de, Thomas of Woodstock, *see* Buckingham, earl of, Humphrey Plantagenet, his son
Col, Maistre Gontier, secretary to Charles VI 3457
Cornüay, Conway, Conwy, north Wales 610, 641, 768, 866, 1178, 1252,

INDEX OF NAMES

1317, 1322, 1402, 1646, 1678, 1740, 1795, 2107, 2186, 2255; p. 191, l. 4; p. 201, ll. 1, 4; p. 305, ll. 2, 9; map p. ii
Corsique, Corsica p. 317, l. 15
Covimtry, Coventry, in the Midlands p. 207, ll. 11, 22
Creton, Jehan, author of the *Prinse et mort* p. 301, ll. 10, 12, and note at head of page; p. 309, l. 23; p. 321, l. 1; p. 323, l. 1; p. 327, l. 1

de Noth, Thommas, Sir Thomas Dymoke, King's Champion 2954
Douvre, Dover, main port opposite Calais p. 213, l. 2; 3479
Dureme, evesque de, Walter Skirlaw, bishop of Durham 3325
Duveline, Dublin, Ireland 271, 287, 393, 447

Edouart, Saint, King Edward the Confessor 377, 1329, 2825
Empire, l', the Holy Roman Empire p. 325, l. 19
Esaü, son of Isaac 2534
Espaigne, Spain 282
Ethimologies, the *Etymologiae* of St Isidore of Seville p. 317, l. 24
Excestre, duc de, John Holland, duke of Exeter, Richard's half-brother:
  with Richard in Wales 827, 1073, 1083
  embassy with Surrey to Lancaster at Chester 1159, 1462, 1502, 1507, 1556, 1746; p. 203, ll. 16, 20
  Deposition Parliament 2489
  Epiphany Rising 3014
  his death 3185, 3199

Ferbric, William Ferriby, one of Richard's clerks 851, 1185; p. 187, l. 18; p. 191, l. 9; p. 195, l. 10; p. 201, l. 15
Flamencs, Flemings 2330
Flint, castle in Flintshire, north Wales 1683, 1693, 2217, 2274; p. 187, l. 3; p. 191, l. 29; p. 201, l. 29; p. 305, ll. 8, 10; map p. ii

Gale, Gaule: France p. 199, l. 27; Gaul p. 317, l. 15
Gales, Galles, Wales 613, 634, 746, 994, 1620, 1962, 1966; p. 191, l. 28; 3702; p. 311, l. 6; p. 319, l. 9

Galles, prince de, Henry of Monmouth, later King Henry V 1082, 2798
Galoiz, the Welsh, Welshmen 549, 677, 882, 995, 1004, 1030, 1035, 1046, 1062, 1277; p. 207, l. 12; 2802
Gaule, *see* Gale
Gaulx, the Gauls p. 319, l. 17
Gayus Figulus, Gaius Figulus, Roman consul p. 317, l. 14
Genico, Jenico, Janico d'Artasso, Navarrese soldier of Fortune 853; p. 187, l. 24
Gerlic, Guerlille, *see* Kerlille
Glocestre, *see* Clocestre
Guenelon, Ganelon, who betrayed Charlemagne's army to the Saracens 1492

Harford, Hereford, close to the Welsh borderland 2408
Henart de Kanbenart, Charles VI's usher of arms 3353–3354
Henry de Lancastre, known as Henry Bolingbroke, 3rd duke of Lancaster, later King Henry IV:
  his departure from Paris 2383
  in Cheshire and Wales 683, 1054, 1143, 1599, 1609
  embassy of Exeter and Surrey to him at Chester 1157, 1175, 1452–1453, 1457, 1513, 1554
  capture of Richard 1653, 1686, 1734, 1811, 1839, 1868, 1882, 1921, 1965, 2159, 2193, 2209, 2269, 2273; p. 187, ll. 4–5; p. 189, ll. 3, 19–20; p. 191, ll. 14, 18, 30; p. 193, l. 20; p. 195, ll. 3, 14, 32; p. 197, ll. 7, 23; p. 199, ll. 5, 14, 19; p. 201, ll. 13, 19, 24; p. 203, ll. 3, 23; p. 205, ll. 4, 29; p. 209, ll. 1, 4; 2398; p. 303, l. 10; p. 305, l. 3
  journey from Chester to London p. 205, ll. 4, 29; p. 207, ll. 6, 28; p. 209, ll. 1, 4, 15, 28; p. 211, l. 11; p. 305, l. 15
  Creton's safeconduct p. 195, l. 32; p. 211, l. 26; p. 213, l. 1
  Deposition Parliament 2419, 2479, 2765, 2768
  elected King 2296, 2635, 2678, 2777
  his Coronation 2823, 2848, 2898, 2935, 2960, 2973
  Epiphany Rising 3002, 3049, 3091, 3105, 3113, 3169

INDEX OF NAMES

Richard's funeral 3255
restitution of Queen Isabella 3313, 3535; p. 307, l. 15
challenged by Louis d'Orléans p. 327, l. 11
eldest son knighted 138; p. 187, l. 22; 2795
Henry of Monmouth, *see* Galles, prince de
Hercules, classical hero of great strength p. 319, l. 19
Heron, Monseigneur Guillaume, William Heron, Lord Say 3332
Hoult, Holt, Denbighshire, north Wales 1566, 1601
Hugueville, Monseigneur de, Jean de Hangest, sire de Hugueville, a member of Charles VI's council 3453, 3487

Ybernie, *see* Irlande
Ylïon, Ilium, Troy p. 311, l. 18
Indees, *les*, India, p. 323, l. 5
Iorc, duc de, Edmund of Langley, 1st duke of York 2481, 2486, 2620, 2874, 3084
Ypothades, Hippotes, father of Aeolus, ruler of the winds p. 307, l. 30
Irlande, Illande, Ybernie, Hybernie, Ymbernie, Ireland 39, 47–48, 73, 105, 226, 379, 407, 716, 796, 901, 1344; p. 187, l. 22; p. 197, l. 14; 2312, 3155, 3681; p. 303, ll. 10, 24; p. 307, ll. 20, 24; p. 309, l. 13
Irlandoiz, Irloiz, the Irish 125, 131, 186, 323, 2313
Isaac, Old Testament figure, son of Abraham, father of Esau and Jacob 2536
Ysabel de France, Queen Isabella, daughter of Charles VI and Richard's child-bride 1414, p. 193, l. 25
Ysidore, St Isidore of Seville, author of the *Etymologiae* p. 317, l. 24
Ytalie, Italy p. 326, l. 9

Jacob, son of Isaac 2533
Jenico, *see* Genico
Jehan, Saint, St John the Baptist 99
Judas Machabee, Judas Maccabaeus, one of the Nine Worthies p. 327, l. 4
Juif, Jew p. 191, l. 12; p. 209, l. 21
Jupiter: the god p. 303, l. 5; the planet p. 315, l. 28

Kanbenart, *see* Henart de Kanbenart
Karnarvan, Caernarvon, Caernarfon, north Wales 1334, 1399; map p. ii
Kerlille, Gerlic, Guerlille, evesque de, Thomas Merk, bishop of Carlisle, 838, 1183, 1838, 1870, 2266; p. 187, ll. 16–17; p. 191, ll. 8–9; p. 195, l. 8; p. 201, l. 14; p. 203, l. 24
Kilkigny, Kilkenny, south-east Ireland 89

Lancastre, Lenclastre, Lencastre, *see* Henry de Lancastre
Lancastre le herault, Lancaster Herald p. 195, l. 29; p. 197, l. 12
Liceflit, Lichfield, in the Midlands p. 205, l. 12; p. 207, l. 10
Lolinghehen, Leulingham, town on the border of English territory in northern France 3502, 3510, 3522
Londres, London 29, 1913; p. 205, ll. 7, 11, 25; p. 207, ll. 3, 9, 24; p. 209, l. 28; p. 211, ll. 5, 7, 22; 2399, 2415, 2448, 2570, 2847, 2859, 3060, 3108, 3118, 3122, 3194, 3250, p. 305, l. 16
Lucan, Roman poet p. 325, l. 13

Madelien, Monseigneur, Richard Maudelyn, one of Richard's clerks 1873, 3154, 3274
Mans, Manxmen, from the Isle of Man 882
Maquemore, Art McMurrough, Irish king 46, 102, 210, 225, 233, 254, 289, 318, 322, 345, 351, 409
Marche, conte de, Edmund Mortimer, 5th earl of March 2503
Marche, conte de, Roger Mortimer, 4th earl of March 354
Marïus, Roman general and consul p. 323, ll. 7, 18, 23
Marquis, le, John Beaufort, 1st marquess of Dorset and 1st marquess of Somerset, half-brother of Henry Lancaster 2497, 2943
Mars, Roman god of war p. 303, l. 5
Merlin, magician and prophet of Arthurian legend p. 199, l. 20
Milleforde, Milford Haven, Pembrokeshire, south-west Wales 53, 809, 1270; p. 191, l. 26; p. 303, l. 28
Mithridates, king of Parthia, Persia, now Iran p. 323, l. 16

INDEX OF NAMES

Mor, Saint, Saint Maurus, founder of the first Benedictine monastery in France 1595
Mortimer, Edmund, 5th earl of March 2503
Mortimer, Roger, 4th earl of March 354

Namur, fortified city, south of Brussels, in present-day Belgium 1561
Neptunus, Neptune, Roman god of the sea p. 303, l. 13
Nevers, conte de, Jehan de Nevers, elder son of Philip the Bold and the future John the Fearless 3611
Nicole, evesque de, Henry Beaufort, bishop of Lincoln, half-brother of Henry Lancaster 842
Norevic, conte de, earl of Norfolk l. 2501, note
Northomberlant, conte de, Henry Percy, 1st earl of Northumberland:
   sent by Lancaster to Richard at Conway 1655, 1696, 1758, 1809, 1823, 2321
   tricks Richard 1929, 2008, 2015, 3703; p. 305, l. 2
   captures the King 2206, 2258, 2269
   at Flint, then Chester p. 191, l. 1; p. 195, ll. 2–3; p. 197, l. 6; p. 201, l. 5; p. 203, l. 21
   in Parliament, 2523, 2711

Orreup, Europe p. 323, l. 4
Osoie, Alsace, western borderland of the Holy Roman Empire 281
Ostie, Ostia, port town for Rome, at the mouth of the Tiber p. 323, l. 24

Panebroc, conte de, earl of Pembroke (mistaken reference since vacant in 1399) 2510.
Pappe de Romme, le, *see* Romme
Paris 26, 264; p. 201, l. 20; 2378, 2385, 3343, 3347, 3411, 3451, 3643
Persi, le sire de 2711; *see also* Northomberlant, conte de
Persi, Messire Henry de, Sir Henry Percy (called Hotspur), son of Northumberland p. 193, l. 20
Persi, Sire Thomas de, Sir Thomas Percy, brother to Northumberland 986–987, 1055; p. 191, ll. 17, 24–25; p. 105, l. 12; 3327, 3533, 3571

Philippe, duc de Bourgoigne, *see* Bourgongne, Monseigneur de
Pilate, Pontius, governor of Judea who presided over the trial of Jesus p. 209, ll. 20, 25
Poitiers, western France 263
Pompee, Pompeïus, Pompey, Roman general and consul p. 323, l. 31; p. 325, ll. 1, 6

Richart, le roy, King Richard II:
   Irish expedition 33, 362, 603, 638, 647, 662, 713, 728, 765, 793; p. 187, l. 21; p. 197, l. 14; p. 300, l. 12
   return to Wales 805, 1057, 1619
   at Conway 1206, 1250, 1441, 1761, 1799, 1818, 1830, 1835, 1928
   at Caernarvon 1382
   Richard's treasury at Holt 1583, 1593, 1602
   capture at Rhuddlan 1727, 2094
   at Flint 1690, 2220, 2263, 2274; p. 187, ll. 3–4, 12, 21, 25; p. 189, l. 17; p. 191, ll. 8, 16, 20; p. 199, l. 13; p. 203, l. 4
   Chester to London p. 205, ll. 13, 26; p. 207, ll. 3–4
   deposition p. 213, l. 7; 2298, 2434, 2483, 2507, 2539, 2557, 2569, 2587, 2611, 2744, 2807, 2842, 2877, 3316
   Epiphany Rising 2993, 3017, 3024, 3089, 3138, 3143, 3149, 3157, 3167
   escape from prison p. 301, l. 12
   Richard's death 3224, 3254, 3279, 3415; p. 319, ll. 2–3
   ally of France 3553, 3686; p. 309, l. 34; p. 311, ll. 11, 22, 28
Rommains, les, the Romans p. 315, l. 1; p. 317, ll. 6, 30; p. 321, l. 14; p. 323, ll. 2, 10
Romme, Rome p. 317, ll. 8, 13, 16, 17, 19; p. 319, l. 17; p. 323, ll. 33, 36; p. 325, l. 30
Romme, le Pappe de, the Roman Pope, Boniface IX 478, 486
Rotelant, Rhuddlan, Denbighshire, north Wales 1697, 2090, 2108, 2202, 2215; p. 305, l. 9; map p. ii
Rotelant, conte de, Edward of York, earl of Rutland and duke of Aumale, Richard's cousin and favourite:
   in Ireland 94, 426, 430, 527; p. 168, l. 23

INDEX OF NAMES

in Wales and Chester p. 191, l. 18; p. 193, l. 8; p. 203, l. 21
Deposition Parliament and Coronation of Lancaster 2485, 2623, 2945
Epiphany Rising 2881, 3006, 3062–3063, 3074, 3102

Saine, River Seine 406
Saint Alban, St Albans, north-west of London p. 207, l. 23
Saint David, evesque de, Guy de Mohun, bishop of St David's, south-west Wales 837
Saint Jehan de Jherusalem, St John's Priory, Clerkenwell, London p. 211, l. 21
Saint Pere, *see* Romme, le Pappe de Romme
Saint Pol, conte de, Waleran III of Luxembourg, count of St Pol 3505, 3567; p. 319, l. 9
Saint Pol, St Paul's Cathedral, London p. 211, ll. 9, 15; 2400, 3269
Salsebery, conte de, John Montagu, 3rd earl of Salisbury, friend and patron of Creton:
  sent in advance from Ireland to Wales 546, 569
  at Conway with Richard 861, 1182, 1293, 1817, 1837, 1869, 2156, 3684
  at Flint, then Chester 2264; p. 187, l. 16; p. 191, l. 8; p. 193, l. 5; p. 195, l. 9; p. 199, l. 18; p. 201, ll. 15–16, 18, 27; p. 203, l. 24
  Deposition Parliament 2512
  Epiphany Rising 2994, 3030, 3058, 3189
Salsebery, contesse de, Maude Francis, countess of Salisbury p. 187, ll. 20–21
Sarrasin, Saracen, Muslim or possibly Turk p. 191, l. 12
Scilla, Sulla, Roman general and consul p. 323, ll. 7, 14, 21
Scipio Nasica, Roman consul and leader of mob that assassinated Tiberius Gracchus p. 317, l. 14
Scroup, messire Estienne, Sir Stephen le Scrope 850, 1190; p. 187, l. 17; p. 191, l. 9; p. 195, l. 9; p. 201, l. 15

Souldray, Soudray, duc de, Thomas Holland, duke of Surrey, Richard's nephew:
  from Milford Haven to Conway with Richard 829
  embassy to Lancaster at Chester, with Exeter 1165, 1439, 1557, 1865
  Deposition Parliament and Coronation of Lancaster 2487, 2875
  Epiphany Rising 2991, 3029, 3057
  his death 3187
Stanforde, conte de, Thomas, earl of Stafford 2505
Suetonius, Roman historian p. 313, l. 22
Surestre, Cirencester, town in west of England 3132

Tholomee, Ptolemy XIII, pharaoh of Egypt p. 283, l. 8
Titus Livius, Livy, Roman historian p. 317, l. 28
Turquie, Turkey 591
Tybere Cesar, Tiberius Caesar, 2nd Roman emperor p. 313, l. 19; p. 315, l. 10
Tyberius Graccus, Tiberius Gracchus, Roman politician p. 317, l. 18

Umestat, conte de, unidentified nobleman 2515

Valerius Maximus, Roman author of *Facta et dicta memorabilia* p. 317, ll. 5, 28–29; p. 325, l. 19
Venus, Roman goddess of love p. 303, l. 6

Watreforde, Waterford, south-east Ireland 72, 551
Wemoustre, Wesmoustre, Wemoustier, Westminster 1850, 1946; p. 209, l. 18; p. 211, l. 6; 2371, 2397, 2447
Werewic, conte de, Thomas Beauchamp, twelfth earl of Warwick 2937
Westmerland, conte de, Ralph Neville, 1st earl of Westmorland p. 203, l. 21; 2524, 2936
Windesore, Windsor 2983, 3039, 3054, 3104, 3125, 3131, p. 307, l. 24

Y, for all entries, *see* under I